NARRATIVES OF INDIAN CINEMA

Narratives of INDIAN CINEMA

edited by

MANJU JAIN

PRIMUS BOOKS

PRIMUS BOOKS
An imprint of Ratna Sagar P. Ltd.
Virat Bhavan
Mukherjee Nagar Commercial Complex
Delhi 110 009

Offices at CHENNAI KOLKATA LUCKNOW
AGRA AHMEDABAD BANGALORE COIMBATORE DEHRADUN GUWAHATI
HYDERABAD JAIPUR KANPUR KOCHI MADURAI MUMBAI PATNA RANCHI

First published 2009
Reprinted 2013, 2019

ISBN: 978-81-908918-4-4 **(hardback)**
ISBN: 978-93-80607-79-5 **(paperback)**

Published by Primus Books

Laser typeset by Digigrafics
Gulmohar Park, New Delhi 110 049

Printed at Sanat Printers, Kundli, Haryana

Contents

PREFACE vii
INTRODUCTION ix

PART I: WRITING CINEMA
THE COLONIAL TO THE GLOBAL

1. The Natives are Looking: Cinema and Censorship in Colonial India 3
M. Madhava Prasad
2. Cinema and Hindi Periodicals in Colonial India: 1920–1947 19
Lalit Joshi
3. History Matters 53
Valentina Vitali

PART II: FRACTURED POLITIES

4. The Panoramic Vision and the Descent of Darkness: Issues in Contramodernity 69
Rashmi Doraiswamy
5. Melodramatic Imaginings: Representations of Sectarian Violence within Hindi Popular Cinema and Indian Documentaries 85
Anuja Jain
6. A New Universalism: Terrorism and Film Language in Mani Ratnam's *Kannathil Muthamittal* 97
Priya Jaikumar

PART III: NEGOTIATING IDENTITIES

7. Merit and Opportunity in the Child-Centric Nationalist Films of the 1950s 123
Nandini Chandra
8. Reading Rape: Sexual Difference, Representational Excess and Narrative Containment 145
Karen Gabriel
9. Frames of Cinematic History: The *Tawa'if* in *Umrao Jan* and *Pakeezah* 167
Shweta Sachdeva Jha

PART IV: LITERARY AND CINEMATIC IMAGINARIES

10. The Art of Film Adaptation: *The Remains of the Day* 195
Seymour Chatman

11. Screening Reality: *The Remains of the Day* as Fact, Fiction and Film from a Postcolonial Perspective 211
Ved Prakash Baruah

12. 'Filmi' Shakespeare 229
Poonam Trivedi

13. A Dramatic Film: Performative Politics in Peter Brook's *Mahabharata* 249
Sonali Pattnaik

NOTES ON EDITORS AND CONTRIBUTORS 261

INDEX 265

Preface

THE NUCLEUS OF this volume of essays is the seminar on 'Reflexions: Film, Literature, and Culture', organized by the Department of English, University of Delhi, in March 2004. Six of the articles published here were presented at the seminar: 'The Art of Adaptation: *The Remains of the Day*' by Seymour Chatman (presented at a video conference organized by USEFI); 'Panoramic Vision and The Descent of Darkness: Issues of Contramodernity' by Rashmi Doraiswamy; 'Cinema and Hindi Periodicals in Colonial India: 1920–1947' by Lalit Joshi; 'The Natives are Looking: Cinema and Censorship in Colonial India' by Madhava Prasad; '"Filmi" Shakespeare' by Poonam Trivedi; and 'History Matters: Film Theory as an Obstacle to Film Historiography and Analysis' by Valentina Vitali. I am grateful to the Department of English, University of Delhi, for permission to include them in this volume. The essays by Rashmi Doraiswamy, Lalit Joshi, Poonam Trivedi, and Valentina Vitali have been substantially revised for publication. Madhava Prasad's essay has since been published in *Law's Moving Image* (London: Glasshouse Press, 2004).

The seminar on 'Reflexions' was funded by the University of Delhi and the Department of English. Grateful acknowledgement is made to them. Warm thanks are due to Manjit Singh who, in his capacity as Finance Officer, University of Delhi, generously made funds available and gave his unstinting support. Thanks are also due to the Director and the staff of the India International Centre for providing excellent facilities and space for holding the seminar, to Sumathi Ramaswamy and the Ford Foundation for providing the airfare for two of the participants whose papers could unfortunately not be included in this volume, and to USEFI for organizing the video conference with Professor Seymour Chatman. I should like as well to thank my colleagues on the Seminar Committee: Alok Rai, Udaya Kumar, Subarno Chatterjee, and Rimli Bhattacharya; Ira Bhaskar for her valuable suggestions and help; the students who helped with the organization of the seminar: Anuja Jain, Sangeeta Gupta, Shweta Sachdeva, and Simran Chadha; and the office staff of the Department of English for their hard work and organizational skills: S.K. Chauhan, Hari Singh, Kavita Talwar, Sahib Singh, and Krishan Chander.

Priya Jaikumar's article 'A New Universalism: Terrorism and Film Language in Mani Ratnam's *Kannathil Mutahmitta*' originally appeared in *Post Script: Essays in Film and the Humanities*, vol. 25 (3) (Summer 2006): 48–64, and is reprinted here with the permission of the publisher.

Madhava Prasad's article 'The Natives are Looking: Cinema and Censorship in Colonial India' originally appeared in *Law's Moving Image*, edited by Leslie J Moran, Emma Sandon, Elena Loizidou and Ian Christie (London: The Glasshouse Press, 2004); pp. 161-72 and is reprinted here with the permission of the publisher.

New Delhi MANJU JAIN

Introduction

CINEMA EMERGED a little more than a century ago to become one of the most potent forms of expression that has made an impact on practically every sphere of theory and praxis. From the very outset it has raised a host of issues that have challenged the premises of art, aesthetics, philosophy, psychology, and politics. Some of the questions that it has continued to pose are its relationship to the other arts as well as to technology; the ways in which consciousness and perception are influenced by this new medium; and its impact in the public sphere because of its mass appeal and wide outreach. Also, how do we theorize the specificity and the commonality of film, literature, and other modes of cultural expression in an age of increasing interplay among these forms? How do changes in the public sphere—through state intervention and regulation, changes in structures of dissemination and spectatorship, and processes of globalization—inflect the history of cinema in various locations? How do cinematic representations construct and negotiate the politics of identity? How do these representations map the transitions and the continuities, the filiations and the ruptures, from the colonial to the postcolonial, as well as grapple with the schisms, fissures, and conflicts of the colonial state, and later of the postcolonial nation state which is increasingly marked by the economic and cultural processes of globalization, accompanied paradoxically, and perhaps inevitably, by bitter local and ethnic conflicts? This volume aims to address some of these questions with a focus particularly on issues related to the shifting responses by the colonial state, the Indian nationalists and intellectuals, and the popular press to the emerging medium of cinema with its creative potential, its threats as well as its challenges; the local, national, and global financial networks within which cinema is located; the politics of violence, communalism, and terrorism as negotiated in cinema; the representation of identitarian politics; and the complex ideological underpinnings of literary adaptations.

WRITING CINEMA: THE COLONIAL TO THE GLOBAL

The emergence of cinema in the early twentieth century in India as a powerful tool for the manipulation of the masses generated deep anxieties in the colonial state about its relationship with the colonial subjects. At the same time, there were debates and controversies among the Indian nationalist leaders, the intellectuals, and the writers about the advantages and the disadvantages of this new medium. A study of these varying responses therefore throws important light on the history and political conflicts of the period, many of which continued into the postcolonial nation state.

These issues are explored by Madhava Prasad in his examination of the Report of the Indian Cinematographic Committee (ICC Report) and the accompanying volumes of evidence. The Committee was set up in 1927 to investigate the issue of censorship and the question of Imperial preference for the film industry to counter the popularity of American films. As Prasad explains, the ICC Report 'bears witness to a singular moment in world history when a colonial order encounters in cinema a threat to the social order that was built up by a consensus among the elite leadership of the different communities'—Hindus, Muslims and 'Europeans'. The need for censorship was felt by the colonial rulers not only because of the corrupting influence of American films but also because of the intrusion of the unwelcome 'native gaze' into the private domain of the ruling race, especially when it came to representations of Western women and the use of the cinematic technique of the close-up in kissing scenes. Ironically, Prasad argues, before the advent of cinema, it was only the native communities that had sought to protect their 'inner domain' from the reformist, interventionist gaze of the colonizers. The Report also raises the complex issue of spectatorship and the often paradoxical identification of the colonized with the colonizer. There is an interesting citation of an incident witnessed by the Chairman of the Committee, Diwan Bahadur T. Rangachariar, when the 'native' audience of a film sympathized with the white heroine rather than with her 'Oriental' persecutors! While the colonial rulers and the conservative Indian elite highlighted the corrupting threat of cinema, nationalists such as Lala Lajpat Rai took an uncompromisingly radical position as harbingers of modernity, opposing censorship and Imperial preference. Prasad goes on to show, however, that for several decades after Independence, the Indian state 'would continue with the same censorship rules informed by the same colonial logic', with the nationalists taking refuge in the conservative opinion that they had so firmly opposed earlier.

Many of the ramifications of Prasad's article are further explored by Lalit Joshi, with reference specifically to responses to cinema in four Hindi periodicals from 1920–47: *Sudha*, *Madhuri*, *Chand*, and *Hans*. Joshi has chosen this period because it marks the extraordinary development of the film industry well as of vernacular print capitalism. It is also representative of the most decisive phase of India's anti-colonial struggle in which the colonial elements of modernity were being negotiated in an attempt to foreground an 'Indian' identity. In this context, Joshi investigates the interrogations of nationalist positions on the merits and demerits of cinema in popular journalism. He further examines the generation of multiple concepts of art, aesthetics, language, and culture in the contested space created by cinema in Hindi journalism. Joshi also argues that the Hindi public sphere emerged around this time when cinema in India was undergoing a period of metamorphosis. He shows how cinema entered the Hindi public sphere and engaged with the contentious issues of the period, and how issues related to censorship, art, aesthetics and the market, ethics and morality, glamour and fashion, became part of the larger debate on what constituted an Indian identity and Indian culture.

Finally, Valentina Vitali takes up the issue of the historiography of Indian cinema. She maintains that with the burgeoning of film studies as part of the curriculum of universities, it was primarily Lewis Jacobs' *The Rise of the Film: A Critical History* (1939) that was adopted as a model for writing histories of cinema in many parts of the world. Jacobs relied on a unilinear trajectory of history that posited the nation state as the natural result of an evolutionary development. Vitali, however, questions the use of this historiographic template for Indian cinema since it conceptualizes the nation as an organic entity, ignoring local and global networks. In her study, Vitali foregrounds the neglected issue of film exhibition. She also emphasizes the importance of reframing Indian cinema within local, national, and global financial networks as well as marketing and distribution strategies for an understanding of cinema in India as a practice constitutive of Indian civil society.

The three articles in this section then throw light on the trajectory of Indian cinema from the earlier colonial period to its imbrication in a globalized economy, contributing to an understanding of its historical development and role in the public sphere.

FRACTURED POLITIES

The articles in this section take up further the interventions of cinema in the public sphere and its engagement with the political conflicts and divisions of the time from Partition onwards, focusing primarily on issues of communalism and terrorism. Rashmi Doraiswamy discusses the traumatic communal violence depicted in films on Partition through her deployment of the panoramic vision as a narratorial mode and as an effect of the technological apparatus of cinema. She explores what Homi Bhabha terms the 'contra-modernity' that is at work in everyday acts such as walking in colonial and postcolonial societies. She discusses this unfolding of the panoramic gaze in connection with the routine act of walking and the motif of the train as a narrative strategy in literary and cinematic texts on Partition, specifically with reference to Bhisham Sahni's novel *Tamas* and its adaptation by Govind Nihalani into a teleserial and film and to Ritwik Ghatak's *Komal Gandhar*, using the theories of Michel de Certeau and Walter Benjamin. Doraiswamy argues that a great deal of Partition fiction is concerned with the topography and charting of one's small, intimate, lived space, which is threatened by the horror and violence of political events such as riots. What is evoked in *Tamas*, Doraiswamy elaborates, is the sense of micro-histories that unfold to give a panoramic view of the violence and hatred of the communal passions of the time. In Ghatak's *Komal Gandhar* too, there is a complex interweaving of micro-narratives, while the walk of the protagonists through the landscape and the outing of the drama troupe into the countryside evoke memories of an undivided Bengal. Doraiswamy sensitively shows that rather than follow the path of New Realism as in Italy, or of modernism as in the French New Wave, 'Ghatak combined realism with the rituals of the everyday on the one hand, and of the archaic on the other', creating what she calls 'geological images that encapsulate within themselves many time frames, archaic and contemporary, mythical and achingly real'. The train too haunts Partition fiction and film, functioning as the paradoxical image of modernity, combining notions of connectivity, industrialism, and automation, with notions of flight, dislocation, and uprooting, thus encapsulating the darkness and the trauma of this historical moment.

Anuja Jain's essay carries forward the discussion of representations of the politics of communalism to recent times, in the context of the demolition of the Babri Masjid on 6 December 1992 and the subsequent communal violence in Bombay in 1992–3. Jain argues that it is the visual representations and complex struggle over their interpretations that have dominated the discursive field about these events. She takes up the cinematic representations of these events both in the fiction film and in the documentary, exemplified by Mani Ratnam's popular Hindi film, *Bombay* (1995) and Suma Josson's documentary, *Bombay's Blood Yatra*/ 'Bombay's Journey of Blood' (1993), to argue that the intervention of the documentary filmmakers in the socio-political conditions within India use many of the strategies and idioms that are common to mainstream popular Hindi cinema, such as melodrama, in order to negotiate such apocalyptic moments. In doing so, documentary films play with the expectations of the audiences of popular cinema and also interrogate its status as the most pervasive source of insight into the public sphere. Jain concludes that whereas a film such as *Bombay* uses the melodramatic mode to endorse the Nehruvian, utopic ideals of national unity and progress, a documentary such as 'Bombay's Journey of Blood' deploys it in order to compel the audience to interrogate their utopic desires as well as to confront the deep-seated sectarian conflicts that fracture the Indian nation state.

Priya Jaikumar takes up another film of Mani Ratnam's—*Kannathil Muthamittal* (A Peck on the Cheek, 2002)—to discuss contemporary representations of terrorism in cinema, while also including in her ambit Ratnam's other films on communal violence and terrorism—*Bombay*, *Roja*, and *Dil Se*. Her objective is to interrogate Ratnam's films for their coupling of terrorism with reconstitutions of regional identities as bourgeois, cosmopolitan, and trans-regional in an attempt to attain a new universalism in the postcolonial Indian nation state marked by processes of incomplete nationalization and uneven globalization. In the process of this interrogation, Jaikumar also engages with questions of cinematic form, aesthetics, spectatorial pleasure, and cultural recognition in order to analyze the politics of the film. She takes up the negotiation of political issues with the personal and familial realm in Ratnam's films on terrorism as well as his use of the mode of melodrama for this negotiation. Jaikumar extends the discussion on terrorism further by suggesting that terrorism in *Kannathil Muthamittal* is interpreted not purely through the language of a nation state but also as a critique of bourgeois modernity, of which the nation state is just one powerful manifestation. She uses Søren Kierkegaard's idea of melancholy, as sadness for no apparent reason, with which he opposed the philosophical underpinnings of European modernity that was vital to colonial nation formation. Jaikumar invokes notions of faith and melancholia as responses to modernity because, she claims, they are resuscitated in Ratnam's portrayal of female suicide bombers in *Kannathil Muthamittal* and *Dil Se*. She suggests, in conclusion, that the conditions through which films from regional industries arrive at national and global centres of film circulation reveal the political stakes of their new universalism. To this end, in *Kannathil Muthamittal*, a middle-class Tamil family is confronted with an LTTE militant in an attempt to address a fractious regional identity and to find a centrist consensus acceptable to a national and global audience.

Negotiating Identities

The representation of identitarian politics is further explored in this section, with the focus on marginalized figures such as the child, the raped woman, and the *tawa'if*. Nandini Chandra discusses the manner in which children have been represented in the social realist films of the 1950s. These films, she argues, pioneered visions of childhood that have continued to haunt Hindi cinema. She focuses on the depiction of marginalized children in five films—*Munna*, *Ab Dilli Door Nahin*, *Boot Polish*, *Jagriti*, and *Ferry*—analyzing them from perspectives of class, caste, and gender. She locates these films within the historical context of Nehruvian socialism as well as the promises belied by the rhetoric of new beginnings promising a nationalist utopia in the newly independent nation state where all children would be equal. She also exposes the contradictions in the directors of the progressive Indian People's Theatre Association (IPTA) marked by the conflict between their elitist paternalism and the pretensions of their socialist programme in their depiction of children. She then goes on to look at the self-narratives of the child artists, based on her interviews with them, showing how the internalization of their roles impacted their lives as child artists and later as adults struggling to find a foothold in the film industry.

In 'Reading Rape: Sexual Difference, Representational Excess and Narrative Containment', Karen Gabriel discusses the several meanings that have been assigned to rape and to the raped body in Bombay cinema. Within a patriarchal sexual economy, she argues, the raped woman's discourses on as well as of pain and violation are transformed into ones on the exchange and violation of ownership. In the depiction of the female subject of pain, the camera movements are also deployed to 'transform testimony into spectacle'. Gabriel destabilizes the distinction between the popular and the supposedly politically correct avant-garde by analyzing a rape sequence from Ramesh Sippy's *Bhrashtachar* and juxtaposing it with Shekhar Kapur's *Bandit Queen*, thereby unveiling the ideological and discursive orthodoxy of Kapur's film. She discusses also the differences between Mala Sen's literary version and Shekhar Kapur's cinematic one on Phoolan Devi's life, as well as the off-screen controversies about the film, including Phoolan Devi's own objections to the cinematic representation of her life and the subsequent claims to ownership of her story by Shekhar Kapur and Channel Four, who maintained that her version was a lie. This, ironically, resulted in a denial and silencing of *her* narrative. There is, then, a complex interplay of lives, roles, mythification, and motives, resulting in a silencing of female subjectivity, turning her into a spectacle of eroticized violence and an object of consumption for the producer, director, and male spectator.

Shweta Sachdeva Jha, in 'Frames of Cinematic History: The *Tawa'if* in *Umrao Jan* and *Pakeezah*' also takes up the relationship of 'real' and 'imagined' identities in order to show how popular Hindi films negotiate history through cinematic representations of the *tawa'if* within the context of the postcolonial imaginary. She discusses how these films frame the *tawa'if* as a historical subject and an artefact as well as an embodiment of the nation, with the focus especially on the syncretic performative traditions of a composite Hindu–Muslim culture, or '*ganga-jumna tehzeeb*'. Sachdeva Jha argues that this reimagining of the *tawa'if* culture as representative of a desirable religious and cultural unity is particularly significant in the context of conflicting religious discourses on communal and religious identities in postcolonial India. She locates these historical negotiations within recent debates on the construction and narrativization of history and also situates them in relation to the historical *tawa'if* as well as her literary representations. She explores the complex relationship between films, history, filmmakers and the audience within the postcolonial imaginary, focusing on the cinematic narratives, the *mise en scène*, and the choice of famous actresses whose 'star texts' further enhance the imagination of the *tawa'if* as a performer.

Literary and Cinematic Imaginaries

Several articles in the preceding sections deploy literary strategies in their analyses of films. This section is concerned specifically with the symbiotic relationship of film and literature as manifested in the adaptations of literary texts into films. From its earliest beginnings, film has owed a great deal to literature. Eisenstein's and Griffith's acknowledged indebtedness to John Milton, Gustave Flaubert, and Charles Dickens is well known.[1] Film, as some of the earlier essays have shown, engages deeply, as does literature, with issues of representation, telling and showing, visuality and textuality, narrativity and language, image production, point of view, identification, form, genre, and authorship, as do literary texts. It is film, in fact, that provides an interdisciplinary site *par excellence*, requiring a multiplicity of disciplinary and theoretical grids for an adequate understanding.

Although the relationship of literature and film is not merely one of adaptation to literary texts, adaptation nevertheless is a key issue in a discussion of the relationship of the two media, raising several hermeneutical questions pertaining to both. The major debates concern questions of fidelity to the 'original' text; the parasitism of the filmic adaptation to the literary text; the supposed hierarchy of literature over film; of word over image, of what W.J.T. Mitchell terms the 'protracted struggle for dominance between pictorial and linguistic signs'.[2] As Robert Stam succinctly puts it: 'Terms like "infidelity", "betrayal", "deformation", "vulgarization", and "desecration" proliferate in adaptation discourse, each word carrying its specific charge of opprobrium…the standard rhetoric has often deployed an elegiac discourse of loss, lamenting what has been "lost" in the transition from novel to film, while ignoring what has been "gained"'.[3]

Also, any discussion of fidelity will assume the notion of a stable, unified text, with a fixed essence or 'kernel' (to use Joseph Conrad's phrase in *Heart of Darkness*) of meaning, which has been questioned by contemporary critical theory. For instance, if there is an adaptation of the *Mahabharata*, to which version of the text should the adaptation be faithful? This is the case especially with oral narratives that have accumulated with variations over centuries. There is also the question of length. How can a film be a faithful adaptation of a novel, or of an epic, because of the relative differences in the temporal length? If a film is of the duration of three hours, how can it faithfully render a novel such as *War and Peace* which runs over several hundred pages? It is the reverse situation with the short story. For a story of a few pages will need to be expanded for a film. Consequently, there will be principles of selection, reduction, expansion, concentration, and exclusion in the process of adaptation involving multiple choices—conscious as well as unconscious. These principles, moreover, are mediated not merely by the vagaries or visions of individual directors, producers, and screenplay writers but also by their cultural and historical situatedness.

The articles in this section explore these problematics of literary adaptation (as do those by Doraiswamy, Sachdeva Jha and Gabriel in earlier sections of this volume). In doing so, they venture beyond the specifities of Indian cinema and literature and examine the complex negotiations of Indian filmmakers with other literatures, and of a Western filmmaker, Peter Brook, with the Indian epic, the *Mahabharata*, in changing and shifting political, social and cultural contexts. Indian cinema is thereby situated within a larger global, historical, and transcultural framework and questions are raised about the relationship of the local and the transnational in terms of modes of production and processes of narrativization. The scope of the book is thus widened and enriched by the debates and issues raised by these articles.

At first glance, it may seem anomalous to have included Seymour Chatman's paper on *The Remains of the Day*, a film based on a novel by a Japanese, set in the English countryside, about the memories of an English butler, in a volume of articles that focuses on Indian cinema. However, as Ved Prakash Baruah points out in his response to Chatman's paper from a postcolonial perspective, 'the intellectual and cultural legacy' of the film is 'a veritable mélange of peoples, places and purposes'. Kazuo Ishiguro, the author of the novel, is an *émigré* of Japanese birth and ancestry settled in Britain; the screenwriter, Ruth Prawer Jhabvala, a novelist in her own right, is of Jewish descent, who spent her childhood in Nazi Germany, lived as a refugee in England and was educated there, married an Indian and lived in India for some time, before settling in New York. The filmmakers, James Ivory and Merchant Ismail, are an Indo-American team. James Ivory is an American Protestant who is deeply interested in India, and Ismail Merchant (now deceased) was a Muslim born in Bombay. This mélange results in a fascinating interplay of cultural, racial, and historical subject positions in the making of the film which, however, is not the focus of Chatman's discussion.

Chatman's paper is a fine illustration of the problematics of adapting a novel into a film, taking into account the divergences of the two different media. While dismissing the question of 'fidelity', he emphasizes that the real issue is 'not literal fidelity, but whether a film gives a good cinematic *equivalent* of the novel'. Consequently, in his discussion of the adaptation of *The Remains of the Day*, he is concerned with showing 'how a film can use certain techniques to present interesting equivalencies of a novel's effects'. He further clarifies that while he will 'concentrate on changes in form to accommodate the new medium', he 'cannot avoid implications for content as well'. In his analysis of the content, he is concerned primarily with Stevens' reminiscences of his own personal affairs, especially his relations with his father and with Miss Kenton. Chatman illuminatingly discusses the use of the first person unreliable narrator in the novel as well as the omission of this narrative strategy in the film, but he focuses mainly on the theme of the unlived life. In the process, he minimizes the political and historical dimensions of both the film and the novel, referring cursorily to Stevens' blindness, to the import of Lord Darlington's sympathy with the Nazis, to 'the evil enterprise being hatched in the house', to the series of secret meetings arranged among British and European dignitaries at the manor, culminating in the one between von Ribbentrop and Chamberlain that led to the sell-out of Czechoslovakia, and to Lord Darlington and his associates being modelled after the 'Cliveden Set'.

Chatman concludes that '[I]n their openness, both the novel and the film are modernist or post-modernist endeavours, but they achieve openness in different ways, unique to their respective media.' While the novel achieves this openness through the narrative strategy of unreliable narration, the film, Chatman argues, 'eschewing direct verbal access to Stevens' mind, requires us to read out of Anthony Hopkins' face and gestures what his inhibitions do not permit him to say', thus depending on visual details and on the acting prowess of the lead actor.

While Chatman therefore highlights the effects achieved by the literary and the cinematic media respectively, Baruah argues, in his response to Chatman, that what is outside the frame, that is, the larger picture of Britain's history, is what Chatman overlooks in his article, thereby tacitly undermining the relationship of form and content. Consequently, while attending to the formal aspects of cinematic representation, Baruah discusses the adaptation of *The Remains of the Day* from the vantage point of content, especially from a postcolonial perspective, foregrounding the historical and political contexts of both novel and film (public as well as private), arguing that it is essential to consider what is excluded as well as included in both, and that 'ambivalencies' are as important as 'equivalencies' in the process of adaptation. He views the representation of history in both novel and film from the perspective of recent debates about the relativity of constructions of history where the subject position of the author and its 'reciprocity with cultural epistemes' need to be foregrounded. Unlike Chatman, therefore, Baruah explores the complexities of the individual subject positions of the novelist, producer, director, and scriptwriter as vital factors in any discussion of the relationship of the novel to the film. He foregrounds, especially, the nuances of the role of the scriptwriter, Ruth Prawer Jhabvala, which Chatman does not consider.

Consequently, while Chatman highlights the formal aspects of the process of adaptation, focusing largely on personal relations and on the theme of the unlived life, Baruah explores its political and historical facets. The two articles therefore illustrate divergent approaches to the adaptation of the same text, complementing each other, but also showing that a purely literary and rhetorical reading occludes the complex ideological factors involved in the adaptation.

The complexities of adaptation are further explored in Poonam Trivedi's article, 'Filmi Shakespeare', where she discusses how Shakespeare has nourished Indian, particularly Hindi cinema in diverse forms, 'as appropriations, recreations, relocations and as "after life" or presences'. This varying use of Shakespeare, Trivedi argues, not only illuminates changing colonial attitudes to Shakespeare, but more significantly, helps to chart the shifts in the politics of an interculturalism that infuses the 'cultural imaginary' of mainstream Indian cinema. She traces the influence of Shakespeare on Parsi theatre, from which Indian cinema originated, going on to discuss Indian cinema's engagement with Shakespeare from its earliest days in the silent era to contemporary times. In the process, she historicizes this engagement first in relation to colonial educational policies that aggressively propagated the study of English with Shakespeare as the literary icon, and then, the cultural resistance to these imperial policies in the subversive appropriation of Shakespeare in the vernaculars, often in bold, hybrid performative modes. She then goes on to discuss the second stage of negotiations with Shakespeare in the 1940s and 1950s, following the widespread impact of the study of English literature in India, which was marked by anxieties of authenticity versus populist appropriation, as manifested especially in the intercultural appropriation of Kishore Sahu's *Hamlet* (1954). The next stage in the negotiation of this colonial legacy was fully to relocate Shakespeare into 'a pervasive local *mise en scène*', often infused with indigenous literary and performative traditions. Trivedi illustrates this trend with an analysis of two recent films directed by Vishal Bharadwaj: *Maqbool* (2004) and *Omkara* (2007), third-generation postcolonial adaptations of Shakespeare, 'cross-over' films that together constitute a paradigm shift in the reconfiguration of Shakespeare on the Indian screen. These films, 'adaptations' of *Macbeth* and *Othello* respectively, she argues, 'demonstrate not only a postcolonial "play" with Shakespeare's text, but also a confident postmodernist reimagining of literary heritage'. Further, she shows how Shakespearean traces in terms of theme, character, imagery, fragments of scenes and sequences, and lines of dialogue are testimony to the manifold ways in which Shakespeare, once an iconic colonial text, has been assimilated into the 'cultural imaginary' of the nation.

Sonali Pattnaik, in her article on 'Performative Politics in Peter Brook's *Mahabharata*', eschews discussion of the film as a successful or failed adaptation of the epic. She is interested, rather, in examining the question of the relationship of cinema to literature and writing via Brook's radicalization of cinematic space, and thereby concentrating on ongoing controversies regarding textuality, orality, and reading practices. Her article seeks to explore the method of representation deployed by the film which, she argues, contests the false dichotomy between text and context as well as the larger thematic debate between constructivism and essentialism. She uses the Deleuzian/Artaudian critique of presence in cinema to question the dominant representation of the text as allegory, thereby highlighting the undercutting of cinematic realism. She discusses as well the absence of a complex reading of transculturalism in the film, the play of identity and difference in the spectator, and the manner in which the mechanical tools of cinema can be manipulated to acquire political and cultural value. What emerges, she concludes, is not a seamless whole but a fractured, fissured text.

These articles on adaptation then, of novel, play, and epic, are significant contributions to the debates in adaptation studies, exploring as they do the complex interplay of forms, genres, subject positions, cultural mediations, and ideological constructions, often teasing out the 'unsaid (the *non-dit*)' of the textual utterances as well as of their cinematic adaptations.[4]

It is hoped that though the topics covered are by no means comprehensive, the articles in this volume will contribute towards an enhancement of an understanding of the complex role that cinema and its narrativization have performed and continue to perform in the public sphere in India and will raise issues and debates for further exploration.

Notes

1. Braudy and Cohen, 1999.
2. Quoted in Stam, 2005.
3. Ibid., p. 3. See the entire Introduction for a detailed and comprehensive discussion of issues pertaining to adaptation (pp. 1–52).
4. Ibid., p. 10.

References

'Dickens, Griffith and Ourselves', in Leo Braudy and Marshall Cohen, (eds.), *Film Theory and Criticism: Introductory Readings*, 5th edn, New York and Oxford: Oxford University Press, 1999, pp. 426–34.

Robert Stam, 'Introduction: The Theory and Practice of Adaptation', in Robert Stam and Alessandra Raengo, (eds.), *Literature and Film: A Guide to the Theory and Practice of Adaptation*, Oxford: Blackwell, 2005, p. 4.

PART I
WRITING CINEMA
THE COLONIAL TO THE GLOBAL

1

The Natives are Looking: Cinema and Censorship in Colonial India

M. Madhava Prasad

IN 1927, THE Indian Cinematograph Committee began its project to 'report on the system of censorship of cinematograph films in India and to consider whether it is desirable that any steps should be taken to encourage the exhibition of films produced within the British Empire generally and the production and exhibition of Indian films in particular'.[1] The Committee was set up by an order of the Government of India's Home Department (Political), on the recommendation of the Council of State in India. The terms of reference were as follows:

1. to examine the organization and the principles and methods of the censorship of cinematograph films in India;
2. to survey the organization for the exhibition of cinematograph films and the film-producing industry in India;
3. to consider whether it is desirable that steps should be taken to encourage the exhibition of films produced within the British Empire generally and the production and exhibition of Indian films in particular; and to make recommendations.

The third point was a direct consequence of a resolution passed at the Imperial Conference of 1926[2] seeking to extend the policy of Imperial preference to the film industry. The order in which the terms of reference were presented, however, was designed to de-emphasize the question of Imperial preference and to highlight the issue of censorship.

The Committee was headed by Diwan Bahadur T. Rangachariar, C.I.E., Vakil, High Court, Madras, and had in addition the following members:

1. The Hon'ble Khan Bahadur Sir Ebrahim Haroon Jaffer, *Kt*
2. Colonel J.D. Crawford, D.S.O, M.C., M.L.A.
3. Mr K.C. Neogy, M.L.A., Vakil, High Court, Calcutta

4. Mr A.M. Green, I.C.S., Collector of Customs and Member of Bombay Board of Film Censors
5. Mr J. Coatman, M.L.A., Director of Public Information

The government had been careful to provide representation for the two communities that, according to the by then well-established colonial common sense, constituted the principal population segments of the subcontinent: Hindus and Muslims. Giving the Chair to an Indian was also a noteworthy symbolic gesture. The three 'European' members who represented different interests of the ruling race in the colony together appended a minute of dissent to the final report, demonstrating a degree of solidarity that was not always in evidence during the proceedings of the Committee.

In the only detailed consideration of the Committee's proceedings available, Brian Shoesmith[3] pointed out that in 1927, several other countries—Australia, England, France, Germany and Japan—had conducted similar inquiries to gauge the impact of film on society, and in particular to find ways to protect national markets against Hollywood's dominating presence.[4] The Indian inquiry was also motivated by similar concerns, but here the dyarchic colonial regime then in place gave an interesting twist to the proceedings. For in the colony it was not only a question of the influence of cinema in general, but of the impact of American cinema. Further, it was not just a question of its impact on everybody, but of its impact on the natives in particular.

Already in 1921, a 'cinema expert' by the name of W. Evans had been sent to India to report on the film industry in the country. Evans had recommended stiffer censorship rules and better implementation. Calls for stricter censorship had been voiced since 1913[5] in England and India, and in 1918 the Cinematograph Act was put in place in response to widespread concern. But Evans' mission and subsequent discussions in England and India showed that it was by no means a settled issue. The colonial structure's anomalous coexistence with the idea of a comity of nations contributed to the peculiar tonality of the discussions about films in the colonies, and in particular in India. This was in part because while in other colonies the audiences for films were predominantly comprised of Europeans, in India the natives also rushed to experience this new form of amusement in large numbers.

The need for special attention to censorship of cinema was explained thus on the first page of the report:

> There are two reasons for differential treatment of the cinema. One reason is that the cinema appeals to a much wider audience. The number of persons who witness a successful play is infinitesimal compared with the vast numbers who witness a

successful film. The second reason is that the film has a special and peculiar appeal. It has to achieve its effect visually, without the aid of the spoken word. The result is an exaggeration of physical expression and suggestive action. Every device is employed in order to intensify the visual impression, such as the well-known device of the 'close-up', and thus a peculiarly direct and vivid impression is produced upon the mind of the spectator.

Following Evans' report, a debate ensued in the British press with the predominant view being 'that much harm was being done in India by the widespread exhibition of Western films'. According to Rangachariar, who examined a number of the articles, 'The general trend of them is that, owing to difference of customs and outlook, Western films are misunderstood and tend to discredit Western civilisation in the eyes of the masses in India....' Thus a Bishop: 'The majority of the films, which are chiefly from America, are of sensational and daring murders, crimes, and divorces, and, on the whole, degrade the white women in the eyes of the Indians' (p. 3). Questions were raised in Parliament (p. 4) and in 1926–7, 'The British Social Hygiene Delegation' visited India and mounted some 'drastic criticisms'. It claimed that all over India, 'the evil influence of the cinema was cited by educationists and the representative citizens as one of the major factors in lowering the standard of sex conduct, and thereby tending to increase the dissemination of disease' (pp. 4–5). In Burma, the National Council of Women advised that sex and crime pictures should be banned. In India, in the Legislative Assembly, questions were raised about the extent and nature of censorship. Indian members such as Hon'ble V. Ramadas Pantulu and Hon'ble Rao Saheb Dr U. Rama Rao agreed with the British view and called for measures to restrict or prevent the screening of films likely to have a bad influence. H.G. Haig, Home Secretary, agreed: 'The censor has to decide not only what is tolerable from a Western standpoint in the representation of Western manners but what is tolerable from an Eastern standpoint, or even what is tolerable from the standpoint of probable error or misrepresentation' (p. 7). He felt that more British films might be better, but 'a still greater improvement would lie in a considerable extension of the production of Indian films,—showing Indian stories in an Indian setting'.

The Committee issued 4,325 copies of the questionnaire, of which 320 were received back with answers. 353 witnesses were examined, of whom 114 were Europeans/Anglo-Indians/Americans. Of the remaining 239 natives, the following ethnic profile is provided: 157 Hindus and 82 non-Hindus (38 Muslim, 25 Parsi, 16 Burmese, 2 Sikhs, and 1 Christian). There were 35 women in all, 16 Europeans, and 19 Indians, Parsis, and Burmese. The ethnic composition of the witnesses was a matter of great importance to the entire enterprise, for it was precisely a matter of finding a way in which the 'privacy' of ethnic groups in India could be protected against the cinema's tendency to make everything public. In his summation, Rangachariar notes:

> The majority of the European witnesses who take the view that film misrepresentation does harm, seem to consider that this misrepresentation lowers Western, especially European civilisation in the minds of Indians, and that *therefore the effect is injurious to Europeans.* In some cases they consider that the result is also injurious to Indians. Those Indian witnesses, however, who agree that Western life is misrepresented, consider that the misrepresentation is *definitely harmful to Indians* because it either induces them to ignore what is good in Western civilisation or to copy what is bad.[6]

In order to show that there was no danger of misrepresentation of Western life demoralizing the spectators, Rangachariar cites an incident that he witnessed in a theatre in Madras:

> The white heroine in every reel was being persecuted by a cosmopolitan band of villains whose leader was an Oriental and whose rank and file comprised other Orientals. Whenever the white hero made a timely appearance or the heroine escaped from the toils, spontaneous applause broke forth, and on one occasion when the screen showed the heroine about to fall into the hands of her Oriental persecutor an excited voice cried out in Tamil: 'Look out, Miss, look out!' No more convincing argument could be adduced to show that the sympathies of Indian audiences are not alienated or seriously affected by the portrayal on the screen of a life that is strange to them, always provided that an appeal is made to their human emotions.[7]

The question of representation and misrepresentation arises in a context where relations between a ruling race and a 'subject race' are suddenly restructured by the entry of a third element—here, the institution of cinema, already dominated by the American product. Britain carried on free trade with the rest of the world, but wanted a different regime of Imperial preferences to be enforced in its colonies. These preferences related to trade in all kinds of goods, cinema being a relatively minor element. However, the anxieties expressed by various sections of British public opinion as well as members of the British Parliament came as a handy excuse to propose preferences. It was not that the need for Imperial preference led to the invention of a threat from American cinema, since this threat perception was in existence long before the Imperial Conference. Imperial preference was also seen by some as a solution to the problem posed by American films, since British films, produced in a climate of stricter moral values, were considered more healthy, less prone to presenting the 'seamier side' of European life.

The social hygienists might already have been the inspiration behind the questions frequently raised in the British Parliament about the possible relation between American cinema and declining native respect for its rulers. Gandhi's views on cinema, which he expressed rather bluntly in a two-line response to the committee's questionnaire[8] may also have been indirectly influenced by the hygienist movement in Britain, which must have been an important influence during his time in England. In a memorandum following its visit, the delegation said, 'In every province that we visited, the evil influence of the cinema was cited by educationists and the representative citizens as one of the major factors in lowering the standard of sex conduct and thereby tending to increase dissemination of disease'.[9] From all accounts this appears to have been a crackpot delegation but its alarmist claims, which were later discredited by the very people who were cited as sources of information by the delegation, may have played an important role in pushing the government to order the inquiry. In India, the Council of State and the Legislative Assembly discussed the issue. Sir Haroon Jaffer (who was later to be included in the inquiry committee) expressed concern about the low quality of films that were circulating in India, and the Home Secretary agreed with him that 'gross misrepresentations of Western morals, of Western culture, and Western civilisation ... have not infrequently found their way into cinema exhibitions'.[10] Thus, the terms of reference of the future committee were based on the *solutions* that had already been decided upon by the rulers. The Report noted that the Home Secretary had already expressed a hope that more British films would find their way to India to improve the quality of the fare available to the audiences in the colonies. The colonial officer clearly felt obliged to suggest that British films were of a better quality than the American imports, but he also knew that it was difficult to sustain such an opinion when everybody knew that even in England, British films were no match for the Hollywood product. Thus, it was on the question of encouragement to Indian film production that all the diverse interests represented in the entire debate seemed to arrive at some kind of consensus. The Home Secretary had already given expression to what was to become the only point on which the Committee members were all in agreement: 'But it seems to me that a still greater improvement would lie in a considerable extension of the production of Indian films—showing Indian stories in an Indian setting'.[11]

American cinema contained scenes set in nightclubs, highlighting the lives of women of loose morals and the like. On the other hand, even the more normal aspects of Western life, such as couples kissing or hugging or dancing 'in public' were equally a cause for worry because the uneducated native was gaining access to views of the private lives of the ruling race. Cinema, and in particular 'close-ups', provided a view of the white woman's body to all and sundry; even the most impoverished Indian could, for a small fee, walk in and look at the bodies of white women and their amorous activities. The repeated reference to 'close-ups' shows a preoccupation with the public exposure to which the white people's private lives were susceptible: one witness suggested that much of the harm could be prevented by simply cutting out the close-ups. It was a question, quite simply, of a collapse of order and hierarchy, an alarming leveling of the rulers and the ruled. Throughout the volumes of evidence, it is repeated again and again: it is not the educated Indians who are familiar with cultural differences and can be relied upon to appreciate the films in a proper manner, it is the illiterate masses and what impressions they will form of the ruling race that is at issue. Encouragement to Indian cinema, especially to mythologicals, was seen by many as one way of keeping the 'low class of Indians' away from theatres that showed Western films. Rangachariar, for his part, tried to reassure the ruling race that the illiterates were far from getting wrong ideas about white women. His anecdote is revealing: the Indian spectator sympathises with the white hero and heroine to the extent of crying out to the heroine to escape and seems not to regard colour as a basis for identification. This spectator is in no danger of being alienated, Rangachariar says, with unintentional irony. Giving evidence of one kind of alienation, he reassures the white residents of India that another kind of alienation—disenchantment with the Empire—is unlikely.

Cinema thus put the social order of British India into an ideological crisis, at a time when it was hardly seen by more than a small fraction of the population. The nationalists among the witnesses were fully aware of this, and resolutely refused to say that American films were doing any harm to Indians. Various versions of the problem were presented: 1. the image of British women will suffer; 2. the minds of gullible Indians will be corrupted; 3. all races should be treated with respect, there should be no bad images of Indians in Western films any more than there should be bad images of Westerners in films screened in India. On all these fronts, the nationalists remained firm that the minds of Indians were not so weak as to be corrupted by a few films; if the image of British women suffered, Indians were not at fault, it was the Westerners who were making these films; and so on.

Other committees, set up by the government of free India to inquire into the film industry, repeated many of the ideas of the ICC Report and tended to pose the problems in the same way, with the same terms and concepts. In this way, the Report had a lasting impact on thinking about cinema in India. But beyond this, the true value of the document lies in the four volumes of evidence, including the written answers to the questionnaire as well as the full details of the oral examinations conducted. It is a text of tremendous historical value, documenting a dramatic confrontation between two or more different conceptions of the nature of the Indian polity and culture in a colonial state. In the next section, I discuss some aspects of the Report that concern the disruptive role played by cinema vis-à-vis the existing colonial relations of governance and social relations between the three most important ethnic groups in the colony—Hindus, Muslims and 'Europeans'.

II

The Chairman of the Committee, in his words to 'the first European gentleman' to give evidence, posed the crucial question in these terms: 'We have heard complaints from European gentlemen and ladies that the exhibition of Western life to an Easterner produces a lowering effect concerning the European'.[12] J. Stenson, Supervisor, Bombay Entertainments Duty Act, replied that it was not his view, that he did not think it a serious issue. The Chairman persisted: 'We have all different ideas of decency; for instance, we have different notions of decency and the Europeans have different notions of decency, and as long as the Europeans live here we do not expect them to give up their notions of decency, and their manners unless there is something extraordinarily indecent in the pictures shown. We often hear these complaints, but when pressed to a point they are not able to tell us where the trouble actually lies, and I seek your assistance in this matter'.[13] Stenson confessed that he could not answer the question. The Chairman persisted, pointing out that there were 'certain things in your mode of life' which Indians would not care to adopt and vice versa, but that was no reason to judge these things as immoral. Stenson responded that he found nothing objectionable among Indians. On further questioning by other members, he agreed that 'Western films as shown today, including all these cabaret scenes and scenes of the underworld, are a definite misrepresentation of Western life'.[14] However, in Bombay at any rate, the 'people in the cheaper seats' who were the main cause for concern were not seeing these films in large numbers, particularly because there were very few 'four-anna' seats in theatres showing Western films. Only the educated Indians went to see these films and they were 'not likely to be seriously deceived'.[15] As Mr Green summed it up, 'the people who would misunderstand them do not see them'.[16]

Thus at the very beginning, the tone of the Committee's proceedings was set. But the theme of the unwelcome gaze of the uneducated Indian kept coming back. Thus R.K. Mhatre, Assistant Director of Public Health, in his written statement: 'Western films are greatly misunderstood by the uneducated Indian as evidenced from their behaviour at the cinema theatres. Innocent action such as embracing or kissing are hissed and jeered at through their ignorance of Western social life and customs'.[17] In his oral deposition, Mhatre confirmed his views, but averred that the remedy was not censorship but to 'raise the educational standard'.[18] Others considered that a bad impression about Western culture was being created by the Europeans in India, some of whom led 'bad lives', and not just by the films.[19]

An interesting encounter occurred between the Chairman and a journalist with nationalist leanings, R. Venkataram. The journalist was firmly against censorship based on the misrepresentation thesis, and argued for a 'widening in our outlook of mind', which provoked the Chairman to ask:

> Q: Would you like Indian ladies to be shown in the way Western ladies are shown?
> A: You can't help it.
> Q: I mean in Indian pictures; would you like a Madrassi lady—a Madrassi Brahmin lady—shown in an Indian picture dressed in a Western costume?
> A: If she were so shown I would not object to it.
> Q: On what grounds would you not object to it?
> A: Because these things are happening in real life.

The nationalist refused to budge on his principles. The Chairman's irritation mounted.

> Q: Supposing they depict Rangachariar [referring to himself] without a turban, in a hat?
> A: What would be wrong?
> Q: Supposing your character was being portrayed as addressing a public meeting without a Gandhi cap and khaddar dress, and you were dressed in a Bond Street costume ... do you think it would be right?
> A: I do not know what a Bond Street costume is. If somebody took a fancy to represent me in full English costume I would not object to it.[20]

The issue came down to individual representation, with Rangachariar trying to highlight the absurdity of representing a man who wears a turban in a hat. Of course, from a biographical point of view, this raises problems, but what happened meanwhile was that Rangachariar had turned a question of cultural representations applicable to complex social formations into one of individual representation.

The difference between the two broad viewpoints that are opposed to each other throughout these proceedings hinges on two different conceptions of the polity. Nationalists like Venkatram proceeded on the assumption that Indians were modern individuals, (future) citizens of a democratic country, whereas the conservative opinion took the colonial polity as the natural and durable state of affairs. The nationalist objected to misrepresentation of 'Orientals' in Hollywood films, but saw no evidence of objectionable misrepresentation of white people in them. A European subject, Major W. Ellis Jones, M.L.C., insisted that the 'class of film depicting so-called "Society Life" in Europe and America, these types of pictures are harmful to young people of all races and must convey to the uninformed Indian an entirely false view of the woman of these continents'.[21] He recommended that 'such low cabaret scenes should be deleted'.[22] Jones also claims that his educated Indian acquaintances want such films to be banned. Here, a commonality of interests between Indians and Europeans began to appear: while Europeans were against exposing European women (through their representations) to the uneducated Indian gaze, it was also proposed that educated Indians were also not comfortable with the general availability of such views. In other words, a paternalist compact between right-thinking Europeans and Indians was hinted at.

Faced with a situation where its own skills of voyeuristic observation and reformist intervention, the former in any case, were suddenly available for the native to use against it, the colonial authority was clearly on the defensive. What Partha Chatterjee has called the 'rule of colonial difference', on which colonial power rested, required the preservation of the 'alienness of the ruling group',[23] its transcendence of the social order over which it exercised power. Chatterjee has also shown how, on the other hand, the nationalists also sought to separate the public domain of politics (where colonial power held sway), from the socio-cultural 'inner world' which would be out of bounds for the colonial gaze. The nationalists won for themselves the freedom to interpret modernity in their own way by insisting on this demarcation of spaces.

Chatterjee places this development in the mid-to the late nineteenth century and tracks the theme with particular reference to the 'women's question'.[24] It was not coincidental, therefore, that it was precisely the 'image of the white woman' in the eyes of the natives that precipitated a brief reversal of historical roles. With the advent of cinema, an unexpected situation developed, where the colonial authorities found themselves identifying with their ethnic origins, something they did not have to do before. Under the impact of cinema, the British seemed to lose their footing in the universal, as it were. If earlier British authorities could, without damage to their despotic status, undertake social reform informed by universal values, now the native, a colonized subject, was occupying the universalist position of viewing offered by Hollywood cinema, an intolerable situation for the logic of colonial difference.

Sometimes, the compulsions of colonial representationalism would generate some unusual modes of thinking symptomatic of the untenable, indefensible nature of the colonial presence. Major Jones, continuing with his oral evidence, explained a remark in the Written Statement, where he had objected to the depiction of 'kept women' in an Indian film.

> Q. (Chairman): Do you mean to say that there should be no play or drama or story in which kept women should be referred to?
> A: What I really intended to convey was that as far as possible they should be of the same race. If the film was produced by the Indians it should be all Indians. If they are produced by Englishmen they should be all Englishmen. If they are produced by Madrasis they should all be Madrasis. There should be only one race engaged in it, I mean the actors and actresses of films.
> ....
> Q: You say a female character was taken by an Englishwoman in life?
> A: Yes. The film was produced in Calcutta. It was a local product.
> Q: (Mr Green): Do you say that she was represented on the screen as an Englishwoman?
> A: No.
> Q: As a Bengali herself?
> A: Yes. She was represented as an outside woman altogether.
> Q: She was dressed as a Bengali?
> A: No. She was dressed as an ordinary outside Indian woman.
> Q (Chairman): She was dressed as an Indian?
> A: Yes.
> Q: She was not represented as a European?
> A: No.
> Q: She consented to take that part. She was not represented as an Englishwoman?
> A: I have objections to showing to the general public a film of that nature.
> Q: If she was represented as an Indian what is your objection? I thought it comes within your meaning that they should have the same race. You would bar English actresses taking the part of Indian girls?
> A: Yes.
> ....
> Q: On what grounds would you ban it?
> A: On the same grounds as I would protest against a Madrasi woman being employed with a Bengali man. I think the people of the race would object. They do object. We know in India they object very strongly to their women acting with men of other races. . . .Indians object to it very strongly and we object on the same basis.
> ....

> Q: Do you object to Frenchmen taking the part of Englishmen on the stage?
> A: We are of the Western race. The Bengalis, the Madrasis, and the Rajputs think themselves separately.
> ....
> Q: (Mr Green): ...Do I understand you to object to a European actress appearing in an Indian film even if she acted so well that she would not be recognized on the screen as a European?[25]

Jones's answer to that was an emphatic yes. Jones represented 'cotton', that is, the community of European cotton traders. His objection, as the Chairman restated it, was 'generally to any race representing another race'. For a colonial polity to survive as a stable formation, there must be no neutral currency through which colonizer and colonized can interact. Democracy would have been one such currency, which one stream of British opinion understandably opposed.[26] Cinematic representation also threatened to function precisely as such a currency, where the substance (European blood) was hidden behind the mask (representation of Indian womanhood). Even if the representation was so perfect as to conceal any hint of European origins, it would still be a problem because for Jones it was not a question simply of representations; it was a matter of actual social/sexual relations. Here realism functioned as a moral–political norm. Second, Jones' testimony also pointed to the way in which the European community perceived itself as one of the many communities of India: the Rajputs, the Madrasis, the Bengalis, etc. Thus it was by analogy with these communities,[27] and their strict enforcement of endo-sociality that Jones made a case for the Europeans' right to their racial separateness. H.W. Hogg, Secretary of the Punjab Boy Scouts Association, summed up the dangers posed by films which show 'a white woman being easily led astray say by an Arab ... a white woman leading a loose idle life ... that is bound to lower the respect of Eastern races for white women of the Western races'.[28] Where 'a small number of English people' lived amidst a large number of Indians, says Hogg, hinting at more sinister possibilities, women 'living in isolated stations where very often law and order is not maintained', 'the dignity and the respect which is due to a woman ... would certainly be lowered.[29] Among the natives, there were several who agreed with this point of view. Thus, a Diwan Bahadur from Punjab objected to foreign films which showed revolutions, because he was confident that grievances 'can be redressed without having recourse to revolution or rowdyism', to which the Chairman replied, 'You are very optimistic that way'.[30]

The underlying logic of Jones' reservations was far more tellingly revealed in the repeated discussions of the question of kissing. The common refrain, which began to be used by many people in these proceedings, and which was repeated until recently as an explanation, was that Indians do not kiss in public and therefore they should not be shown doing so. In addition, this was also used to explain why the native spectator might end up with a low opinion of Europeans, whom he saw on screen kissing. Rangachariar exposed the faulty logic of this claim, pointing out that while the image of kissing was shown in public, the act itself was depicted as taking place in private.[31] This difference, which seems obvious to us, was imperceptible to people then: kissing in public meant being seen in public kissing. This was another version of Jones's argument, which saw, in the images on screen, not a set of cinematic signifiers strung together to tell a tale, but the actual people behind it, who acted out those scenes so that they may be displayed in public. The logic of the colonial social order was revealed here: Ideally, there must be no public space as such—the social fabric must consist entirely of the communities each with its separate, closed social order, its moral and cultural leaders, its rules of conduct, etc. The inner life of one community must not be made public, made visible to the gaze of an individual from another community. Cinema came in the way of such a conception of colonial society. Its realistic images of private life caused an acute sense of violation of the right of communities to privacy in a polity organized as a series of discrete, mutually exclusive units. Before the advent of cinema, it was only the native communities which sought to protect their 'inner domain' from the reformist/universalist interventionist gaze of the British rulers. With the advent of cinema, the modern suddenly came loose from its presumed immanence to white society. It was the nationalists who suddenly occupied centre-stage as harbingers of a modern future and who dismissed British and Indian conservatives alike as representatives of a passing order.

Thus, the nationalist Lala Lajpat Rai was uncompromising in his rejection of proposals for censorship and Imperial preference. He also told the Committee in no uncertain terms that in his opinion, Imperial preference was the actual intention behind the whole enterprise. Asked about cabaret scenes, underworld scenes, and scenes that 'tend to lower the Western womanhood in the estimation of our people here', Rai replied: 'I don't want the youth of this country to be brought up in a nursery. They should know all those things, because then they will be better able to resist those things when they go out. They should see all those things here and they will be able to understand better all the points of modern life'.[32] The Chairman asked whether 'knowledge of other portions of the Empire' was not essential. 'A: I think knowledge of the world is essential.... I don't know if there is any special reason why we should know more of the Empire than of the rest of the world.... You will pardon me, Mr. Chairman, I have no use for the Empire at all. The Empire treats us as helots everywhere, and therefore I have no affection for this Empire. My point of view cannot agree with those who love this Empire'.[33] No danger to morality was posed by such films because if Indians were to get educated in Western morals (which the West wanted them to learn), then it was necessary for them to watch such films.

A ban on American films was not a realistic option for a number of reasons: First, being a schizophrenic entity, British political authority could not have adopted colonial trade practices towards a free country like the USA. Second, British films were no match for the racier American product, even in the eyes of the ordinary British residents of India, who would certainly have objected to a ban. It would have been very difficult to impose a restrictive policy of showing the films only to white people. Most important, the nationalist gaze was taunting the colonial regime for its political backwardness, the hollowness of its claims to participate in the Enlightenment. The RICC reveals to us the irresolvable dilemma faced by the colonial authority in the cultural domain in the face of a new cultural technology, which the ideology of colonialism had not anticipated.

In place of a ban and a blanket imposition of Imperial preference, therefore, the Committee's report contained some compromise proposals. Of these, one is interesting because it targets a cinematic device: the close-up. 'Avoid close-ups as much as possible. That is the main thing',[34] said Mrs V.G. Coulson, a representative of the Bengal Presidency Council of Women. The close-up, Mrs Coulson argued, brings the image of the Western woman too close to the viewer, who experiences a sense of possession of the image, and by extension, of the woman herself. But the Chairman wanted to know why only the Indians should be deprived of such an illusion of possession. 'The close-ups are in evidence everywhere. In England also it is in evidence very largely. How is it then that the English society does not revolt against it? May I put to you how the Indians view it? The thing is done in the West. It is not we who misrepresent them, but it is the Westerner himself who represents himself or herself in that light, and why don't they tap the very source of mischief without coming here and asking to put a stop to it?'.[35]

The Chairman's questions here exposed a weakness in the argument of the conservatives. The witness could not claim ethnic solidarity with those who produced these films, but the *images* gave the impression that the women on screen and the white women in India belonged to the same race. On the other hand, the Europeans in India did want to identify with the 'white race' as far as the situation in India was concerned. There was no racial leadership who could be appealed to in order to stop the production of objectionable films: the white race's *imaginary* unity was not complemented by a *symbolic unity*. Unlike the Madrasis, the Rajputs, and the Bengalis, who appeared to function as communities with a recognized leadership, the British in India could not claim to belong to a community called Europeans, with an identifiable position of authority to which complaints could be addressed. Coulson's comments suggested that since neither she nor the colonial authorities could intervene to change the free market to suit the needs of the colonial moral order, the Indians who ordered the films should be asked to desist.

The ICC Report bears witness to a singular moment in world history when a colonial order encountered in cinema a threat to the social order that was built up by a consensus among the elite leadership of the different communities. Cinema exposed these communities to the gaze of a non-denominational public, but perhaps it also exposed the falsity of the claims of the leadership that such communities existed at all. The gaze of the film spectator came to haunt the conservative desire for closed community spaces, and in the most interesting development of all, many European groups found themselves seeking the very communal right to non-interference from outside that the nationalists had demanded from them. But cinema, a product at the forefront of a newly aggressive American capitalism's global drive, harbinger of a new logic of universality, could not be held to account, it would not abide their question. They tried to inveigle the Indian community leaders into a pact that could save them all, but the nationalists stood firm against such a compact. Censorship guidelines ended up reflecting the concerns of the conservatives on both sides, and for several decades after independence, the Indian state would continue with the same censorship rules informed by the same colonial logic. The nationalists, with power in their own hands, began to find comfort in the conservative opinion they had so firmly opposed. While cinema aroused moral anxiety wherever it was introduced all over the world, in India these unique circumstances gave rise to the idea of a 'backward spectator', one who lacked the qualifications for watching films, which continues to be operative to this day.

Notes

1. *Report of the Indian Cinematograph Committee, 1927-28*, Madras: Madras Government Press, 1928, p. xi. (henceforth *RICC*).
2. Ibid., p. xii.
3. Brian Shoesmith has given a detailed account of the politics behind the setting up of the commission and the fate of its recommendations. See Brian Shoesmith, 'The Problem of Film: A Reassessment of the Significance of the Indian Cinematograph Committee, 1927–1928', *Continuum*, vol. 2, no. 1, 1988–9, pp. 74–89. See also E. Barnuow and S. Krishnaswamy, *Indian Film*, 2nd edn, New York: Oxford University Press, 1980.
4. Shoesmith, p. 74.

5. Ibid., p. 77.
6. *RICC*, p. 111.
7. Ibid., pp. 111-12.
8. This was Gandhi's reply: 'Even if I was so minded, I should be unfit to answer your questionnaire, as I have never been to a cinema. But even to an outsider, the evil that it has done and is doing is patent. The good, if it has done any at all, remains to be proved', *RICC*, vol. 4, p. 56.
9. *RICC*, pp. 4-5.
10. Ibid., p. 6.
11. Ibid., p. 8.
12. Ibid., vol. 1. p. 41.
13. Ibid.
14. Ibid., p. 43.
15. Ibid., p. 44.
16. Ibid.
17. Ibid., p. 50.
18. Ibid., p. 55.
19. Ibid., p. 209.
20. Ibid., pp. 542-3.
21. Ibid., p. 306.
22. Ibid., p. 309.
23. Partha Chatterjee, *The Nation and its Fragments: Colonial and Postcolonial Histories*, Delhi: Oxford University Press, 1994, p. 10.
24. Ibid., pp. 116-34.
25. *RICC*, pp. 310-13.
26. Chatterjee, op. cit., pp. 16-18.
27. In actuality these were not actually existing communities in any real sense; they were, rather, national cultures with further internal divisions. Usually, when a Madrasi community was referred to, it was the Brahmin or upper-caste groups that were meant.
28. *RICC*, vol. 2, p. 69.
29. Ibid., p. 70.
30. Ibid., p. 141.
31. For a more detailed consideration of the ban on kissing (with reference to independent India), see Madhava Prasad, *Ideology of the Hindi Film: A Historical Construction*, New Delhi: Oxford University Press, 1998, Chap. 4.
32. *RICC*, vol. 2, p. 201.
33. Ibid., p. 202.
34. Ibid., p. 925.
35. Ibid., p. 926.

2

Cinema and Hindi Periodicals in Colonial India (1920–1947)

Lalit Joshi

Yon swargiya cinema ke
Sab khel manohar rozana
Kaun dikhata hai baitha
Maya-machine par wah syana
Hai kaun wah adrishya drishya
Jo dikhlata yeh manmana
Kabhi udhar bhi drishti phiri
Kya kabhi use bhi pehchana
(Everyday the pleasant sights of the cinema heavenly
Will he show them, the skilled one who sits besides the magic machine?
Which invisible scene will he show at will?
Ever seen him? Ever recognized him?)

—Excerpted from Hanuman Prasad Goel '"Lalaam", Swargiya Cinema', *Sudha*, year 3, vol. 2, no. 2, 1929, pp. 188–9

THIS ARTICLE AIMS to map the contested space created by cinema within Hindi journalism and to see how, within the confines of this space, multiple notions of language, art, and culture were generated. I try to examine the extent to which popular literature was able to transfigure cinema into a topic of debate and discussion. My objective is also to see how nationalist positions on what was good and bad about cinema began to be interrogated in popular writings and how writers began selectively to redraw the normative boundaries of art and culture.[1] The period 1920–47 has been chosen as it marks the spectacular development of the film industry on the one hand, and the extraordinary growth of vernacular print capitalism on the other. Moreover, this period is representative of the most decisive phase of India's anti-colonial struggle in which the diverse colonial elements of modernity were being negotiated in the hope that a pan-Indian identity could eventually be forged.

I focus on three Hindi periodicals published from the United Provinces, the Hindi heartland of the Indian subcontinent. These are: *Madhuri* (1922–50), *Sudha* (1927), and *Chand* (1923).[2] Unlike some conservative journals (*Sammelan Patrika*, *Nagari Pracharini Patrika*, *Saraswati*) of this period, *Madhuri*, *Sudha* and *Chand* provided adequate space to cinema. The three also enjoyed a committed readership. In its heyday *Chand* had a circulation of about 15,000, while the circulation of *Madhuri* and *Sudha* ran into 4,000 and 7,200 copies respectively.[3] *Sudha* and *Chand* published regular cinema columns captioned *Chhaya Path*, while *Madhuri*'s cinema column was called *Chhaya*. *Sudha* also featured *Sampadakiya Sahmati* (Editorial Consent) where cinema-related comments and letters were published.[4] At another level the three periodicals competed with each other in publishing pin-ups of the famous actors of those times.

Who were the people writing for these periodicals? Biographical details of the authors are not available, but they were certainly not drawn from the professional group of *littérateurs* who had begun to make their presence felt in the world of Hindi publishing. Except for two entries by Surya Kant Tripathi 'Nirala' in the *Sudha* of November 1934 and January 1935 respectively, I did not find a single essay written by an author of literary repute. This is not to suggest that the literary sphere did not have its own viewpoint on cinema. In fact, right from the 1930s through the 1950s, well-known writers, who had been drawn to the industry, had been documenting their experiences, often warning aspiring writers about the slippery world of cinema. In addition to the illustrious Munshi Premchand, the film industry was able to entice story writers and poets such as Bhagwati Charan Verma, Narendra Sharma, Amrit Lal Nagar, Pradeep, Sudarshan, Upendranath Ashk, Gopal Singh Nepali, and many others. For example, Ajanta Cinetone of Bombay employed Premchand while Sudarshan was in Calcutta working for New Theatres. Again, Filmistan in Bombay hired Pradeep, Nepali, and Ashk. The experience of literary men in the film industry was far from satisfactory. Two instances of this can be cited. In a letter addressed to a friend in 1935, just before he quit the film industry in Bombay, Premchand wrote:

> It is pointless to hope for any improvement in cinema. The profession is organized in the same way as the trade in liquor. Dancing naked, kissing, petting, men assaulting women...all this is rightful in their eyes. Tastes have become so inferior that the public does not enjoy cinema unless such harmful and shameful scenes are included. Through cinema all the vulgarities of the West are being thrust on us and we are helpless. People are not organized and a sense of good and bad is completely absent. However hard you plead in the newspapers it is of little use. Having given it much thought I feel that it would be best to leave this world.[5]

Premchand posted another indictment of cinema in the 1935 edition of *Lekhak*, a periodical published from Allahabad. Differentiating literature from films in the essay entitled *Cinema aur Sahitya*, Premchand wrote that while literature strove for 'idealism and beauty', films were only concerned with making profits.[6] He also felt that it was early to think of an age when 'cinema and literature would come together and when popular tastes would become so refined that any depreciation in art would be treated with contempt'.[7] Upendranath Ashk, who reached Bombay a decade later, went a step further in the condemnation of the industry. In 1946 he put together a drama script called *Maskebazon Ka Svarga* (The Heaven of Sycophants),[8] which dared to expose the behind-the-screen activities of the industry. Evidence from other sources also demonstrates that the literary community was generally less comfortable within the industry and writing for films was often looked down upon as an unfortunate compromise.

Hindi periodicals would not have been publishing essays on cinema with such abandon had it not been for the popularity achieved by the essay as a modern prose form. There seems to be unanimity among literary historians that the trend of essay writing in Hindi started with the Bhartendu era and continued well into the Dwivedi and Chhayavada eras.[9] Furthermore, with the advent of the essay was inaugurated a free (*unmukta*) and liberal (*udaar*) style of Hindi prose.[10] Ramchandra Shukla, who published the first comprehensive history of Hindi literature in 1945, mentions three kinds of essays constituting modern Hindi prose, namely *vicharatmaka* (ideational), *bhavatmaka* (emotional), and *varnanatmaka* (descriptive). Critical, that everything was getting published in the name of *nibandh* (essay), Shukla regretted that despite the freedom enjoyed by the writers, most essays lacked what he thought was the 'fresh and miraculous force of language' and the 'outpouring of new ideas'.[11] The essays on cinema cannot be slotted into any one of the categories suggested by Shukla: a single entry could be *vicharatmaka*, *bhavatmaka*, or *varnanatmaka* or a combination of the three. What is perhaps more important to underscore is that it was through these essays that 'the areas in which consensus needed to be established were first reconnoitered...and public opinion organized...the essays developed into a fully-fledged literary form flexible enough to cover a wide variety of issues....'[12] The authors of cinema-related essays were perhaps self-taught critics who shared a deep love for cinema, and who were driven by a sense of responsibility to educate innocent readers about the perils of the tinsel world. For the wide variety of subjects that they chose they seemed to have been guided by the literary and cultural *samskaras* of this period.[13] Topics were not confined to contemporary trends in Indian cinema. Often recent developments in British and American cinema were debated. Thus, there is little room for doubt that the authors were bilingual and often sourced materials from American and British publications.

Nationalist Ambivalence towards Cinema

With the advent of mass nationalism in the 1920s, it began to get clearer that pressing art and culture into the service of the nation was no less a problematic issue than the mobilisation of the Indian people in politics. Dhundiraj Govind Phalke expressed this in unambiguous terms:

> In 1910 I happened to see the film *Life of Christ* at the American-Indian Picture Palace in Bombay.... While the life of Christ was rolling before my physical eyes I was mentally visualizing the Gods, Shri Krishna, Shri Ramchandra, their Gokul and Ayodhya.... I felt my imagination take shape on the screen. Could this really happen? Could we the sons of India, ever be able to see Indian images on the screen? [14]

Phalke was convinced that both in terms of industrial and ideological production, cinema could serve as a truly *swadeshi* enterprise.

> During this period, I was constantly preoccupied with the analysis of every film which I saw, and in considering whether I could make them here. There was no doubt whatsoever about the utility of the profession and its importance as an industry ... this was the period of the *Swadeshi* movement and there was profuse talking and lecturing on the subject. For me personally, this led to the resignation of my comfortable government job and taking to an independent profession. I took this opportunity to explain my ideas to my friends and leaders of the *Swadeshi* movement. Even people who were familiar with me for 15 years found my ideas impracticable. [15]

These and other articles of Phalke, which were serialised in the Marathi magazine *Navyug* between 1917–18, reflect both—a sense of betrayal as well as rage at being unable to mobilise support for what he thought was a perfectly nationalist project. One way to assess Phalke's sense of loss could be by reading his article against the scanty source materials available on the nationalist positions regarding cinema. For example, Bal Gangadhar Tilak, Phalke's contemporary, and leader of the extremist faction of the Indian National Congress, took the lead in establishing the connection between cinema and the national movement. This comes across clearly in columns in the Marathi newspaper *Kesari*, which Tilak edited from Poona. In fact, when *Raja Harishchandra* was released in 1913, the *Kesari* was one of the first nationalist newspapers to review it and acclaim it as India's first *swadeshi* film. Tilak even suggested to Phalke that he launch a film company (which Tilak proposed could be called the Hindustan Cinema Film Company) with American assistance to make films for the domestic and the international markets. Phalke politely declined, asserting that he wanted to make films exclusively for the Indian audience with *swadeshi* themes.[16] One does not come across any correspondence between Phalke and Tilak after this incident but there is evidence to suggest that until his death in 1921, Tilak remained in constant touch with prominent Indian filmmakers. It did not therefore come as a surprise when his funeral procession became one of the most extensively filmed events of the 1920s.[17] In addition to Tilak, the most vocal support to cinema came from Rabindranath Tagore. Tagore's interest in the medium was stirred when some of his stories began to be filmed in the 1920s. The first among these was *Manbhanjan* (1923), followed by *Balidan* (1927), *Bicharak* (1929), *Dalia* (1930), *Giribala* (1930), and *Naukadubi* (1932). In his famous letter to Murari Bhaduri, Tagore explained how silent cinema had been able to develop its own grammar.

> The principal element of a motion picture is the 'flux of image'. The beauty and grandeur of this force in motion has to be developed in such a way that it becomes self-supported without the use of words. If some other language is needed to explain its own, it amounts to incompetence. If music can achieve profundity without the words of the cadence of a melody, then why should not this 'motive force' be considered as a distinct aesthetic experience? [18]

In 1932, New Theatres announced that Tagore himself would direct their forthcoming production—*Natir Puja*. In the absence of any surviving print it is unclear whether or not Tagore was actually able to direct the film, but after the film was released he is reported to have been unhappy with the results. Yet this did not diminish his enthusiasm for cinema. By 1936 he was ready to experiment again, this time as a music director along with Pankaj Mullick, in P.C. Barua's *Mukti* (1937). [19]

Like Tagore, Jawaharlal Nehru's first memories of cinema belonged to the films of the silent era. As a student in England, Nehru had watched theatre and cinema with unwavering passion and met many stage and film artists of that time, including the famous Charlie Chaplin.[20] The earliest reference available is Nehru's participation in the Madurai Conference of 1931, organized by the Tamil Nadu Actors Association, where he exhorted filmmakers and artists to work towards the fulfilment of the objectives of the freedom struggle. Five years later, after he had watched *Achhut Kanya* with rapt attention at the Roxy Theatre in Bombay along with Sarojini Naidu, he wrote a congratulatory letter to Devika Rani. But there is barely anything in the letter that can be construed as Nehru's preliminary statement on Indian cinema. A more precise formulation had to await the first Indian Motion Picture Congress in Bombay in 1939, when Nehru dispatched a personal communication to the organisers. He asserted:

I am far from satisfied at the quality of work that has been done. Motion pictures have become an essential part of modern life and they (*sic*) can be used with greater advantage for educational purposes.... So far greater stress has been laid on a type of film, which presumably is supposed to be entertaining, but the standard or quality of which is not high. I hope that the industry will consider now in terms of meeting the standards and of aiming at producing high-class films that have educational and social values. Such films should receive the cooperation not only of the public but also of the state. [21]

Nehru's reservations about the poor quality and content of Indian cinema notwithstanding, several policy initiatives were taken during his prime ministership that were to change its course in the future. These included the setting up of the Patil Committee of Enquiry, the Khosla Commission on Censorship, and the creation of the Film Finance Corporation. Moreover, the credit for organising the First International Film Festival of India in 1952 goes entirely to him.

It was Gandhi, more than any other nationalist leader, who shocked the film community with his consummate hostility towards cinema. It is paradoxical that by the early 1920s Gandhi, whose indigenous methods of political mobilization had elevated him to India's undisputed leader of the national movement, could envisage no role for cinema as an instrument of political intervention. Thus, when the Indian Cinematograph Committee[22] placed before Gandhi a questionnaire to know his views about cinema in 1937, Gandhi returned the document with a letter addressed to T. Rangachariar, the Chairman of the Committee. Describing cinema as 'sinful technology' he replied:

Even if I was so minded, I should be unfit to answer your questionnaire as I have never been to a cinema. But even to an outsider, the evil that it has done and is doing is patent. The good that it has done at all remains to be proved. [23]

By the 1940s, Gandhi's patience with cinema had begun to wear out rapidly. An interview in the *Harijan* of 3 May, 1942 reveals this:

Mahatma Gandhi: You will be surprised to hear that I have never tuned in to a radio, nor have I been to a cinema

Question: Do you think these things are bad?

Mahatma Gandhi: I will not say so. I may say that cinema films are often bad. About the radio I do not know. [24]

The film community squirmed with disbelief. It took enormous courage on the part of writer and filmmaker Khwaja Ahmed Abbas to mount a frontal attack on Gandhi through a letter published in the October 1939 issue of *Filmindia.* I have reproduced the letter in detail to demonstrate the crucial questions it raises about the relationship between cinema and ethics and its implications for the nationalist project as a whole. Abbas wrote:

In two of your recent statements I have been surprised and pained to find cinema mentioned in (what appears to me) slightly contemptuous terms...you briefly state that you never saw pictures. In a more recent statement you include cinema among evils like gambling, satta, horse racing etc., which you leave alone 'for fear of losing caste'. Now if these statements had come from any other person, it was not necessary to be worried about them.... But your case is different ... even the slightest expression of your opinion carries much weight.... And one of the worlds' most useful inventions would be allowed to be discarded ... to be abused by unscrupulous people.... I have no knowledge of how you came to have such a poor opinion of cinema.... I can only imagine that rushing from one political meeting to another, you chanced to catch a glimpse of some lewd cinema poster ... and concluded that cinema is evil. I frankly confess that there are many films that are morally and aesthetically bad.... I also confess that you and most of your generation will not like the playful romanticism that my generation gloats over in most films.... The concept of morality changes from age to age.... I sincerely hold that the national movement led by you has indirectly caused much purification and regeneration in the realm of Indian cinema.... You are a great soul, Bapu.... Give this toy ... a little of your attention and bless it with a smile of tolerance.[25]

Gandhi did not respond. His silence evoked another impassioned outburst. This time from Baburao Patel, the editor of *Filmindia:*

Let this champion of the *daridranarayan* come down and meet us and we shall try to convince him or be convinced. Surely as workers in the film field, we are not worse than the poor untouchable for whom the old Mahatma's heart bleeds. And if he thinks we are, the more reason why he should come to our rescue. [26]

Gandhi was finally able to watch *Ram Rajya,* his first film, in 1943. Despite being unwell, Gandhi watched the entire film but maintained a stoic silence afterwards.[27]

Thus, there were two ways in which the nationalist leadership approached cinema. First, as 'low art' it aimed to provide vulgar entertainment to the masses. Gandhi, who viewed cinema as a corrupting influence, could not envisage a role for it in the construction of a *swadeshi* culture. There were others who compared cinema to other vices like gambling and prostitution and demanded a strict censorship over it. But leaders such as Tilak, Tagore, and Nehru felt that cinema could effectively integrate the transformative agendas of the nationalist project. Hence they continued to impress upon filmmakers the need to make films with powerful social and educational themes. Even critics of this time like Aurobindo Ghosh and Ananda Coomarswamy, who wrote extensively about art and culture, made little attempt either to treat cinema as a rich and varied register of popular culture or to understand the new regime of aesthetics that it had inaugurated. These ambivalences, as we shall see, were articulated in complex and imbricated ways, in the Hindi periodicals from the 1920s through the 1940s.

The Language Question

The story of how eighteenth century Hindustani was recast in the nineteenth century and appeared in its twentieth century Sanskritized avatar as *khari boli* has already been told in much detail by Dalmia, Rai, and Orsini.[28] This transformation would not have been possible had it not been for the emergence of what Orsini has termed the 'Hindi Public Sphere'. Borrowed from Habermas's *Structural Transformation of the Public Sphere* (1989), Orsini uses the term to imply 'a discursive and institutional space, a common language, set of procedural principles ... activism and the awareness of a public "out there".[29] In practice, this meant that if Hindi had to claim autonomy it would have to be separated for Urdu, 'standardized' and 'historicized'.[30] The Hindi public sphere, which expanded in somewhat concentric circles around the towns of Benares, Kanpur, Agra, Allahabad, Patna, Delhi, Calcutta, and Bombay, attracted people of landed wealth who belonged to Brahmin, Rajput, Kayastha, Bania, and Khatri families. Members of these castes '... produced the first wave of activism and created institutional space for Hindi in the form of periodicals, literary and public associations, and text-book writing'.[31]

By the turn of the nineteenth century, the stage had been set to probe into the mixed heritage of Hindi and to reclaim it as a derivative of Sanskrit. As the Hindi public sphere expanded rapidly, the Hindi Sahitya Sammelan (1910) of Allahabad became active in articulating the demands of the Hindi nationalists. The Congress politicians from the United Provinces (the erstwhile North-West Provinces) began to patronize the Sammelan in different ways, often participating in its annual activities. Gandhi, among others, was quick to comprehend the role which language would play in the politics of mobilisation. As early as 1916, at the inaugural ceremony of the Banaras Hindu University, he had rejected the notion of English as the unifying language of the country and had cast his vote in favour of Hindi. It was therefore natural for Gandhi to be invited to attend the eighth annual conference of the Sammelan at Indore in 1918. At Indore, his proposal to evolve a scheme to popularise Hindi in the south was met with much support from the delegates. But as time wore on, Gandhi became increasingly aware of the troubled histories and genealogies of 'Hindi'. [32] He made his intentions clear during the twenty-fourth conference in 1935, when he successfully persuaded the Sammelan to formally accept Hindi-Hindustani as the future *rashtrabhasha* of India.[33] The Hindi press reacted with fury. Gandhi's proposal was proclaimed as an act of betrayal.[34] Orsini has suggested that the language debate 'took the form of a struggle for authority: should it rest with national politicians or with Hindi experts?'[35] The Hindi-Hindustani controversy, which began to be articulated in cinema-related essays published by Hindi periodicals, needs to be examined in this context.

Reviewing *Achhut Kanya* in *Madhuri*, a writer complimented the filmmaker for making a beautiful film on village India by exposing the nakedness of Indian society.[36] He also attributed the success of the film to the birth of a mature audience, which had begun to appreciate the worth of art.[37] The writer, however, ruefully observed that:

> A Bengali gentleman has written the plot of *Achhut Kanya*. One fails to understand how the stories of Bengali writers achieve extraordinary success in cinema. Our Hindi has not produced a writer whose story is as beautiful and famous as Sharatchandra's *Devdas* and *Manzil*. One also does not hear [these days] about Premchand or Sudarshan.[38]

Another writer, Shyamnarayan Kapoor, slammed filmmakers for showing callous disregard to the purity of language. The attempt to use Urdu and Persian words in Indian mythologicals or Sanskrit words in films with stories set in Iran was cited as a case in point. Kapoor wished the language of cinema could be Hindi so as to enable filmmakers to serve the cause of the nation.[39] Concerned that very few papers in India published serious essays and critiques about cinema, he proposed that more comments on the subject be frequently published in Hindi.[40]

In the case of some writers Hindi nationalism no longer meant a repudiation of Urdu alone, but assumed aggressive posturing towards other languages which posed a challenge to Hindi's bid to supremacy in the film industry.

> The astonishing thing is that most films are made in Hindi but their stories are translated from Marathi, Gujarati and Bengali. Is there an immediate scarcity of Hindi stories.... Recently, Bengali newspapers, jealous of Pandit Sudarshan's success, have by propaganda created a feeling that 'Foreign Dogs' have been banned in the lands of '*Swadeshi Thakurs*'. Regionalism is on the rise in Bengal. Realizing that Hindi has acquired the stature of a national language, the Saturn eye of Bengali has now fallen upon it. Hindi *wallahs* better be careful. [41]

Here, the Hindi nationalists seem to show utter contempt for history. In fact, right from the second half of the nineteenth century, Bengali intellectuals like Rajendra Lal Mitra, Keshub Chandra Sen, and Bankimchandra Chattopadhyaya had been campaigning to make Hindi the administrative language of the North-West Provinces. Bankim and Bhudeva Mukherji had even proposed declaring Hindi India's national language.[42] Hindi nationalists thus gave the language controversy a new twist. By targeting Bengali along with Urdu, they wanted to remind readers that Hindi was no longer a regional language, but represented the linguistic aspirations of the Indian people at large. Writing in the strife-torn environment, just before the partition of India, Umesh Joshi censured Indian cinema for denying Hindi its rightful place within the medium:

> Hindi appears in a distorted form in Indian films.... Difficult Arabic and Persian words are promoted in the name of Hindi. Hindi films run with the help of the Hindi speaking people; crores of rupees are collected from the Hindi territories.... Today Hindi writers are doing the rounds of film companies.... Hindi cinema values [today] Urdu writers, or those Hindi writers who have swallowed their pride. Only writers with some self-esteem view producers and directors with contempt ... they do not bow before [them] ... they do not value money as much as they value ideals.[43]

Joshi further explains why Hindi had descended to such levels of apathy and neglect:

> Today most producers and directors in cinema are Gujarati, Marathi or Bengali and have no idea of the character of Hindi. The Urdu *munshis* who proudly call themselves the 'linguists of Lucknow', have succeeded in bluffing the filmmakers. Sycophancy is the family trait of the *munshis*.[44]

Urdu came to be privileged, observed Joshi, because many actors and actresses in Bombay belonged to the Urdu-speaking districts of Punjab:

> They are well versed in Urdu. But however much they rehearse they will not be able to pronounce Hindi in its natural way.... Hence, Hindi words are expunged for their convenience and replaced by Arabic and Persian equivalents. Such films with a mixture of Urdu words are screened regularly. No one protests. The producers are convinced that the language of North Hindustan is the one which is spoken in cinema.[45]

Pakistani film historian Mushtaq Guzdar laments that the Bombay film industry had 'lured men of substance into its fold, enriching itself, and causing a brain drain at other film centres'.[46] It has also been suggested that India's film industry was heading towards cultural rootlessness because some of the film industry's finest talents had to 'exert themselves in a language not their own, spoken by people from whom they were both physically and culturally removed'.[47] Indeed, by the mid-1930s, alongside Bengali directors and Gujarati producers, the number of Urdu writers who sought refuge in the burgeoning Bombay film industry was disproportionately high. Drawn from the undivided Punjab, Delhi, United Provinces, and Bihar, not all of them were Muslims. In fact Premchand, Rajendra Singh Bedi, Krishna Chander and Ashk—all non-Muslims—wrote in Urdu.[48] It was because of the presence of such writers that Hindi cinema was able to retain its eclectic flavour. But the Hindi nationalist in Joshi found the situation unsavoury.

> It is the foremost duty of the Hindi-speaking public to openly boycott such films so that the producers are made to understand that the character of Hindustan's national language was not the one portrayed in films.[49]

Condemning the use of Arabic–Persian mixed Hindi in Indian mythologicals, he declared that the trend was 'dangerous and humiliating for our culture'.[50] Furthermore, it was a matter of shame for Hindu producers and Hindi-speaking people alike that 'Muslim writers were trying to force Islamic culture into our films through dialogues and songs'.[51] Joshi's diatribe ends with the suggestion that the Hindi Sahitya Sammelan take immediate stock of the situation. [52]

Harish Trivedi has recently argued that Urdu writers continued to thrive in Bombay because they were the 'inheritors of a … different and pliable tradition of literary patronage and of literature being regarded as entertainment'.[53] However, this is only part of the explanation. Indeed, by the 1860s, a nascent yet discernible Urdu public sphere had emerged. However, the language policy of the colonial government demolished the hopes of the Urdu protagonists. By 1900, Hindi had been formally declared as the language of administration in Bihar and the Central and United Provinces. The negative consequences flowing out of this enactment impacted the Urdu publishing industry as the demand for Urdu progressively declined in schools and colleges. [54] Hence, it was more than the 'pliability of tradition of literary patronage' that facilitated Urdu writers' relocation to Bombay. The film industry offered them security of tenure when similar opportunities had dwindled considerably in north India. Hindi writers, on the contrary, had a choice of returning to their former careers. Also, as Trivedi has argued, their exodus from Bombay brought an abrupt end to the 'wishful thinking' that there had ever existed a possibility of developing Hindi cinema as a pure literary genre. [55]

The Nature of Film Criticism

By the beginning of the twentieth century, film news and columns began to appear as regular features in most newspapers of India.[56] A somewhat similar trend was perceptible in magazines and periodicals. In the 1920s, entrepreneurs began to feel the need to publish magazines exclusively devoted to cinema. The first among these to be launched was the Gujarati magazine *Mauj Majah* (1924).[57] The success of *Mauj Majah* prompted others to venture into film journalism. Shailjananda Mukherjee, novelist and director, cobbled together the Bengali film periodical *Bioscope* (1930)[58] and later *Shahana*.[59] The first Hindi film periodical, *Chitrapat*, was started by Hrishamcharan Jain from Delhi in 1934. Another Bengali periodical, *Ruparekha*, began to be published by Jyotishchandra Ghosh around the same time. English language readers were able to savour film journalism for the first time in 1935 when Baburao Patel brought out *Filmindia*, a magazine notorious for the 'politically partisan views' of its editor.[60] *Filmindia* (reborn as *Mother India* in 1949) remained the market leader until *Filmfare* arrived in 1952. The 1930s and the 1940s witnessed several waves of film magazines. These included, among others, Jogiban Bandopadyaya's *Kheyali* (1934), Wadia Movietone's *The Indian Screen Gazette* (1938), V.P. Sathe's *Sound* (1942), and Kailash Mukhopadhyay's *Rupamancha* (1943). Targeted at the middle-class reader, film magazines provided a curious blend of film reviews, film news, advertisements of new releases, and abundant gossip. Unfortunately, most magazines had a high mortality rate and very few specimens have survived. [61]

Cinema related essays in Hindi periodicals differed from their counterparts in film magazines in three respects. First, cinema was viewed not as art-in-itself but in relation to other art forms such as theatre and dance. In the second place, there was an overriding concern to evolve a methodology for understanding and interpreting cinema. Third, cinema columns avoided frivolous writings on the subject. Hindi writers viewed film criticism as serious business. They firmly believed that there existed a deep connection between good cinema and a discriminating public. For example, Lakshman Prasad Gargya discussed the method of Gajanand Sharma, a contemporary critic whose reviews, Gargya suggested, helped shape viewer preferences.

> In the early days of the talkies Gajanand Sharma M.A, drew much respect as a critic. It has been my experience that cinema lovers decided to see a certain film only after they had read Sharma's review in the Delhi periodicals '*Chitrapat*' and '*Movies*'. Sharma's style was as follows—He began with plot description so that readers could understand the sequence of events. This was followed by a description of the characters and their roles in the film. Finally, Sharma focused on … the

technique of direction, acting etc. Sometimes Sharma also made a funny comment about a certain character. [62]

Another critic discussed by Gargya is J.R.Shastri:

> Shastri began his career with *Rangabhoomi*. Later he also wrote for *Chitrapat*. But some of his best critiques were published in *Rangabhoomi*. Shastri's viewpoint was shaped by psychological facts. He believed that 'scathing' and 'sarcastic' criticism as well as 'ridiculing' destroyed the seriousness of our views....The question before us is not to reform the companies ... the question ... is to make the people *parkhi*. If people become *parkhis*, reform is bound to follow. [63]

Thus, Gargya leaves little room for doubt that the objective of film criticism was not to engender sterile pedantry but to transform ordinary people into *parkhis* or connoisseurs of cinema. If this were to happen then India could produce better films.

Writing for *Sudha* in 1935, Govind Ballabh Pant analysed the causes of cinema's ultimate supremacy over theatre. According to Pant, cinema enjoyed four distinct advantages. In the first place, while the depth of the field in theatre was always constricted, 'panning' and 'tracking' enabled cinema to expand it infinitely. Second, cinema could project reality in a more natural way. For example, scenes depicting large 'crowds' or 'wars' could not be simulated on stage while in cinema they could be shot easily on location and realistically depicted. Third, cinema by controlling movement in time through devices such as 'fade in', 'fade out', 'mixing', and 'superimposition' had actually altered the norms of narration. Fourth, unlike theatre, in which the scenes were very long, cinema had shortened them so that the audience did not get bored. [64] More than a tribute to cinema, Pant's essay is an exposition of cinematic techniques which is aimed to help readers identify the causes of the technological superiority of cinema over other art forms.

Pant's arguments about the demise of theatre and the emergence of a rival regime of visuality did not find favour with other writers. J.P. Srivastava read a paper entitled 'Cinema Tatha Rangmanch' at the annual Hindi Sahitya Sammelan conference in 1936; it was subsequently published in *Sudha* in the same year. In this paper, Srivastava asserted that though theatre had not been able to compete with cinema in evoking natural performances from its actors, in enabling quick changes of scenes, or in preventing melodramatic performances, it was far from becoming an art in decline. Hence, when 'some people are confounded whether theatre has lost its lustre because of the talkies', they need to be reassured that 'just as photography could not destroy painting, the talkie cannot destroy or paralyze theatre'. [65]

In yet another essay, drawing a connection between cinema and dance, Kapildev Singh lauded the efforts of film companies like Prabhat, New Theatres, and Bombay Talkies for reviving extinct dance forms. Citing examples from films like *Mahatama*, *Amrit Manthan*, *Amar Jyoti*, *Maya*, *Mira*, *Karorepati*, *Mukti*, *Vidyapati*, *Jeevan Prabhat*, *Achhut Kanya*, and others, Singh stated that 'Cinema has certainly contributed to the betterment of the dance form, on which hinges the development of our culture.'[66]

Rajkishore Sharma indicted every film company in India, except New Theatres, for making films that were inferior in terms of direction and cinematography. He asserted that the nascent film industry in India required a clear sense of direction from its critics. For this purpose, Sharma attempted a frame-by-frame analysis of the New Theatres film *Dhoop Chhaon*. He found the 'photography brilliant', the 'sound design clear', 'no faults in the scenario', and the 'direction excellent'.[67] Sharma also described the camera positions of an entire sequence.

> A close up shot where Rajkumari's eyes meet Deepak's in the driving mirror, a long shot of Deepak's entry into Roopkumari's house, a medium shot of the rich banker's brother tearing a letter inside the car and a middle shot of a startled banker watching a car take away the child followed by a medium close up shot of the same.[68]

The May 1938 issue of *Sudha* carried an essay by Ramasrey Sharma in which the author devoted eight pages to the systematic analysis of the film *Jeevan Prabha*. He divided his essay into four separate segments—plot, acting, scenes, and language. The nuances of the film were worked out in detail under each segment.[69] In a separate essay published in the *Chand* of 1938, Sharma's contemporary Gargya laid down the principles for good film criticism.[70] Gargya insisted that good film criticism meant placing the least emphasis on plot illustration and description of characters. What needed to be attempted, instead, was a comparative evaluation of all aspects of cinema. This was possible if a psychological approach was adopted. Finally, identifying the reasons and the categories of audiences who derived satisfaction in watching certain kinds of films formed the last component of Gargya's enquiry. Gargya's last formulation is particularly interesting because for the first time, a writer was trying to understand the phenomenon of reception in cinema. There is no evidence to show that his methodology had any impact on readers, but the fact that he proposed a basic guideline for film criticism cannot be ignored.

Kamalkumar Sharma attempted a classification system for Indian films by dividing them into 10 genres. These were: 1. ballad films (*Natir Pooja*); 2. play films and musical films (*Bridegroom Wanted*); 3. cartoon films (*Silly Symphony*, *Mickey Mouse*, *Jambu Kaka*); 4. comic films (*Manmayi Girls*

School); 5. story films (*Devdas, Ruplekha*); 6. epic films (*Sita, Queen Christina*); 7. church films (*Shri Gaurang, Dakshyaksh*); 8. art films (*Vasantsen*); 9. jungle films (*Trader Horn, Mahua*); and 10. fantasy films (*Hatimtai, Magic Flute*).[71] Though simplistic in his approach, Sharma's typology must have been one of the first of its kind in Hindi journalism.

Thus, throughout the 20s and the 30s, Hindi writens groped for the key metaphors through which the cinematic process could be elaborated and understood. In the absence of a tradition of critical thinking about cinema such as the one obtaining in Europe and America (Münsterberg, Arnheim, Eisenstein, Bàlàzs) in this period, what the Hindi periodicals set out to achieve was nothing short of extraordinary.

The Ethics of Good Cinema

Even before the Indian Cinematographic Committee had formally published its voluminous findings in 1928,[72] the debate on what constituted good cinema had already become an integral part of the Hindi public sphere. In fact, many of the issues highlighted by the Committee had already been examined and reported by Hindi periodicals. For example, the Editorial Board of *Sudha* had, in its first issue of 1927, studied the impact of cinema on Indian youth and had recommended strict control over films that were corrupting young minds.

> The bioscope-cinema *tamasha* is becoming very popular in India. We have seen ourselves that in Benares, children aged eight to ten years—who cannot get good education, but can easily acquire bad habits—buy two-anna tickets and watch cinema daily. We have even seen that because of this habit ... students of Sanskrit are selling lemonade-soda inside.... In this situation it is imperative for the government to exercise control over cinema.[73]

Blaming American films for corrupting the Indian youth, the writer further noted:

> Until now most of the films shown are made in America.... Some are made in England ... very few made by Indian companies are shown.... It is true that audiences do not prefer them [Indian Films]. Audiences prefer films that have scenes of violence, looting, daring and adventure. Such films are generally made in America. People learn bad things by watching them. In fact, this is an art if put into good use, will benefit people. However, its misuse can be terrible.[74]

The editor of *Chand* also strongly condemned cinema for beguiling young minds. He cited the views of the distinguished Bengali scientist P.C. Roy who, in reference to cinema at the annual conference of the Suniti

Sangh in Dacca, had issued an appeal for imposing restrictions on all films promoting obscenity and immorality. Roy had remarked that 'parents were sending money to their children for education, but children were wasting it on cinema'.[75] *Chand* also reported that the Women's Conference in Madras (1935) had resolved to seek parental assistance in notifying the Commissioner of Police whenever they found an obscene film or a poster on display.[76]

Hollywood bashing continued in other writings as well. Pannalal Srivastava warned Indian readers of the ideological undercurrents of American cinema. American cinema was actually undermining India's freedom struggle. 'Today, cinema is the most powerful weapon of propaganda.... American film companies make ... films to defame India.... *Storm Over Bengal*, *Siege of Lucknow*, *Gungadin* ... are a blow to our freedom struggle.'[77] Srivastava advocated public awareness instead of censorship. He reminded the readers that when 'the *Siege of Lucknow* and *Gunga Din* arrived in India, the provincial governments had banned them. But this did not bring much benefit. The aim of the foreign capitalists is to defame India.'[78]

Another writer argued that Indian cinema had not been able to protect its audience from the challenge posed by Western cinema because it had already entered a period of stasis. Unlike Western films, Indian films were made only to entertain and not to propagate transformative agendas.

> Hindustani cinema attaches much value to entertainment. The objective is similar in Europe except that in Russia and Germany it plays the role of a literary person and an interpreter. Cinema has played an important role in changing the conditions in Russia while it has contributed to the growth of a chivalrous spirit in Germany.... Films in India are made with the object of entertainment. All the films made so far have mythology and trickery. There is no reference to the social or the contemporary.[79]

Mohan Lal Gupta disagreed. He observed that Indian cinema had fallen into disrepair because it had failed to fulfill its basic function, namely, to entertain.

> When we enter a cinema hall with a tired mind and a heavy heart, to banish our fatigue, our only objective is entertainment. The aim of the filmmaker should be to fulfill our objectives. But in ninety percent of the cases when we come out of the cinema hall we appear more tired and preoccupied.[80]

Another scribe blamed the mass production of films in India for their inferior quality.

> Every year new films are being released in India. The Talkie has grown so big that its head cannot be distinguished from the tail. The foremost objective is to

produce a film in seven days! Whether such haste vitiates the sequence of the story, kills art, destroys the language—is nobody's concern. A film is released so that third class seats in the theatre can be occupied and the pockets of owners, directors and the leading cast can be filled with money.[81]

He also questioned the flawed nature of the film narrative, accusing Indian directors for having completely neglected the pedagogical aims of cinema.

Our directors feel that without incorporating 'fight-sequences' and 'chase' scenes, a film does not become lively … they cannot picturize a 'climax' without 'kissing' and 'embracing' scenes.... They have never tried to see how useful cinema can be for the spread of education. Indians … prefer films with Indian plots, but those with taste watch foreign films as they find Indian films 'loud' and 'uninteresting'.... In many places they embellish their plots with situations and scenes … lifted from foreign films … which does not make them more beautiful than a jute rag with silk patches over it.... There are historical errors in the scenes....[82]

Indian films also lagged behind in other aspects. Their 'photography is not satisfactory … the editing ordinary' or 'there is not a single owner of an Indian film company who has been able to make a film for the international market'.[83] Finally, Gupta urged the Indian film industry to pay heed to Sheikh Iftikar Rasul, a London-based filmmaker of Indian origin who, on a visit to India, had recommended redemptive measures for making the Indian film industry more competitive. These included: 1. Actors be encouraged to specialise in just one or two roles; 2. actors of one film company be allowed to work in another; 3. talented actors be given due publicity; 4. films be made to provide education along with entertainment; 5. industry be reoriented to attract educated people; 6. more attention be paid to photography; 7. film stars be encouraged to visit theatres where their films were being screened; 9. only skilled craftsmen be employed; and 10. every scene be well rehearsed before a take.[84] It would have been of crucial importance if we could have devised a mechanism to determine if Rasul's prescriptions were adopted by the industry at large or whether any filmmaker actually benefited from them. But the fact that a vernacular periodical of the 1930s had the insight to publish an essay that demanded an overhaul of the film industry so that its products could become competitive in the national as well as the global markets, assumes significance in a period when the flow of capital and technology was unidirectional.

In another detailed analysis of contemporary cinema Lakshmishankar Mishra, 'Arun' B.A., observed remorsefully that 'it is an unpleasant truth that most of our Indian film companies have been successful in making inferior quality films'.[85] But unlike Gupta, Mishra expressed satisfaction that there were still 'some companies whose objective from the very beginning had been not only to encourage art and literature but also to make films that are exemplary'.[86] Drawing a distinction between 'good' films and bad 'mythologicals', Mishra argued that there was little value in making religious films as they lacked proper subject treatment and were made to satisfy the tastes of a small audience. Such films could attract audiences earlier as taste for good cinema had not then developed.[87] But things had started changing with time. The audience wanted to see good films as much as it recognised the value of money. With refinement in art, progress had become the order of the day. A critical viewpoint (*aalochanaatamak drishti*) had finally emerged.[88]

There were others who did not share the optimism of Mishra. Alarmed at what he felt were declining standards of Indian cinema, Kapoor wrote:

> How competent and enlightened a director should be becomes clear when we watch a European or American film.... In India except for one or two directors none knows the ABC of direction.... Except for the New Theatres of Bengal and Pune's Prabhat, no film company has made artistic films. Bombay filmmakers are completely commercial. Their objective is to fool people and make money somehow...Beginning from the silent era, the few good films which can be counted are '*Devdas*', '*Meerabai*', '*Chandidas*', '*Pooranbhakt*', '*Rooplekha*', '*Taruni*', '*Manmayi Girls School*', '*Excuse Me Sir*', '*Amritmanthan*', '*Bhagyachakra*'.[89]

Kapoor cautioned against treating Hollywood as a measure for good cinema. Blaming American films for misrepresenting India in American films, he alleged that in *Behind the Curtain*, the dramatization of the bazaar scenes as well as the portrayal of Indian women was aimed at tarnishing India's image in the eyes of the world. Likewise, *Son of India* distorted reality to such an extent that it did not remain a film about India. Kapoor exhorted Indian audiences to protest against such misrepresentations so that American filmmakers would in the future try to exhibit India with greater accuracy.[90] Finally, Kapoor also castigated Indian filmmakers for making films that were inferior, with poor narratives and narrow choice of themes.

> Talkies are the newest mode of entertainment for the Indian audience and their popularity is steadily growing.... Rarely is a film made that makes us proud.... Most films have weak plots....They are full of songs ... whether a person is dying or living, a song has to be sung. Whether one is a king, beggar, thief, bandit or a *goonda*—he must sing a song.[91]

Agitated by the glamour and publicity that preceded the release of every film, Kapoor contended that it inevitably resulted in the press indiscriminately declaring all films to be good, arguing that he was not against publicity as long as it reflected the truth.[92] Also, concerned about filmmakers being lured by 'mythologicals', he lamented that the genre was targeted only at a small audience consisting of the women and the elderly. Moreover, mythologicals had little contemporary relevance.[93] Instead, he advocated a cinema that highlighted the eradication of social evils.[94] Appalled by a report that prostitutes had started entering the profession, Kapoor warned that the process would deleteriously impact women and children.[95] Clearly, Kapoor emerges as an uncompromising votary of the nationalist project. Under the new role envisaged for it, cinema could not be allowed to become an embarrassment to nationalist imaginings in art. By purging it of all pre-realist yearnings, Indian cinema could be brought closer to the goal of creating a purely nationalist aesthetic.

Reflections on Cinematic Techniques and Inventions

Essays on technical aspects of filmmaking were rare though, when these were published, they reveal that a nuanced rendering of the craft was possible in vernacular literature. '*Bioscope Ke Chhipe Rahasya*' (Hidden Secrets of the Bioscope) explores the production of special effects in cinema. The essay highlights the use of 'double exposure' and 'reversing gear' for producing such effects. According to the author, special effects such as making a man spring to a treetop or an ocean disappear, turning a human being into a dwarf, or creating a monster on the screen have become possible only with the advent of new technology.[96] The objective of the essay is clearly to banish the element of *rahasya* (mystery) from cinema. This was necessary if the screen had to be prevented from being turned into a site for irrational imagination.

In 1933, a correspondent of *Chand* wrote an essay on the art of 'make-up' in cinema. The essay included a photo illustration from the film *Mr Jekyll and Mr Hyde*. The correspondent noted that though the use of effective 'make-up' had caused wastage of valuable raw stock, the results were spectacular.[97] The correspondent also pointed out that the success of films like *The Hunch Back of Notre Dame* and *Frankenstein* could be singularly attributed to good 'make-up'. He lamented however, that Indian filmmakers required developing greater skills. Pointing out that Ezra Mir's make up in *Zarina* was not realistic, he hoped that one day India would produce its indigenous 'make-up' artists like Boris Karloff and Fredrick March in the West.[98] What the *Chand* correspondent perhaps implied by realistic 'make-up' was the attainment of versimilitude.

In another essay, readers are informed about a machine invented by a scientist— Vamadasa Chatterjee of the Science College at Calcutta. The *swadeshi* machine, we are told, is not being commercially produced, but a large-scale production of the machine would be desirable as it would facilitate the making of low-cost films.[99] Kapoor also mentions that the support for the inventor has been overwhelming, as the owners of the local theatre (*Chavighar*) have announced that any film made with Chatterjee's machine would be screened on a priority basis. Without doubt, Kapoor's appeal to the industry is patriotic. Earlier in the century, the *Swadeshi* movement had created the right conditions for scientists and inventors like P.C. Ray and J.C. Bose to turn into entrepreneurs. Kapoor deploys Chatterjee's camera as a metaphor so that the imbricated relationship between nationalism, art, industry, and the anti-colonial movement could be explored.

Star and Corporate Profiles

In addition to reviews and critiques of cinema, brief sketches of film stars were also published. Different authors deployed different criteria to distinguish good/great from bad ones. Some used these distinctions to imagine the arrival of an ideal citizen-actor. For example, Sarju Prasad Prem pronounced Prithviraj Kapoor as a good actor because of Kapoor's ability to learn Hindi in a short period of time.[100] Kapoor was regarded great also because of his untarnished reputation in society. According to Prem, Kapoor was perhaps among the few actors in India who, despite their riches, refrained from women,[101] drinking, and smoking.[102] A similar sketch of Navinchandra, a star of successful action and stunt films of the 1930s, reveals how vernacular writers were trying to establish the subtle connection between art and social responsibility. Many of Navinchandra's films, including *Pawagarh ka Patan*, *Young India*, *Chalta Purza*, and *Badmaash ka Beta*, we are told, became very popular at the box office.[103] However, Navinchandra's box office success is not attributed to his superior dramatic skills but to his simplicity and humility. Navinchandra, it appears, had to 'struggle much during his student days',[104] but when he became successful, he decided to repay his debts to society by supporting the education of 5–6 students at a time.[105] The essay ends with the hope that Navinchandra would continue to serve both cinema and society with the same dedication as before.[106]

Essays in this category also dealt with great directors of the Indian talkies. Sachidananda Nigam claims that in order to become a great director one had first to prove oneself to be a great artist.[107] Nigam's inquiry takes him deep into the study of some of the prominent directors of his time.

Shortlisting six directors (Chandulal Shah, Ramashankar Chaudhry, Nitin Bose, Pramathesh Barua, Shantaram, and Devakikumar Bose), Nigam proclaims Devakikumar Bose to be the greatest artist-director among them all. Chandulal Shah is rejected because of his failure to make any impact on the audience after his film *The Barrister's Wife*. Besides, Nigam accuses Shah of first being a trader by mentality and an artist later. Ramashankar Chaudhry is discredited for not making great films after *Madhuri* and *Temple Wells*. Likewise, Nitin Bose is cast aside for not being able to exploit the best team of musicians and sound engineers at New Theatres. He is also criticized for directing a commercial film like *Daku Mansur*. Nigam also discusses three films of Barua, namely *Grihadah*, *Manzil*, and *Devdas*. Declaring *Grihadaah* to be a better work than *Devdas*, Nigam argues that whatever little success *Devdas* had achieved was due to Saratchandra Chatterji's story and the songs of K.C. Dey and Sehgal. Shantaram is proclaimed a great director but not the best. His films have 'powerful dialogues, gorgeous settings, enchantment, and great dramatic turning points'.[108] The harshest indictment is reserved for Barua. Barua's problem, alleges Nigam, is succumbing to the charms of the box office. For example, Barua does not hesitate in including a song even when little need exists for it. The net result is that all of Barua's films have become theatrical.[109]

Devakikumar Bose's portrait, on the contrary, stands out in sharp contrast. Nigam calls him a poet at heart, whose films are marked by a relegation of theatrical elements and a progression towards what Nigam refers to as a trend of 'natural acting'.

> When the country was celebrating films like *Laila Majnu*, *Shirin Farhad*, *Savitri Satyavan*, *Ayodhya Ka Raja*, *Subah Ka Sitara* etc., Devakikumar Bose, by making *Chandidas* and *Puranbhakta*, enhanced the prestige of the country.... When the entire film industry was progressing along the path set by theatre.... When dialogues were being uttered in the theatrical mode, songs added inappropriately, and magical and unnatural scenes abounded ... he introduced a natural element in *Chandidas* and *Puranbhakta* and reversed the flow of tide single handedly. [110]

Alongside 'natural acting', argues Nigam, Bose's films always explore socially relevant themes. For example, *Inqalab* is the story of a young revolutionary who wants to create a just society. Similarly in *Kaun,* the protagonist abandons the comforts of modern life to live close to nature.[111] Each film of Bose is unique because it brings to the fore new conflicts, new *rasa*, and new thought:

> Those who worship the works of Milton, Keats, Shelley, Victor Hugo, Turgenev, and Gorky would find Bose's films admirable. Laced with complex psychological riddles and profound philosophy, there are few in India and the world who can match his technical brilliance.[112]

Thus, even though Nigam could not define or explain what he implies by 'art' or its nuanced connection with 'great direction', European classics constitute the reference point for artistic greatness. But what is startling in the list of authors provided by Nigam is the absence of any Hindi author. Nigam's contemporary Ram Kishan Lal Bhatnagar, endorsed the view that Devakikumar Bose was India's foremost director, but cited different reasons for it. According to Bhatnagar, Bose's greatness lay in his correct understanding of history. While other directors distorted the narratives of history, Bose was able to engage them creatively.[113] This was possible because Bose was the only director who understood the true nature and purpose of art and worked towards its perfection, thus vindicating Nigam's stand that in order to be a great director one had to be a great artist as well.[114]

In some issues of the vernacular periodicals, synoptic sketches of India's prominent film companies were also published.

> There are only three Film Companies among Indian talkies that are famous—Prabhat, New Theatres and Bombay Talkies. In order to establish its importance Prabhat made *Amrit Manthan*. It did what the *rishis* and *munis* did ... use the narrative style to influence public minds. *Amrit Manthan* condemned human sacrifice, *Mahatama* attacked untouchability, *Amar Jyoti* spoke about the freedom of women, and *Duniya Na Maane* rejected child marriage.... Thus Prabhat Film Company ... tried to set ideals for a better life by seeking inspiration from religious ... texts.... We hope that it will continue to make good films.[115]

New Theatres' selection of social themes and the rejection of mythologicals was recalled as its single most important contribution to Indian cinema. Sri Krishna argued that this was a reflection of the company's policy of pragmatism. By the repudiation of the mythological, New Theatres had demonstrated that it was the only company in India to realise that 'if all companies made films of a similar *rasa* then the cinema-art of India would not make any collective progress'.[116] Sri Krishna also praised New Theatres for making films that were not obscene.[117] Bombay Talkies too made films in the social genre. However, Bombay Talkies scored over Prabhat by its exemplary use of Hindi, which made its films 'interesting, emotional, poetic, natural, and pure'.[118]

A rare sample, found among the periodicals surveyed, is an essay about a certain East Indian Film Company of Calcutta. The essay reads like publicity material, for the proprietors of the company. Admiring the picturesque surroundings, the author notes that 'everyone in the company behaves courteously ... the studio can be hired at reasonable rates'.[119] He also describes Bajranglalji Khemka, the proprietor, as 'a lover of art who is willing to invest any amount of money for its promotion'.[120] What the author seems to be suggesting is that in order to be regarded as a 'good' film company it must fulfill the social criteria of being an organization that is affordable, professional, and dedicated to art.

SHOULD RESPECTABLE PEOPLE JOIN THE PROFESSION?

In 1938, *Chand* reprinted two brief articles earlier published in the Hindi film periodical *Chitrapat*, along with remarks by Saryuprasad Prem. Both the articles deal with women and moral values prevailing in the film industry. The first, authored by Rajbahadur Singh, begins with a testimony of film actor Prabha who, according to Singh, belongs to a 'respectable family of freedom fighters'. Prabha highlights the importance of *sadhana* in the making of a successful actor:

> Sisters ... regard cinema as a ... mine of fame and wealth.... I consider it my bounden duty to warn them. They should understand that neither a filmmaker awaits them, nor is the audience desperate to honour them. In order to carve out a place for themselves in cinema as well as in the hearts of the audiences, they will have to make the same kind of sacrifices as have been made in other fields.... What is beauty in itself, unless kindled by *sadhana* ... many hurdles will have to be crossed before reaching the peak.... This will require extraordinary will-power.... Few film companies have a clean environment.... Only these should be approached by married women. [121]

Prabha's patriotic credentials are further established when the reader learns that she had been earlier imprisoned for participating in a political demonstration. Readers are also told that Prabha spends most of her time in sharing her anguish with other women.[122] But Singh, who can be credited for successfully rescuing the woman's voice, fails to tell us why Prabha became so bitter towards the end. The question whether she was a victim of sexual harassment or whether her career was marred by a series of flops as she herself had failed to measure up to the levels of *sadhana*, which she mentions in her testimony, remains unanswered. In the concluding part of the article Singh documents the experience of an educated male actor, who incidentally is also a victim of the industry.

> Before coming to Bombay I had thought that a film studio was akin to heaven ... if we express our views about them [now] we can say that they are wrestling pits for modern devils.[123]

Singh does not provide any background about the male actor, except that he was an educated and respectable young man. There is also no information about why the actor is compelled to label the entire industry as 'wrestling pits for modern devils'. The thrust of the article clearly seems to be to forewarn its readers that the industry is not an appropriate career for respectable people.

In the second article, two other depositions made by people from the industry are documented. In the first we come across the opinion of the owner of Vijaya Pictures who, upon being probed, admitted to a reporter that the environment inside the industry was 'far from clean'.[124] In the second case, an actor employed by the Imperial Film Company acknowledges that the 'environment inside the studio was not sacred and no woman could remain pure for long'.[125] The article ends with an emotional appeal to India's youth:

> I appeal to the hard working youth of our country not to enter this field until [it] has been cleansed. Time does not stand still. Change is inevitable. Until cinema is reformed the entry of good people would not be proper.[126]

Jyotindranath conjectured that degeneration had set in because of the increasing presence of prostitutes in the profession.

> There are very few women of good moral character in cinema. Our young men are attracted towards prostitutes who have suddenly acquired the status of film stars.[127]

A number of social reformers and nationalist leaders who had assembled in 1939 to celebrate the 25th anniversary of Indian cinema in a programme organised by the Indian Motion Picture Congress expressed dissatisfaction at the growth of cinema in India. Some speakers, without directly alluding to the entry of prostitutes in the film industry, seemed disturbed at cinema's portrayal of women. K.M. Munshi spoke at length about how Nadia as 'Hunterwali' made a mockery of Indian womanhood.[128] The connection between prostitution and the performing arts began to be established for the first time in the second half of the nineteenth century. This can be seen as the culmination of a concerted movement mounted by administrators, missionaries, and social reformers to bring to an end the evil profession of the *tawaif* or the *nautch* (dancing) girl. It was alleged that Indian classical music had entered a phase of degeneration because of its association with prostitutes who had successfully managed to privilege the erotic *thumri* over its spiritual counterpart, the *khayal*. Vidya Rao, who has analysed the issue, suggests that two musicians from Maharashtra, namely Vishnu Digambar Paluskar (1873–1931) and Vishnu Narayan Bhatkande (1860–1931), campaigned aggressively against *thumri* and its proponents so that Indian classical music could be restored to its spiritual domain.[129] Evidently, Paluskar and Bhatkande did not explore other causes such as diminishing patronage from local rulers and feudal elements for the apparent decline of the *khayal* tradition.

Indeed, during the colonial period, a 'new morality' seemed to have emerged which, as Nair has pointed out, viewed women as its sole guarantors.[130] Men came to be regarded as inherently promiscuous while women came to be seen as endowed with the virtue of monogamous fidelity. Further, no one shared this burden more disproportionately than did middle class women of colonial India.[131] Talwar's survey of women's journals in Hindi between 1910–20 further confirms this. Men not only edited women's periodicals but also wrote about women's issues, adopting distinct patriarchal positions, often appealing for a return to an 'ideal womanhood' of an imagined past. On their part, women writers advocated education of women and adult suffrage, but rarely attacked patriarchy or demanded its ultimate dissolution.[132] The question of moral values was therefore actually addressed to women. It represented the anxieties of men, who saw in the emergence of a professional woman actor the possibility of a reappraisal of the 'woman's question' which had conveniently been relocated to an 'inner domain of sovereignty' by the national movement.[133]

Conclusion

As the number of films steadily rose between 1920–47, and as more and more people thronged to cinema houses, the number of film periodicals also shot up significantly. Rajadhyaksha and Willemen have listed some of these.[134] A similar pattern, though of a smaller magnitude, was seen in the case of cinema-related articles published in Hindi magazines. So when Kapoor bemoaned in 1932 that 'there are very few papers that publish essays and critiques on cinema.... The popularity of cinema demands that useful comments on cinema be published.... There is dearth of cinema based literature in Hindi',[135] he probably misread the situation. His contemporary, Nandkishore Tiwari, alluded to a trend which was just the opposite. Tiwari wrote: 'recently with the progress of the talkie cinema, there has also been an expansion of film literature. Where only few cinema related periodicals were published there are many more now. Growth in periodicals has produced a flood of writers and critics.'[136] Tiwari's observation merits some probing. The May 1936 of *Madhuri* carried a full-page advertisement about the publication of two special issues. The first of these was to focus on stories and the other on films. The advertisement claimed that 20,000 copies of each issue would be printed. A readership of such scale was impressive indeed. Brahmaswarup Gupta asserted that cinema had become a part of everyday life.

Try to sit in the upper class of a cinema hall and you are bound to hear from someone that a certain film star lacked one thing or another, that a star acted miserably in a certain film.... While you are in a train just try to initiate a conversation by saying that 'Sehgal sahib's acting is great' and you will find people comment on all the actors and actresses.[137]

But had cinema spawned good journalism?

> Pick up any cinema-periodical. Read it from the beginning to the end. You will find it full of half-naked and obscene photographs.... The photographs will carry beautiful captions 'The Queen of Emotions Miss ...' or 'The Harbinger of Indian Art Abroad' etc. Fertile minds will ... write poems about them or compile their biographies.[138]

Indeed, when the Hindi poet Mahadevi Verma expressed disdain for such journalism, the editor of a film magazine in Delhi cheekily retorted that the magazine was 'not meant for minors'.[139] Jyotindranath made it clear that he was not against cinema periodicals: 'I agree that cinema periodicals are required. But their main objective should be to reform the profession, to make people aware of its ills, to protect them from obscenity, and to encourage true artists....'[140]

In sum, the radicalization of the national movement from the 1920s onwards and the extraordinary growth of Hindi periodicals created a favorable environment for literary people to intervene in contemporary debates. Many of these were generated within the Hindi public sphere and writers often tried to mediate as mentors of a national culture-in-the-making. This they hoped to achieve by transforming cinema into a subject of critical reflection and debate. Thus, Indian cinema—its narrativity, cinematography, dramaturgy, aesthetics, morality, and social relevance—became the foci of intense literary contemplation. This was in striking contrast to the nationalist discourse, which had either overlooked cinema or treated it as an instrument of nationalist propaganda but had refrained from engaging it theoretically. Cinema had, by altering the traditional forms of narration, had threatened the literary and moral framework of society. Cinema, therefore, required careful interrogation before being assigned a proper place within the domain of cultural production. The continued use of Hindustani by the film industry was seen as a transgression intended to subvert the basis of the 'Hindi' movement which, most believed, had reached a decisive phase of struggle. Writers regretted that Indian films were technically and aesthetically inferior to Western films, but still constituted the best defence against the latter, which were trying to spread an alien culture in India in the time of *swadeshi* and boycott. Nonetheless, people had to be cautioned about the dangers of cinema. If good cinema were to be made in India, it was necessary to develop a critical approach to the medium. Hindi periodicals strove to transform people into *parkhis* or connoisseurs of cinema. This in turn would restore the balance between cinema's quest for providing healthy entertainment as well as realising its educational goals. The woman's question re-emerged as an issue concerning the vulnerability of women in the industry. The Hindi public sphere ensured that women's voices were not heard directly. In most cases, men claimed to speak on behalf of women. Incidentally, I did not come across any essay on cinema authored by a woman writer, although by this time women had started writing for Hindi periodicals. In one essay after another, women were constantly warned that a career in cinema would be disastrous. Lastly, what is of enduring value is that those who wrote for the periodicals have left behind a corpus of rich materials that helps us to rethink the history of the reception of Indian cinema in the climactic decades of India's freedom struggle.

Notes

1. Madhava Prasad's argument that 'the screen was a political site not by nature, but because the situation compelled the filmmaker to define it as such' can be extended to include writings on cinema as well. (2000, p. 123).
2. *Madhuri* and *Sudha* were published from Lucknow while *Chand* was published from Allahabad. Lucknow had been a centre of Urdu journalism from the second half of the nineteenth century, Newal Kishore Press being the driving force. In the 1920s its publishers decided to step into the unfamiliar territory of Hindi journalism. As it turned out, the publisher reaped rich dividends. *Madhuri* and *Sudha*, the two periodicals published by them, became benchmarks for other aspiring publishers in north India. Newal Kishore Press attracted many talented writers and creative people from the neighbouring districts. Among these were Suryakant Tripathi 'Nirala', Ila Chandra Joshi, Krishnabihari Misra, Badrinath Bhatt, Matadin Shukla, and others (Orsini, 2002, p. 37). Joshi rose to become the co-editor of *Sudha* in 1929. In the second year of its publication, *Sudha* enjoyed an unrivalled circulation of 7,000 (1928). The figure fell down precipitously to 2,000 in 1937 (Statement of Newspapers and Periodicals published in the United Provinces, Allahabad, cited in ibid., p. 65). Allahabad emerged as a major centre for Hindi publishing towards the turn of the nineteenth century. Ramnarayan Lal, Chintamani Ghosh and Ramnaresh Tripathi took the initiative. Ramrakh Singh Sahgal launched *Chand* in 1922 without much financial investment but with great commitment.
3. Orsini, 2002, pp. 65–6. The aim of such periodicals was, as Dwyer has suggested for a different context, to create 'desires and fulfill them, but the readers can subvert them so that their own desires are met. The content of the magazine must be relevant to the fantasies and anxieties, which dominate the readers' concerns' (Dwyer, 2004, pp. 247–85).
4. It is not clear whether *Sampadakiy Sahmati* was authored by the editor or scripted by others. An incident that took place during Harivansh Rai Bachchan's early career throws much light on the question of authorship. *Chand* had employed Bachchan in 1927. He was asked to contribute essays for the magazine. But the editor Sehgal did not approve of Bachchan's work and fired him. Later Bachchan found out that

all his essays had been published but under fictitious names with fictitious degrees (*Kya Bhooloon Kya Yaad Karoon*, 12th edn, Delhi: Rajpal & Sons, 1993, p. 176).

5. Rai, 1992, p. 591.
6. Ibid., p. 600.
7. Ibid.
8. The drama has been republished in Ashk, 1969, pp.12–143.
9. See Shukla, 1999, p. 277; Chaturvedi, 1999, p. 88; and Nagendra, 1991, p. 475.
10. Chaturvedi, 1999 p. 154.
11. Shukla, 1999 pp. 276–7.
12. Dalmia, 1997, p. 315.
13. Francesca Orsini has identified them as the promotion of public good (*lok hit*), nation building and the need to view everything novel as a sign of foreignness (p. 173).
14. *Close Up*, January–March 1969, p. 28.
15. Ibid.
16. Kaul, 1998, p. 38.
17. Ibid., p. 39.
18. Rajadhyaksha and Willemen 1995, p. 209.
19. Ibid.
20. Charles Chaplin met Nehru and Indira Gandhi several years later in Switzerland. He recalls the memorable journey from Lucerne to Manoir de Ban with Nehru, where they discussed among other things, the political and economic situation in India (Chaplin, 1964, pp. 470–1).
21. The message was printed in the July 1939 issue of *Filmindia* and cited in Kaul, 1998, p. 41.
22. Ibid., p. 44.
23. The Indian Cinematograph Committee was constituted in 1927 with two British members and an Indian lawyer, Diwan Bahadur Rangachariar, as its chairman. The Committee recorded the testimonies of 114 Europeans, Americans, and Anglo-Indians and 239 Indians. Witnesses belonged to the film industry as well as other professions. Three issues that were carefully examined by the Committee included 1. the impact of Western films on the Indian audience; 2. the need for censorship; and 3. viewing conditions in Indian theatres. The Committee published its voluminous findings in 1928. The Report clearly reveals that Indian audiences were worried that foreign films were encouraging crime in India and corrupting young men with their explicit love scenes. European witnesses complained that European and American cinema deprecated Western culture and showed women in negative roles. The Committee was unanimous in declaring that all Western films, regardless of the countries of their origin, were alien to Indian regimes of taste. Therefore there was need for censorship. But censorship being a sensitive matter, it needed to be handled carefully. The Report also acknowledged that the real issue at stake was not censorship but the question of evolving a mechanism to facilitate the growth of Indian cinema. Though the recommendations of the Committee were not implemented, they provide, *inter alia*, a glimpse of the film culture of the 1920s and 1930s.
24. Kaul, 1998, p. 45.
25. Ibid., pp. 45–50.

26. Ibid., p. 51.
27. Seen in this light, it should not appear ironical that a comprehensive documentary on Gandhi could not be made during his own lifetime and that audiences had to wait more than 32 years for Richard Attenborough to make the first feature on his life.
28. Dalmia, 1997; 2001; and Orsini, 2002. Alok Rai distinguishes between the syncretic Hindi—the common language of north India (which was synonymously known as Hindustani, Rekhta, Hindavi, and even Urdu) and 'Hindi'—which evolved as a result of the language controversy during the colonial period.
29. Orsini, 2002, pp. 11–12.
30. Ibid., p. 27. There were other factors as well. Throughout the nineteenth century, the colonial government demonstrated much interest in the study of India's diverse cultural and literary traditions. This led to a voluminous production of grammars, dictionaries, and lexicographies. The study of a language led to its objectification, that is, a language began to be identified with a specific region or community. Missionary encounters with Indian languages complemented this process. In the case of Hindi, the missionaries took the lead in the 'actual substantive development of modern Hindi prose and the standardisation of vocabulary and orthography' (Dalmia, 2001, p. 147). By the time the rebellion of 1857 had been subjugated, a small but influential community of Hindi proponents had emerged in the Punjab, Delhi, and the North-West Provinces. Those who saw merit in the promotion of Urdu contested the move. The supporters of Hindi sought the replacement of Persian as the language of provincial administration by Hindi written in the Devanagari script. The adversaries of Hindi clamoured for the recognition of Urdu as the official language. According to Alok Rai, the lead was taken by literary associations such as the Banaras Institute and Allahabad Institute in the 1860s (ibid., p. 38). Thus, Bhartendu Harishchandra's campaign to establish Hindi as *nij bhasha* (language of the individual and community) snowballed into a full-fledged movement for the establishment of Hindi as *rashtrabhasha* (language of the nation). What was lost in the war of words was that Hindi (or Hindustani as it was called then) actually reflected a complex system of borrowings from local dialects and was a kind of '*ur*' language, as Rai has argued (2001, p. 25). The language debate spilled into the twentieth century. By this time there were many who suggested the purging of all Urdu words from Hindi and the adoption of *khari boli*, a more sanskritised form of Hindi. A smaller minority, however, continued to draw upon the rich diaglossia it had inherited.
31. Orsini, 2002, p. 4.
32. Lelyveld, 1994, pp.189–91.
33. For these details see Orsini, 2002, pp. 358–61.
34. Describing Gandhi's views as shortsighted and ill-informed, 'Nirala' labelled his Presidential address as an affront to Hindi ('*Sammelan Aur Mahatama*', *Sudha*, June 1935, reprinted in *Nirala Rachnavali*, ed., Nand Kishore Naval, vol. 6, Delhi: Rajkamal, pp. 46–8.
35. Orsini, 2002, p. 361.
36. 'Achut Kanya', *Madhuri*, June 1939, Year 17, vol. 2, no. 5, p. 597.
37. Ibid.
38. Ibid.
39. 'Bharat ka Bolta-Balta Cinema', *Madhuri*, 1932, Year 11, vol. 1, no. 5, pp. 553–6.

40. Ibid.
41. Mohan Lal Gupta, 'Bhartiya Cinema', *Madhuri*, December 1937, Year 16, vol. 1, no. 1, p. 630; Rai, p. 53.
43. Joshi, 'Bhartiya Filmon mein Hindi ki Rooprekha', *Madhuri*, 1946, Year 25, vol. 2, no. 4, p. 327.
44. Ibid.
45. Ibid., p. 328.
46. *Pakistani Cinema (1947–1997)*, 1997, p. 8.
47. Barnouw and Krishnaswamy, 1980, p. 107.
48. For details see Mufti, 2000, pp. 1–36.
49. Joshi, p. 327.
50. Ibid.
51. Ibid.
52. Ibid.
53. Trivedi, 2006, p. 60.
54. Christopher B. King's study of the growth rate of the production of vernacular books and periodicals between 1868–1925 demonstrates that in 1868 the figure for Urdu stood at 217,153. The figure continued to rise steadily until 1914 (688, 505) after which it declined to 513,085 in 1925. The data for Hindi in the same period is more impressive. In 1868, the total production of Hindi books and periodicals was 392,316. By 1925 it had peaked to 3,078,241 (1994, pp. 38–9). In the 1920s, Hindi also began to be taught as a subject at the university and college levels in the United Provinces, fuelling the demand for Hindi books and teachers (Kumar, New Delhi: 1991, pp. 129–31).
55. Trivedi, p. 61.
56. Dwyer, p. 251.
57. Ibid.
58. Rajadhyaksha and Willemen, 1995, p. 143.
59. Ibid.
60. Chakravarty, 1996, p. 69.
61. Ibid.
62. 'Cinema Chitron Ki Alochana', *Chand*, 1938, Year 16, vol. 1, no. 2, pp. 344–6.
63. Ibid., p. 345.
64. 'Natak Banam Cinema', *Sudha*, March 1935, Year 8, vol. 2, no.1, pp. 67–9.
65. 'Rangmanch Tatha Cinema', *Sudha*, 1936, Year 9, vol. 2, no. 2, p. 150.
66. 'Nrityakala Aur Cinema', *Madhuri*, 1939, Year 17, vol. 2, no.1, pp. 32–4.
67. 'New Theatres Ki Teen Bahumulya Bheint', *Madhuri*, April 1936, Year 14, vol. 2, p. 370.
68. Ibid.
69. 'Jeevan Prabha', *Sudha*, May 1938, Year 11, vol.1, no. 2, pp. 441–9.
70. Gargya, p. 346.
71. 'Cinema Sahitya', *Madhuri*, March 1936, Year 14, vol. 2, p. 241.
72. For details see *Report of the Indian Cinematograph Committee, 1927–28*, Madras: Madras Government Press, 1928.
73. 'Cinema Enquiry Committee', *Sudha*, 1927, Year 1, vol. 1, no. 4, p. 470.
74. Ibid.
75. 'Bharat Mein Cinema Ke Bure Prabhava', January 1935, Year 13, vol. 1, no. 3, p. 402. Just as the Indian Cinematograph Committee had observed, the issue for the writer was not American versus Indian cinema, but Western films versus Indian films. Thus,

'If too much exhibition of American films in the country is a danger to the national interest, too much of other Western films is as much a danger... The British social drama is as much an enigma to the average Indian audience as the American' (cited in Barnouw and Krishnaswamy, 1980, p. 56).

76. Ibid., p. 402. Prasad points out how the social reformer Muthulakshmi Reddy, who herself belonged to the *devadasi* community, had told a journalist in 1939 that cinema was facilitating a surrogate revival of the *devadasi* system ('The State in/Of Cinema', pp. 126–7).
77. 'Bharat Ke Viruddh Dushprachar', *Madhuri*, August 1939, Year 18, vol. 1, no.1, p. 139.
78. Ibid.
79. Radhakant Sharma, 'Bharat Ke Talkie Parde Ki Kuchch Abhinetriyan', *Sudha*, 1933, Year 6, vol. 2, no. 4, p. 321.
80. 'Bhartiya Cinema', *Madhuri*, December, 1937, Year 16, vol. 1, no. 1, p. 629.
81. 'Bhartiya Film Vyapar Ki Unnati', *Sudha*, March 1932, Year 5, vol. 2, no. 2, pp. 263–4.
82. Ibid.
83. Ibid.
84. Ibid.
85. 'Hindi Ki Kuch Mahatvapurna Talkie Filmein', *Sudha*, August 1934, Year 8, vol. 1, no. 1, p. 56.
86. Ibid.
87. Ibid.
88. Ibid.
89. *Madhuri*, April 1936, Year 14, vol. 1, no. 1, p. 312.
90. *Chand*, 1932, Year 10, vol. 2, no. 4, p. 438.
91. Ibid., p. 554.
92. Ibid., p. 555.
93. Ibid.
94. Ibid.
95. Ibid.
96. *Madhuri*, 1925, Year 4, vol. 1, no.1, pp. 47–9.
97. 'Make-Up', *Chand*, 1933, Year 11, vol. 2, no. 1, p. 91.
98. Ibid.
99. Kapoor, p. 553.
100. Sarju Prasad Prem, 'Chhaya Path Ka Suprasiddha Kalakaar', *Chand*, 1938, Year 16, vol. 2, no. 2, pp. 196–7).
101. Ibid., p. 196.
102. Ibid., p. 197.
103. 'Navinchandra', *Chand*, May, 1933, Year 11, vol. 2, no. 1, p. 90.
104. Ibid.
105. Ibid.
106. Ibid., p. 91.
107. Satishchandra Nigam, 'Bharat Ka Sarvashreshtha Kalakar Kaun Hai', *Madhuri*, 1937, Year 15, vol. 2, no. 1, p. 107.
108. Ibid, pp. 107–9.
109. Ibid.
110. Ibid., p. 109.
111. Ibid., p. 110.

112. Ibid., p. 111.
113. 'Devakikumar Bose Ki Kala Par Drishti', *Madhuri*, 1936, Year 15, vol. 1, no. 1, p. 359.
114. Ibid.
115. Sri Krishna, 'Bharat Ki Teen Shrestha Fim Companiyan', *Sudha*, June, 1936, Year 9, vol. 1, no. 3, p. 155.
116. Ibid., p. 157.
117. Ibid.
118. Ibid., p. 160.
119. Kamla Kant Nautiyal, '*East Indian Film Company*', *Madhuri*, 1936, Year 15, vol. 2, no. 1, p. 593.
120. Ibid., p. 594.
121. 'Cinema Pravesh', *Chand*, April 1938, Year 16, vol. 2, no. 5, p. 604.
122. Ibid.
123. Ibid., p. 605.
124. Ibid.
125. Ibid.
126. Ibid., p. 606.
127. 'Vartaman Cinema Patra', *Madhuri*, 1939, Year 17, vol. 2, no. 5, pp. 732–3.
128. Cited in Prasad, p. 125. Munshi urged filmmakers to help the freedom struggle by turning towards Indian themes, scenarios, and sentiments.
129. 'Thumri and Thumri Singers: Changes in Style and Life Style', in Banga and Jaidev, eds., Shimla: IIAS 1996, pp. 278–315. Susie Tharu and K. Lalitha have rightly argued that all social reform movements in colonial India carried powerful hidden agendas. These included 'massive ideological reconstructions of patriarchy and gender' (1993, p. 152).
130. Nair, 1996, p. 146.
131. Ibid.
132. Veer Bharat Talwar, pp. 206–25.
133. Chatterji, 1994, p. 117. For a highly detailed discussion of how cinema tried to achieve this see Zutshi, Calcutta: 1993, pp. 83–142; and also Rajadhyaksha, 1993, pp. 47–82.
134. Rajadhyaksha and Willeman, 1995, pp. 17–30.
135. Kapoor, p. 556.
136. 'Cinema-Sambandhi Vichcharon Ki Chori', *Madhuri*, February, 1936, Year 14, vol. 2, no. 1, p. 106.
137. '*Bhartiya Film Kala*', *Madhuri*, August 1937, Year 16, vol. 1, no.1, pp. 135–7.
138. Jyotindranath, p. 732.
139. Ibid., p. 733.
140. Ibid., p. 734.

References

Ashk, Upendranath, *Maskebazon Ka Svarga*, in *Filmi Duniya Ki Jhalkiyan*, vol. 1, Allahabad: Neelabh Prakashan, (1996) 1969.

Barnouw E., and S. Krishnaswamy, *Indian Film*, New Delhi: Oxford University Press, 1980.

Chaplin, Charles, *My Autobiography*, England: Penguin, 1964.

Chakravarty, Sumita S., *National Identity in Indian Popular Cinema, 1947–87*, New Delhi: Oxford University Press, 1996.

Chatterjee, Partha, *The Nation and its Fragments*, New Delhi: Oxford University Press, 1994.

Chaturvedi, Ramswarup, *Hindi Sahitya Aur Samvedana Ka Itihasa*, Noida: Mayur Paperbacks, 1991.

Dalmia, Vasudha, *The Nationalization of Hindu Traditions: Bhartendu Harishchandra and Nineteenth Century Benares*, New Delhi: Oxford University Press, 1997.

Dwyer, Rachel, 'Shooting Star, The Indian Film Magazine *Stardust*', in Rachel Dwyer and Christopher Pinney, eds., *Pleasures of the Nation, The History, Politics and Consumption of Public Cultures in India*, New Delhi: Oxford University Press, 2004.

Gazdar, Mushtaq, *Pakistan Cinema 1947–1997*, Karachi; New York: Oxford University Press, 1997.

Joshi, Umesh, 'Bhartiya Filmon Mein Hindi Ki Rooprekha', *Madhuri*, Year 25, vol. 2, no. 4, 1996, p. 327.

Kaul, Gautam, *Cinema and the Indian National Struggle*, New Delhi: Sterling Publishers, 1998.

King, Christopher R., *One Language Two Scripts: The Hindi Movement in Nineteenth Century North India*, New Delhi: Oxford University Press, 1994.

Kumar, Krishna, *The Political Agenda of Education*, New Delhi: Sage Publications, 1991.

Lelyveld, David, 'The Fate of Hindustani', in Carol A. Breckenridge and Peter Van Der Veer, eds., *Orientalism and the Postcolonial Predicament*, New Delhi: Oxford University Press, 1994.

Mufti, Aamir R., 'A Greater Story-writer than God: Genres Gender and Minority in Late Colonial India', in Partha Chatterjee and Pradeep Jagannathan, *Subaltern Studies*, vol. xi, New Delhi: Permanent Black, 2000.

Nagendra, *Hindi Sahitya Ka Itihasa*, Noida: Mayur Paperbacks, 1991.

Nair, Janaki, *Women and Law in Colonial India*, New Delhi: Kali for Women, 1996.

Orsini, Francesca, *The Hindi Public Sphere*, New Delhi: Oxford University Press, 2002.

Prasad, Madhava, 'The State and Cinema', in Partha Chatterjee, ed., *Wages of Freedom*, New Delhi: Oxford University Press, 2000.

Rai, Alok, *Hindi Nationalism*, New Delhi: Orient Longman, 2001.

Rai, Amrit, *Qalam Ka Sipahi*, Allahabad: Hans Prakashan, 1992.

Rajadhyaksha, Ashish, 'The Phalke Era: Conflict of Traditional Form and Modern Technology', in T. Niranjana, P. Sudhir, and V. Dhareshwar, eds., *Interrogating Modernity*, Calcutta: Scagull Books, 1993.

Rajadhayaksha, Ashish, and Paul Willeman, eds., *Encyclopaedia of Indian Cinema*, New Delhi: Oxford University Press, 1995.

Rao, Vidya, 'Thumri and Thumri Singers: Changes in Style and Life Style', in Indu Banga and Jaidev, eds., *Cultural Orientation in Modern India*, Shimla: IIAS, 1996.

Sharma, Radhakant, 'Bharat Ke Talkie Parde Ki Kuchch Abhinetriyan', *Sudha*, Year 6, vol. 2, no. 4, 1933, p. 321.

Shukla, Ramchandra, *Hindi Sahitya Ka Itihasa*, 34th edn, Varanasi: Nagari Pracharini Sabha, 1999.

Trivedi, Harish, 'All Kinds of Hindi: The Evolving Language of Cinema', in Vinay Lal and Ashis Nandy, eds., *Fingerprinting Popular Culture: The Mythic and the Iconic in Indian Cinema*, New Delhi: Oxford University Press, 2006.

Tharu, Susie, and K. Lalitha, eds., *Women Writing in India, vol. 1, 600 B. C. to the early 20th Century*, New Delhi: Oxford University Press, 1993.

Zutshi, Somnath, 'Women, Nation and the Outsider in Contemporary Hindi Cinema', in T. Niranjana, P. Sudhir, and V. Dhareshwar, eds., *Interrogating Modernity*, Calcutta: Seagull Books, 1993.

3

History Matters

Valentina Vitali

OVER THE LAST FEW years, a growing number of universities in India have begun to offer, or are thinking of offering, film studies as part of their curriculum. A central part of these new courses, as distinct from programmes of literature and cultural studies, is a history of cinema, in India and elsewhere. This offers great opportunities: the purpose of a history of cinema is to arrive at an understanding of where cinema must have come from, of how it functions within a global process of industrialization as encountered by diverse societies, and of the nexus between that and the reshaping of people's habits and lives through the narrative strategies of individual films. But the institutionalization of this type of enquiry is not without its dangers. Film historiography developed alongside cinema and, since the end of World War I, has been directly implicated in the promotion of national film production. Early instances of national film histories emanated, significantly, in the years between the two World Wars from the two countries that then competed most fiercely to globalize their industrial empires: the United States, with Lewis Jacobs' *The Rise of the American Film: a Critical History* (1939) and the Third Reich, with Oskar Kalbus' *Vom Werden Deutscher Filmkunst* (1936). Immediately after World War II, these were followed by a series of film histories that took stock of the proliferation of national film industries over half a century in a variety of European countries, as well as by that milestone of film historiography that is Siegfried Kracauer's *From Caligari to Hitler* (1947). Kracauer's account successfully fused the industrial and the national dimensions of cinema all the better to foreground the nexus between, on the one hand, the functioning of films as commodities and, on the other, the changing of people's thoughts through their engagement with films as cultural items. But in spite, or perhaps precisely because of this achievement, it was Lewis Jacobs' model that was adopted as a template for the writing of film histories in much of the world.

Divided into six parts, entitled 'Fade In', 'Foundations', 'Development', 'Transition', 'Intensification', and 'Maturity', Jacobs' book relied on a linear notion of history that understood the nation state as the natural result of an evolutionary trajectory. In adopting this as the framework appropriate to chronicle both the cultural and the industrial dimensions of cinema, Jacobs effectively collapsed the intellectual task of a history of the cinema as a cultural terrain where social positions that may and may not be in line with the state of affairs dominant at any point in time are mediated, with the objectives of the capitalist forces dominant within the American film industry. The outcome was a back-handed celebration of Hollywood films that erected a handful of filmmakers as exemplary film artists for the world to emulate.[1]

Since the publication of *The Rise of the American Film*, the writing of film histories in terms of some intuited national ethos that determines both the industrial arrangements and the aesthetic modalities of the films produced has become the norm. Seeking to compete with Hollywood, individual countries have tended to narrate the histories of their cinemas along Jacobs' model. Only a handful of film histories to date have questioned this template, and Barnouw and Krishnaswamy's *Indian Film*, a book that has demarcated the study of Indian cinemas since its publication in 1963, is not one of them. *Indian Film* narrates the history of the cinema in India as a linear trajectory that, not unlike literary histories, mirrors nationalist accounts of the rise of the nation: the beginnings of cinema in 'India' with the Lumière brothers' screening in Bombay in 1896; the founder, Dadasaheb Phalke, a photographer born into an upper-caste family and a committed nationalist; the coming of sound, which helped consolidate a domestic film industry producing and exhibiting films in the local languages; the rise of a studio system around New Theatres in Calcutta (producing Bengali films), the Prabhat Film Company in Pune (making films in Marathi, Hindi and some in Tamil), and Bombay Talkies in Bombay; and finally, in the run up to 1947, the emergence of an indigenous form of film realism and concomitant *auteurs* out of New Theatres.

I have discussed elsewhere the enormous problems of this account of the cinema in India.[2] The two limitations of *Indian Film* that need emphasising here are 1. its focus on film production, which the authors uncritically prioritise to the exclusion of the other sectors constitutive of any cinema; and 2. its conceptualisation of the nation as an organic entity, disconnected from local and global networks. Whereas by the 1930s Hollywood cinema was the product of a fully corporate venture the economic priority and operational emphases of which were on production, this has never been the case for the cinema in India. Nor was cinema in India immune to the difficulties that other industrial sectors faced because of India's positioning in a global, colonial economy. Since its beginning, cinema in undivided India was marked by a scarcity of equipment that made exhibition, not production, the one activity most immediately accessible to South Asians. Licenses were issued by the Raj, not to the exhibition site, but for the use of film projectors. Consistent production of Indian features did not kick off until well after World War I. Imported (mainly American and Italian) films could be acquired cheaply and circulated rapidly, while films produced locally were expensive to make. To recover the high cost of production, Indian films would be screened for weeks at a time. Madan Theatres, which dominated Indian cinema throughout the silent period with a monopoly on exhibition, did produce films but in its own cinemas Madan only screened the imported fare. Exhibition of foreign films, not Indian film production, generated Madan's operating capital.

Because the historiographic model dominant in film studies to date was developed on the nationalist blueprint of a cinema, Hollywood, that until the 1960s at least, made film production its priority, little or no research so far has been done on film exhibition in India. And yet, there is evidence that, from the beginning, this is the sector that lent early cinema in India the cohesiveness of a distinct national industry. In the 1920s, the population of undivided India, and in particular the urban population, began to increase at a very high rate.[3] Again, preliminary and inconclusive research suggests that exhibition outlets increased in number, from 175 in 1921 to 275 in 1924 and 406 in 1927.[4] In Bombay exhibition began to stratify, with films released first in the upmarket theatres of Grant and Lamington Roads and then traded off to suburban and mill-area halls.[5] Indian production companies like Sharda proliferated and successfully competed against American distributors with similar fare. Sharda produced as much as one film every three weeks. However, unlike other companies at the time, Sharda did not have stable access to exhibition. Throughout its short life, for the exhibition of its popular stunt films, Sharda remained entirely dependent on the limited number of exhibitor-producers such as Krishna, which, in the theatres they controlled, would alternate their own productions with those of other Indian producers. As a way to secure for itself exhibition spaces, Sharda was quick to adopt a strategy until then relatively untested in Indian cinema: the creation, more or less overnight, of a 'film star' who was entirely bound to the company. And yet, in spite of the popularity of Sharda's 'Master Vithal–Indian Douglas Fair Bank', the company's precarious base in exhibition led to its collapse in 1929, after an unsuccessful attempt at corporate floatation.

As is also evident from the 1928 *Indian Cinematograph Committee* report, by the mid-1920s an exhibition sector had come into place that was *de facto* determining the terms by which producers worked. Today, funding for film production is, as a rule, raised by distributors. Madhava Prasad has observed that, unlike in the 1920s, today exhibitors' profits are rarely reinvested into cinema; hardly ever in film production and only very sporadically in exhibition. Exhibitors' capital does tend to circulate across other sectors of the economy, most notably in real estate, but this does not make such capital any less crucial to an understanding of the functioning of cinema in India. On the contrary, it is precisely the modes which characterize the circulation of the exhibitors and other sectors' money that offer a glimpse of the ways in which the cinema is embedded in the socio-economic fabric of the country. Exhibitors may not fund production directly, but this is not to say that distributors are in a position to define the modalities of film production. India has one of the world's lowest number of cinemas. Restrictions on new cinema buildings, enforced by Nehru in 1947 and in place until the late 1960s (depending on state governments' individual policies), have meant a chronic shortage of cinema houses across the country that gives exhibitors the upper hand over both distributors and producers.[6] The developments which, in the 1970s, led to the rise of Amitabh Bachchan as a superstar and which, over a few years, shaped Hindi cinema as we know it today, indicate that exhibition remains the locomotive of the Bombay film industry to this day.

In the early 1960s, unlike in the rest of India, Bombay's industry underwent radical changes and growth. As the old cotton mills began to close down, new industries, mainly chemicals and pharmaceuticals, emerged. Between 1961 and 1981 the number of factories in Maharashtra doubled, from 8,233 to 16,594.[7] Unlike the mills, which were situated in the city, the new factories grew in the extended suburbs east of the island, on the eastern railway route along the Bandra–Kurla belt, or in the area around Trombay, to the south-east. The years of the Third Five–Year Plan and the Annual Plan also registered a high growth of employment, primarily in the newer branches of manufacturing.[8] And as in these sectors wages were much higher than in the mills,[9] the disposable income of a significant share of the population also increased.[10] Third, migration and employment in factories meant a certain regularization of 'productive' and 'unproductive' labour time. Unlike small farmers, factory employees possess what is generally referred to as 'leisure time'.

Bombay's industrial boom was also experienced in Hindi cinema, but not in a homogeneous, concerted way across the three sectors of the film industry. Stimulated by higher disposable incomes and commodities' consumption across a sensibly larger share of the Indian population, in the early 1960s box office revenues increased by 25 per cent. Under pressure from escalating inflation and, from 1966, of currency devaluation, the two main Indian production centres, Bombay and Madras, saw a sharp rise in production costs which led to a significant polarisation of the production sector. Whereas in 1963 13 per cent of all Indian films were made by 'studio-owner producers', 41 per cent by 'regular producers', and 46 per cent by 'other than regular' or ad hoc producers, over a period of two years, 'regular producers' were responsible for no more than 23 per cent of all Indian films, with 'studio-owners' and ad hoc producers representing 19 and 58 per cent respectively of all cinema production.[11]

The insistent calls, made by the trade press of the period to producers and films stars, to help reduction of production costs even as box office revenues were increasing, are a good indication of the Bombay film industry's mode of functioning. On the one hand, rising production costs forced distributors, the sector which generally advances the money for production, to demand a higher share of the box office from exhibitors; on the other, exhibitors, who were simultaneously paying higher entertainment tax, also demanded from distributors either higher theatre rental rates or a larger share of the box office, or both, in the process effectively eating into the capital available for production. In India in the 1960s, the power relations among the three sectors were such that these pressures resulted in higher exhibition costs, shouldered by the distributor and producer. As independent producer J. Om Prakash stated in 1960 in an article entitled 'The Invisible Sieve',

> Of the many problems facing the industry today, the most pressing that calls for immediate consideration is the problem of equitable sharing of revenue of our pictures. Statistics of the box-office collections in all territories show that there has been an increase. [B]ut simultaneously the share of the distributor has gone down by about one third. These two aspects of the film business reveal the fact that exhibition of films in our country is not based on fair terms. Mostly the distributors have to submit to the dictates of the exhibitors, for whose exclusive benefit pictures are apparently screened.[12]

India's chronic shortage of cinema and the exhibition sector's capacity to enforce its terms on distributors and, indirectly, on producers, led to a situation where, by the mid-1960s, less 'regular producers' found themselves capable of affording to make a sufficiently high number of films to deserve that name. If the few who could shifted to the category of 'studio-owners', the majority was forced to reduce production to an ad hoc basis. And as a smaller number of producers could also afford exhibition, at least in large central cinemas, the number of films produced and released dropped, reaching, from 1962, record lows not touched since the first half of the 1940s, during World War II. Tamil film production also decreased in the same period.

By the second half of the 1960s, the stand of the exhibitors had not changed. Rising production and exhibition costs and higher box office revenues had led to increasing competition among producers and distributors, a situation that further strengthened exhibitors. When, in 1966, a few producers looked for an alternative way to break through an exhibition sector that was reluctant to expand along with the rest of the industry and began marketing their films through Radio Ceylon, thereby hoping to pressure exhibitors into accepting terms of exhibition more advantageous to the producers, the executive committee of the Central Circuit Cine Association (CCCA), the Indian Motion Picture Producers Association (IMPPA), and the Film Producers' Guild of India issued a statement declaring that 'We will not acquire the films of those producers who violate the [IMPPA and Guild's] decision and if the films of such producers have already been acquired, they shall not be taken delivery of by the respective distributors of the circuit.'[13] Two years later, still confronted with distribution and production sectors that effectively complied by the terms of—because under direct and indirect pressure from—exhibitors, 11 Bombay producers, headed by J. Om Prakash, decided to distribute their own films themselves in the east Punjab, Delhi, Uttar Pradesh, and CPCI circuits. This time around the small group of producers found support in the sector's representative bodies, the IMPPA and the Guild, which suspended the release of all new productions in the central circuit.[14] With a freeze on new Hindi releases and the IMPPA and the Guild's threat to stop production completely, in February 1968 Delhi cinemas were reduced to showing foreign films only, a situation that cut significantly into Delhi exhibitors' revenues. A month later, when Bombay producers organized a huge rally 'against exhibitor's high rentals',[15] the Theatre Owners Association counteracted by stopping exhibition in Bombay for 'an indefinite period'.[16] The following week, exhibitors announced the founding of Pradarshak Sahakar Chitra, 'a newly floated concern for motion picture production by exhibitors and theatre-owners in Bombay' with an initial investment of Rs 1 crore to go into production immediately. Typically, they invited producers to 'cooperate', including J. Om Prakash who, four months later, was elected president of the Guild.[17]

At one level, this series of events and their outcome was a symptom of the exhibitors' continuing stronghold on the industry as a whole—a power that is reflected in the official figures for the Indian film industry's distribution of capital across the sectors. In 1968, out of a total investment in cinema of Rs 41 crore, Rs 26 crore or 63 per cent were invested by exhibitors, while small and large producers were responsible for no more than Rs 6 crores (15 per cent), leaving the remaining Rs 9 crore (22 per cent) to distributors.[18] At another level, producers' attempts to put pressure on exhibitors clearly indicate that in a situation of rising production costs and demand, that is, in a situation of industrial growth, the exhibitors' reluctance to expand along with the rest of the industry was perceived as increasingly unsustainable. And yet very little could be done about that.

In November 1968, the state of Maharashtra relaxed existing regulations for cinemas and granted licenses for semi-permanent cinemas in areas where the proportion of cinema was lower than one per 10,000 inhabitants.[19] Significantly, the only opposition to these measures came from exhibitors, who saw in the new regulations the threat of competition. One year later, however, Bombay witnessed the opening of a new type of venue: the suburban upmarket cinema hall. Among the first was the Shreyas in Ghatkopar, one of the areas of Bombay which had developed to host the growing population of white-and blue-collar workers that provided the labour force of Bombay's new industries. Unlike existing suburban cinemas, the Shreyas was equipped with 1, 071 seats, state-of the-art sound and projection technology, air-conditioning and a large car park. Simultaneously, in 1969, figures for Indian film production showed a significant recovery. By then, however, Madras had overtaken Bombay as India's largest production centre, in spite of Madras' lower allocation of raw stock: out of the 351 films made in India that year, only 89 were produced in Bombay, while Madras made 227, 14 of which were in Hindi.[20] A year later, the situation catapulted: Bombay production jumped up by 223 per cent to 199 films, while Madras fell to 208. In the same year, 400 new cinemas opened across the country, three of which were in Greater Bombay, with a few more under construction.[21]

The factors behind this expansion, an expansion which eventually led to the rise of Amitabh Bachchan and, within a few years, to the multi-starrer or blockbuster, is not to be found in the rise of production costs, for these were an effect of the expansion, not its cause. The questions to be asked which may offer an explanation to the changes that took place in the Hindi film industry in the 1970s cannot be asked within a frame that gives priority to production, as current film historiography tends to do. Production costs had been escalating since the early 1960s, but a powerful and cohesive exhibition sector contained the expansion of this sector, in effect causing the further fragmentation and polarization of production and the proliferation of so-called 'small-budget' films.

The social dramas of the 1950s and 1960s were expensive, glossy productions, at times with extremely long turnover times, so that producers, depending on district-based distribution networks, remained more or less confined within the allocated linguistic and financial district belt. By contrast, as film director and former stuntman Kamran explained in an article entitled 'Faith in Small Budgets',

> Small budget [films] [e]ntertain the public even in small stations. [They] are numerically more than big-budget-pictures [and] keep [a] lot of people alive by giving them work. [W]hile big ones take 2½ to 3 years or even 5 years for

> completion it is possible to complete six small budgets within the time of making one big-budget picture. While big-budgets consume about 70 lakhs per picture not less than ten small budgets could be made within the cost of one big-budget picture. [T]he chances of failure of small budgets are always negligible, the distributors are all happy having not only covered their investment but having made a decent profit. The producers are also happy in making a small profit. [I]t is very difficult for a small-budget picture to make a jubilee. If they run to eight weeks it is itself a jubilee and a feat. They are generally within 7 to 7½ lakhs and their modest run in all places is enough to make them commercially successful.[22]

This type of film circulated much faster than big social melodramas. Until the late 1960s at least, small-budget films were to be seen primarily at the margins, in cinemas in the suburban and rural areas, where distributors could bypass powerful exhibitors and their exorbitant terms of trade. The Indian wrestling champion Dara Singh, who became a popular starlet in 1962 with Babubhai Mistri's *King Kong*, from then on owed his cinematic fame to this circuit. By the late 1960s he began to be cast in cheap urban action films where, as in *Hum Sub Chor Hain/The Criminals* (Maruti 1973), he plays 'the criminal'. Centring on a discourse of 'corruption', including the police's, these films featured an illegal hero that preceded, if only by a few years, Amitabh Bachchan's. Only a historiographic framework that gives due weight to the role of exhibitors in India and, second, which reframes the Hindi cinema within financial networks that are simultaneously local, national, and global can explain why Amitabh Bachchan, unlike Dara Singh, became a superstar.

Worldwide, the 1970s were marked by profound changes in the American economy. As a consequence of the reduction of trade barriers at the end of the 1950s, from the early 1960s the growth of global trade accelerated unexpectedly. Finding its markets under increased pressure from lower cost exports from the developing blocs, in the early 1970s the United States redirected its economy towards the finance, insurance, and real estate sectors. While this new regime enabled the world's most powerful economy to run large deficits in its balance of trade, it also allowed it to reflate investment. Demand for those industrial products that North American businesses no longer found profitable to produce expanded.[23] As a result, during the 1970s, relative to First World countries, all Third World regions increased their degree of industrialization and urbanization to a far greater extent than they improved their GDP per capita. Unlike the First World's economic boom in the post-War period, Third World economies financed this expansion by borrowing on the international money market.[24]

India and China were the two exceptions: unlike, for instance, South Korea, whose total long-term debt services rose from 3.1 per cent of GNP in 1970 to 10.2 per cent in 1986, India's total debt services over the same period, like those of China, barely changed (1.1 in 1970 and 1.6 in 1986).[25] Indian manufacturing, primarily Bombay's, increased; trade, commerce, and the tertiary sector also grew significantly. However, by far the most important economic measure undertaken by the Indian state in this period was the nationalization of the 14 largest Indian banks, in 1969. Credit centralization was part of a broad programme of economic and political centralization that responded to the rise of finance capital in the United States by sheltering India from its pressures. Indira Gandhi's administration, not the IMF, took full control of the capital flow within and out of the country. Centralization of credit had huge repercussions on the shape of the Indian industry and finance that grew under the State's protectionist aegis. Although large sections of the Indian capitalist class were dependent on the government not only for industrial licenses, quotas, and import allocations, but also for investment funds from nationalized banks and other government-controlled industrial and agricultural development programs, the hostility of this class to the Congress took the form of withholding fresh investment into now state-controlled, financial institutions.[26] Indeed, the sector to grow most as a direct result of the centralization of finance was the so-called 'black' economy.[27] Although a black economy first developed in South Asia during World War II, with the 1969 nationalization of the banks, a spiralling share of Indian capital seeking to flee State control found a parallel, faster and, on the whole, cheaper channel of circulation in the film industry.

At this point, and at this point only, Indian exhibition opened up. Within a year from the nationalization of the banks, 400 new cinemas opened across the country. In Bombay, but not only there, new and well-equipped suburban cinemas like the Shreyas formed a larger and faster circulation network for both films and money-fleeing government control and red tape. Bombay film production, which had been falling steadily since 1961, also went up sharply within a year from the nationalization of the banks (by 223 per cent, *Screen*, 9 January 1970, pp. 1, 14). The link between the two were, of course, the distributors, who did invest larger amounts in films, but not, initially, directly into production. *Zanjeer* (Chains, dir. Prakash Mehra), released in 1973, is a case in point. When *Zanjeer* went into production, many stunt actors were available at the low end of the market. Amitabh Bachchan was not one of them. A former stage actor and radio announcer who was deemed a 'bad' film actor because he seemed to lack the established stars' capacity to emote on stage,[28] Bachchan was cast in *Zanjeer* because he was as cheap a male body as those already available within the mainstream sector. In comparison to contemporary melodramas, *Zanjeer* was a cheap production, with no star value, poor sets, and poor quality stock and prints. The only unusual investments for this kind of production were the script, a practice that was then, and remains today, uncommon in the Hindi cinema, and, significantly, an unprecedentedly extensive advertising campaign.

Gradually, exhibition priorities began to feed back on production. Costs, which had been rising and had been contained since the mid-1960s, were finally allowed full play. Films began to be made that combined the generic conventions of the small budget, quickly produced, and quickly distributed film that until then had circulated exclusively at the margins of the industry with the necessity to invest and circulate larger amounts of money. Within less than two years from *Zanjeer*, larger amounts of money came to be wrapped up also around those production ingredients that were deemed to guarantee high box office returns at the higher end of the market. The longest running film in the history of Hindi cinema, *Sholay* (Flames of the Sun, dir. Ramesh Sippy, 1975) was a more costly feature that relocated *Zanjeer*'s story of urban crime into a rural setting heavily inscribed with the tropes of the social drama, including notions of nationalism and social modernization. In addition, Dharmendra, then an established star, was cast in the lead role; Bachchan as the star's sidekick. *Sholay* set the template for a new marketing and distribution strategy, the 'multi-starrer' that, feeding back on production via the script, reinscribed the 'lower' market's proven ingredients into, or *as*, the mainstream's formula. As a consequence, and unlike less quoted Hindi action actors such as Dara Singh and Feroz Khan, throughout the 1980s Amitabh Bachchan retained the versatility of the 1950s stars: he was available for action films and for romance. Significantly, while in 1972 lack of facial expression or emotional charge was regarded as a lack of acting skills, by 1975 reviews of Bachchan's performances elevate the same lack of expression to a quality—the skills of looking unperturbed, steely, cool, and invulnerable were built into the image of the star, thus radically altering the mainstream's generic stock. And finally, whereas in Dara Singh's and in other 1960s action films the hero remained, on the whole, wedded to notions of national loyalty, the nature and mode of circulation of the capital underpinning the 1970s action productions left its mark on their hero. For a few decades at least, he would move outside the structures of the State, which emerges in the films as a corrupt entity, its agents either too rotten or ineffective. It is precisely at this level—the interface of the economic and the cultural—that the adoption of a historiographic model based on a nationalist biography of Hollywood (such as Jacobs') has created, and will continue to create, enormous obstacles to the visibility, the documenting and the understanding of Indian cinemas as social practices with material functions and effects.

For Hollywood, India has historically been a financially insignificant market.[29] But the operation of American distributors in India over the past decades cannot be fully grasped if reduced to purely financial terms. The purpose of the Motion Pictures Export Association of America (MPEAA) is to secure the distribution of its members' films where severe currency shortages exist. American foreign distributors meet once a year at the Cannes International Film Festival and determine programme prices according to what price a market can bear. The longer a nation's audience has been cultivated to consume their programmes, the higher the prices. Once the market is secure for American films, the MPEAA leaves distribution to individual member companies. Until the 1970s, American domestic film consumption sufficed amply for Hollywood majors to make large profits. Anything added to that was regarded as a bonus. As a result, in India as in other select markets, American films were made available at very competitive prices, often well below the prints' actual value. In industry terms, cheaply exported American films were intended to 'cultivate' the market.

But the crisis which swept American industries in the late 1960s and early 1970s also affected its film industry and, within it, Hollywood's export operation. Prior to the 1970s, vertically integrated studios operated on the basis of annual production schedules. Banks and other lending institutions provided revolving credit which left individual companies free to allocate the funds themselves. From the mid-1970s onwards, following an over-production boom which landed Hollywood into a huge financial crisis, banks began to extend loans on a picture-by-picture basis, with the films themselves as collateral. Veteran industry leadership was replaced by a mélange of agents, lawyers, bankers, and business executives who saw filmmaking primarily as an investment strategy that, not unlike commodities trading, combined the risks of high-stakes speculation with a virtually limitless potential for corporate tax sheltering. Over a period of less than 10 years, production line studios were transformed into production marketing divisions of a broader entertainment sector controlled by global conglomerates. Finance capital, which in the previous two decades had been only one aspect of the film business, from the mid-1970s onwards became its determining, dominant factor. Studio bosses no longer had to account to their backers on the basis of annual production and profit plans. Annual production slates were turned into a series of autonomous bets closely tied in to the marketing divisions of 'synergetic' industries, such as the music business, computer games, theme parks, tourism, and publishing. As finance capital's gambling syndicates took over the business, costs exploded—[30] individual films were replaced by 'franchises' (as was the case for the *Star Wars* and the *Jurassic Park* franchise) and marketing costs mushroomed.[31] In this context, foreign markets that were previously insignificant, such as South Korea, became central to Hollywood's overall turnover and profits. As each of these countries opened up to American capital, the onslaught of aggressive Hollywood distribution and marketing also gradually led to the collapse of their national film production, or to its subsumption to a new Hollywood, just as had gradually happened in many European countries from the end of World War II.

Until recently, India's policy of relative closure against American finance capital has protected its film industry from the same fate. But the situation has changed and it would be unwise to underestimate the potential of the institutionalization of the study of cinema as an instrument of globalizing American capital and its commodities. History teaches us that film historiography developed alongside with, and can be shaped uncritically by, the rules governing the market. By advancing an argument about the function of exhibition as the locomotive of the Hindi cinema, my intention has not been to propose an alternative history of the Hindi film industry as one of the sectors of the cinema in India. Much research still needs to be done before we can contemplate anything near a history, let alone an alternative one. Instead, somewhat provocatively, I have sought to stimulate a debate by pointing to the possible productivity of a line of inquiry that is shaped by a differently motivated model of historiography—one critically intent on opening up, rather than erasing, the interface between economics and culture, between the functioning of a film industry and the aesthetics of individual films—all the better to understand how, precisely through their narrative strategies, films mediate, at any point in time, our encounter with global capital.

Notes

1. For the economic and historical background to Lewis Jacobs' work see Gomery, 1984.
2. Vitali, 2006.
3. Desai, 2004, pp. 22–3.
4. Figures from Bharucha, 1938.
5. Bhaumik, 2001, p. 36.
6. Desai, 2004, p. 52.
7. D'Monte, 2002, p. 84.
8. Ibid., pp. 79–80.
9. Ibid., p. 84. Whereas the average wage of a mill worker was Rs 7,120 a year, a chemical worker would earn a yearly average of Rs 14,367.
10. Chatterjee, 1975, pp. 54–5.
11. Figures and categories terminology from *Screen*, 7 November 1966, p. 11.
12. *Filmfare*, 1960. The 'invisible sieve' of the title is the cinema screen, because, according to the writer, that is where most of the revenues and profits end up.
13. *Screen*, 1966, p. 1.
14. *Screen*, 1968a, p. 1.
15. *Screen*, 1968b, p. 1.
16. *Screen*, 1968c, p. 1.
17. *Screen*, 1968d, p. 1.
18. *Screen*, 1968e, p. 13.

19. *Screen*, 1968f, pp. 1, 12.
20. *Screen*, 1969, pp. 1, 11.
21. *Screen*, 1970, pp. 1, 14.
22. *Picture Post*, 1968.
23. See Brenner, 1998.
24. Arrighi, 1991.
25. Vanaik, 1990. See also Desai, 2002.
26. Chandra, 2003, pp. 29-30.
27. Vanaik, 1990, p. 36.
28. See *Filmworld*, 1972a; *Filmworld*, 1972b; and *Filmworld*, 1972c.
29. Between 1955 and 1962, for instance, gross revenues of American majors in India grew from under US$2 million to just over US$3.2 million. As a percentage of Hollywood's foreign revenues, these figures represented then 0.65 per cent and 1.08 per cent respectively. Compare this to the 80 per cent of foreign revenues represented in the same period by the numerically smaller market of Europe (figures from Manjunath Pendakur, 1985.
30. Between 1972 and 1979, costs increased by 450 per cent (Cook, 2000).
31. By the late 1990s, the average cost of releasing one film in the American domestic market was estimated by the Motion Pictures Association of America to be some $76.8 million, while the average marketing budget per film amounted to some $100 million (ibid.).

References

Arrighi, Giovanni, 'World Income Inequalities and the Future of Socialism', *New Left Review*, no. 189, 1991, pp. 39–65.

Bharucha, B. D., ed., *Indian Cinematograph Year Book*, Bombay: Motion Picture Society of India, 1938.

Bhaumik, Kaushik, 'The Emergence of the Bombay Film Industry 1913–1936', Ph.D. thesis, University of Oxford, 2001, p. 36.

Brenner, Robert, 'The Economics of Global Turbulence', *New Left Review*, no. 229, 1998, pp. 1–264.

Chandra, Bipan, *In the Name of Democracy: JP Movement and the Emergency*, New Delhi: Penguin Books India, 2003, pp. 29–30.

Chatterjee, Partha, 'Indian Democracy and Bourgeois Reaction', in *A Possible India: Essays in Political Criticism*, (1975) 1997, pp. 54–5.

Cook, David A., *A History of the American Cinema*, vol. 9, *Lost Illusions: American Cinema in the Shadow of Watergate and Vietnam, 1970–1979*, Berkeley: University of California Press, 2000.

Desai, Meghnad, *Marx's Revenge: The Resurgence of Capitalism and The Death of Statist Socialism*, London: Verso, 2002.

———, *Nehru's Hero: Dilip Kumar in the Life of India*, New Delhi: Roli Books, 2004.

D' Monte, Darryl, *Ripping the Fabric: The Decline of Mumbai and its Mills*, New Delhi: Oxford University Press, 2002, p. 84.

Filmfare, 16 December 1960, p. 42.

'Amitabh Bachchan walks across the screen like Alice in Wonderland', *Filmworld*, vol. 8, no. 3, May 1972a.

'Amitabh is lifeless', *Filmworld*, vol. 8, no. 7, September 1972b.

'Amitabh looks like a patient of insomnia', *Filmworld*, vol. 8, no. 8, November 1972c.

Gomery, Douglas, 'Film Culture and Industry: Recent Formulations in Economic History', *Iris*, vol. 2, no. 2, 1984, pp. 17–28.

Pendarkur, Manjunath, 'Dynamics of Cultural Policy Making: The US Film Industry in India', *Journal of Communication*, vol. 4, Autumn 1985, pp. 52–72.

Picture Post, December 1968, pp. 119–21.

Screen, 19 January 1968a.

———, 22 March 1968b.

———, 12 April 1968c.

———, 19 April 1968d.

———, 5 July 1968e.

———, 22 November 1968f.

———, 10 January 1969.

———, 9 January 1970.

Vanaik, Achin, *The Painful Transition: Bourgeois Democracy in India*, London and New York: Verso, 1990.

Vitali, Valentina, 'Not a Biography of the "Indian Cinema": Historiography and the Question of National Cinema in India', in Valentina Vitali and Paul Willemen, eds., *Theorising National Cinema*, London: British Film Institute, 2006.

PART II
FRACTURED POLITIES

4

The Panoramic Vision and the Descent of Darkness: Issues of Contra-Modernity

Rashmi Doraiswamy

THE PANORAMIC VISION

WHILE 'POINT OF VIEW' as a narrational mode in literature and cinema has received extensive critical attention, the 'panoramic view' has remained largely unexplored. I define this view as a motivated unfolding of land or cityscape in the narrative, bearing within it actual or possible micro narratives. The panoramic vision is a constitutive one of our everyday lives, accompanying even such acts as walking and travelling. Its embedding in imagery, in literature, and in the visual arts has a long history. As Anne Freidberg points out: 'The *mobilized gaze* has a history, which begins well before the cinema and is rooted in other cultural activities that involve walking and travel. The virtual gaze has a history rooted in all forms of visual representation (back to cave painting), but produced most dramatically by photography. The cinema developed as an apparatus that combined the "mobile" with the "virtual".'[1]

Even though panoramic vision predates modernity, it has its own links with it, being part of modernity's project of bringing the mobile, virtual gaze into being. Along with the diorama (1823) and the panopticon (1791), the panorama,[2] which evolved out of the panoramic painting (1792), created possibilities of virtual spectacles hitherto unknown.

There is thus a convergence in the modern period in the West between a representational, narrational form that pre-existed it in the arts and new technological apparatus that further facilitated this panoramic vision. There is a sense of teleological aspiration and realization. The issue that Freidberg and many other theorists do not address, however, is that the panoramic gaze is also linked to another facet of the modern period in the West, which is colonialism. The history charted is a technological one, very specific to the history of the West. In colonized and postcolonial societies, in place of this teleological convergence of aspirations, there is non-teleological simultaneity, which is not aspirational. Here it is the product of another specific historical conjuncture, the encounter of the colonizer with the colonized. There is a sense of the imported modes overlapping with local representational ones. Eastern modes of scroll painting, such as the Chinese, for instance also posit a panoramic vision, a vision that was ironically tapped for the juxtapositional aesthetics of montage in film by Sergei Eisenstein. Indigenous forms of the representation of the panoramic vision combine with Western representational forms and apparatus to produce a vision specific to a given historical conjuncture. There is a panoramic vision of the colonizer, just as there is a panoramic vision of the colonized, both born of the encounter between the two.

This article examines panoramic vision as a narrative strategy in fiction on Partition, a cataclysmic event that accompanied India's achievement of independence from the British in which nearly three million are estimated to have died. My article deals with the panoramic vision in the context of what Homi Bhabha calls 'otherwise than modernity': 'Such cultures of a postcolonial contra-modernity may be contingent to modernity, discontinuous or in contention with it, resistant to its oppressive, assimilationist technologies; but they also deploy the cultural hybridity of their borderline conditions to "translate", and therefore reinscribe, the social imaginary of both metropolis and modernity.'[3] I take up the unfolding of the panoramic gaze in connection with the everyday act of walking and the motif of the train in literary and cinematic texts on Partition.

The Walk

The everyday act of walking in the city has been defined in critical theory in two different registers—that of modernity and of postmodernity—by Walter Benjamin and Michel de Certeau, respectively. While Benjamin defines the *flâneur* as one who walks the arcades, making leisure of the time that could have been put to 'useful' labour producing commodities, de Certeau contrasts the totalising but hazy view of the city from skyscrapers to the immediacy and intimacy of walking the streets.

NEW HEROIC TYPES

It takes a heroic constitution to live modernism, says Benjamin.[4] Benjamin refers to conspirators, ragpickers, street walkers, dandies, and *flâneurs* as the 'new types' of modern city life in Baudelaire's France and relates the poet/man of letters and the commodities he produces analogically to them. Of these 'types' who inhabit the underbelly of the city, it is the *flâneur* who is different from the rest, in that he strolls the city in boredom/leisure, while the others do so as part of the cycle of commodity production. It is interesting to see that Benjamin associates the *flâneur* only with the modern city, with its crowds, and most importantly, with its arcades. Narrow pavements, before the coming of the arcades, according to him, 'afforded little protection from vehicles. Strolling could hardly have assumed the importance it did without the arcades.'[5]

How do other 'heroes' of modernity walk and stroll through *their* cities? Is the stroll any less a stroll because it lacks the ease of leisure? Is it any less of a stroll because far from being an antidote to boredom, it is fraught with anxiety? Is the city any less a city for not including in its built-up *being* horizontal expanses or skyscraping verticality?

Russian literature in the nineteenth century focused on an entirely different emergent social type: the 'small man', the 'superfluous man', and the 'underground man'. Modernity everywhere, as part of the larger historical processes of capitalism, industrialisation, and the rapid growth of cities produced its own representational types who faced modernity with what Benjamin has called a 'heroic constitution'. Russia, cut off from the mainstream history of Western Europe, in a sense 'lagged' behind temporally, but caught up and raced ahead when it came to debates on realism and modernism. The *flâneur* could haunt glass-covered, marble-panelled arcades that seemed like cities in miniature in the relatively more advanced capitalist countries of Western Europe of the nineteenth century; the Russian type, in contrast, was not a stroller, but a scurrying clerk trying to make ends meet to buy an overcoat (Gogol) or an impoverished student committing murder to test his conscience (Dostoevsky's Raskolnikov). In contrast to the *flâneur*, Russian literature had the superfluous man in works such as Goncharov's *Oblomov*, a leftover from the leisure of the *feudal* order, who could not rouse himself to any activity, let alone that of commodity production.

A great number of the fiction narratives on the Partition of the subcontinent deal with walks through the city. One of the most remarkable of such narratives is Mohan Rakesh's short story *His Heap of Rubble*[6] for its depiction of city-turned-traitor, city as arch-deceiver. Ghani Miyan's revisiting of his 'hometown' in this story is the site of a terrifying dual reading—he sees with innocence, the city looks back with deception.

The even more contra-modern hero is one who is an outcast, in terms of social hierarchies. He walks through the city and is the 'narrative trigger' for an unfolding vision of that city. In Bhisham Sahni's 1971 novel *Tamas*, too, many spaces unfold through Nathu's walking through the city: Nathu, walking through the city in the morning after he has, with great difficulty, killed the pig, wondering what made Murad Ali ask him to do the job, wondering if it was 'his' pig lying in front of the mosque.... This is a very different stroll from that of the dandy/*flâneur* strolling through the arcade. Nathu too is a creature of the city, but of a different sort, engendered by a different kind of city: a contra-modern character, walking a contra-modern city.

This contra-modern walk through the city is fraught with anxiety, all the more so because the city in the grip of riots is a city gone awry. Nathu, who only wanted to make that extra little money when he undertook Murad Ali's assignment, cannot walk the leisurely walk of a bored *flâneur* seeking to amuse himself. His walk has lost the destination-bound nature of the walk and has mutated into a stroll, but a stroll shorn of all ease. Through this act of passing through the city, he discovers a new link between himself and the city, as one who may have actually, god forbid, started the riots. The marginal has moved centre-stage in the events of the city, unwittingly, and only he is in possession of this dark secret. This is a walk of terror in which the 'boulevard does not become interior', as Benjamin says it does for the *flâneur*: 'The street becomes a dwelling for the *flâneur*; he is as much at home among the façades of houses as a citizen is in his four walls.'[7] The road, the *gali*, in *Tamas*, becomes for Nathu more alienated and alienating than ever before.

Gyanendra Pandey unfairly criticizes Bhisham Sahni's *Tamas*: 'The story marks a return to a less subtle nationalist statement in which *agent provocateurs* and mysterious evil folk pulling the strings from behind the scenes mislead an innocent and bewildered, but brave people. Partition is represented here, moreover, in the likeness of natural disaster in which human actions play little part; far removed from the run of daily life ... this is also the line that respectable, academic nationalist historiography has followed.'[8] Pandey is not sensitive to the fact that in *Tamas*, *everyone* is implicated. Sahni begins his novel with a scene that evokes 'darkness' (*tamas*) literally and metaphorically. Nathu is surreptitiously trying to kill a pig that is stubbornly refusing to die. He has been paid in advance for this job by Murad Ali. The sole lamp in the room in which he is enclosed is threatening to go out. This first powerful scene—powerful in its repulsiveness—is in the nature of a prologue to the novel. The protagonist to whom we are introduced is not the only lead character of the novel. It is his *act* that is more significant, for it sets the motor of the narrative running and is the immediate cause of the riots that follow. One can reverse the well-known quotation from Goethe's *Faust* used, among others, by Mikhail Bulgakov as an epigraph to his *The Master and Margarita* and referred to in the text of the novelette and the film, *The Meek One*, by Dostoevsky and Bresson, respectively: '"Say at last—who art thou?" "That Power I serve which wills forever evil, Yet does forever good".' Nathu in *Tamas* could well say the opposite: 'I meant no harm, yet unwittingly served a Power that willed evil and did evil.' The same is true of the young Parsi girl Lenny in Deepa Mehta's *1947—Earth*, who unwittingly gives her ayah, Shantabai, away to the mob.

SILENCED SPEECH

In *Walking in the City*, Michel de Certeau compares walking with the speech act. It has the same relation to the city that the act of speaking has to language: 'On the most elementary level it has a threefold "uttering" function: it is a process of *appropriation* of the topographic system by the pedestrian (just as the speaker appropriates and assumes language); it is a spatial *realization* of the site (just as the act of speaking is a sonic realization of language); lastly, it implies relationships among distinct positions, i.e. pragmatic "*contracts*" in the form of movements (just as verbal utterance … sets up contracts between fellow speakers).'[9]

If walking is like the speech act, what then of walking as silenced speech? What when language, or silence, submerges the utterance, or the city overwhelms the one who walks? What happens when the 'known' topography becomes alien? As Nathu walks this city it uncovers itself, little by little, but nothing makes sense. It is this disjunction between each of the characters and the great totality of which they are a part that is the essential characteristic of the frightening vision that *Tamas* offers. Nathu walks and the city unfolds as panorama, but it is a panorama that perplexes him: 'Ever since he had come out of that despicable hole, he had been wandering from one street to another…. Nathu had been feeling extremely restless. The more nervous he became, the more confused he felt. He could not talk to any one…. The whole day passed thus, wandering about the streets….'[10] The other characters, too, only see little portions of this city gone awry that are given to them, and act according to their impulses in this little framework. It is possible to say that Nathu's 'ethical self' actually comes into being through the everyday practice of walking through this 'alien' city.

Nathu, doubly silent—on the one hand, for being subaltern by caste and class, and on the other, dumbfounded by the enormity of the events he has unknowingly unleashed—walks through the city, a city that is no longer playing by known rules. One of the most interesting scenes in the book and the film *Tamas* is that of Nathu spotting Murad Ali in the crowd and running after him, trying to engage him in conversation, and somehow to get a confirmation that the pig thrown in front of the mosque was not the one he had killed. But by now events have overtaken them so much that this question cannot even directly be articulated. Murad Ali, moreover, does not want to talk to him; he pretends not to know or to hear him and hurriedly makes a getaway. Thus, if de Certeau compares the everyday practice of walking to the speech act, it is possible to posit, within the realm of pre-modernity/modernity, when the city is riot-torn, walking as the act that silences speech.

'"Walking" affirms, suspects, guesses, transgresses, respects, etc., the trajectories it "speaks". All modalities play a part in it, changing from step to step and redistributed in proportions, successions, intensities that vary with the moment, the route, the stroller. The indefinable diversity of these operations of utterance. They cannot be reduced to any graphic tracing,'[11] says de Certeau. One can 'affirm, suspect, guess or transgress' that which relates to the parameters of the known. What does one do with a town/city that itself does the transgressing of all expected codes? What if the known city becomes a labyrinth? To de Certeau's thesis, which deals with the late modern/postmodern city, we can provide a reading of the city that is incompletely modern, non-secular, from which emanate radiations of power and hatred. 'The city becomes the dominant theme of political epic but it is no longer a theatre for programmed, controlled operations. Beneath the discourses ideologizing it, there is a proliferation of tricks and fusions of power that are devoid of legible identity, that lack any perceptible access and that are without rational clarity—impossible to manage',[12] says de Certeau of the postmodern city. How much more true this is of the city during and after riots!

TOPOGRAPHY OF THE CITY UNDER SIEGE

A great deal of Partition fiction has to do with the topography and charting of one's lived space. But this is not the panoramic mapping of a land seen from above. This is the charting of the small intimate space, the house, the neighbour's house, the *mohalla*, the street beyond. In a state of siege, that is as far as the horizon stretches. These are topographies of fear, where the world shrinks to exclude the Other next door:

> Right in front of the gurudwara, across the lane, was a row of shops belonging to the Sikhs, behind which a slope went right down to the bank of a stream. Beyond the stream lay a big orchard of *lukat* fruit. Therefore, there was little danger of an attack being mounted from the front....
>
> To the left of the gurudwara, some of the houses near the end of the lane belonged to Muslims, behind which stood the Khalsa school. Beyond the Khalsa school stretched the fields. To the right of the gurudwara, where the lane ended, there was a *mohalla* of Muslim houses....
>
> The Sheikh's house with the green balcony, however, was located at the back of the gurudwara, beyond two narrow lanes. It was Sheikh Ghulam Rasul's double-storeyed house and, according to the information brought by the informers, it had been turned into a fortress by Musalmans.[13]

Big geographical realities are of no immediate perceptual significance to people in times such as these.

PANORAMA FROM ABOVE

There can be a panoramic view from above (a god's or a bird's eye view, for instance); there can be panoramic views from the same plane. In fiction on Partition, the panoramic view from above is almost absent. This is in contrast to Anne Freidberg's assertion that 'The ideology of representation in the panoramic painting must be placed in the context of concurrent reconceptualization of the idea of the horizon and of perspective (the first hot air balloon was launched in 1783 and aerial balloonists found vistas that radically changed the landscape perspective) and the "cult of immensity" in painting, where scale was a factor in the concept of illusionist immersion.'[14] In our state of contramodernity, in the depiction of a cataclysmic event such as Partition, the aerial panoramic view and the immensity of canvas are not viewed as possibilities for representation. The intimate topography of this fiction, intertwined inextricably with hate and terror, of necessity stands opposed to the overarching panoramic vision from above, for it cannot see beyond itself. In *Walking in the City*, Michel de Certeau contrasts this all-embracing view from above to the view offered by the actual walking processes in the city where 'History begins at ground level, with footsteps.'[15] New York, for him, as seen from the World Trade Center heights, the highest man-made construction, offers him '... the pleasure of looking down upon, of totalizing this vastest of human texts'.[16] The view from above of the observer/outsider stands in opposition to those 'insiders' who perforce have to live through the everyday experience of communal hatred and violence. In an ironic reversal we have instead, in the novel, *the look from below to above*. This 'inverse look' represents the equation of power between the colonised and the coloniser, of an incomplete modernity. The height allowed these postcolonial viewers is not that of the skyscraper that gives the feeling of God looking down upon the 'vast human text' that is offering itself up for reading, but the very 'low' height of the homely terrace, from where the city on fire and the *galis* of conflict can be seen. The enveloping haze of greater heights, which would shield the eye from such enactments of violence, is not available to those who live in the non-vertical, narrow-streeted cities of contra-modernity. This view from a height-in-proximity is captured by Deepa Mehta in *1947—Earth*: it is this view that almost decisively turns the ice-candy man, still suffering from the sight of his family lying slaughtered in the train from Gurdaspur, into a fundamentalist.

In fact, a reference to the politics of the 'totalizing view' is present in Karim Khan's narration of the parable of Musa and Khizr in *Tamas*: 'The moral of the story is—a ruler can see what you and I, ordinary folk cannot see. The British ruler has all-seeing eyes, otherwise how can it be possible that a handful of *firangis* coming from across the seven seas should rule over such a big country?'[17] The panoramic view was given to the colonizer. The colonized could only live through the particular, immediate horrors of their land that was being split into two.

In an ironic reversal we have instead *the look from below to above* in the novel. Incomplete modernity has internalized trains as everyday experience, but not aeroplanes as yet. When the worst rioting was nearly over, a sound arrests the attention of the dwellers of the town:

> It was an aeroplane. Flying over hills and valleys, with its wings outspread.... The aeroplane was, it would seem, out on a joy-flight.
>
> As it approached the village, people came out; they stood on raised platforms on roofs of houses and stared hard at the aeroplane with breathless curiosity.
>
> ....
>
> Over whichever village the aeroplane flew, hostilities ceased, drums stopped beating, slogan-shouting ceased, looting and burning stopped.[18]

This ironic scene has unfortunatly been left out of the film.

The Structure of the Novel

What *Tamas* the novel offers us is a double panoramic movement: one of the form, the other of the events that unfold within the plot. The novel is structured like a collection of short stories in which the protagonists pass through, disappear, reappear, or die. In this structure, the narrative sometimes carries the panoramic memory of other stories of Partition in Indian literature. There is remembrance of Manto's *Thanda Gosht* (Cold Meat), for example, in the novel. A group of men are chatting on the terrace of Sheikh Ghulam Rasul's house. 'They too had not had time to bury their dead', says the narrator of the story in a chilling, conversational tone:

'The *mujahids* sitting on the Sheikh's terrace had come from outside. They were narrating their exploits and experiences to one another.

'... A Hindu girl went up to the roof of her house. As soon as we saw her, we ran after her. There were nearly ten of us. She was trying to jump over the low wall on the roof to go over to the adjoining house when she fell into our hands. Nabi, Lalu, Mira, Murtaza all had a go at her one by one.

'... When my turn came there was no sound from her; she wouldn't move. I looked at her; she was dead. I had been doing it to a dead body,' he laughed a hollow kind of laughter, and turning his face to one side, spat on the floor.[19]

Necrophilia has been encountered in Manto's story in a different context; the horrors, however, are the same, whatever the protagonists' religion.

Narratives about big historical events, when they are not set up as belonging to the genre of the historical, often dispense with the plot line evolving around fixed characters. One of the most celebrated examples illustrating this is Eisenstein's *Battleship Potemkin*, made to mark the twentieth anniversary of the 1905 revolution. The sailor who leads the mutiny, Vakulinchuk, dies, but the people, as a collective, fill the vacuum that he leaves. This was a narrative affirming the power of collective action to change the course of history. *Tamas*, on the contrary, is about the dispersal of communities and neighbourhoods as they are engulfed by violence. Thus, the 'episodic structure' of the novel represents this dispersal. There are no heroes and leading lights; there are only humans, who act in a lowly or magnanimous manner in the situations into which they are thrown. Well-meaning individuals like the Congress leader Bakshiji are quite ineffective. He is left exclaiming sadly in the end: 'Kites shall hover, kites and vultures shall hover for long....'[20] It is only the communists who try actively to preach the idea of peace and harmony, but they too are outnumbered by the bickering representatives of the various secular and non-secular parties. It is the episodic structure that also gives power to the ending. We once again encounter the same set of leaders we had in the beginning. Having passed through the irrational violence of the times, a cynicism towards their petty bickering is evoked. The protagonists too make up with each other, keeping short-term interests in mind, but the deep rifts cannot be bridged.

Bhisham Sahni's *Tamas* has been criticized for its episodic structure. 'As a novel *Tamas* is episodic in structure, which from the point of view of literary craftsmanship may not exactly be considered flawless,' says Nihalani,[21] who adapted it into a tele-serial and film. It is precisely this 'episodic' structure, in my view, that is the novel's strength. It retains the sense of little histories that unfold to give a panoramic view of the violence and hatred of the inflamed communal passions of the time.

Writing of panoramic literature as a specific genre in France in the 1840s, Benjamin says: 'In this literature, the modest-looking, paperbound, pocket-size volumes called "*physiologie*" had pride of place. They investigated types that might be encountered by a person taking a look at the marketplace. From the itinerant street vendor of the boulevards to the dandy in the foyer of the opera house, there was not a figure of Paris life that was not sketched by a *physiologue*.'[22] Elaborating on Benjamin's writing on panoramic literature, Margaret Cohen says,

> Panoramic texts evince a characteristic narrational mode: They are composed of micronarratives with no direct continuity from plot to plot. Their narratives'

temporal concentration is accompanied by a concentration of subject matter. Panoramic texts focus on a knowledge that the structuralists might have called a 'Parisianeme', a distinctive minimal unit of Parisian life. This minimal unit is presented from the viewpoint of a single narrator. The micronarrative is a textual index of the panoramic text's scientific ambitions. Brevity is a principle of encyclopedic narrative, as the encyclopedic article 'concentrates the *maximum* of knowledge in the *minimum* of time.[23]

Bhisham Sahni's novel portrays a gallery of characters of all political persuasions. The narrative is woven around several protagonists and their microhistories. It is this characteristic that gives it a distinct panoramic sense. Although Sahni's work cannot directly be traced to this genre, it is a historical modernity and contra-modernity that engender this form, with its vast fund of new character types.

The Motif of the Train

Images of the panoramic vision from the train abound in literature and cinema. According to Leo Charney and Vanessa Schwartz, 'Modern forms of experience relied not simply on movement but on the juncture of movement and vision: moving pictures. One obvious precursor of moving pictures was the railroad, which eliminated traditional barriers of space and distance as it forged a bodily intimacy with time, space, and motion. The railroad journey anticipated more explicitly than any other technology an important facet of the experience of cinema: a person in a seat watches moving visuals through a frame that does not change position.'[24] Modernity, in addition to being defined socially, economically, and politically, is also defined neurologically. The new regimes of the visual that modernity gave birth to contribute significantly to its neurological definition. These new regimes of the visual were characterized by the mobility, the diegetic and spectacular nature of the images that were engendered.

In popular literature, Ian Fleming's *From Russia with Love* comes to mind. The panoramic unfolding of the cityscapes and the crossing of the Iron Curtain into the 'free world' is loaded with political significance, yet the varying worlds that are crossed do not affect the protagonists of the novel in any essential way. The landscape is a *passive* one, changing the very demeanour of people and their character. The section 'Train to the Urals' in Boris Pasternak's *Dr. Zhivago*, is an opposite kind of panoramic unfolding. This is a *reflective* one, putting on display the contrary and contradictory images of a country in turmoil after the Revolution, showing the complete severance of the doctor from his surroundings. The travel shows up the differences of life in Moscow and the provinces, the new social compartmentalizations, and the changing relationships between people. The feel of a country in churning and the emotional and mental distance of Zhivago from this churning, even though he is in its midst, is brought out through this journey into the interiors of Russia.

Bhisham Sahni's *We Have Arrived in Amritsar* is an amazing example of this panoramic view from the train of land/townscapes whose meanings have changed after Partition. It is, in fact, a rare example of an *active* landscape: it does not passively unfold, but actively exerts influence on the psychology of opposing groups in the train who interpret the changing landscape. The behaviour of the babu changes from weakling to aggressor in tune with the towns they are passing by:

> Suddenly the feeble-looking babu peeped out of the window and shouted, 'We have passed Harbanspura!'…
>
> 'Eh babu, why are you shouting?' the Pathan with the rosary said surprised. … He laughed jeeringly. It was obvious he knew nothing about the significance of Harbanspura….
>
> The babu made no attempt to explain anything….
>
> A little later, a loud clicking sound was heard; perhaps the train had changed the tracks. The babu peeping out of the window looked towards the direction in which the train was advancing.
>
> 'We are nearing some town,' he shouted. 'It is Amritsar.' He yelled at the top of his voice and suddenly stood up and addressing the Pathan sitting on the upper berth, shouted, 'You son of a bitch, come down.'[25]

The panoramic vision of the train journey thus serves to show up contrasts of opposing worlds, free/totalitarian, city/provinces, city/nature. The unfolding panorama may be passive or active depending on how the protagonists and the panorama influence each other.

In Kumar Shahani's *Tarang* and *Kasba*, the train is itself part of a larger panoramic view. In *Tarang*, the lead protagonist narrates to a fellow radical worker the story of the disintegration of her family and her migration to the city. They are sitting in a small hut by the railway tracks, and as she recalls her life, we see trains in the twilight circling and passing by through the open quadrangles that pass for windows. Uprooting, migration, the pull of the city on the margins of which such lives are destined to be lived, and industrialization—all these complex themes are poetically embedded in this sequence. Another interesting sequence with a train is in *Rasayatra*, directed by Nandan Kudhyadi and scripted by Madan Gopal Singh. The film is based on the life of the great Hindustani music vocalist, Mallikarjun Mansur. Mansur, a young man, desirous of learning music from a maestro in Bombay, is all set to travel out for the first time from the small town of Miraj to the big city. As he stands on the platform, the engine gives off great clouds of smoke that engulf him. Instead of the train moving, we have the musician pulled out of the frame in a tracking movement (on tracks). To the strains of a *tarana*, we see the panoramic tracking view giving us a strangely close view of buidings and train tracks and yards in Bombay in the light of dawn, signalling the singer's entry into the city. The image of the singer getting *pulled* into modernity is complemented by the abstract syllables of the *tarana*, as the first-time experience of the singer entering the big city, not yet moulded into words, yet welcoming the experience through the lively percussive beat.

The train haunts literary and cinematic imaginaries in Partition fiction, as that one motif that contains the paradoxical image of modernity: notions of 'the industrial', of 'connectivity' (linking distances together), of 'automation' (running on tracks with great force) combine with the historically specific notion in the Indian subcontinent, with *flight*. Thus, while the first three attributes outlined above can be encountered in many works of European fiction, it is the last characteristic, that of flight from extenuating social/religious/political circumstances, that makes it specifically 'local'. The traumatic moment of Partition, which is encapsulated in the image of the train, writes 'the nation's modernity as the event of the everyday and the advent of the epochal'.[26] It is the train that transported people in flight, whether as living or dead bodies. Many narratives of Partition recount how trains would arrive filled with dead bodies, as evidences of communal riots elsewhere. One recalls Deepa Mehta's *1947—Earth,* where the Ice-Candy Man waits on the platform for the train from Gurdaspur to arrive and is restless at its being late. When it does arrive, he finds his family members and other passengers lying butchered inside. Amar Kanwar's *Season Outside*, too, a reflexive documentary on the dividing lines between communities, in its section on Partition, has very minimalist, but moving images of the train, filled with fleeing people, crossing borders.

RITWIK GHATAK

What are the reasons for Ghatak being the unique figure he is in the post-independence cultural landscape? While others focus on the event, Ghatak focuses on memory. He had seen the splitting of his beloved Bengal, of the left movement, and of the cultural movement led by the IPTA. The anguish of these separations did not leave him till the end of his life. He, more than others, his contemporaries or filmmakers who came after him, questioned the aesthetics of realism as it had been formulated in the West and what Madan Gopal Singh has called 'realist balance'[27] in representing events that were searing in their destructive intensity. In Ghatak's works, the car, the train, the aeroplane are mythic and modern at the same time.

In post-War Europe, two movements that tried to come to terms cinematically with recent history came into being. Italian neo-realism, in many of its works,[28] had its protagonists walk through devastated cities. The French New Wave had its characters walk in and out of cafés, hotels, and homes onto streets. According to Deleuze, both these film movements gave up the pretence of constructing plots based on cause-and-effect actions, in response to the magnitude of the War: 'The French New Wave cannot be defined unless we try to see how it has traced the path of Italian neorealism for its own purposes—even if it meant going in other directions as well. In fact, the New Wave, on a first approximation, takes up the previous route again: from a loosening of the sensory-motor link (the stroll or wandering, the ballad, the events that concern no one, etc.), to the rise of optical and sound situations. Here again, a cinema of seeing replaces a cinema of action'.[29] Ghatak, working contemporaneously in the 1950s and 1960s, does the same with regard to recent subcontinental history.

In *Komal Gandhar* (E-Flat, 1961), strolling through the landscape, the protagonists relive the memory of the separation of Partition. While the walk in other Partition fiction and films unfolds a changing topography that the eye sees and registers, in *Komal Gandhar,* the outing of the drama troupe into the countryside and the protagonists' walk through the landscape evoke memories of the undivided Bengal to the mind's eye. This is not a sequence that charts action and reaction, but calls up the impress in memory of undivided land and river. In a moment of nostalgic and angry narration, which is also a moment of emotional bonding, Bhrigu tells Anusuya of his home on the other side of the river Padma: 'On this side is the Padma, and on the other side too is the same river', sings a swaying Bijon Bhattacharya, while other artistes of the troupe take a boat ride, also singing another song in chorus. There is thus a complex interweaving of micro-narratives, of the three autonomous segments—Bijon and his companion, the theatre group in the boat, and Anusuya and Bhrigu—which are visual as well aural (given the coming together of so many different fragments of song). This sequence once again underlines the importance of panoramic micro narratives in memory—'recall narratives' (as, in a sense, *Tamas* is for Bhisham Sahni). Suddenly, we have the image of tracks leading nowhere and the crescendo of voices—mainly of women—singing *Duhai Ali.* The polyphony of voices and chants turns into a hysteric cry. The camera moves forward, as if on an invisible train, and comes to an abrupt, though expected halt at the dead end. In this sequence, memory creates an image that intervenes forcefully as sensuousness into the real present. The force with which this image calls up the splitting of the nation, with all its associations, cleaving into the pastoral, idyllic peace that envelops the different narratives of the players of the troupe, remains unsurpassed in Indian cinema. Rather than follow the path of a new realism, as in Italy, or the path of modernism as the French New Wave did, Ghatak combined realism with the rituals of the everyday on the one hand, and of the archaic on the other. He created what I call geological images that encapsulated within themselves many time frames, archaic and contemporary, mythical and achingly real. Madan Gopal Singh says, 'Ghatak chose to address Partition through a maze of carefully invoked oralities in defiance of all established conventions in Indian cinema. The idea was to arrive at a mode of articulation through a cleft tongue—at the same time partial and excessive in its expression. Though extremely well-read, Ghatak was primarily a man of the epic sensibility embedded in the oral tradition where discourses of memory freely mingled with mythology, folklore and classical narratives'.[30]

Ghatak, so fond otherwise of circulars (even if cut) and pans, dispenses with the panoramic vision in this sequence. The panorama of nature unfolds in a slow rhythm through Anusuya and Bhrigu's leisurely walk, or the swaying of the people to the music. But when it comes to the train, it is a headlong movement into a dead end. The curved horizon of the panorama is split by the relentless and inexorable linearity of the train-camera. It is also of interest that the movement is accomplished through the train-camera, a strange being that is an amalgam of both the train and the camera. We are given the movement associated with both, but shown neither the train nor the camera. The tracks, too, laid in lush nature, could belong to the train or the camera. This unseen index of modernity—or, should we say, in this sequence of destructive contra-modernity—the camera-train rushes onto an idyllic, pastoral landscape. Ghatak, however, does not fall into the trap of simple binary oppositions of pre-modern/ modern, or nature/industry. The idyll is already split, severed from its unity with the land on the other side of the Padma, as are the traumatised beings of the protagonists.

Notes

1. Friedberg, 1994, pp. 2-3.
2. 'The panorama was a 360 degree cylindrical painting, viewed by an observer at the centre. The illusion presented by the panorama was created by a combination of realist techniques of perspective and scale with a mode of viewing that placed the spectator at the centre of a darkened room surrounded by a scene lit from above.' Ibid., p. 21.
3. Bhabha, 1999, pp. 937-8.
4. Benjamin, 1983, p. 74.
5. Ibid., p. 36.
6. 'His Heap of Rubble', in Mushirul Hasan, 1997.
7. Benjamin, 1983, p. 37.
8. Gyanendra Pandey, 'Defence of a Fragment', quoted in Bhatia, 2002, p. 200.

9. de Certeau, 2000, p. 106.
10. Sahni, 2001, pp.125-6. Henceforth referred to as *Tamas*.
11. Ibid., pp. 107-8.
12. de Certeau, 2000, p. 104.
13. Sahni, 2001, pp. 232-3.
14. Friedberg, 1994, p. 22.
15. de Certeau, 2000 p. 105.
16. Ibid., p. 101.
17. Sahni, p. 124.
18. Ibid., pp. 296-8.
19. Ibid., p. 288.
20. Ibid., p. 351.
21. Nihalani, 1988, p. 5.
22. Benjamin, 1983, p. 35. Benjamin then adds, 'The leisurely quality of these descriptions fits the style of the *flâneur* who goes botanizing on the asphalt', p. 36.
23. Cohen, 1995, p. 232.
24. Charney and Schwartz, 1995, p. 6.
25. Hasan, 1997, p. 121.
26. Bhabha, 1990, p. 293.
27. Singh, 1993, p. 47.
28. Rosselini's *Paisa* and *Germany Year Zero*, for instance.
29. Deleuze, 1989, p. 9.
30. Singh, 2004.

References

Benjamin, Walter, *Charles Baudelaire: A Lyric Poet in the Era of High Capitalism*, London: Verso, 1983.

Bhabha, Homi K., 'Dissemination' in *idem*, ed., *Nation and Narration*, London: Routledge, 1990.

———, 'The Location of Culture', in Julie Rivkin and Michael Ryan, eds., *Literary Theory: An Anthology*, Oxford: Blackwell, 1999, pp. 937–8.

Bhatia, Nandi, 'How Long Does Lahore Burn', in S. Setter and I. B. Gupta, eds., *Pangs of Partition*, vol. II, New Delhi: ICHR and Manohar, 2002.

Charney, Leo, and Vanessa Schwartz, 'Introduction', in *idem*, eds., *Cinema and the Invention of Modern Life*, Berkeley: University of California Press, 1995.

Cohen, Margaret, 'Panoramic Literature and the Invention of Everyday Genres', in Leo Charney and Vanessa Schwartz, eds., *Cinema and the Invention of Modern Life*, Berkeley: University of California Press, 1995.

Certeau, Michael de, 'Walking in the City', in Graham Ward, ed., *The Certeau Reader*, Oxford: Blackwell, 2000.

Deleuze, Gilles, *Cinema 2: The Time-Image*, Minneapolis: The University of Minnesota Press, 1989.

Friedberg, Anne, *Window Shopping: Cinema and the Postmodern*, University of California Press, 1994.

———, 'Introduction', in *The Partition Omnibus*, New Delhi: Oxford University Press, 2002.

Mohan Rakesh, 'His Heap of Rubble', in Mushirul Hasan, ed., *India Partitioned: The Other Face of Freedom*, New Delhi: Roli Books, 1997.

Nihalani, Govind, 'Introduction', in Bhisham Sahni, *Tamas*, trans. Jai Ratan, New Delhi: Penguin Books India, 1988.

Sahni, Bhisham, *Tamas*, trans. Jai Ratan, New Delhi: Penguin Books India, 1988.

———, 'We Have Arrived in Amritsar', in Mushirul Hasan, ed., *India Partitioned: The Other Face of Freedom,* New Delhi: Roli Books, 1997, p. 121.

Singh, Madan Gopal, 'Ray and the Realist Conscience', *Cinemaya* 20, Summer 1993, p. 47.

———, 'Ghatak's Partition Trilogy', unpublished paper presented on 17 March 2004 at the international seminar, 'Reflexions: Film, Literature and Culture', organized by the Department of English, University of Delhi, at the India International Centre, 17-19 March, 2004.

5

Melodramatic Imaginings: Representations of Sectarianism within Hindi Popular Cinema and Indian Documentaries

Anuja Jain

ON 6 DECEMBER 1992, the Babri Masjid was demolished in Ayodhya and the subsequent 'communal' conflagration consumed the city of Bombay in 1992–3. Significantly, the debate over who destroyed the Babri Masjid, and who was responsible for the horror and frenzy of this sectarian violence that engulfed the city of Bombay and transformed one of the most cosmopolitan, multi-ethnic, and religiously tolerant cities has been much debated by historians, anthropologists, political scientists, intellectuals, academics, and cultural theorists. It is the visual representations of the demolition of the Masjid as well as of the terror of the Bombay riots that have dominated this large discursive field. These representations are characterized by a complex struggle over the interpretation of the photographic and cinematic imaginations.

Positioned within these discourses, my article aims to analyse the cinematic representations—both in fiction and in documentary cinema of this catastrophic moment which not only had a lasting impact on the Indian polity and its socio-economic conditions, but also became symptomatic of the ethnic conflicts within many other South Asian societies. Analysing Mani Ratnam's popular Hindi film *Bombay* (1995) and Suma Josson's documentary film, *Bombay's Blood Yatra* (Bombay's Journey of Blood, 1993), I will argue that the documentary filmmakers, as they engage with this historic moment of sectarianism and intervene in the socio-political conditions within India, use many of the aesthetic strategies and idioms that are similar to those used by popular Hindi cinema. The melodramatic mode is one such technique that is most commonly associated with popular Hindi cinema in its negotiation with the experiences of the apocalyptic moments such as those of the sectarianism of 1992–3.[1] My article will explicate the use of the aesthetic strategy of melodrama as employed by documentry cinema and analyse its implications for the representation of the horror, despair, desolation, and frenzy of the sectarian strife.

Indian cinema is still to a large extent synonymous with 'Bollywood' or 'art' cinema. As opposed to popular Hindi cinema, a medium that dominates largely and single-handedly the viewing culture of Indian society and shapes middle-class conceptions of politics and society, Indian documentary cinema still exists outside the sustained public discourse. Documentary films are framed by a complex nexus of production, circulation, exhibition, and consumption within India—the absence of any state funding and infrastructure; political interference and the consequent absence of these texts from transmission on the national TV channels; the absence also from privately owned TV channels which are not only imbricated within the demands of entertainment but also constitute a viewing culture that is not inclusive of these documentary films; long battles with censorship; exhibition mostly at film festivals, within India or internationally, or screenings by non profit organizations, educational institutions, and film clubs.

My article will explicate how working in these material conditions, documentary filmmakers employ the melodramatic modality, which enables the victims to narrate the pain and loss caused by the moment of communal conflagration. However, by using this modality that is familiar to audiences of popular Hindi cinema, documentary cinema also plays with the expectations of the audience, which is informed by its knowledge and acceptance of popular cinema's narratives and techniques. Documentary cinema therefore not only creates a discursive space that reconfigures the public, informs the spectator-citizen who interrogates the dangerous *Hindutava* constructions of 'potent' Hinduism and its nature of violence, but it also mobilizes a serious interrogation of the popular audio-visual media forms as the most pervasive source of insight into the socio-political conditions.

I would like to begin with a discussion of Mani Ratnam's *Bombay* (1995), one of the first Indian films to respond almost immediately to the 1992–3 sectarian violence of Bombay. *Bombay* engages with the pertinent issue of the possibility of a united 'nation' and the consequent mobilization of a 'national' identity, particularly that of an *Indian,* which has been fragmented by the communal conflagration and religious divisions within Indian society following the Babri Masjid demolition.

Ratnam deploys the melodramatic mode, and the family becomes the space that allows for socio-political conflicts to be 'symbolically rendered' and not 'produced as allegorical abstractions'.[2] In the film, the family functions as a means of, and becomes symbolic for, the nation state itself. It enters into dialogue with the socio-political conflicts brought forth by the moment of sectarian violence and becomes the site for the addressal of the question of a possibility of reconfiguring the 'nation' that has been ruptured by Hindu–Muslim conflict. Throughout the movie, the narrative builds up the answer to this question in an affirmative. Within the narrative, a space is created where the protagonist Shekhar Mishra (a Hindu) is able to marry Shaila Bano (a Muslim), and kinship relations between their estranged families are regrouped within the space of the family with the birth of their twin sons. The twins with their names—Kabir Narayan and Kamal Bashir—function as the 'idyll of reconciliation'.[3] Thus, with names that are a mixture of Hindu and Muslim identities, 'the children are drained not only of the signs of religious differences but of any marks of difference at all'.[4] Ratnam thus creates a sense of a national identity that negates any difference and is essentially *Indian*.

The film follows the conventions of a melodramatic Hindi film, and in the last sequence we witness the family, which has been torn apart within the vortex of the riots, getting united. The twins who had been lost are restored within the fold of the family and the film ends with a human chain formed by people of different castes and communities. In this sequence, we see the constant circular panning of the camera, the expression of the intense emotions of pain and trauma in the lyrics, the hysterical outcries of both Shekhar and his wife Shaila Bano, the *mise en scène* composed of charred bodies, amputated arms, badly wounded children. All these create a hyperbolic melodramatic matrix and subject viewers to extreme emotions, from the intense horror and nightmare of the 'communal' conflagration, to the cathartic reunion of the twins, and the final restoration of the family. Throughout the film, and especially in this sequence, what we witness is the way in which the melodramatic mode allows for the narrative enactment of the intense experiences and emotions of the horror, pain, and frenzy of sectarian violence. The mode of melodrama allows Ratnam to represent 'events at once so apparently senseless and so predictably routine that neither narratives nor images seem to be able to encompass them'.[5] However, I would like to argue that though Ratnam embraces melodrama's larger impulse to 'reverse time, to return to the time of origins and the space of innocence … reconcile the irreconciliable',[6] he also goes on to construct a consensus narrative. He does not merely deploy the melodramatic mode to attain a resolution or to make a revelation of moral and emotional truths; he weds the moral, wish-fulfilling, melodramatic impulse to recognise and regain a lost innocence to a larger desire of his—that of constructing the utopia of a 'secular' India. The melodramatic resolution, 'the retrieval of an absolute innocence and good in which most thinking people do not put much faith'[7] becomes the utopic imagining of a 'nation', precariously balanced on a forced cohesion of Hindus and Muslims. Ratnam's great *hamartia*, his tragic flaw, becomes this much desired utopia, which needs to be constructed and then reaffirmed as real.

In his vision of modern India, all through the film, Ratnam does make a bid to register the particular demands and interests of each separate group in society. But his model of secularism becomes problematic, as it is defined by a 'national' unity that negates the scripting of the modern nation state as a contrapuntal narrative in which voices and identities are given to the varied ethnic and social groups instead of suppressing them under the homogenizing discourse of the 'national' identity of an *Indian*, especially given the long history of Hindu–Muslim conflict and the complex relationship of Muslims and Indian citizenship, in the face of continuous demands by the militant Hindu Right for a 'pure' Hindu nation. Though economic as well as cultural differences between the two communities are represented, Ratnam attempts to resolve the long-standing conflict between them by presenting mythical solutions, such as the construction of the human chain to restore a utopian world. With the construction of the human chain, he not only attempts to naturalize tensions, but also to subsume all the Hindu–Muslim conflicts, in the film's desire to reconfigure the political and social structures of contentions.

For critics such as Tejaswini Niranjana, the burden of the film is to 'create the contemporary convergences between the human, the secular and the nationalist and to dramatize the condensation of these characteristics in the Hindu male who has discarded marks of caste and community'.[8] I do not agree with the views of Niranjana or Vasudevan that Ratnam is attempting to create a sense of an essentially Hindu national identity or that in his 'bid for inter-communal integration' he is proposing 'modernity as evolving from the trajectory of Hindu subjectivity'.[9] Ira Bhaskar also effectively argues that in the context of the riot Ratnam holds both the communities responsible, and that, in fact, 'it is not difficult to see that the ultimate responsibility does rest with the aggressive and unrepentant intransigence of Hindu fundamentalism'.[10] While it is evident that Ratnam is clearly not attempting to create a Hindu majoritarian narrative, yet what still makes the film problematic is that, as a Nehruvian socialist, he follows the rhetoric of *national unity* and *progress*. He attempts to instate this aura of a 'national community', a nation which positions itself as representing the common unity and interests of all groups. Thus, he perpetually attempts to reconstitute the fractured identity of a Muslim as an *Indian*. However, the faultlines are revealed within Ratnam's imagined nation despite the continuous process of preserving and protecting his myth of a common 'national' identity from potential ruptures due to communalism, long-standing differences, and the opposition of minorities to a nationalism that saw their demands and voices as narrow political demands, often creating barriers in the way of *national unity* and *progress*. We witness this especially in the sequence when Shaila Bano goes to post a letter to her mother. As she is walking towards the post-box, she witnesses the *rath yatra*, the procession that began in September 1990 from the rebuilt Somnath temple in Gujarat and was supposed to conclude in Ayodhya. It was organized by the Hindu Right under the leadership of L.K. Advani and it mobilized thousands of members of the militant *Sangh Parivar*, the *karsevaks* who finally demolished the Babri Masjid in Ayodhya on 6 December 1992, unleashing communal conflagration throughout the country. As many scholars and critics have pointed out, this *yatra* was a political strategy by the Hindu Right to disseminate the imaginings of the Indian nation state as a 'pure' Hindu nation, and to project the utopia of restoring the nation to its *true* Aryan Hindu glory. As Shaila Bano looks at this procession—the aggressive slogans, speeches, and placards—we have a close-up shot of Shaila looking terrified and worried, anticipating the impending doom. Most importantly, we also see her instinctively, unwittingly, covering her head with the sari that she wears, a gesture that traditionally characterises Hindu married women. This marks the moment when the same Shaila who could defiantly respond to her Hindu landlady's displeasure at having a Muslim in the house by asserting, 'Yes, I am a Muslim', begins to realize the implications of being a Muslim in a nation ruled by the fascist Hindu regime. After this point, she becomes a helpless bystander, who realizes that as a minority Muslim, she does not even have the privilege, which her high-caste Hindu husband has, to critique the riots. Seeing the sight of the rioting mobs burning each other, her own burnt house, dead parents, lost children, and hundreds of injured children, Shaila can only ask in agony and pain, 'so many children, poor small children, why did this have to happen—what did we all do, suppose my own children....' Thus, despite allowing Shaila Bano her Muslim identity all through the film's narrative—creating the space where it is Shekhar who proposes to convert to Islam in order to marry her, Shaila continuing to practice Islam even after marriage to a high-caste Hindu Brahman, the couple's sons having mixed Muslim and Hindu names—with this moment of the *rath yatra* Ratnam unwittingly ends up constructing the Muslim as the Other, someone like Shaila Bano, a Muslim who needs to be assimilated through marriage within the dominant Hindu 'national' community.

Significantly, this integration, despite Ratnam's attempt at being even-handed in his treatment of the role of the two communities in the riot, is not simply the conventional stereotypical representation of the Muslim within mainstream cinema,[11] but exemplary of the question raised by scholars like Gyanendra Pandey: 'Can a Muslim be an Indian?'[12] We are forced to deliberate whether the 'secular' imaginings within the Indian nation state are inevitably predicated upon the integration of the Muslim within the majoritarian fold. Is appropriation the only way in which a

Muslim can survive today in the given political and social circumstances of a fascist Hindu regime, an India where the militant Hindu Right frames Muslim identity as a normative 'other', a 'fanatic' or a 'terrorist', an India that is constitutive of an almost 83 per cent Hindu majority, who believe in the Right Wing's rhetoric of a 'pure' Hindu nation?

Richard Dyer in 'Entertainment and Utopia' has suggested that 'Entertainment offers the image of "something better" to escape into, or something we want deeply that our day-to-day life doesn't provide. Alternatives, hopes, wishes—these are the stuff of utopia, the sense that things could be better, that something other than what is can be imagined and may be realized'.[13] In a similar vein, for Ratnam also these melodramatic imaginings and resolutions of a unified 'nation', and the 'secular' identity as *Indian*, are structured upon the dual recognition of how things are and how they should be. The narrative of the film carries an awareness of the absence of such 'communal' harmony in the contemporary socio-political conditions within India. Ratnam does give us a nuanced representation of the complex relationship between Hindus and Muslims. For example, in the last sequence, Shekhar questions the leaders of both communities and raises the issue of their responsibility for the carnage. But *Bombay*, like many other popular Hindi films, performs the ritual function of being a socially integrating force and insists upon 'forcing the status quo to yield signs of moral legibility'.[14] For Ratnam, the pressures of mass appeal, the desire for box office success, the demands of his own Nehruvian nationalist ideology, necessitate the construction of and belief in this discourse of the 'nation' and 'national' identity as the only hope amidst the stark pessimistic reality of a country torn apart by sectarian carnage.

Linda Williams points out that 'the greater the historical burden of guilt, the more pathetically and the more actively the melodrama works to recognize and regain a lost innocence'.[15] In a similar vein, in the last sequence, Shekhar emphatically asserts that he and his family 'are only *Indians*'. This call to be an *Indian* is deeply flawed, and what we need to realise is how often this ideology of secularism, which is often associated with slogans like 'we are Indians first, Hindus second' or 'we are Indians first, then Sikhs'[16] is precarious. This vision of an *Indian* is underlined by a desire for a 'national' unity that carries the danger of naturalising the deeply problematic relationship between Hindus and Muslims, and of offering a resolution through a common hegemonic identity. This imagining of an *Indian* for both, a Hindu as well as a Muslim, comes across as a hollow utopic imagining and overlooks the complex relationship between the Muslim identity and Indian citizenship; it negates the fact that in the Bombay riots, the state was criticized for being ineffective in protecting Muslims and for having a prejudiced attitude towards them at such moments of sectarian violence.

Ira Bhaskar significantly argues for melodrama within Hindi popular cinema as a powerful mode of public mourning, and deems the intense emotional responses that melodrama elicits as enabling a confrontation of the spectres that haunt history and give voice to a desire for reparation.[17] However, in her discussion of Mani Ratnam's *Bombay,* though she recognises that melodrama may simplify and binarise political issues, she deems melodrama's 'rhetorical strategies' and 'moral vision' as needed in extreme situations of sectarian violence. She thus argues: 'Its resolutions are *projected desires* rather than achieved ends'.[18] However, I would like to argue that it is precisely in this desire for a resolution and vindication of a utopic vision in extreme situations of sectarian violence, this desperate faith in the possibility of redemption, that the melodramatic mode in *Bombay* becomes problematic and needs to be critiqued. This kind of deployment of the melodramatic modality that Bhaskar suggests leads to the negation of real conflicts in the choice for utterly faulty premises, such as mixed marriages, human chains, and other ideologies of integration, which are often presumed to resolve such conflicts and to reconfigure the political and social structures of contentions. Instead, what is needed is the recognition that these moments of sectarian violence are becoming a routine and hence call for an urgent interrogation of the 'secular' and 'secularism' within the Indian nation state, instead of each time negating the long-standing, deep-seated conflicts within Indian secularism for these hollow and dangerous utopic imaginings.

It is here that the pervasiveness of the melodramatic narratives of popular Hindi cinema becomes dangerous and needs to be challenged by other cultural discourses. This is where the documentary film, *Blood Yatra* (Bombay's Journey of Blood, 1993) by Suma Josson becomes so significant. The documentary film also deploys the melodramatic mode to question not just the plausibility, but also the very desire for such utopic imaginings as those of Ratnam, of a 'national' identity which subsumes the individual religious identity within a larger homogenous 'secular' one in the given contemporary social, material, and political conditions of India, where the Hindu Right Wing is coalescing religion with nationhood, and a Hindu identity with the national identity, in its reordering of the Indian nation state on the lines of the Hindutava ideology.

The film uses the interview mode, and the documentary filmmaker, abandoning the conventional voyeuristic objectivity, does not hesitate in manipulating the subjects in order to mobilize the emotional excess. Josson begins the film with an interview of a lower middle class woman, a slum dweller who narrates the tragic incident of her young son, the only bread earner of the family, being shot by the police during the riots. During the interview the camera slowly zooms into the face of the mother as she finishes narrating the incident and silently waits for her emotional breakdown. As it records the breakdown, and as we hear her sobbing, the camera pans down to a medium close-up shot of the weeping young child in her lap. This interview is followed by a montage of black and white images intercut with images of the Right Wing leader L.K. Advani before the demolition of the Babri Masjid, and close-up stills of the inhuman wounds of the victims of the riots. Thereafter, Josson quickly mobilizes the iconic images and sounds of the brutally wounded victims, weeping orphan children, abused women, debilitated houses, and other spaces with traces of human blood and amputated limbs. This takes up about 15 minutes of the screen time, and what we as spectators witness is a kind of emotional investment and narrative enticement in the fashion of the melodramas of popular Hindi cinema. We see a 'text of muteness'—the use of gestural and visual excess, tableaux, and spectacle, generating 'meanings which cannot be generated from the language code'.[19] This allows the identification of the filmmaker and the audience with the 'Other', the interviewed subject, and generates meanings which language alone cannot convey. This also becomes a perfect example of protagonists becoming the objects of pathos, victims of forces that lie beyond their control and understanding, as in melodramatic narratives.[20]

Further, along with creating the melodramatic hyperbolic matrix in the fashion of Ratnam's *Bombay*, the trope of the family is once again used to narrate the deep pain and loss caused by the moment of 'communal' conflagration. Though the documentary film uses the same familiar trope of the family, significantly, it does not allow the narrative a melodramatic resolution in the manner of popular Hindi cinema. There are no utopias that instate the visions of a composite 'secular' nation. Unlike Ratnam's *Bombay*, there is no utopic resolution, no restoration of the family, and no homogenizing discourse of the 'national' identity of an *Indian*. Thus the documentary film underlines how, in the given socio-political conditions, there is no possibility of the 'moral occult' of the melodrama where, in the struggle between the spiritual forces, there is an eventual victory of the ethical impulses ....[21] The interviewed subject, along with the other subjects in the film, expresses no hope of their kith and kin returning, as either they are dead, shot by police bullets, or burnt or butchered in front of their own eyes by the members of the other community.

Significantly, in the film Josson is not the 'self obscuring voyeur of *verité* realism'[22] and, abandoning the conventional voyeuristic objectivity, she does not hesitate in manipulating the subjects in order to elicit useful confessions from them. These are moments of an intense emotional realism, evocations of melodramatic excess, familiar to audiences of popular Hindi cinema. They have a discursive status, where the filmmaker is not using them to give 'evidence', or trying to hide her privileged position as compared to the interviewed subject. She is aware of the fact that it is she who would function as a historiographer, who would finally *mediate* these narratives. But what makes these accounts invaluable is that there is no 'referential illusion, where the historian tries to give the impression that the referent is speaking for itself'.[23] In such excessively emotional moments, the filmmaker does not attempt to create an illusion of a spontaneous textural or behavioural quality, but works with the understanding that the documentary performers 'act' in much the same way as their dramatic counterparts in commercial cinema, except that they have been cast for their social representability, and their roles are composites of their own social roles as well as of the dramatic requirements of the filmmaker. These personal memories and traumas are narrated by the victims with a clear consciousness that it is only by narrating their stories about their loss in moments such as those of sectarian violence that they can be heard. Thus, on the part of the victims, the melodramatic excess evoked by the interviews legitimizes an element of 'performance' for them. There is a consciousness within the documentary filmmaker also that she is not functioning merely as a cinematic recording eye and, instead, with a valence of activism and interaction, she 'approximates the human sensorium: looking, listening, and speaking as it perceives events and allows for response'.[24] I would like to emphasize that as the filmmaker mobilizes an emotional realism, she is aware of certain questions that these images pose not only to her, but also to their viewer. These images ask their audience what rights or prerogatives does the victim retain, as the filmmaker uses the images of a victim's pain and trauma. Is there a danger of an aestheticization of powerlessness? What is the relation between the subject and the privileged observer who is often in the position of power? Do these images often assume the danger of reassuring the viewer of our own secure social position?

In conclusion, I would like to underline that the melodramatic mode in documentaries such as Josson's 'Bombay's Journey of Blood' not only gives voice to the physical and psychological trauma of the voiceless victims, but also allows the filmmaker to contest the widely prevalent representations of 'communal' violence in the public sphere, and to intervene in the constitution of the modes of perception and terms of understanding of the Hindutva project. The film forces the spectators to interrogate the role and function of popular cinema and its dangerous utopias, which time and again overlook the already prolonged suppression of many social, ethnic, and religious voices in India. The documentary film uses the melodramatic mode, highlights the impossibility of attaining utopic resolutions, and forces the audience to interrogate this very desire for such utopias, reiterating that it is no longer possible to sanitize and naturalize sectarian violence which has torn apart the social and moral fabric of society. A documentary film, such as *Blood Yatra,* leaves its audience with the question: Can we unburden ourselves of the images of the innumerable charred bodies and the mass-scale inhuman violence to reinstate the mythic utopic ideals of a united 'nation', and a homogenous 'national' identity of an *Indian*?

Notes

1. Ira Bhaskar, '"The Persistence of Memory": Historical Trauma and Imagining the Community in Hindi Cinema', unpublished thesis, New York University, 2005. See also Bhaskar Sarkar, *Mourning the Nation: Indian Cinema in the Wake of Partition*, Durham NC: Duke University Press, 2009.
2. Christine Gledhill, ed., *Home is Where the Heart is: Studies in Melodrama and the Woman's Film*, London: BFI, 1987, p. 30.
3. Ravi Vasudevan, 'Bombay and its Public', *Journal of Arts and Ideas*, vol. 29, January 1996, p. 46.
4. Ibid., p. 47.
5. Thomas Elsaesser, 'Subject positions, speaking positions', in *Holocaust, Our Hitler,* and *Heimat* to *Shoah* and *Schindler's List*', in Vivian Sobchak, ed., *The Persistence of History: Cinema, Television and the Modern Event*, New York and London: Routledge, 1996, p. 146.
6. Linda Williams, 'Melodrama Revised', in Nick Browne, ed., *Refiguring American Film Genres: Theory and History*, Berkeley, Los Angeles, and London: University of California Press, 1998, p. 75.
7. Ibid., p. 61.
8. Niranjana, p. 164.
9. Vasudevan, op. cit., pp. 49, 61.
10. Bhaskar, op. cit., p. 299.
11. Ibid.
12. Gyanendra Pandey, 'Can a Muslim be an Indian?', *Comparative Studies in Society and History*, vol. 41, no. 4, November 1999.
13. Richard Dyer, *Only Entertainment*, New York: Routledge, 1992, p. 222.
14. Williams, op. cit., p. 53.
15. Ibid., p. 61.
16. Ashis Nandy, 'The Politics of Secularism and the Recovery of Religious Toleration', in Rajeev Bhargava, ed., *Secularism and Its Critics*, Delhi and New York: Oxford University Press, 1998, p. 326.
17. Bhaskar, op. cit., p. 87.
18. Ibid., p. 496. Emphasis in original.
19. Peter Brooks, *The Melodramatic Imagination: Balzac, Henry James, Melodrama and the Mode of Excess*, New York: Columbia University Press, 1984, p. 72.
20. Thomas Elsaesser, 'Tales of Sound and Fury: Observations on the Family Melodrama', in Christina Gledhill, ed., *Home is Where the Heart Is: Studies in Melodrama and the Woman's Film*, London: BFI, 1987.
21. Brooks, op. cit., p. 19.
22. Williams, op. cit., p. 383.
23. Ronald Barthes, *Mythologies*, Paris: Seuill, 1970.
24. Bill Nichols, *Representing Reality: Issues and Concepts in Documentary*, Bloomington and Indiannapolis: Indiana University Press, 1991, p. 44.

References

Barthes, Ronald, *Mythologies*, Paris: Seuill, 1970.

Bhaskar, Ira, '"The Persistence of Memory": Historical Trauma and Imagining the Community in Hindi Cinema', unpublished thesis, New York University, 2005.

Brooks, Peter, *The Melodramatic Imagination: Balzac, Henry James, Melodrama and the Mode of Excess*, New York: Columbia University Press, 1984.

Dyer, Richard, *Only Entertainment*, New York: Routledge, 1992.

Elsaesser, Thomas, 'Tales of Sound and Fury: Observations on the Family Melodrama', in Christina Gledhill, ed., *Home is Where the Heart Is: Studies in Melodrama and the Woman's Film*, London: BFI, 1987.

———, 'Subject positions, speaking positions: From *Holocaust*, *Our Hitler*, and *Heimat* to *Shoah* and *Schindler's List*', in Vivian Sobchak, ed., *The Persistence of History: Cinema, Television and the Modern Event*, New York and London: Routledge, 1996.

Gledhill, Christine, ed., *Home is Where the Heart is: Studies in Melodrama and the Woman's Film*, London: BFI, 1987.

Nandy, Ashis, 'The Politics of Secularism and the Recovery of Religious Toleration', in Rajeev Bhargava, ed., *Secularism and Its Critics*, Delhi and New York: Oxford University Press, 1998.

Nichols, Bill, *Representing Reality: Issues and Concepts in Documentary*, Bloomington and Indiannapolis: Indiana University Press, 1991.

Niranjana, Tejaswani, 'Cinema, Censorship, Communalism: The Case of Mani Ratnam', *Bombay Voices: Special Issue on Censorship and Freedom of Expression*, vol. 4, no. 2, 1996.

Pandey, Gyanendra, 'Can a Muslim be an Indian?', *Comparative Studies in Society and History*, vol. 41, no. 4, November 1999.

Sarkar, Bhaskar, *Mourning the Nation: Indian Cinema in the Wake of Partition*, Durham NC: Duke University Press; 2009.

Vasudevan, Ravi, 'Bombay and its Public', *Journal of Arts and Ideas*, vol. 29, January 1996.

Williams, Linda, 'Melodrama Revised', in Nick Browne, ed., *Refiguring American Film Genres: Theory and History*, Berkeley, Los Angeles, and London: University of California Press, 1998.

6

A New Universalism: Terrorism and Film Language in Mani Ratnam's Kannathil Muthamittal

Priya Jaikumar

WRITING ABOUT contemporary representations of terrorism in cinema reopens questions of primary concern to film theorists. Asking how a film defines a terrorist requires an interrogation of the visual, aural, and narrative conditions through which subjects enter the realm of discourse. Exploring the relationship between a film's depiction of political violence and the traumas of people forced to adopt, resist, or live with brutality reiterates suspicions that the referent or real escapes complete representation. The obscene opportunism in writing about terrorism today, at a time when it is receiving an ideologically defined global profile to entrench reactionary and racist anxieties, echoes concerns about the ethical responsibilities of intellectuals. These questions nearly blighted my ability to write this article, before I came to the conclusion that they were in fact the motivation behind my writing. Consequently my analysis of Mani Ratnam's depiction of Tamil militancy in Sri Lanka in *Kannathil Muthamittal* (A Peck on the Cheek, 2002; henceforth *KM*) is offered as a reflection on the affiliations and limits of a particular cinematic language that makes sense of terrorism.

At a mundane level, such an analysis demystifies the film's representative process. It also discloses the aesthetic vocabularies, cultural functions, and opportunities for national and global circulation potentially available to a Tamil film today. Recent hype about the globalization—or what Ashish Rajadhyaksha has called the 'Bollywoodisation'—of Hindi cinema rarely extends to regional films. Ratnam's Tamil films, however, constitute an exception. His internationally competitive production values and thematic validations of a culture of neo-liberalism qualify him to exploit opportunities beyond a regional market. With other Tamil directors venturing into bilingual productions (as with Kamalahasan's *Mumbai Express*, Hindi/Tamil,

2005), Ratnam's films may portend an alternative to Tamil films that assume a purely local audience and regional returns. But it is too premature to suggest a trend at a time when Tamil cinema remains a primarily local industry compared to its Hindi language counterpart.[1] My interest in this article lies in interrogating Ratnam's films for their repeated coupling of terrorism with reconstitutions of regional identity as distinctly cosmopolitan and trans-regional.

When cinema—a medium deeply implicated in the commercial competition over regional, national, and international audiences—casts its gaze on terrorism, a simultaneously local and global crisis on the political agenda of multiple nations, it activates a fundamental social and spatial conflict. It permits a Tamil film to connect with national (popular) and international (primarily film festival) audiences through tropes of terrorism made globally familiar by an increasingly prevalent, normative, urban middle-class perspective. But the film's politics and aesthetics are also constituted in relation to its local culture, state structure, and class formations. The film succumbs, on the one hand, to a material drag to its immediate environment, and on the other to an impetus to iconise that context into something broadly generalizable. I argue that as a post-colony's economic liberalization allows filmmakers from seemingly peripheral film industries to aspire to universal status—producing their families as every family, their cities as every city, their values as normative values—the problematic relationship of the particular to the universal is exacerbated, and the mechanics of universalization exposed by the processes of incomplete nationalization and uneven globalization. The conditions through which films from regional industries arrive at national and global centres of film circulation divulge the political stakes of their new universalism.[2]

Mani Ratnam's Films

Kannathil Mutthamittal tells the story of Amudha, an irrepressible adoptive daughter of an urban Tamil family in present-day Chennai (formerly Madras). Amudha's birth mother Shyama is a rebel leader of a Sri Lankan LTTE (Liberation Tigers of Tamil Eelam) cell. The film narrates the disruption and reintegration of Amudha's foster family around two key events: her foster parents Indra and Thiruchelvan's revelation to the young girl that she is adopted, and Amudha's restless search for her birth mother which takes her from Chennai, India, to Sri Lanka.

Though this film did not achieve the box-office success of some of Ratnam's previous productions (like *Nayakan*, Tamil, 1987; *Roja*, Tamil/ Telugu/Hindi, 1992; *Bombay*, Tamil/ Hindi, 1995), it received critical acclaim. Nationally, *KM* won awards for Best Child Artist, Best Audiography, Best Editing, Best Music Direction, Best Lyrics, and Best Feature Film in Tamil. The film circulated well, and was screened at international film festivals in North America, including the Palm Springs Film Festival (2002) and San Francisco International Film Festival (2002) in California, the Toronto International Film Festival (2002) in Canada, the 26th Asian American International Film Festival (2003) in New York, and the 12th Philadelphia Film Festival (2003). It won the Best Film Award at the Indian Film Festival of Los Angeles (2003).

Ratnam's *Roja*, *Bombay*, and *Dil Se* (Hindi, 2000)—three films dealing with terrorism and communal violence in India—won him a high national profile, allowing him to attract Hindi cinema's leading stars and find commercial distribution beyond the south Indian market.[3] *Roja* and *Bombay* also drew considerable attention from India's intellectual left. Scholars argued that Ratnam's films were symptomatic of a number of economic and social transformations initiated in the nation during the 1990s. His films were seen to consolidate a national bourgeoisie's desires in a neo-liberalizing society by legitimating the breakdown of Nehruvian welfarism and by aligning India's new economy of consumption with a communal-national consensus, wherein Hindutva nationalism masqueraded as a form of secularism.[4] Rather than speak from within the terms of analysis outlined in these discussions, I discuss *KM* with a view toward interrogating, rather than equating, a Tamil film's vision of a family and community with the presumptive national consensus.[5]

Regional language films may produce themselves as nationally paradigmatic, and strong arguments suggest that Ratnam's terrorist cycle of films do just that. But evading possible differences between mainstream Hindi films and Ratnam's films in relation to the production of a hegemonic nationalism is troubling, particularly given Tamil cinema's orthogonal, rather than overlapping, development to Hindi cinema, Tamil linguistic separatism, Tamil Nadu's push for state autonomy, and the Dravidian Anti-Hindi Imposition Movement that have defined the state's (and the director's) past.[6] Without denying that dominant political agendas in this southern state have frequently overlapped with that of the central government, I think red flags may yet be planted on the question of when and why Ratnam's films count as national as opposed to regional, how they traverse or overcome (rather reinforce or produce) those divisions, with what ambitions, and at what costs.

By following this line of questioning, I also extend challenges mounted by Nicholas B. Dirks, Lalitha Gopalan, Madhava M. Prasad, and Ravi S. Vasudevan, who in separate instances and to different ends express dissatisfaction with scholarly interpretations that read commercial films as a cultural entrenchment of hegemonic politics in the last instance, ignoring questions of cinematic form and pleasure. The questions of aesthetics, pleasure, and cultural recognition are central to my analysis, which enters a discussion of the film's politics by way of examining film form. A tropic negotiation of political issues through the personal and familial realm characterizes all of Ratnam's films on terrorism, investing them with a melodramatic quality. Urging film scholars to recognize the Chinese box nature of melodramas, Laura Mulvey has suggested that we escape the potentially endless (Chinese box-like) debates over the genre's progressive or regressive nature. Contradictions that save melodramas 'from belonging blindly to the bourgeois ideology that produced them' are the 'overt mainspring and specific content of melodrama, and not a hidden, unconscious thread to be picked up only by special critical process'.[7] With her argument, Mulvey pushes debates about a film's politics through the prism of its multiple social functions, suggesting as well that spectatorial pleasures are located precisely within a melodrama's internal contradictions.

KM is a melodrama that attempts to reconcile contradictions between the particulars of ethnic (Tamil) identity and the manufactured universals of (bourgeois) class identity. Opposing historical forces modernizing Tamil Nadu's bourgeoisie provide a central incitement to the contradictory pleasures of this film, in which a regionally defined class identity cannot be extended to connote universal representability without explicit symbolic renegotiations. Focusing on the divisions between regional and national identity in his essay on *Roja*, Vasudevan notes that 'in labouring to transform the text of Tamil identity into that of an Indian one, the film came up against a symbolically intractable edifice'.[8] Arguably, a larger conflict is at play when ethnic identity, imagined in culturally specific terms, gets reconstituted as bourgeois identity, wherein a Tamil middle class collaborates with an imagined national and global class cohort to equate prosperity, success, and secularism with economic neoliberalism, producing a generalised social axiomatic. I turn to *KM*, a film that (umblically) connects Chennai's urbanity with Sri Lankan Tamil militancy to show the kind of cultural work that goes into transforming potentially 'intractable' local, ethnic 'edifices' into narratives and images viable on translocal screens. Irrespective of the film's actual success with audiences outside the regional market, a desire for broad-based legibility produces the film's cinematic vision and its idioms of pleasure.

The Role of Cultural Specificity

Kannathil Mutthamittal Ullamthaan Kalvery Kolludhadi
Unnai Thozhuvidhilo Kannamma OOnmathham Aagudhadi

—Subramania Bharati, 'Chinnanjiri Killiye', 1917

> A kiss on your cheek and my heart
> Is a drunkard dazed;
> When I hold and hug you [my dearest], I am
> Completely crazed.
>
> —P.S. Sundaram's translation, 93

Mani Ratnam's film draws its title from a Tamil poem by Subramania Bharati or Bharatiar (1882–1921).[9] Ratnam had intended to call the film *Kodai* (Umbrella), after the title of a short story that the film's male protagonist Thiruchelvan writes about the infant he adopts from a camp for Sri Lankan Tamil refugees in Rameswaram, India. Rejecting a literal link to the film's narrative, Ratnam borrows from the poem 'Chinnanjiri Killiye'. The poem is part of a series of songs (called 'Kannan paattu') well known in Tamil literature and alive in contemporary music. One can purchase P. Unnikrishnan's renditions of Bharatiar's poetry at any Chennai music store today and, not unusually, I grew up listening to Bharatiar's poems being hummed by family members.

Bharatiar first published his patriotic songs in 1908, galvanizing modern Tamil poetry and literature.[10] A Tamil Brahman who rejected India's caste-based hierarchies, the poet called himself a 'Shakti *dasan*' (a '*dasan*' or devotee of the Goddess of Strength), a 'Shelley *dasan*' (a devotee of English Romantic poet P.B. Shelley), and a proud son of 'Mother Tamil'. He cut a contradictory figure with his celebration of Tamil despite the Brahmanical preference for Sanskrit as the 'higher' language of Hindu scriptures. In Tamil Nadu, where post-Independence politics have been defined by the dominant political party's rejection of Brahmanism and Sanskrit, by a 'Thani Thamizh' (Pure Tamil) movement, and by a rationalist–socialist critique of casteism, Bharatiar's reclamation by a Tamil Brahman film director is politically charged.

Bharatiar's persona and lyrics serve two important functions in the film. First, they enable associative unities across regional, caste, linguistic, and national divisions that would be near impossible in view of the postcolonial politics of Tamil Nadu. In discussing the contestatory developments of regional modernities in the early twentieth century, historian Karthigesu Sivathamby notes that the anti-Hindi movement spearheaded by Periyar's 'Self Respect Movement' in 1937 'united the Tamils on the slogan of protecting the virtues, the vigour and the uniqueness of the Tamil language against the onslaught of Hindi'.[11] The year 1937 saw the first of many unpopular efforts by India's (colonial and later national) central government to make Hindi the official language of southern India (a predominantly Tamil, Telugu, Malayalam, and Kannada speaking constituency), politicising the Madras Presidency along linguistic lines. The coercion unified a 'Tamil' people otherwise divided along caste and class lines.

Caste disparities were central to the evolution of the Dravidian Nation ('Dravida Kazhagam') movement in the south. The mass popularity of the Dravidian movement of the 1940s arose from a genuine lack of social justice for a range of non-Brahman castes and classes, historically disenfranchised by a caste system that placed Brahmans at the caste apex as interpreters of scriptural texts; a social hierarchy entrenched under colonial modernity when Brahmans moved to positions of administrative power. Opposing this structure of privilege, the DMK won electoral victory in the modern state of Tamil Nadu in 1967, and political parties hailing from the legacy of the Dravidian movement have since occupied electoral office. Opposition to Brahmanical consolidations of class privilege led to complex caste formations of the region's postcolonial middle class. As Sivathamby (2002) argues, non-Brahman castes (the Pillais, Nairs, Kapus, Kammas, Reddys) found an affinity with each other and the Dravidian movement, which provided them with a forum to redress social inequalities and find opportunities for social mobility. At the same time, new power cliques were born.[12] Party factionalization (into the DMK, AIADMK, and MDMK) and an idolatry cult of personality persisted. Tamil Brahmans, eased out of state institutions, prevailed upon the region's cultural and private enterprises.[13]

In this context, Bharatiar—a Brahman who was an active social reformer, a crusader against casteism, a devout Tamil scholar, and a linguist who spoke English and various north Indian languages—becomes a fantasy figure. He signals the retention of upper-caste identity while supporting social justice. He effaces elevated caste identity while marking the preservation of Tamil language, and suggests conversance with Hindi and English. The promise extended by Bharatiar allows Ratnam to produce a cinematic vision where Tamil Brahmans subtly reclaim their moral place alongside non-Brahmans to become part of an apparently caste-neutral, composite urban middle class. In *KM*, the male protagonist is called Thiruchelvan, a non-Brahman name. Thiru's sister Kamalee is given to what may be construed as Brahmanical prejudices: she is fearful that an adopted child will be *karruppu* with *vyaadi*, diseased and dark-skinned. But mostly the characters are kept clean of caste markers, reflecting a homogenized urban society where names, speech patterns, and prejudices are shared easily across caste lines.

Overt caste or cultural parochialisms would be a handicap for the film's larger ambition for a cinematic cosmopolitanism. The motivating desire is for a locally meaningful but transportable film language that will gain rather than lose from its flexibility. The desire for mobility involves the film in a series of strategic abstractions. This is the second function of Bharatiar's song in the film. The pleasure of recognizing a reference to Bharatiar may belong to Tamil audiences, but it is a subtle reference that does not announce itself. Bharatiar's song merely enhances the operative emotionalism of the film available to all audiences. In the original poem, the 'peck on the cheek' leaves the speaker in a state of extreme rapture: in the opening verse quoted above, for instance, *OOnmathham* evokes the image of a frenzied tusker and *kalveri* refers to the madness (*veri*) of intoxication. In the film, the kiss to and from an adoptive child of a Sri Lankan militant who is (biologically and nationally) an 'other' for the Indian Tamils serves as a similarly transformative contact. As I argue further, the film's kiss mediates between the Thiruchelvan family's Tamil identity and its bourgeois identity by establishing that both self-definitions are derived from a compassionate exchange with an entity who is both familiar (a Tamilian) and estranged (a child of a militant Sri Lankan). When Amudha kisses her foster parents from Chennai and her terrorist birth mother from Sri Lanka, the film stages a political reconciliation between India and Sri Lanka and constructs a unified Tamil identity, with Chennai as a centripetal force. The kiss seals the Indian Tamil's paternity over the Sri Lankan Tamil, and at the same time renders the bourgeois family moral, by defining the family in relation to a humane and tactile transaction rather than a financial and impersonal one.

From Referential Specificities to Emotional Abstractions

> 'Nee yenga ponnu illai.' (You are not our daughter).
>
> —Thiruchelvan to Amudha in *KM*

As with the writings of the English Romantic poets whom Bharatiar admired, in his 'Kannan pattus' as well the sensation of touching the infinite is made intimate; mind-altering ecstasy is experienced through the ordinary. The collective of Bharatiar's enraptured songs are written to an unnamed 'Kannan' or 'Kannamma', which are male and female terms of endearment. In the series of poems, the poet's addressee remains mysterious, the shape shifting into his lover, mother, child, nation, and Krishna or a form of divinity. 'Chinnanjiri Kiliye' is widely understood as addressed to Parashakti, manifesting the combined power of goddesses Lakshmi, Saraswathi, and Parvathi, though Shakti itself can also suggest the androgynous energy of Shiva and Parvathi's union. In the poem, Parashakti appears in the form of a (male or female) child. Translations of the poem show possibilities of word play over the addressee's identity. 'Chinnanjiri Kiliye' literally translates into 'My darling little parrot'. P.S. Sundaram's translation renders this as 'My little poppet', while T.N. Ramachandran titles the poem 'Sri Krishna, the Little Daughter', whose kiss so moves the poet.[14]

The kiss on the cheek in the film's title is equally ambiguous. It could refer to a kiss from Amudha to Thiruchelvan and Indra, her foster parents; to birth mother Shyama's kisses showered on Amudha; to Amudha's long kiss to Indra when the child finally re-affirms her love for her foster mother. Two song sequences incorporating the film's title put its lyrical abstractions to use in a manner enhanced by our knowledge of Bharatiar but not debilitated by an ignorance of it. Indra sings the first iteration of the lyrics 'Kannathil Muthamittal' to Amudha, and later the same song is picturized between Amudha and Thiruchelvan.[15] There are two additional differences between the first sequence and its repetition: the first occurs in Chennai and the second in Sri Lanka, and the father–daughter sequence follows Amudha's repeated efforts to run away from her foster home, given her progressive alienation from her foster mother. Notably, both songs are sung after Thiruchelvan conveys a traumatic truth to the little girl. On her ninth birthday, Thiruchelvan tells Amudha: You are *not* our daughter.

1. In a relay of kisses, Amudha kisses her foster mother Indra.

There is a textual logic to the harshness of this revelation that connects to the narrative's subtext rather than to the narrative itself, in that the trauma of Amudha's birth exceeds her life and enacts the trauma of a community or a people. Consider the film's opening and closing sequences. *KM* starts sometime in the recent past in Mankulam, north-eastern Sri Lanka. (North and east Sri Lanka are LTTE strongholds). Shyama has just wed Dileepa. They are bathing in the ocean when Dileepa playfully asks Shyama whom she likes best. She begins in ascending order, placing her husband above Tamil film star Kamalahasan. Above her husband she places 'Sami' (God). To indicate the entity she loves best, Shyama silently takes the dark wet soil of her land and smears it on Dileepa's face. (The erotics that unite the land with God and her husband in this scene mimic, again, the transcending abstractions of Bharatiar's 'Kannan' songs). At the film's conclusion, we find Shyama waging a war for a separate Tamil state in Sri Lanka. When Indra, Thiru, and Amudha finally seek her out, Shyama begrudgingly makes herself available to her long separated daughter. This sequence visually refers to Thiruchelvan's short story about the Sri Lankan Tamil refugees who come to India seeking, according to his metaphorical story, no more than the shelter of an umbrella. He paternally holds an umbrella over a newly articulated family of his wife, their adopted daughter, and her terrorist birth mother.

2. Shyama, the birth mother, kisses her daughter Amudha.

A reading sensitive to the ethnic and national work of this resolution might (justifiably) argue that Amudha is the agent that leads a Sri Lankan Tamil militant to accept an obligation to an Indian family, and an Indian Tamil family to extend protection to their Sri Lankan counterpart.[16] In the strife of Sri Lanka's LTTE territory, a scattered Tamil identity finds emotional solidarity when a Sri Lankan/Indian child is held and kissed by her Chennai family as well as her Sri Lankan mother. *KM* stages an encounter between two kinds of Tamils—the first belonging to an upwardly mobile Chennai family and the other to Sri Lanka's militant Tamil separatists—in a coming together that makes the militants less threatening to the former, and less anomic in their anti-statist, territorial passions.

In fact, *KM* appropriates the militant's fervour for the urban Indian Tamil family, giving them access to a sense of identity and community *while* retaining their claim to individualism. In this dimension, the 'pecks on the cheek' to and from Amudha are what allow a Tamil family access to a bourgeois identity without losing their connection to the passions identified with land and community. Witness the scenes when Kamalee and her husband criticize Thiruchelvan's newfangled ideas of parenting, which involve telling Amudha of her adoption. Thiruchelvan and Indra's model of parenting, which brooks no interference from their extended

3. Amudha, in a final affirmation, kisses Indra in the last scene.

family and honours the needs of a child, is marked as patently non-traditional. Within the film, certain forms of non-traditionalism portend crudeness and superficiality, as shown in an early sequence by one of Indra's potential suitors. Much to the writer Thiruchelvan's contempt, the suitor loves the horoscope and gossip sections of a newspaper, extending his inappropriate curiosity to Indra's past. In contrast, Amudha and her foster parents' quest into Amudha's identity is born of love and mediated through two self-interrogative documents: Amudha's personal diary and Thiruchelvan's short story (discussed further). The film ameliorates the weakness of an alienated bourgeois subject by placing its faith in the possibility of authentic self-awareness and communication across difference.

I offer this textual reading to propose that a feared *loss* of regional identity underlies Ratnam's films, even though they appear to assimilate regional identity within a dominant national economic mode.[17] Tamil Nadu's domination by DMK politics has meant that in their emergence as a modern middle class, Tamil Brahmins and non-Brahmins have been in positions of simultaneous centrality and marginality to each other, to the state, and to the central government.[18] Paradoxically, the diverse elements of regional class and caste formations in Tamil Nadu were *politicized* (rather than homogenized) with the creation of a postcolonial Indian nation state, because class and caste identity were reified as part of a reaction formation against internal (regional) and external (national) hierarchies. The complex Tamil identity thus constructed has been placed under threat of erasure only with the region's induction into a transnational economy, which leads the middle class to *willingly* reimagine itself as spatially mobile and culturally cosmopolitan without the antagonizing presence of state coercion (reserved today for classes explicitly disenfranchised by globalization). To take a quotidian example, in 2005 the city of Chennai was plastered with prominent advertisements for training centres that would

'Neutralise Your MTI (Mother Tongue Influence)'. Unlike the 1930s or 1960s, when devotion to the mother tongue was inextricably linked to the production of political subjectivity in Tamil Nadu, young Tamilians seeking work at US call centres desire to excoriate linguistic markers of difference.

Ratnam artfully balances (through art) this push for a new uniformity against the pull of desires for regional identity and difference. His films dramatize encounters between Tamil middle-class subjects and terrorists to realize a regional class's ambition for economic mobility and global/national visibility while allowing them meaningful linguistic and regional affiliations. The urban Tamil bourgeoisie competes with its alter ego—the militant fighting for a separate nation in Sri Lanka—because the latter appropriates the position of a passionate subject. Recall the debates between Fredric Jameson and Aijaz Ahmad over the allegorical nature of Third World literature. Though Jameson's essay is often interpreted as an assertion of the nationalist character of all Third World literature, his proposal is that capitalism creates a division between the libidinal and public spheres, so that the literature of advanced capitalist nations (unlike that of incompletely capitalist or quasi-socialist 'Third World' societies) operates within the private, libidinal terrain. Ahmad finds such a cognitive mapping untenable as it presupposes a static 'Third World' whose literature perennially and organically connects the libidinal to a communal life. Capitalism, Ahmad notes, does not remain an externality, but becomes a shaping force in the formation of postcolonial societies through its characteristic separation of the public from the private realms. With an expansion of neoliberal policies, the Indian nation today is at a stage of capitalism where the libidinal must be reinvested in the political by narratives that find ways to personalise politics. The new bourgeoisie seeks ways to re-unify with the idea of community to demonstrate its legitimacy.

This process is fraught with difficulty for the *regional* bourgeoisie because of their proximity to a subject who radically personalises politics: the militant. In using her body as a tool to fight for her land, the terrorist embodies a non-alienated subject. The figure of the terrorist threatens to expose the regional bourgeois protagonists' alienation from their land and their fellow humans. In *KM*, the Sri Lankan Tamil militants' presence potentially derides the Chennai family with a sense of their superficiality. In the first narrative segment, Dileepa tells Shyama that he does not want a child until there is peace in his land. Years later, when Shyama learns that her daughter has come to meet her, she dismisses Amudha's claim over her, calling the 300 trainees of her camp her real 'children'. Through choosing the possibility of death in pursuit of a homeland, Shyama places a burden of responsibility on the family that has the luxury to live in peace. Reconciliation with the Tamil Sri Lankan militant presence is crucial because it mocks the Chennai family with a sense of its potential irrelevance.

In Sri Lanka, Amudha asks a man why he speaks Tamil strangely. The man replies, 'Idhuvun Tamil daan'. This is *also* Tamil. He is later revealed to be an LTTE suicide bomber. In the persistence of such difference, the Thiruchelvan family cannot only fail to symbolise India's middle class, it can barely represent all Tamils. In *KM*, the social fragment represented by Thiruchelvan's family simulates consensus to compensate for its actual historical absence, and to increase its own political purchase. Defining Amudha as the child of a national/social 'other' and accepting her difference is crucial to this family's new class valuation. In other words, the Tamil terrorist whose obsession to a cause interrupts and embarrasses the bourgeois family's individualism becomes the very presence that allows the family its point of entry into a new kind of bourgeois discourse: a discourse that articulates its values in terms of a universal humanism that, surprisingly, reveals its investment in identitarian, ethnic, and territorial politics.

Bourgeois Valuations

> When you think of socially relevant issues, it becomes a tool to have a character in the media. Merging micro and macro story becomes possible.
>
> —Mani Ratnam

Tamils constitute approximately 20 per cent of Sri Lanka's population, and in a Buddhist majority state, this Tamil population is primarily Hindu with Muslim and Christian minorities. Onwards of the sixteenth century, Portuguese, Dutch, and British colonisers divided the island's three kingdoms comprising Tamil and Sinhala people into colonial administrative units, politicizing differences that were further accentuated under the postcolonial policies of modern Sri Lanka. Genocidal attacks by the Sinhala state against its Tamil population (particularly in 1956, 1958, 1961, 1971, and 1983) and a discriminatory national Constitution in 1972 (ratifying a 'Sinhala-only' language policy, Buddhism as state religion, attempted repatriations of Sri Lankan Tamils) met with demands for a separate Tamil state ('Eelam') within Sri Lanka. These demands turned intractable by 1976, with a violence that has left civilians of all political sympathies devastated in a continuing crossfire between the Sri Lankan army, the LTTE, and extremist Sinhala groups like the Janata Vimukta Peramuna.[19]

The film empathizes with Sri Lankan Tamils in a few ways. First, Sri Lanka is depicted as an idyllic countryside under military attack. Urban territories such as Colombo (with its state-declared Economic Promotion Zones to attract direct foreign investment) remain unseen.[20] Consequently, the film identifies upper middle class Tamils with Chennai rather than Sri

Lanka, belying the existence of an urban Sri Lankan Tamil population invested in economic growth and disinvested (or contradictorily invested) in anti-state militancy. Second, as a spokesperson for Sri Lankan Tamils, Shyama demands peace as the sole condition for abandoning her life as a militant, but the specific terms of peace remain vague. The film interrogates the personal rather than political consequences of Shyama's terrorism. Upon meeting her, Amudha asks, 'Why did you leave me and go away?' Shyama must explain her maternal recalcitrance to an uncomprehending child, but never her militancy to her state.

The film's accusation of personal betrayal applies, nevertheless, to a Tamil diaspora's attitude towards Sri Lankan Tamils. Historically, Sri Lankan Tamils perceived Indian Prime Minister Rajiv Gandhi's efforts to broker peace between the Sinhala government and the Tamil Tigers in 1987 as India's betrayal of the Tamil cause. The two and a half year campaign by the IPKF (Indian Peace Keeping Force) resulted in the death of approximately 12,000 Sri Lankan Tamils, the destruction of much of Jaffna, and a protracted guerilla war with the Tamil Tigers.[21] But Indian Tamils, caught between the political sympathies of India's central government and Sri Lankan Tamil separatists, found themselves alienated from both when LTTE suicide bombers assassinated Gandhi in 1991. Produced over a decade after these events, a film attempting to establish Indian paternity over a child of Sri Lankan militants navigates an explosive emotional minefield of guilt, culpability, and disenchantment.

KM is haunted by the presence of Sri Lankan Tamil militancy, which activates the film's central trauma. Amudha's need to find her birth mother transforms her adoptive family's ordinary lives into extraordinary ones, as it leads them outside their accustomed world. Personal trauma connects the child's distress to her family's existential crisis, allowing the political realm to enter the film and structure its plot. The plot is divided into three segments, moving from Sri Lanka to India and returning to Sri Lanka again. The first sequence of events in Sri Lanka concludes with a newly-wed Shyama discovering that the Sri Lankan army is hunting down her husband as a wanted member of the LTTE. To escape state repression, Shyama abandons her nation after her husband is presumed dead. On a small boat in turbulent waters to India, a pregnant Shyama overhears that he is alive. Shyama delivers her child in the refugee camp in Tamil Nadu and returns immediately to Sri Lanka, abandoning her infant. The child's cries open the credit sequence.

The next narrative segment jumps to Chennai a few years later and adopts a radically different tone. A little girl called T. Amudha replaces the omniscient narrator, and she talks directly to the camera to describe what sounds like a comfortable upper middle class family. Her father Thiruchelvan is an engineer and a respected Tamil writer. Her mother Indra is a newscaster and a familiar face on Chennai television. A song sequence establishes Amudha as a precocious girl. These exuberant portraits of normalcy are punctured on Amudha's ninth birthday with her father's revelation. At this point, Amudha's voice-over ceases, only to reappear briefly in the third narrative segment that begins with the family's flight to Sri Lanka. The disclosure of adoption jars in the midst of Amudha's childish complaints about school and siblings, evoking the emotional timbre of the earlier narrative segment. In the overused allegory of nation as mother, Amudha is transformed into a child of two nations and two mothers: a personification of splintered allegiances.

Who is truly hurt by this sundering? Despite its explicit backdrop of Sri Lankan militancy, *KM* is a crypto-bourgeois text that claims the dynamics of trauma and reconciliation for India's middle class Tamils. Though the film's structure hinges around Shyama's decision to return to Sri Lanka and Amudha's crisis, the cycle of trauma and symbolic recompense belongs to her adoptive Chennai family. The Chennai family must confront the Sri Lankan militant who exercises an emotional control over their lives to renew their bonds with each other: consequently, the last shot of the film is that of Thiru, Indra, and Amudha under Thiru's umbrella, finally at peace with each other as a new, reintegrated family. When Thiru and Indra accept their duty as surrogate parents, they realize a fantasy of ethnic solidarity while assimilating the Tamil militant into two dominant bourgeois civic institutions: that of a monogamous, patriarchal family, and that of mass media.

Ratnam's films frequently use protagonists who are media professionals or translators. With such characters, Ratnam affirms the utopian possibilities of electronic or digital media controlled not by special interests but by a socially committed, morally responsible bourgeoisie. The protagonists of *KM* are equally well-meaning in their efforts to translate the militant's world into their own domain of comprehensibility and deliver it to the film's audience. So a narration of Thiruchelvan's 'Umbrella' is provoked by Amudha's need to know the story of her adoption. As if in response, Thiruchelvan's short story begins in his voice-over. Enunciated in 'pure' Tamil, the words of the story appear in blue letters inscribed on the upper half of the film screen as black and white images unfold below. The story ends with a frozen image of a mother's hand leaving an infant, which transforms into a sketch in a magazine article being read aloud by Indra. This is one of many instances when a shift in mediating subjectivities leads to a change in the film's style of textualization. The formalism through which a social problem (here, of Sri Lankan refugees in India) is dealt with as a semiotic event and resolved by imposing a stylized visual coherence binds the director and his spectators in a modernist complicity. Ratnam's media-oriented characters and Ratnam himself deliver to the spectators a

4. Thiruchelvan's story about Sri Lankan refugees in India appears on the screen.

terrorist made legible through familiar interpretive grids. A disturbing subject is domesticated through networks of signification drawn from bourgeois discourses of print and radio journalism, or televisual and photographic images.[22]

Incomplete Appropriations

> Amudha (persuading her birth mother to leave Sri Lanka): 'There is no war in Madras. No army. We can watch TV and go to the movies. There's a beach.'
> Shyama: 'I have work here.'
>
> —*KM*

If characters that use media serve as directorial tools to connect micro-narratives with macro issues, the terrorist who makes the same connection through violence competes with the former figure. Formalist sleights of hand do not placate the socio-political crisis of terrorist violence in every instance. Physical violence remains largely unrepresented in Ratnam's films (or represented through glamorized spectacles, as in *Dil Se*). In *KM*, we are protected from images of Shyama as a killer. When Amudha shows Shyama her diary and album with photographs of her grandfather, of her school dance, and of famous media characters (like the popular A.R. Rahman, in a self-conscious reference to Mani Ratnam's favoured music composer), Shyama offers no reciprocal gesture. There are no photographs of film stars and siblings to record her life; only a silence and cinematic ellipses to designate a life lived in violence. The film's varying articulacy with regard to its protagonists and its differing portrayal of their need to auto-narrate their lives maintains Shyama's enigma.

Shyama's work as a militant is not portrayed in detail.[23] Towards the narrative's conclusion we see an LTTE camp for female recruits, where Shyama coordinates their training as Dileepa sits in a wheelchair. Like all Ratnam's filmic narratives, *KM* is elliptical in its construction. Shyama's transformation from a carefree young woman (in the first narrative segment) to a grim LTTE fighter (in the last) remains unseen. Similar to Amudha and Thiruchelvan, we must imagine the interim. To Amudha's questions about her abandonment of maternal duties, Shyama replies, 'The situation was such . . . I had no choice.' Amudha and Thiruchelvan indict a mother who abandons her newborn child ('This cruel act can never be justified,' Thiruchelvan writes in 'Umbrella'), and the explanation of Shyama's maternal lapse lies somewhere in a narrative gap.

The film offers meagre narrative, but substantial elliptical, non-narrative explanations for its inexplicable female—the maternal militant. Narratively, *KM* (like *Dil Se*) suggests that a woman accepts killing as an act of duty or conscience because she has borne or witnessed unbearable privation. The film abstracts state oppression, which is represented through a series of impressionistic images of attacks directly or indirectly experienced by the female. Attribution of psychological trauma partially alleviates the unfathomable nature of the mother who is also a terrorist, by constructing her as a pathological (rather than a political) creature. Moreover, through Amudha's plot structuring quest, the narrative's obsessive desire to decipher Shyama's compulsion to return to her husband and land replicates the mechanisms of a modern, liberal state that, in the first instance, must comprehend an act and classify its nature in order to pass judgment. Modern penal systems, as Michel Foucault reminds us, evolve from the notion that the State must be assured that a subject understands the nature of her crime, and possesses sufficient motive to perform it. Criminal violence must be convincingly assimilable with the 'global behaviour of the subject', because the 'more clearly visible this integration, the more clearly punishable the subject'.[24] Foucault presciently predicts a moral–legal state system that will base itself on profiling criminals according to the causal probability of their perpetrating unruly acts. Within the cultural and aesthetic morality of Indian cinema, the mother is the very antithesis of a 'dangerous', 'unruly' subject. So the mother who kills or abandons her child becomes a deified figure (as in Mehboob's *Mother India*, Hindi, 1957), precisely because she makes an unthinkable sacrifice for her nation–state's greater good.

Shyama, who sacrifices motherhood not for India but for a Tamil nation in Sri Lanka, is a confusing figure within this signifying system. She is neither completely rationalized within a bourgeois liberal state discourse nor deified in a nationalist one. To comprehend her, we must question two things: the aforementioned presumption that a film's narrative coherence is consonant with the rationalizing impulse of state discourse, and the efficacy of the nation as an analytic trope. In her essay on terrorism in Indian films, Sumita Chakravarty argues that representations of terrorism are liminally threatening and regenerative to an imagined national collectivity. In some disagreement, I would argue that though Ratnam's films are clearly nationalist and often pitch conflicts between national selves and their atavistic others, there is more than a perpetually renegotiated binary at stake here.

By keeping the motives for Shyama's decision partially inexplicable and making her act incomprehensible, *KM* imagines an individual operating under a different system of morality, self, and history than the film's central protagonists. In fact, the film's cinematic defences for its idiom of normativity are revealed when it ceases to manufacture narrative causes for the female terrorist's recalcitrance, configuring her radical intransigence through style. At these moments, *KM* does not interpret terrorism purely through the language of a nation state but begins to consider it as a critique of bourgeois modernity, of which the nation state is but one powerful manifestation. Grasping this requires that we devise tools to assess elements that lie outside the vocabularies of the nation state and bourgeois modernity, though they may be produced in relation to them.

The person who withdraws from our way of life is more damning of it than one who actively attacks it, because the former leaves no basis for communication. In her essential incommunicability, Shyama (like the unsmiling Meghna of *Dil Se*) is a melancholic (rather than a criminalized or deified) figure. Melancholy, as Sigmund Freud and Søren Kierkegaard show us, has everything to do with modernity. I do not wish to transplant philosophical meditations from late nineteenth century Europe to early twenty-first century India, but I linger briefly on Kierkegaard's idea of melancholy because he opposed the philosophical underpinnings of European modernity crucial to colonial nation formation. He, therefore, provides us with a clue to what was remaindered in the coupling of modernity with rationalism, specifically, the absurdity of faith.

According to a Hegelian concept of history, the consciousness of freedom progresses with the development of social organizations (through Christianity, the Reformation, the French Revolution and so on), materializing in a rational being who perceives in himself the unity of subjective (individual) and objective (State) spirit.[25] Kierkegaard was deeply critical of this Hegelian notion of a dialectical progression, central to Western notions of history and foundational to the evolutionary concept of a rational subject, who was to emerge as the legimitating basis of a contractual, modern, liberal state transported to the colonies. Religiosity motivated Kierkegaard's critique of this coherent, rational subject, as he found belief offensive to reason. In exegetic tales, Kierkegaard allegorizes religious faith's transcendence over all human categories, making the melancholic subject a counterpoint to the rational subject who manifests the spirit of modern consciousness.

By his account, melancholy as sadness for no apparent reason may be defined as something 'essentially incommunicable' and 'appropriate to the condition of modern life', serving as counter-current to modernity by its non-productivity and inwardness.[26] I invoke notions of (transcendental, non-rational) faith and melancholia (as complete disengagement from society) as responses to modernity because they are resuscitated in Ratnam's potrayal of female suicide bombers. Like *Dil Se*'s Meghna, *KM*'s Shyama's lack of words is non-productive by the standards of her interlocutors—in this instance, an incessantly communicative Chennai family in which Indra is a newscaster, Thiruchelvan a writer, and Amudha a diarist. As noted earlier, Shyama's silence and absence stand for her cinematically unrepresented life of militancy in Sri Lanka. By showing her commitment to her mission in a manner that brooks no rational dissuasion and abjures familial ties, Ratnam creates a subject outside the realm of what is valued by his protagonists. Shyama is not reducible to an atavistic other of nationalist discourse or a statist rationalization of criminality; she lies at the limit of modernity's vocabulary and is partially incomprehensible within its terms. Notably, LTTE philosophy—influenced in equal measure by Gandhian asceticism, Swami Vivekananda's and Subhash Chandra Bose's nationalist militancy, and Marxist-Leninism—confounds easy categorizations.

By bringing bourgeois protagonists into contact with such a figure, *KM* risks revealing their restricted comprehension. These limitations are partially allayed by Amudha's obsessive mother fixation that motivates *KM*'s narrative (or by Amar's romantic love for Meghna in *Dil Se*). Amudha's (and Amar's) *un*reasonable love exceeds 'acceptable' limits of affections in that it disrupts family lives, but such excess is necessary in the pursuit of a monomaniacally melancholic subject and in creating 'secular' counterparts to the terrorist's transcendent faith. Despite this pursuit, however, neither Meghna nor Shyama rehabilitate into middle-class normalcy. No secular emotion counter-balances or 'cures' the female terrorist's transcendence of desires—for marriage, home, child, television shows, and trips to the beach—which the film confirms as normative. (Shyama promises her daughter she will return when Sri Lanka is at peace. The ensuing childish question of '*When*, mother?' is redolent, then, with multiple yearnings.) Minimally (because passively rather than radically), in melancholic Shyama the film represents a modernity of incomplete promise, because she betokens the possibility of a partial base of consensus, poorly apportioned benefits, and an irrational state.

Conclusion

The transition from European colonial to US-dominated structures of imperialism are frequently described as a shift from 'a model of empire based on a network of clearly defined geographical powers to one which is radically de-spatialized', controlled by transnational corporations and international monetary and judicial organizations.[27] Both modes of empire have depended on cultural narratives that manufactured parochially European or US perspectives as equivalent to the plenitude of humanity, the former assuming a universalism through colonially enforced education systems that corralled normativity around canonical texts, and the latter through a market-induced cultural imperialism.

With an increasing dispersal of technology, training, and bourgeois values, and a rise in privatizing nation states and diasporic audiences, our contemporary period is equally characterized by the global presence of products from regions historically marginalized in a US-dominated world economy. Ratnam's *KM* is one such product. In *Roja* and *Bombay*, Indian film scholars note that terrorist kidnappings and communal riots provide an opportunity for Tamil protagonists to prove their nationalist and Hindu (coded secular) credentials. *KM* uses its encounter between the middle class and militant subject to a greater end, despite its apparently regional address. The film rewrites ethnic and regional identity by circumventing the nation, and staking a humanist and ethical position for its bourgeoisie.

In the film, Sri Lanka remains an unreal fantasy, Shyama a mystery, and both a troubling presence for India. Several Sri Lankans remind Amudha to not forget them, and they tell Thiruchelvan to 'write something nice about Sri Lanka'. By assimilating Sri Lanka as a personal memory and a storied location for the Thiruchelvan family, the film fictionally consolidates urban Chennai's centrality to all Tamils. Simultaneously, it mediates between the LTTE's fixed demand for territory and the Chennai family's easy mobility across territorial boundaries by using the militant to establish the bourgeois family's humanitarian concern for community and its link to territorial identity. The desire to give the family representative status beyond ethnic or regional identity is expressed, in this instance, *through* regional and ethnic politics.

This hermeneutic is particular to a postcolonial regional middle class's historical predicament in this era of economic globalization. Narratives that negotiate the two handles of the term 'regional bourgeoisie' must do double the work of similar narratives produced by the national or global north, because the regional bourgeois subjects' proximity to differentiated and incomplete modernities, their historical sympathy for a politics based on territorial demands, and their use of (linguistic, cultural) systems tagged for their particularity obstruct an easy production of universals. To manufacture its universalism, a regional film like *KM* must satisfy two potentially variant cultural needs: the need to address a fractious ethnic identity, and the need to find settling points for a visual, moral, political centrism acceptable to a national and global audience. The film puts a middle-class Tamil family face to face with an LTTE militant to this end.

Notes

1. See Ashish Rajadhyaksha, 'The 'Bollywoodization' of the Indian Cinema: Cultural Nationalism in a Global Arena', *Inter-Asia Cultural Studies* vol. 4, no. 1, 1 November 2003, pp. 25–39. See also, Shreedhar Pillai, 'Year 2004—A Flashback', *The Hindu*, Friday, 31 December, 2004, FR1.
2. This discussion parallels efforts to define cinemas that translate local (particularly East Asian) cultures for a non-local audience as a form of 'decipherable localism' (Shu-mei Shih, 'Global Literatures and the Technologies of Recognition', *PMLA* vol. 19, no. 1, January 2000; James Schamus, 'Aesthetic Identity: A response to Kenneth Chan and Christina Klein', *Cinema Journal*, vol. 43, no. 4, Summer 2004). Though Ratnam does not have the global stature of an Ang Lee (he operates from Madras Talkies, his studio in Chennai), aspects of my analysis of his film may be productively considered in relation to this scholarship.
3. Communalism in the Indian context refers to religious sectarianism, and violence against any faith may be described as communal violence.
4. See Tejaswini Niranjana, '*Roja* Revisted', *Economic and Political Weekly*, 21 May 1994, p. 1299; Chakravarty, Venkatesh and M.S.S. Pandian, 'More on *Roja*', *Economic and Political Weekly*, vol. 29, no. 11, 12 March 1994; Rustom Barucha, 'On the Border of Fascism: Manufacture of Consent in *Roja*', *Economic and Political Weekly*, 4 June 1994 and, V. Srinivas, '*Roja* in Law and Order State', *Economic and Political Weekly*, 14 May 1994.
5. This is akin to Ravi S. Vasudevan in 'Voice, Space, Form: *Roja* (Manirathnam, 1992), Indian Film and National Identity', in Stuart Murray, ed., *Not on any Map: Postcoloniality and Cultural Nationalism*. Exeter: Exeter University Press, 1997. See also Nicholas B. Dirks, 'The Home and the Nation: Consuming Culture and Politics in *Roja*', in Rachel Dwyer and Christopher Pinney, eds., *Pleasure and the Nation: The History, Politics and Consumption of Public Culture in India*, New Delhi: Oxford University Press, 2001.
6. Ratnam grew up during the height of the anti-Hindi movement in the south, so he did not have the opportunity to learn Hindi. (This and other information and quotes from the director are from a personal interview with Mani Ratnam, 14 August 2004). For more on Tamil linguistic separatism, consult Sumathi Ramaswamy, *Passions of the Tongue: Language Devotion in Tamil Nadu, 1891–1970*, Berkeley: University of California Press, 1997.
7. Laura Mulvey, 'Notes on Sirk and Melodrama', in Christine Gledhill, (ed.), *Home is Where the Heart Is*, London: BFI, 1987, p. 75.
8. Vasudevan, op. cit., p. 163. See also Sumita Chakravarty, 'Fragmenting the Nation', in Mette Hjort and Scott Mackenzie, eds., in *Cinema and Nation*, London: Routledge, 2000, p. 235.

9. *Roja* incorporates Bharatiar's compositions as well, at a critical moment when the male protagonist Rishi Kumar wraps himself in a burning Indian flag (Nicholas B. Dirks, 'The Home and the Nation: Consuming Culture and Politics in *Roja*', Rachel Dwyer and Christopher Pinney, eds., *Pleasure and the Nation: The History, Politics and Consumption of Public Culture in India*, New Delhi: Oxford University Press, 2001, pp. 161–2).
10. In the Tamil literary canon, the secular poetry of Sangam literature (circa first century AD) is considered the golden period of old Tamil writing. The post-Sangam period (eleventh to thirteenth centuries AD) was characterized by epics such as Ilangovadigal's *Silapadigaaram* (about a woman whose righteous wrath destroys the kingdom of Madurai); couplets for everyday life and one-line aphoristic compositions [like Thiruvalluvar's *Thirukkural*; Auvaiyar's *Aathichoodi*]; the devotional turn towards Bhakti poetry popularized by Shaivite and Vaisnavite saints; and Kamban's *Ramayana* under the Chola kings. The modern period of the eighteenth and nineteenth centuries brought Islamic and Christian (missionary) influences to the language, as colonialism put new pressures on Tamil literature and on the Dravidian language which predated Sanskrit but absorbed north Indian influences.
11. Karthigesu Sivathamby, *Understanding the Dravidian Movement: Problems and Perspectives*, Madras: New Century Book House, 1995, p. 7.
12. The practice of reserving state quotas for backward classes socially integrated the middle sector of backward classes (the Thevars and Vanniars) with elite non-Brahmans, while excluding the truly underprivileged (Dalits).
13. Robert L. Hardgrave Jr, *When Stars Displace the Gods: The Folk Culture of Cinema in Tamil Nadu*, Austin: University of Texas Press, 1975; M.S.S. Pandian, *The Image Trap: M. G. Ramachandran in Film and Politics*, New Delhi: Sage Publications, 1992; Karthigesu Sivathamby, *The Tamil Film as a Medium of Political Communication*, Madras: New Century Book House, 1981 and Sivathamby, 'De-ideolgization of Politics is the Tragedy of Tamil Nadu', interview with *Frontline*, vol. 19, no. 22, 16 October–8 November 2002, http://www.frontlineonnet.com/fl1922/stories/20021108002409200.html. See also *Seminar*, Special Issue on Chennai, March 2004, http://www.india-seminar.com/semframe.html.
14. T. N. Ramachandran, *Bharati Patakal*, Tanjavur: Tamil University, 1989, p. 265.
15. The lyrical and visual abstractions of the song's affective references give the sequence with father and daughter a near incestuous feel.
16. I use 'militant' and 'terrorist' interchangeably in this article to convey the instability of terms that shift according to the context and source of definition.
17. As proposed by Niranjana in 'Integrating Whose Nation? Tourists and Terrorists in *Roja*', *Economic and Political Weekly*, 15 January 1994.
18. Brahmans, as an example, benefited from centuries of caste and class privilege (vetted by the British Indian government and the Indian National Congress at the centre), resisted the increase in state quotas (against the state government and non-Brahmans), fought Hindi imposition (against the centre and with Tamil non-Brahmans), and largely supported their neighbouring Sri Lanka's Tamil militancy (in shifting relations with the centre).
19. Nihal Parera, *Society and Space: Colonialism, Nationalism, and Postcolonial Identity in Sri Lanka*, Boulder, CO: Westview Press, 1998; David J. Whittaker, ed., *The Terrorism Reader*, 2nd edn, New York : Routledge, 2001, p. 85; Jonathan Spencer, 'On not becoming a 'Terrorist': Problems of Memory, Agency, and Community in the

Sri Lankan Conflict', in Veena Das et al., eds., *Violence and Subjectivity*, Berkeley: University of California Press, 2000, pp. 121-40, and Patricia Lawrence, 'Violence, Suffering, Amman: The Work of Oracles in Sri Lanka's Eastern War Zone', in Veena Das et al., eds., *Violence and Subjectivity*, Berkeley: University of California Press, 2000.

20. Parera, op. cit., p. 172.
21. Whittaker, op. cit.; Spencer, op. cit.
22. *Dil Se* and *Bombay* portray radio and newspaper journalists, *Roja* a computer cryptologist, and *KM* an activist writer. According to Ratnam, the inspiration for *KM* came from an article about an adopted child from Asia in *Time* magazine, and several details of the film drew from reportage on the LTTE (personal interview with Mani Ratnam, 14 August 2004).
23. However, a range of disconnected sequences builds emotional justification for Tamil militancy. A village is shelled by the Sinhala army even as Tamils lie injured or clinging to their temples; Thiruchelvan and his Sinhala friend Harold talk of a guerrilla warfare of attrition in Sri Lanka, Palestine, Chechnya, and Bosnia, angrily arguing that capitalist nations harvest commercial profits from micro wars fought in the global south; Thiruchelvan repeats combative lines from LTTE trench poetry when attacked by LTTE guerrillas. These sequences offer an implicit suggestion that violence may be a form of agency for victims of state repression, but the idea is not dwelt upon at any length.
24. Michel Foucault, 'About the Concept of the "Dangerous Individual" in Nineteenth Century Legal Psychiatry', in James D. Faubian, ed., *Michel Foucault: Power*, vol. 3, New York: The New Press, 1994, pp. 188, 189.
25. Tom Bottomore, ed., *A Dictionary of Marxist Thought*, Oxford: Blackwell, 1983, p. 198.
26. Harvie Ferguson, *Melancholy and the Critique of Modernity*, London: Routledge, 1995, pp. 4-5, 18-19.
27. David Morley, 'EurAm, Modernity, Reason and Alterity or, Postmodernism, the Highest Stage of Cultural Imperialism?' in David Morley and Kuan-Hsing Chen, eds., *Stuart Hall: Critical Dialogues in Cultural Studies*, London: Routledge, 1996, p. 327.

References

Ahmad, Aijaz, 'Jameson's Rhetoric of Otherness and the 'National Allegory', *Social Text*, 1987, vol. 17, pp. 3-25.

Barucha, Rustom, 'On the Border of Fascism: Manufacture of Consent in *Roja*', *Economic and Political Weekly*, 4 June 1994, pp. 1389–95.

Bottomore, Tom, (ed.), *A Dictionary of Marxist Thought*, Oxford: Blackwell, 1983.

Chakravarty, Sumita, 'Fragmenting the Nation', in Mette Hjort and Scott Mackenzie, eds., in *Cinema and Nation*, London: Routledge, 2000, pp. 222–37.

Chakravarty, Venkatesh and M.S.S. Pandian, 'More on *Roja*', *Economic and Political Weekly*, vol. 29, no. 11, 12 March 1994, pp. 642–4.

Dirks, Nicholas B., 'The Home and the Nation: Consuming Culture and Politics in *Roja*', Rachel Dwyer and Christopher Pinney, eds., *Pleasure and the Nation: The*

History, Politics and Consumption of Public Culture in India, New Delhi: Oxford University Press, 2001. pp. 161–85.

Ferguson, Harvie, *Melancholy and the Critique of Modernity*, London: Routledge, 1995.

Foucault, Michel, 'About the Concept of the "Dangerous Individual" in Nineteenth Century Legal Psychiatry', in James D. Faubian, ed., *Michel Foucault: Power*, vol. 3, New York: The New Press, 1994, pp. 176–200.

Gopalan, Lalitha, *Cinema of Interruptions: Action Genres in Contemporary Indian Cinema*, London: BFI, 2002.

Hardgrave, Robert L. Jr, *When Stars Displace the Gods: The Folk Culture of Cinema in Tamil Nadu*, Austin: University of Texas Press, 1975.

Jameson, Fredric, 'Third World Literature in the Era of Multinational Capitalism', *Social Text*, Fall 1986, vol. 15, pp. 65–88.

Kierkegaard, Søren, *Repetition*, trans. Walter Lowrie, New York: Harper Torchbooks, 1941.

Lawrence, Patricia, 'Violence, Suffering, Amman: The Work of Oracles in Sri Lanka's Eastern War Zone', in Veena Das et al., eds., *Violence and Subjectivity*, Berkeley: University of California Press, 2000, pp. 171–204.

Morley, David, 'EurAm, Modernity, Reason and Alterity or, Postmodernism, the Highest Stage of Cultural Imperialism?' in David Morley and Kuan-Hsing Chen, eds., *Stuart Hall: Critical Dialogues in Cultural Studies*, London: Routledge, 1996, pp. 326–60.

Mulvey, Laura, 'Notes on Sirk and Melodrama', in Christine Gledhill, ed., *Home is Where the Heart Is*, London: BFI, 1987, pp. 75–9.

Niranjana, Tejaswini, 'Cinema, Femininity and the Economy of Consumption', *Economic and Political Weekly*, 26 October 1991, WS 85–6.

———, 'Integrating Whose Nation? Tourists and Terrorists in *Roja*', *Economic and Political Weekly*, 15 January 1994, pp. 79–82.

———, '*Roja* Revisted', *Economic and Political Weekly*, 21 May 1994, p. 1299.

Pandian, M.S.S., *The Image Trap: M. G. Ramachandran in Film and Politics*, New Delhi: Sage Publications, 1992.

———, 'Nationalism Refigured: Contemporary South Indian Cinema and the Subject of Feminism', in Partha Chatterjee and Pradeep Jeganathan, eds., *Community, Gender, and Violence: Subaltern Studies XI*, New York: Columbia University Press, 2000, pp. 138–66.

Parera, Nihal, *Society and Space: Colonialism, Nationalism, and Postcolonial Identity in Sri Lanka*, Boulder, CO: Westview Press, 1998.

Prasad, Madhava M., 'Signs of Ideological Re-Form in Two Recent Films', in Ravi Vasudevan, ed., *Making Meaning in Indian Cinema*, New Delhi: Oxford University Press, 2000, pp. 145–67.

Pillai, Shreedhar, 'Year 2004—A Flashback', *The Hindu*, Friday, 31 December 2004, FR1.

Rajadhyaksha, Ashish, 'The 'Bollywoodization' of the Indian Cinema: Cultural Nationalism in a Global Arena', *Inter-Asia Cultural Studies*, vol. 4, no. 1, 1 November 2003, pp. 25–39.

Ramachandran, T. N., *Bharati Patakal*, Tanjavur: Tamil University, 1989.

Ramaswamy, Sumathi, *Passions of the Tongue: Language Devotion in Tamil Nadu, 1891–1970*, Berkeley: University of California Press, 1997.

Schamus, James, 'Aesthetic Identity: A response to Kenneth Chan and Christina Klein', *Cinema Journal*, vol. 43, no. 4, Summer 2004, pp. 43–52.

Seminar, Special Issue on Chennai, March 2004, http://www.india-seminar.com/semframe.htm.

Shih, Shu-mei, 'Global Literatures and the Technologies of Recognition', *PMLA*, vol. 19, no. 1, January 2004, pp. 16–30.

———, 'Globalisation and Minoritization: Ang Lee and the Politics of Flexibility', *New Formations*, vol. 40, Spring 2000, pp. 87–101.

Sivathamby, Karthigesu, 'De-ideolgization of Politics is the Tragedy of Tamil Nadu', interview with *Frontline*, vol. 19, no. 22, 16 October–8 November 2002, http://www.frontlineonnet.com/fl1922/stories/20021108002409200.htm.

———, *The Tamil Film as a Medium of Political Communication*, Madras: New Century Book House, 1981.

———, *Understanding the Dravidian Movement: Problems and Perspectives*, Madras: New Century Book House, 1995.

Spencer, Jonathan, 'On not becoming a 'Terrorist': Problems of Memory, Agency, and Community in the Sri Lankan Conflict', in Veena Das et al., eds., *Violence and Subjectivity*, Berkeley: University of California Press, 2000, pp. 120–40.

Srinivas, V., '*Roja* in Law and Order State', *Economic and Political Weekly*, 14 May 1994, pp. 1225–6.

Sundaram, P. S., trans. *Poems of Subramania Bharati*, Delhi: Vikas Publishing House, 1983.

Vasudevan, Ravi S., 'Bombay and its Public', in Rachel Dwyer and Christopher Pinney, eds., *Pleasure and the Nation: The History, Politics and Consumption of Public Culture in India*, New Delhi: Oxford University Press, 2001, pp. 186–211.

———, 'Voice, Space, Form: *Roja* (Manirathnam, 1992), Indian Film and National Identity', in Stuart Murray, ed., *Not on any Map: Postcoloniality and Cultural Nationalism*, Exeter: Exeter University Press, 1997, pp. 153–69.

Whittaker, David J., ed., *The Terrorism Reader*, 2nd edn, New York: Routledge, 2001.

PART III
NEGOTIATING IDENTITIES

7

Merit and Opportunity in the Child-Centric Nationalist Films of the 1950s

Nandini Chandra

IN EARLY APRIL 2007, the Supreme Court in India put a stay on OBC (Other Backward Classes) reservations in response to a petition by the 'Youth for Equality' (YFE), a mainly upper-caste urban group which advocates the preservation of 'merit'. This group's appeal for the Indian media during the year-long span of its existence has been attributed to the enormously popular film *Rang De Basanti* (*RDB*, 2006), which depicts the righteous anger of youth who spontaneously take to the streets in frustration at the state's corruption and inefficiency. Candlelight vigils and demonstrations *à la Rang De Basanti* have become the symbol of an authentic popular nationalist recovery, whose self-righteousness spills over from anti-reservation battles to fighting for justice in criminal cases (provided the victim's profile resonates with their yuppie upper-caste profiles). The repeated publishing of the pictures of a few AIIMS students braving water cannons in the city tabloids is further proof that the whole battalion of the upper-caste media is behind this alleged plea for equality.

What is significant for the present article is YFE's method of campaigning and the reliance on Hindi films as a source of political posturing. Their sit-ins and election campaigns, during the 2006 JNU (Jawaharlal Nehru University) student elections, for example, resounded with songs from the first Bhagat Singh film *Shaheed* (1965), a resurrection ultimately indebted to *RDB*. At the same time, they had no qualms about borrowing from a rival brand of politics. Even as they claimed their political vocabulary from the revolutionary fervour of Bhagat Singh and his comrades, they also borrowed the Gandhian gesture of turning the other cheek, sending 'get well soon' cards to their opponents as in *Lage Raho Munnabhai* (2006), a film about the viability of using Gandhian methods to combat the stress and strife of everyday life in mafia-dominated Mumbai. It is this inherent lack of a committed political core and an indiscriminately eclectic political vocabulary, bordering on tokenism, that characterize the populist agitprop film in Hindi as much as the lumpen bourgeois student politics that has followed in its wake.

In this article I attempt to trace the seeds of this discourse through an exploration of Hindi cinema's first depictions of children and young people in the 1950s. The social realist films of the 1950s pioneered visions of childhood that have haunted Hindi cinema ever since. School is presented as the only legitimate place for the child in these films and they entertain a conception of innate merit such that any child, even an orphan, with some minimal benevolence from the state, can go on to attend school and live a decent life. The ideal child citizen, whether obedient or rebellious, is one possessed of this innate sense of merit. Merit not only propelled the political and socially empowering message of these social realist films by linking it to the imperative of an equal and just society which makes provisions for everyone, but at the same time naturalized the notion that a certain inborn merit precedes the moment of social equality. Yet the child actors themselves, who articulated this notion of childhood, whether from the working class or the bourgeoisie, never went to school and never accessed this model life, as we will see. The social situation was obviously far more complicated and sinister than the films would lead us to believe.

Daisy Irani,[1] a young girl who played cherubic little boys through the 1950s, had this story to tell of her brief but traumatic encounter with schooling. Her mother, a typically ambitious and controlling woman, asked her to say, 'sorry for the trouble' to Jawaharlal Nehru at the end of a social gathering that he had hosted for the child artists. Not knowing English very well, she instead said, 'sorry for the troubla'. She was 13 years old at that time and had never been to school. Nehru realized this and chided the mother, urging her to send the girl to school. At Nehru's insistence, Daisy was admitted to middle level, Class Seven, where she stayed for three years before dropping out.

The notion of child citizenship enshrined in these films was thus beset by an inherent and basic contradiction between ideals of social justice and claims of entitlement of one group over the other. Our discussion will attempt to unravel some of these threads by studying the depiction of the marginalized children in the films vis-à-vis the life narratives of the child actors who played them. Indeed, all the child actors, irrespective of the roles they played, were pushed out of making any substantive claims on citizenship. On the one hand were the IPTA (the Indian People's Theatre Association) directors' overarching elitist and paternalist assumptions, their rhetoric of the 'new beginnings' promising a nationalist utopia, and on the other hand were the self-narratives of the child artists who had internalized to different degrees a sense of their illegitimacy as an outcome of their distance from the school system. The four films that are taken up for discussion here—*Munna*, *Ferry*, *Jagriti*, and *Boot Polish*—were all produced in 1954.

The Vision of the IPTA Directors, their Manifesto for National Progress

Historically, the birth of child-centric cinema derives from the Italian neorealist cinema's commitment to make contact with 'reality', which was largely sought to be achieved through location shooting.[2] These films foregrounded the figure of the child in the city in order to focus on the heightened vulnerability of the underclass, especially their sufferings in the aftermath of the War. The Nehruvian socialist and Indian People's Theatre Association framework within which the genre was located in the Indian context in the 1950s also sought to emphasize the necessity of identifying with the polarized social reality of the colonial metropolis. This often took the form of encouraging method acting. Balraj Sahani talks about scrupulously observing the coolies in front of Jogeshwari before he could play the role of the rickshaw puller in *Do Bigha Zameen* (1954).[3] Also, K.A. Abbas utilised the one night he had spent on the streets of Bombay to maximum effect in four of his films.

The need for a referential framework and a correspondence to reality was highly crucial. When Sahani enlisted a migrant labourer to play the role of Signalman Duli for Balwant Gargi's play of the same name, the labourer was too intimidated despite and perhaps because of a month's concerted efforts by the whole unit to make him act. He finally begged Sahani to let him off. Sahani was so enraged by what seemed rank ingratitude, that he yelled at him asking if he had any self-respect. After being yelled at and chastised, the actor proceeded to give a sterling performance. Sahani observed that it was as if the labourer was more Duli than Duli. He also added that it took a long time for them to get him out of the world of Duli.[4] In Sahani's perception, the labourer was similar to a recalcitrant child or colonized subject who could be made to perform only through a dose of authoritarian discipline. In addition, he was also seen to be delusional and needed proper guidance to break out of an illusory world. This aspect of the Left cultural vanguard, where the urge to discipline the proletarian is greater than the urge to identify with his class reality, is palpable in the child-centric films too.

The role of the intellectual within the ambit of the Progressive Writers' Association (PWA) and the Indian People's Theatre Association (IPTA) was especially ambiguous when it came to their depiction of children. Thus, despite the radical content of the reality portrayed, there was a hidden desire to keep the working class (like children) in its place. Their view of childhood was based on a sympathy for the occasional orphan who underwent harrowing pangs of homelessness, rather than with those perennially doomed to homelessness for structural rather than accidental reasons. At the same time, the child protagonists were invested with a lot of affect to mark their unbearable and intolerable destitution, as it were. This often bordered on melodrama and precocious posturing, turning a precious realism into artifice.

The IPTA led filmmakers like K.A. Abbas, Raj Kapoor, Hemen Gupta, and Satyen Bose, those who specialized in 'the narratives of the lost and wandering child' were ostensibly close to the state's version of development. In other words, they did not see their commitment to redistributive social justice such as land reforms to be at odds with the logic of an exclusively bourgeois reform. While they believed that the state ought to redeem the destitute and the homeless, simultaneously they conceded its inability to accommodate each and everyone. At the same time, those possessing natural charisma and propensity for leadership, needed for the efficient running of a capitalist state, were invariably upper-caste. The inscription of the greater logic of the market in the state's script of social democracy then produced a nationalism that favoured the bourgeoisie and industrial class. If at all it favoured the poor, it was the 'deserving poor' meaning the upper and intermediary castes within the petit-bourgeois strata. The language of rewards and meritocracy was thus a means to forestall the threat of compensation provided by B. R. Ambedkar's constitutional interventions for SCs and STs. The social realist filmmakers were able to dramatize this conflict between reward and compensation, favouring the one while discounting the other.

What is interesting is that these films consistently enabled this conflict to be imagined in cultural and nostalgic terms—through the loss narratives of the precolonial rural idyll, parents, friends and other affective ties that transcended disciplinary structures and bureaucratic balance sheets—rather than a material conflict in the opportunities and resources available to the poor whether they be Muslims, Dalits or girls. The resulting pathos produced in the films was not because the most destitute were uncompensated, but a result of the anxiety or guilt generated in the hearts of the ones who were rewarded and integrated into the system. By not acknowledging the specific identities of the marginalized public, the films seemed to contribute to a secular class ethos, but in effect they strengthened a denial of class, caste, gender and religious conflict. Also, the presentation of secularism through the juxtaposition of different places of worship or characters of different religions fuelled the implicit practice of so-called secular politics along symbolic lines rather than everyday struggles and engagements. The birth of the unmarked child was a product of precisely such a symbolic politics.

The New Beginnings Package

In these films, it was the unmarked child who became a site for questioning the indifference of the state as well as reaffirming its paternalistic authority. It was through this child, usually enacted by a child actor with a fair cherubic face, that children were sought to be thematized as carriers of an innocent past of plenty and purity, in the criminalized, urban milieu of Bombay. The importance of basic needs like a home, food, and clothing in the wake of terrible famine, and price rise in the years prior to and immediately following Independence was emphasized through the situation of a child being orphaned. It was implied that the colonial masters, however unjust, at least took care of basic needs, and to that extent the onset of Independence was experienced as a loss of parental protection, a state of being orphaned, rehearsing at the same time the trauma of the unacknowledged Partition!

The sign of the child then operated both as a metaphor for rationalizing new beginnings as well as couching those beginnings within the language of protectionism.[5] Thus the demand for parental supervision from the state and public caviling on how Bombay cinema affected their children's morals were heard side by side. K.A. Abbas wrote a letter to Gandhi, remonstrating as well as pleading with him to give up his prejudicial views on cinema. Gandhi counted cinema among evils like gambling, *sutta*, horseracing, etc., which he left alone for 'fear of losing caste'. Abbas' letter reads: 'You are a great soul, Bapu. In your heart there is no room for prejudice. Give this little toy of ours, the cinema, which is not so useless as it looks, a little of your attention and bless it with a smile of toleration.'[6] In support, he drew a list of beneficial educative ends to which the medium could be used such as the making of documentaries, newsreels, anti-crime stories, and political features. He argued that while he could understand and even sympathize with his own father's aversion to the new medium ('an imported vice from the West'), he could not explain to himself Gandhi's rigid stance. After all, he was the Father of the Nation, and his views had a lot of influence. While his opinion on films could account for the works of those filmmakers who only depicted 'love and sex', it did disservice to the good work done by his own brand of filmmaking, the realist–idealist genre inspired by a Nehruvian/IPTA vision of nation building. He ended his letter by saying that Gandhi should not grudge this 'little toy' to his children. The manner in which Abbas played down his own father to endorse a non-biological/symbolic father is characteristic of the state paternalism of these films.

Film had to defend itself against allegations of depravity and counter the moral police by projecting itself as a medium of didacticism, worthy of an audience made of potential citizens. The films of the 1950s explicitly contested the biases regarding the necessarily evil effects of cinema. For example, in 1954, 13,000 women of Delhi petitioned Pandit Nehru, asking him to curb the evil influence of cinema on children as it led to precocious sexual habits, playing truant from school, and leaving home to find film jobs.[7] While this sparked off a fierce debate between the various proponents for and against cinema, it assured schools a central place in the discourse of childhood. The editor of *Filmfare*, Baburao Patel, stridently argued against the view that films had a corrupting influence on children. The fact that he belonged to the denotified Banjara tribe of Maharashtra[8] and was mostly self-taught probably contributed to his refutation of this middle-class opinion. He wrote that the real solution was to impart proper education and not blame films. He added that where talent and inclination did exist, parents should wisely encourage ambition.[9]

In fact, the spate of children's films to come out that year could well have been an unconscious response to this public opinion. These films anticipated the criticism and sought to offset it through the didactic voice of an authority figure advising children to go to school, prying the truants and tramps off the backs of the good school-goers. In short, schools were invoked to suggest a service equally available to all, and it was up to the citizens to make use of the facilities provided in schools to ensure a productive national life. The films carrying this message ironically fed into a concept of education as the responsibility of citizen-clients, rather than a state concern, importing terms of the market into the relationship between the state and its subjects.

However, in tandem with the dominance of symbolic politics, the films continued to invoke the left rhetoric of 'revolution' and 'new dawn'. Within this matrix of social reality, Nehru emerged as an immanent presence, a redeemer of pledges and social justice as in *Ab Dilli Door Nahin* (1957). It is therefore logical that he patronized the filmmakers and child artists who were promoting his vision through films. Nehru's self-endorsement included breakfasting with the kids, premiering their films in the Rajya Sabha, and taking them to Russia for cultural shows. The fact that most of these child artists never went to school assumes a special poignancy in this context.

In light of the nationalist circuit of film production, the terrain of the child-centric film became extremely moral. Orphan after orphan was unleashed upon the streets of Bombay or Delhi, made to balk at the vast cityscape, its industries bellowing fire and smoke, its streets festering with inhumanity and crime. Films such as *Munna, Ab Dilli Door Nahin, Ferry,* etc., were part of this moral landscape even as they endowed the street with a carnivalesque spirit. As is visible from Nehru's canonization in these films, there was no visible moral outrage directed against the Congress leaders who had come to occupy the seats of power. For the IPTA-led vanguard filmmakers who are historically identified as the backers of Congress leadership under P.C. Joshi, the dilemma was not so much about Congress's overtly anti-people policies, but that the Left's sacrifices in the struggle had not been acknowledged. The Left was caught in the bind of hailing the Congress as big brothers instead of formulating a political argument against their right-wing policies. They were continuously waiting to be patted on the back for services rendered. Consequently, the moral core of the films was diffuse, not naming or blaming anyone, but seeking recognition for their moral goodness. Heroism in these films was based on a combination of superior moral and social capital, derived from invoking an eclectic bag of nationally validated thinkers and visionaries. This baggage consisted of an assortment of terms such as socialism, development, secularism, equality, and nationalism. There is no reason to doubt the commitment of these artists to the principles enshrined in the consolidated package. But insofar as they belonged to a landed aristocracy or feudal upper-caste, very often their commitment to secularism or socialism was articulated in terms of the economic magnanimity of having once been the ruling class. The ability to straddle differences of sect and religion also came quite comfortably and unselfconsciously to them. Equipped with these impeccable credentials, these artists then forwarded the cause of a schizophrenic nationalist development.

The films thus operated at the level of a split structure, a narrative of loss as much as of hope. Let us take a typical case portrayed in the film *Ab Dilli* directed by Amar Kumar. The child, played by Master Romi, is about to become an orphan. He has lost his mother and is bracing himself to lose his father, who is falsely framed on a murder charge and is hence due for execution. Imbued with the pure hope and innocent faith of the archetypal child, he sets out for Delhi in order to petition Pandit Nehru to intervene and grant amnesty to his father. Meanwhile, the real killer, apprised of the little child's resolve, is all set to kill him. While on the road to Delhi, the pickpocket Ghaseeta, who has an alibi for his father and is accompanying the little boy to Delhi, is run over by the murderer. While the child is out on the streets of Delhi, looking for Pandit Nehru, he meets with a ragtag bunch of street children who are initially hostile, but eventually give him shelter and help him reach Nehru.

While he is looking for Nehru and also for his father (who himself has escaped from prison to look for him) the state as represented by Nehru gets its act together. Nehru the poster patriarch comes alive as a disembodied voice in a rally in the Ram Lila grounds. The real criminals are caught. The child is restored to his father. He starts going to school and the riff-raff is told to mend its ways. The return of normalcy, however, does not suggest the same degree of joyous abandon as when the school routine was suspended, when the law of the street prevailed, as seen in the deliberately carnivalesque *qawwali* number which the children had performed. Thus, there is a contradiction between the city projected as a den of vice and deceit and the actual warmth and hospitality of those who are seen to project such an idea, resonant of the self-descriptions of the child artists. These street urchins are shown to live in a shed rented from a corrupt milkman, caricatured as a pot-bellied mustachioed tyrant. Here, then, is our OBC figure, and the children have our sympathy only because they lampoon him and mark themselves away from that denigrated caste identity. But while they are as motherless as the protagonist, they are not in the running for a socially advantageous status or dignity. Nehru does nothing for them.

In fact, their status as children is defined in an oblique relationship to the archetypal child. They are mischievous, cheeky, cute, but at the same time very street-savvy. Their dilemma is not one of grappling with the betrayal of national promise, but simply surviving from day to day. Whether this requires a wily determination to pick pockets or a steely resolve to outwit the masters, neither have any connection with the state's imperative to provide free and compulsory education to all below 14 years of age. There is no guilt associated with this particular bunch either, since their endurance and street skills makes it redundant to put them through school in the first place. Their role is to help the individual meritorious (upper-caste) child to gain what is due to him from the state.

Realism and Real Children

The year 1954 seems particularly exemplary insofar as it witnessed four spectacular *naya zamana* (new world) films involving children: *Munna*, *Jagriti*, *Boot Polish*, and *Ferry*. These films could be studied to grasp the relationship between the state's view of children and its development agenda.

As we saw above, while the cute and innocent child protagonist is meant to explore the tension between the state and the individual, he also has to rub shoulders with real children who are removed from the more upscale workings of the nation state. Their national duty is confined to saving this other child from becoming one of them. These other children are outside competition in the market as well as the state. They eke out an existence in the interstices of the two, and the state does not feel accountable for their plight. If anything, the real children represent a threat: the potential to make the obedient child citizen stray from his dutiful and honest path. These children are not singled out for their marginal caste or religious identities; they simply belong to an underclass and are given diminutive names which do not overtly betray caste or religion. In contrast, the upper-caste status of the child hero archetype is made visible quite unequivocally. Thus in *Ab Dilli*, Ghaseeta and Maseeda are pickpockets who spend their time smoking ganja in the cemetery, surely indicative of a low-caste identity. In *Munna*, Lakhiya Majdoor, the determined newspaper boy, is identified in terms of his class but not caste identity. In *Jagriti*, the scholarship boy Shakti is shown to be the son of a domestic worker. In *Boot Polish*, the identity of the main child characters is left vague. While their aunt is shown to be a common whore, their parents are referred to as freedom fighters. The villainous pickpocket is called Bhiku. Finally, the other orphan in *Ferry* is the daughter of a *tawaif* (courtesan) and hence presumably a lower-caste person. Caste identities in these films may be veiled, but they are implicit, and their importance in unravelling subtle points of difference between dominant and residual models of childhood are not entirely lost on the viewers.

It must be recognized that the social realist vision of Hindi cinema was largely articulated within the mythopoeic structure of melodrama, where the world ran according to divinely designed coincidences, where people were forever missing each other by a scrape, and the dénouement always assured the picking up of pieces and wonderful reconciliations. Put simply, the dominant model of childhood was identified with the pure and innocent child protagonist, and was transmitted through a fairy tale structure. The child of this world was then shown to be inspired by love and piety towards parents or the trauma of separation from them, feelings recognized and perpetuated as being part of an immemorial ideology of childhood. The marginal children or the riff-raff, on the other hand, were seen to be completely in tune with the capitalist system, shown in terms of their greater pragmatism in contrast to the child protagonist's idealism. However, this pragmatism was likely and paradoxically closer to the residual models of childhood available in different subcultures, as we shall see. But by presenting their survival strategies realistically, and without the sentimentality attached to the other child, the filmmakers inadvertently imbued the street children and the girls with the prestige of realism.

Realism touched the child protagonist only insofar as he was a beneficiary of the state, thus serving a reality that only lived up to the optimism of a particular class. This privileged status was projected as normatively applicable only to the central child protagonist. Other claimants to the privileged version of childhood were not allowed to share in it. In fact, these lesser children are not even desirous of benefiting from the state. Their playful and recalcitrant urges are part of a different economy, unlike the main child who is deliberately withdrawn from the economy in order to free him from adult burdens. In other words, the films retard his actual growth while seeming to promote his development. This is akin to the process whereby the child actor, who enacts the growth narrative, is still expected to retain her baby face for the sake of a more enduring career (as a child artist). The suppression of growth and age is resonant with a vaguely ruling ideology, where time has no transformative potential other than to produce obedient citizens.

As the ideal child protagonist slowly surrenders to the bourgeois democratic system, abandoning his past, the riff-raff foot-soldiers are intended to maintain their location within a precapitalist hierarchy. The main child can move into the dynamics of a new mode of production only if his past privileges are safeguarded by these members of the subordinate classes.

The important question in the context of the four films under discussion then becomes: if the secondary children do not really give their consent to being marginalized and if their ensuing struggle and conflict is not the focus of the films' pathos, then are not the films undermining their own brand of realism by privileging the melodramatic narrative concerning the loss of an affective world over and above the realistic one concerning the loss of bed and board?

In *Boot Polish* Bela, the younger sister of the main child protagonist Bhola, appears to be perpetually hungry. She remarks to her John Chacha (uncle): 'I feel hungry everyday', to which he replies that this everyday hunger is an epidemic. Indeed, her precocious and exaggerated acting style meant to highlight the fact of an 'epidemic hunger' robs the little girl of her simple hunger. At the same time, her inability to bear hunger pangs violates the code of gracious self-surrender, rendering her ineligible for the status of the chosen child who will accede to the institutions of the state. She proves herself ineligible the moment she extends her hand to beg. It is interesting that 'reservations' are seen (by the middle class) as a form of begging too, a concession for one's disabled status. Having proved her unworthiness, Bela is removed from the theatre of competition. She is adopted by a liberal affluent couple, who are capable of satisfying her every urge, but grief at separation from her brother makes all her urges redundant. She no longer feels hungry. The scene that marks this transcendence of childhood shows everybody, from Bhola to John Chacha to her adoptive father, trying to offer Bela her favourite *bers* (berries) to cheer her up, but she has no desire for them. This transcendence of childhood is then synonymous with the moment when the marginalized female sibling refuses entry into the domain of the fight for resources. Instead, she is invested with the compelling femininity of the adult female who must leave for her husband's house, as shown through the Vaishnava lyrics, '*Jaun piya ke des, o rasiya main saj dhaj ke*' (I'll go to my beloved's house all dressed up). It is not as if Bela has automatically sublimated her childlike desires, but the narrative violence of the film imposes this sacrifice upon her.

In *Ferry* too, the female child is prefigured in an unchildlike role, as a mother even before she makes an appearance. The child protagonist, Raju, a scion of a rich landed family, is waiting for his mother to arrive from across the river. He does not know that she is dead. So when a girlish Juhi (played by Geeta Bali) is washed ashore, the child mistakes her for his mother. She is the daughter of a *tawaif*, who is trying to disown her past and is seeking an ideal mother for herself. Very briefly, she is cast in the role of an orphan in order to establish her background. She gets to spend a brief spell of Edenic happiness with Raju, lasting the duration of the song, '*yahi hai mere sapnon ka sansar*' (Here is the world of my dreams). The little boy is more a playmate than a son. But eventually her past catches up with her and the boy's father, Vikas Babu, asks her to leave by the first morning ferry, so that the painful separation with the son can be avoided while he sleeps. However, unlike the stereotypical *tawaif* figure in Hindi films, who is a paragon of sacrifice acutely conscious of her need to give up unreasonable claims, Juhi is stubborn in her unwillingness to give up the happiness she has secured with Raju. She finds various ruses to keep missing the morning ferry, to the dismay of Vikas Babu. Eventually he has to strike a bargain with her so that she will stop behaving like a recalcitrant child. He accepts her as his wife and in exchange, she has to shed her shiny girly clothes, her girlish sensuality, and adopt the role of mother to Raju. But she makes for a very reluctant wife. It could very well be that this reluctance to give up her claims on childhood comes from being the daughter of a *tawaif*, one of the very few communities with a pronounced tradition of daughter preference and hence a higher degree of investment in girlhood.

Thus we see that traditions and modes of behaviour drawn from residual, precapitalist models of childhood determine the degree to which claims on the fruits of one's labour are made or given up. It stands to reason that those privileged in the past will naturally feel more entitled than those who have been deprived. Consequently, the prerogative of being moody, recalcitrant, and indulging in rage also lies with those with inherited capital, whether social, cultural, or economic. Thus in *Jagriti*, when the Brahman boy from the landlord household, Ajay, has to undergo punishment for his thoughtless violence towards the gardener (*mali*), another OBC figure depicted customarily as a butt of ridicule, his resentment manifests itself as rage against the new order, most emblematically represented by the new Gandhian teacher who believes in treating all children as equals.

Ajay understandably does not find equality and the rhetoric around it alluring. He unleashes a trail of destructive pranks in the boarding house to which he has been sent as penalty, in the process displaying leadership qualities that win him a large brood of devoted fans.

In fact, it is the bookish scholarship boy Shakti who understands and believes in equality, but because he is lame in one leg and cannot command the leadership qualities and physical prowess of Ajay, he has to opt out of the educational competition despite the desire for upward mobility willed by the housemaid mother's sacrifice. It is important to note here that while Shakti is resigned to sacrifice, it is his mother who prods him onto academic pre-eminence. The brutality of the abuse suffered by the mother, who has steaming hot water poured on her by a neurotic mistress, is undoubtedly the lot of those who aspire to social mobility.

The boys mock Shakti's handicap, calling him *langda*, to which he smiles sweetly. It is as the natural and morally ordained leader of the boys that Ajay takes up cudgels on behalf of his friend. The fact that Shakti fares better in studies is not seen as threatening precisely because Ajay's vengeful libidinous energy is seen to be synonymous with a healthy rural robustness, missing sorely from the national curriculum. However, after Shakti has been killed, due to Ajay's carelessness and pride, the latter is truly remorseful and shows himself capable of coming first in class as he had promised his friend and not because of any independent urge for academic recognition. So instead of studying by daylight, he studies on the sly at night. His sense of shame derives not only from having to discipline himself to an entirely new life ethic, but also from having to concede to the superiority of the teacher who is symbolic of the democratic order brought forth by Independence ('*sab kahenge main aapse har gaya*' [everyone will say I've lost to you]). With the teacher's help, however, Ajay is able to integrate the radical forms of nationalism with more moderate ones, to integrate a book heavy curriculum with sports, athletics, calisthenics, craft, and the outdoors—in other words, to integrate Shantiniketan with Wardha (Gandhi's *nai taleem*) as well as with a more basic Nehruvian model of liberal English education.

This integrationist and eclectic spirit is invoked in virtually all the films. In *Munna*, the runaway orphan is so wide-eyed and gullible that he has to be taught to discriminate between authentic and inauthentic parentage, and made to reject the corrupt bourgeoisie as class enemy. At the same time, the film's intention is to showcase the rich collection of people he encounters who are all touched and reformed in some primal way by his innocence, thus diluting the class message into a humanist one.[10] In *Ferry*, the child is shown from the start in a Netaji uniform, signalling an alternative nationalism to the Nehruvian or Gandhian one. In tandem, the film projects a more anglicized identity depicted through a pet Alsatian called Lasso, or the children playing with spades and bucket on the beach, donning Western swimwear. However, despite the clear emphasis on class difference, the film neutralizes a threatening liberalism (where a prostitute's daughter becomes the bride of a respectable family), with a dose of patriarchal authoritarianism. It does this by de-sexualising the *tawaif*'s music and dancing skills in a manner typical of the Indian state's attempt to restore the various arts as part of a sober classical Indian tradition.

In *Boot Polish*, we have seen that the socialist new world—signalled through the song '*tu badta chal*' (keep marching forward)—cannot accommodate women as comrades, but only as sisters, wives, or mothers. It is *Jagriti*, however, which most decisively articulates the eclectic spirit in song after song, whether in the famous *jhanki* (exhibition) song ('*Aao bachchon tumhe dikhayen jhanki Hindustan ki, is mitti se tilak karo, ye dharti hai balidan ki*' [Come on children, today we'll show you the exhibit which is India. Make a *tilak* on your forehead with the soil that belongs to the martyrs]) where the martial races and lands are equated with the places in which the revolutionary socialist leaders have been martyred, or else the *sabarmati ke sant* song which pays tribute to the entire pantheon—Gandhi, Nehru, Subhash, etc—almost indiscriminately. The metaphor of integration is so compelling that it must subsume in the nation the philosophies of Gandhi, Nehru, Bhagat Singh and Subhash Chandra Bose, the rural and the urban, along with countless other contradictions.

The Tyranny of Bourgeois Education

> The young of this country have everything in them. They are honest, educated. They can be beautiful, wonderful citizens of the country if given opportunities. But certain influences have always bogged them down and they have been trapped in a situation where they are helpless.
>
> —Raj Kapoor[11]

Raj Kapoor, one of the most influential and commercially successful filmmakers embodying the IPTA vision, sees the problem of poverty as one arising out of a lack of opportunity rather than any structural reasons. If only there were enough schools, he seems to suggest, things would be fine. For the child artists who mostly did not complete schooling, this becomes a self-fulfilling prophecy. The films they acted in of course projected the message that they should leave films and join schools. But would they be accepted in the schools? Could the myths they enacted on screen help them rationalize the abuse and dispossession of their everyday lives? Would it enable them to dream of a new world, hope for a better future? Or did the contradictions make them cultivate discrimination and cynicism above and beyond the patriotic and hegemonic message of national integration?

In this section, I piece together the recounted memories of the iconic child artists Daisy Irani, Master Romi, and Jagdeep of the 1950s, and Master Raju and Junior Mehmood of the late 1960s and 1970s, as told to me in April 2003. I have also drawn from Dilip Ghosh's 1990 documentary film on child artists called *Aadhi Haqeeqat, Aadha Fasaana*.

To start with, the confusion between fiction and reality was the most pressing problem among the respondents. The social realism of the 1950s reserved the most clichéd and stereotypical roles for children, and some of those stereotypes were uncannily reproduced in the lives of the child artists, the bourgeois child playing the cute kid and the working class playing the riff-raff. While the former were usually chaperoned, their money taken care of by a parent who gave up her/his job to become full-time manager or secretary, the latter traversed the city on their own, negotiating their deals and enjoying relative control over their incomes. But irrespective of class, the children shared two common things. None of them had ever been to school and all of them were Muslim.[12] The better-off may have had private tutors and been trained in Kathak dance and tennis,[13] but they were singly deprived of a school life, and almost all of them had internalized the victimized identity of a childhood forfeited at the altar of cinema.

One of the principles by which the city was organized in their minds was the division between the bourgeois world of school, home, playing truant, friends, homework, and playgrounds as enacted on the screen, and the other lived world of the studio, arc lights, unusual hours, freedom from routine, travel, abuse, exploitation, and the responsibility of earning a living. The tyranny of the bourgeois model was so great that both the working-class, autonomous child as well as the coerced and dependent child artist succumbed to it, discounting any ownership of their role as breadwinners or any attendant pleasure in it.

The city as metonym for the world at large and mediated through the prism of literature was not accessible to them. Films were the only medium through which the city was processed and in these films the city appeared mean and hostile. It was shown variously as a spatial grid, a thicket of traffic, a throng, a concrete jungle, and the child was trapped and beset at every corner by the threat of an accident. The other thing which children (both the child actors and the presumed child audience) unmistakably carried from these films was a heightened state of affect conveyed through a precocious acting style and an accompanying set of exaggerated mannerisms.

The child actors related real experiences of abuse and suffering through the exaggerated sentimentality of Hindi film melodrama. They do not see abusive experiences for what they are, but for what they represent vis-à-vis the grand narrative of Hindi melodrama. Fun on the sets is not absent, and involves a sense of temporality that is not strictly divided between work and leisure, age, class and religious divisions.[14] Old issues of *Filmindia* and *Filmfare* reveal an incredible amount of playfulness on the sets with games and matches of wit played in between scenes or during break hours involving all the crew—whether child or adult, junior or star, technical or acting staff.

Yet, despite having belonged to the city so completely, the children have an immense dread of it, especially the affluent ones. They cannot recall ever being loose on the streets without a protective chaperone. In fact, most child actors remember the first experience of being in the city as the result of a crisis. Daisy Irani remembers biking her way into the neighborhood Dena Bank at the age of 14 to withdraw money because of an emergency at home. Under normal circumstances she would never have gone by herself. Master Romi[15] boarded a bus for the first time at the age of 15 to restart life as an apprentice to a director. For the working-class children, who started out as extras, the city was no alien, and they were extremely comfortable with the back alleys and the back entrances of the studios. In a way, for the working-class child, it was the proverbial doorway to riches and prosperity, but not to the class privileges that come with being a star. They might have earned enough money, but not the freedom to do as they liked. For example Junior Mehmood[16] resented being treated as a social inferior as, for instance, when his sons were denied admission at an elite public school citing his presence in lewd C-grade cinema as the reason. While the bourgeois child artists were equally devoid of the cultural capital that comes from going to school, there was still an edge that came from belonging to a privileged family, but none of the economic independence. The money they earned was mostly monopolised by their guardians for investment in speculative film ventures, as in the case of the mothers of Baby Naaz and Daisy Irani.

For both these types of child artists, however, the world was closed beyond cinema even as they longed to break free from it. And yet, they were unable even to imagine an alternate city, where the cinematic did not intervene or impinge in any significant way. Being rendered unfit for acting mature roles thanks to the childlike quality that clung to their faces, they preferred to take up direction or production. In fact, the working-class child might have done a better job with his post-acting career, in terms of sustaining himself economically, than the bourgeois child artist. Between Lakhiya Majdoor played by Jagdeep and Munna played by Master

Romi in the film *Munna*, the former seems to be better-off, financially at least. While Jagdeep takes pride in his status as a child labourer and flaunts the fact that he has been working since the age of seven, Romi is haunted by the compromises he had to make for the sake of financial security and refuses to submit to the prostitution of his art and sensibilities beyond a point. He would rather retire to his suburban flat than work in B-grade television serials, which is all that he has left. The pragmatic and the sentimental are crudely separated worlds, just as they were depicted in the films. Similarly Master Raju,[17] who claims a gentrified upbringing, scoffs at Junior Mehmood who performs at seedy nightclubs.

Junior Mehmood tells the story of how he became Junior Mehmood in the typically filmy style of *chhote log* (lowlife) dreaming above their station. Despite protests from his engine driver father, he forced his way into Mehmood's party and impersonated Mehmood to such perfection that it won him his famous namesake's lifelong support and patronage. In hindsight, he says, 'I was a fool, I thought why doesn't he invite me to his daughter's anniversary party when he has invited everybody else on the sets.' It was pride at being an artist that made him feel bold enough to gatecrash the party. But the conditioning over the years in the film industry taught him the deep-seated biases that make it necessary for the *chhote log* to remain humble and obsequious.

What unites them besides their self-consciousness as artists is also the fantasy of a safe haven where their children can have the childhood they themselves had lost out on. The fantasy worlds such as amusement parks that the current crop of child-centric films rely on are what they aspire to for their children. But because nothing in life is free, especially children's entertainment, they are forced to live by the rules of the market, playing marginal roles that subliminally feed on their childhood identities. They are deprived of the chance to reinvent themselves, condemned to playing the same roles over and over again. This prolonged career has invariably taken its toll. Master Raju feels that he was reduced to playing the victim roles thanks to the nice boy image he enjoyed in his childhood. He is desperate to ward off the gullible victim image by developing a shrewd, cynical persona. This involves the defensive claims of a normal childhood By normal childhood, he tells you, he means that he attended school, played with the canteen boy, flew kites, played with marbles and *gilli danda* (boomerang), and exchanged love letters with the girl next door. But in a moment of bravado, he reveals how Salman Khan used to be his sidekick and lackey, as he was the star then. They would die to be hanging around Master Raju in the Bandra market square. But even for the cynical and smart Raju, there is lament at the premature exposure, for things taking place before their time. Ultimately he too succumbs to the dominant narrative of wasted years.

Sadly, despite belonging to a period in Hindi cinema which glorified the bond between the child and the dispossessed female, Raju can only recall abusive experiences at the hands of his female colleagues. Consequently, they are dismissed for their threatening sexuality manifested in a couple of unpleasant overtures towards him. The role of the cunning and enterprising child which he played in *Kitaab* (1977), for which he won the national award as well as a scholarship covering his college education, is something which he continues to draw on for his survival. He is happy doing serials for *Doordarshan* after playing a drug addict and sidekick in innumerable films. He has not managed to lose the cherubic look and the baby face in adult life, even as he insists on playing the villain. Salman Khan, who was a childhood chum, and Gulzaar, who almost adopted him, are both resented for not having brought him better luck.

Daisy Irani, who belonged to an earlier generation, was more successful in creating an alternative family in the film world as a refuge from the exploitative mother who would drive her to prostitution just to grab a role. Like Naaz, she was regularly beaten, molested, and abused on the sets. Meena Kumari and Ashok Kumar, whom she adopts as parents in her first film, *Bandish*, are subsequently recruited for the role in real life as well. She talks about several occasions when she could not distinguish the boundaries between acting and real life. This inability to distinguish life from screen would leave her tormented. For a scene in which Meena Kumari was supposed to slap her, for instance, she kept turning her face away. After innumerable retakes, Meena Kumari promised not to hit her if she did not turn her face away. But as a tight slap followed the promise, she recalls how Meena Kumari was in tears for having betrayed her trust and begged the child's forgiveness. Similarly, Ashok Kumar was forced to be a little rude to the child off screen to bring out hostile vibes from her. According to her, one eventually learned the difference between film and reality, but the experience left her bitter, and on the verge of a nervous breakdown. While Daisy Irani distanced herself to enact scenes of melodrama, Master Romi and Baby Naaz describe how they would recall personal tragedies to get the tears flowing. While Baby Naaz wished her parents dead, Romi recalled how he would remember the recent death of his father to cause the tears to well up. Daisy Irani says that her conversion to Christianity was her way of getting back at her parents. Her public crusades against the exploitation of children in cinema, and her running an acting school for aspiring actors, were efforts to come to terms with the exploitation of these early years. In fact, she was so violently put off by the mechanical acting children were forced into that she hated to see herself on screen hamming it up.

In a later generation, starting from Master Raju, we notice a greater appreciation of the codes of acting. There is not as much confusion between real and reel life, and the child is aware that he is part of an exchange relation. While alienation from the film industry is rampant across the board, the sense of coercion for the girls took on the desperation of seeking to get married to escape exploitation by parents. The boys felt that they had nowhere else to turn in order to eke out a living.

But the child actors were no mere victims. They were familiar with the power of money and the hold it gave them over their parents. Daisy Irani would earn Rs 35,000 per film in the late 1950s while Master Raju's rates were anything between Rs 60,000 and Rs 1,00,000 in the mid-1970s. A four-year-old Tabassum realised that it was her labour that had brought 'chicken and mutton' to the plates of her parents. When she taunted her parents by saying this, they 'handled' the situation really well and prevented their daughter from becoming a spoilt brat.

While all wage labour under capitalism involves the expropriation of a surplus by the dominant classes, insofar as the actor's self is always implicated in the personae he plays, this job guarantees a personal surplus extraction, as it were. Romi Saudagar, the actor who played the gullible and innocent boy Munna was caught at the wrong end of this conundrum. He had completely internalized the idea of merit propagated by the social realist films and believed that his talent alone would stand him the test of time. However, when I interviewed him (he was in his late 50s), a note of self doubt crept into his voice as he recounted how he had suffered severely for believing that begging and pushing for something are inimical to the social realist aesthetic he was brought up on. He recently did a role for a television serial without charging a penny as the sum being offered was too little and he felt doing it for free would at least maintain his dignity. His interactions with the servants and labourers who were doing some wood work in his house in remote and suburban Bahisar (to him far from the madding crowd, but to his peers, a sign of his lowly financial status) was proof of the easy comradely spirit imbibed from the IPTA inspired narratives in which the child opens to justice the eyes of those blinded by greed.

Thus even as the child actors were alienated from the city in the obvious sense of labourers not fully integrated into the process of production, doing bit parts without a sense of the whole, abused and exploited, what complicated this history of their labour was the acquisition of performative skills and the identity of an artist, which both enhanced and cast a shadow over the subsequent life of the child. The tag of the child artist, as we have seen, is one that haunts, inspires, and condemns in ways that outlive the actual span of labour delivered as a child, extending into adult life. For instance, almost all child actors develop a lingering cherubic face. It is as if their struggle to prolong the period of their acting tenure in a childhood treacherously fleeting results in traces of their baby looks being permanently etched onto their faces. This may possibly be taken as a sign of the willed or constructed nature of the ideology of childhood itself, which retards only to spur growth and enhance income opportunities.

While there is no doubt that these directors' message of equality for children came from hearts that bled unflinchingly for the socially disadvantaged, their underlying faith in the exclusive logic of capitalism dampened the socialist messages of the films. Under the consolidated onslaught of globalized capital, the labouring classes (including women and dalits) have intensified their attack on the affective universe of privilege, refusing to stick to their given script. The struggle over limited national resources is now out in the open. The response of the child actors (as collected in this article) as well as the many child audiences, to these new circumstances is crystallized in the neo-nationalist *Rang De Basanti*, which was the first to articulate a cynicism with old-style uniformed patriotism and state organs. While *RDB* more than reposes its trust in the institutions of the state, the class politics of the film succeeded in mobilizing an aspirant yuppy student population to leave their books and participate (even if mostly virtually) in a lumpenism that was triggered by a violation of the narrative closures of these fifties' social realist films, which set the precedent for the upper caste boy always winning first place.[18]

To be sure, the implications of using children to describe the experience of coming to Independence and the scripting of a new nation was that it de-historicized the militant/anti-colonial nationalism and turned it into a commodity. Bereft of its actual ideological underpinnings in a socialist praxis, this rebel mode took on the aspect of denying the existence of older hierarchies or examining their own locations of privilege. Thus these films, beyond their rhetoric of exploitation and injustice, in a sense provided the historical pretext for refusing to deal with the issue of how exactly these under-classes were to be compensated, so that they could compete with the privileged. The socially marginalized are either shown to waste their potential away or else they are given the dignity of facilitating the accession of the upper-caste brat or waif in some tragic or poignant way. This morally tragic framework instead encouraged a heroism premised on keeping the system of Brahmanical privilege intact in the name of meritocracy. Simultaneously, the socially marginalized also emerged as reluctant collaborators in this nation-building project that was only meant to enhance the opportunities and prestige of the bourgeois players. Since childhood within this bourgeois symbolic domain is so obviously a narrowly instrumentalized category, what Ariel Dorfman calls the mirror of adult wish-fulfilling fantasies,[19] the only way to work our way through the mist of this ideology in order to record the rhythms and textures of a real creature, it seems, would be to look for the historical conjunctures at which institutionalized childhood meets and struggles with the narratives of different subcultures, where a child does not have such a reified identity.

* The interviews with the erstwhile child actors were made possible by an Independent Seed Grant provided by Sarai, Centre for Studies in Developing Societies (January to July 2003).

Notes

1. Interview with Daisy Irani (15 April 2003).
2. In *Bombay, My Bombay*, K.A. Abbas discusses the way in which his one-time experience of sleeping on the pavement got translated into a big moment in at least four of his films, and how before actually shooting *Shehar aur Sapna*, he wandered all over the city in wet and dry weather to shoot his film 'figuratively'. The outdoors was extremely crucial in terms of a certain urban topography—the electric pylon, the *jhopar-patti* (hutments), the railway line on the edge of the slums, the drainpipes. While everything was shot on location, a cylindrical drainpipe was carried to the studio for realistic interior scenes. See K.A. Abbas, 1987.
3. Bhisham Sahani, *Balraj, my Brother*, New Delhi: NBT, 1981, p. 110.
4. Ibid.
5. The relationship between the fathers of the nation and the children of the film industry is a recurrent theme. For instance, the film industry 'would take on the government' for its perceived 'step-motherly treatment' and 'callous indifference' to its 'plight'. The state controlled the film industry through *regulatory* functions, and 'by granting licenses to import technological hardware…and the issuing of *censorship* certificates'. Moreover, 'the high costs of production, lack of adequate returns on investment, and an unstable financial situation led some producers to call for government regulation, even nationalization, of the film industry' Sumita S. Chakravarty, *National Identity in Indian Popular Cinema 1947–1987*, New Delhi: OUP, 1996, pp. 58–61.
6. Quoted from *Filmindia*, October 1939 in Bandhapadhyay, 1993, p. 145.
7. 'Our Readers Say', *Filmare*, vol. 3, no. 14, 9 July 1954, p. 38.
8. Rao, 2004.
9. Baburao Patel, 'Editorial', ibid., p. 5.
10. About *Munna* (1954), K.A. Abbas, its director says, 'Through the wanderings and adventures of a lost child, I wanted to present a cross-section of our society—criminals and capitalists, clerks and news-vendors, rich families with no children and poor families burdened with a number of children—and to highlight how poverty breeds crime. The simplicity and innocence of the child was to provide a foil for all the stupidities and villainies rampant in our social system'. Retrospective Films of K.A. Abbas: 10th International Film Festival of India, GOI Publication, 1985, p. 3.
11. Nanda, 1991.
12. One very obvious contradiction arose from the fact that all the major child artists of the period prior to 1980 (except for Sachin) were from Muslim backgrounds

and that they played Hindu children, consciously effacing their Muslim identity in terms of renaming themselves, a fact which of course mirrors a larger dichotomy of the film industry. For instance, in the Q&A column of *Filmfare*, February, 1954, a reader asks the blunt question, 'What is Master Rattan Kumar by religion?' to which he gets the crisp reply, 'He is Muslim.'

13. The privileged ones such as Baby Chand were reported to be pursuing studies under private tutors at home and learning classical dance from Pandit Badri Prasad. In fact, 'her star status did not prevent her from being a normal and mischievous little girl and she delights in a game of marbles and badminton with her seven brothers and sisters'. 'Candidates for Stardom', *Filmfare*, August 1954, p. 43.
14. An indication that fun was not merely limited to the moppets is evidenced by the games and wit on the sets that one finds scattered through the gossip columns of the film magazines. For instance, on the sets of Ismat Chughtai's *Darwaza*, six glasses of *lassi* are promised to the composer of the worst Urdu verse. While Manju, the heroine, is disqualified for creating something as apt as '*Is atomic garmi mein shooting Everest par ho*', Nazir Hussain bags the prize with his '*Umas ki raat mein takiya lihaaf hota hai*'. *Filmfare,* April, 1954.
15. Interview with Romi Saudagar (19 April 2003).
16. Interview with Junior Mehmood (18 April 2003).
17. Interview with Rajoo Shreshtha (14 and 20 April, 2003). He won a national scholarship after *Kitaab*, which took care of his education up to graduation.
18. Chandra, 'Young Protest: Finding Merit in Popular Cinema', 2009.
19. Dorfman and Mattelart, 1975, p. 31.

References

Abbas, K.A. (dir,), *Munna*, 1954.

———, *Bombay, My Bombay: The Love story of the City*, New Delhi: Ajanta Publisher, 1987.

Arora, Prakash, *Boot Polish*, 1954.

Bandhapadhyay, Samik, ed., *Indian Cinema: Contemporary Perceptions from the 30s*, Selected by Dhruba Dasgupta and Biren Das Sharma, Celluloid Chapter Documentation, Jamshedpur, 1993.

Bose, Satyen, *Jagriti*, 1954.

Chakravarty, Sumita S., *National Identity in Indian Popular Cinema 1947–1987*, New Delhi: Oxford University Press, 1996, pp. 58–61.

Chandra, Nandini, 'Young Protest: Finding Merit in Popular Cinema' in *Comparative Studies of South Asia, Africa and the Middle East,* Duke University Press, 2009, Forthcoming.

Dorfman, Ariel and Armand Mattelart, *How to Read Donald Duck: Imperialist Ideology in the Disney Comics*, International Genreal, 1975.

Gupta, Hemen, *Ferry*, 1954.

Kumar, Amar, *Ab Dilli Door Nahin*, 1957.

Nanda, Ritu *Raj Kapoor: His Life and Films*, Moscow: Iskusstvo Publishers, Bombay: R.K. Films & Studios, 1991.

Patel, Baburao, *Filmfare*, 5 February 1954a; *Filmfare*, 16 April 1954.

Rao, L. S. Madhava, 'Baburao Patel: A Great Hindu Thinker', Centenary Profile, 11 April 2004, http://www.organizer.org/dynamic/modules.php? name = Content & pa = show page 8 pid = 188 page = 39, accessed 28 March 2008.

Sahani, Balraj, *Yadon Ke Jharoke Se*, New Delhi: Atmaram and Sons, 1974.

Smith, Geoffrey Noel, 'The Cities: Real and Imagined', in Mark Shell and Tony Fitzmaurice, eds., *Cinema and the City: Film and Urban Society in a Global Context*, Oxford: Blackwell Publishers, 2001.

'Our Readers Say', *Filmfare*, vol. 3, no. 14, 9 July 1954c, p. 38.

'Candidates for Stardom', *Filmfare*, August 1954d, p. 43.

8

Reading Rape: Sexual Difference, Representational Excess and Narrative Containment

Karen Gabriel

CINEMA IS ONE of the many institutions that generate discourses on rape. The many meanings that have been assigned to the raped body, and the ubiquitous possibility of rape within much mainstream Bombay cinema, signal an interesting and telling representational surplus. These may be understood immediately, if summarily, as the generative and fecund power of a single act—that of rape—to function as spectacle, as mover of narrative and generator of discourse. It is for this reason that cinematic representations of actual or suggested rape are often spectacular, supply considerable causality, and frequently register and pinpoint codes and zones of control. This last, within a patriarchal sexual economy, transforms the raped woman's discourses on/of pain and violation into ones on the improper exchange and violation of ownership. This radical deflection appears both in discourse and in the ways in which the camera approaches the female subject of pain, *transforming testimony into spectacle.*

Bearing in mind the visceral nature of rape, this article will argue that the impact and discursive usefulness of depicted rape rests on the ways in which its significations and effects are manipulated to reify the visceral experiential into the ideological. While the two are dependent on each other, they are frequently made to appear as if they are independent by isolating the material (feminine) subject of pain from the processes of meaning making. If she appears at all, it is as spectacle, not testifying subject, whose testimony/speech, when it occurs or is solicited, is quickly contradicted (through denial of force or the possibility of her pain, for example ('she wanted it', 'she is of loose morals', etc). Often, she is simply killed off (murder or, more often, suicide) or disappears and is thereby silenced. However, her ordeal is retained, reported, and interpreted. Put differently, the feminine subject of violation is preferable as visible object rather than as speaking subject, spectacle rather than speech, ideological lever rather than material testimony. As a result, what we get is (subjective) interpretation that has been hollowed of experience, a narrative devoid of the (raped) subject's interiority and subjectivity and the ideological deployment of these. Rather than being given a privileged status, the woman's critical narrative is either absent, or distorted or rejected.[1] What takes its place is a set of discourses—on sexual ownership and propriety—that corroborate the logic that led to the rape in the first place.

Such strategies of narrative erasure permit a set of very troublesome discourses about both the woman and the rape to emerge. In the process, the raped woman becomes 'an existential cypher…a symbolic cause… representative of her social group, the very embodiment of its collective identity'.[2] Here, as the processes of abstraction and reification begin, the stakes in claiming the meanings of both act (violation) and the site of enactment (the woman's body) increase exponentially.[3] The consequences of such techniques of appropriation are interestingly contradictory. On the one hand, they require a full acknowledgement of the possibility of pain, and on the other, they require that the subject of violence be relocated, and the victim emerges sometimes in the form of masculine honour, sometimes as community honour, sometimes as national honour. Thus a woman is raped/abused/violated, but an individual male or a larger community is injured/victimized/hurt. What is additionally difficult here is that the female body thus implicated in debates on authentic cultural and national identity is frequently circumscribed within its many demands and their scripts. Consequently, this body and its subjectivity are frozen as iconic and mythic and not emergent, dynamic, or historical.

This article will also show how certain representational paradoxes—such as visible invisibility, narration, and the denial of narrative—are characteristic of a mainstream treatment of women's sexuality, violation, or subjectivity. While there is no scarcity of mainstream Bombay films to elaborate and illustrate these issues, this article will use Shekhar Kapur's *Bandit Queen* (1994) and the analysis of a rape sequence in *Bhrashtachar* (Corruption, 1989, dir. Ramesh Sippy) as exemplary.

The Languages of Rape

Though rape is considered 'unnameable',[4] it is, in fact, a chief and much used metaphor, especially for conflict, as we see in the context of colonial conquest. It is, in fact, the *investment* in rape and its converse—legal sex—that are unspoken.[5] For example rape as an issue could not arise when ownership is legally established (as in marriage). As a sign of 'improper' exchange when 'marriage is the archetype of exchange',[6] it becomes a metaphor of deviance, conflict, illegal appropriation, or even chaos. The taxonomies of rape—e.g. sex with a minor, custodial, statutory, gang rape, rape during conflict and the crucial exception of marital rape—all clarify the instituted *social* meanings of rape. The legal requirement for penetration in rape confirms it as *the* violation, prime signal of power. Correspondingly, shame and impurity devolve on the other side.[7] Yet even after penetration is established, violation is queried via the controversial issue of consent (did she consent or invite it in any way?), bringing to the fore the prime but submerged question of sexual agency (refusing permission for sex in this case).[8] The ingenious and perilous denial of semantic stability in language, especially when it comes to women ('no' means 'yes') mystifies the violence of rape and implicates the woman in it. Yet it also requires considerable subtlety which explains why, in the later analysis of a rape sequence in *Bhrashtachar*, pleasure in the rape is generated not through an ideological approbation of it (it remains bad) but through a patriarchal affirmation of masculine pleasure that is premised on women's pain. Interestingly, we see that though patriarchal injunctions against the improper exchange of women (rape) are underscored, so is the patriarchal understanding that female pain and humiliation are normal. The apparent contradiction (rape is wrong) is accompanied by the reason why it is wrong (because it constitutes improper exchange and not because it is violative/painful).

Assumptions that women are somehow causal agents in rape and that their testimony is unreliable lead to the peculiar way of turning the language of resistance in a rape into a bodily and circumstantial thing. According to this, both the prefatory resistance (physical trauma that signals struggle) and (contrary to any indication of trauma) perfect composure post-rape (an immediate visit to the nearest police station or hospital, a fluent and faultless account of events) become signs of proper victimhood. However, because of the construction of the woman as causal agent, even the bodily evidence may be compromising. For instance, Veena Das[9] has noted the ways in which women get read for marriageability during rape trials. The battered body as evidence, ignoring some established circumstances of rape,[10] is based on the understanding that rape is a fate worse than death, when in fact women may prefer rape to battery or death. It is another matter altogether that the rapist may incorporate battery into the rape for a number of reasons. Moreover, in caste, custodial and marital rapes, for instance—where rape occurs frequently and where the balance of power is so uneven that resistance ceases to be a serious option—neither the extent of battery nor the number of rapes can be decisive in construing 'consent' or assessing violence. Rape and sexual vulnerability are functions of socio-economic relations. So even if it is an individual crime, it needs to be located within the institutionalisation of it: the ways in which violence is organised, assessed, and encountered in a society. For instance the gravity of a rape is often assessed on the basis of who commits it, on whom, and how, rather than as an unequivocal act.[11] It then becomes possible to understand why institutionalized rapes occur, the overlaps between 'institutionalized' and 'individualistic rape',[12] the political hue of rape (as community revenge, ethnic cleansing, mode of terror, etc.), and the logic of conviction in rape trials.[13]

The theory and the legal practice regarding rape are then inflected by factors that exceed the incident itself, though they may contribute to its practice. It is only by understanding the structural violence and social causality that transforms rape from an issue of violation to one on ownership that an understanding of what happened, why it happened, and why it continues to happen may emerge. This is a political issue with a general relevance since the inculcation of cultures of violence against women, while imbued with a local specificity, is a near global phenomenon. The methods and meanings of rape differ, pointing to the crucial question of the ownership of discourse itself. Gestapo rapes, those of the colonizers, of the American soldiers in Vietnam, the cross-border rapes during the Partition of India, rapes during communal riots, 'nationalist' rapes,[14] household rapes, etc. are organized differently, even while they manifest in similar ways and may have broadly similar ideological guidelines.

One common ground for the articulation of the subjectivity of the man or the identity of a community has usually been the body of the woman. Below, Urvashi Butalia[15] quotes Krishna Sharma of the VHP:

> 'Hindus must make sure that they are feared by others. We must also prove our mettle. If they rape 10–15 of our women we must rape a few of theirs to show them that we are no less.'

More than 10 years down the line, the story remains the same. Accounts of the mischievous reportage on the Gujarat violence foregrounded the ways in which the female body and the rape of women became centrepieces in the play of communal identity politics:

> Violation of Hindu honour was now compounded by extreme sexual violence and bestiality. Both the abduction and the cutting of breasts were lies—totally baseless stories, which were denied by the Police...The murder and rape of Hindu women, emblazoned in banner headlines across the vernacular press became the excuse, the emotional rallying point, the justification for brutalizing Muslim women and children in ways not ever seen in earlier communal carnages.[16]

If rape has been sentimentally conceived of as the imagined point at which the male imagination fails, it cannot be for lack of trying or experience.[17] The problem is not with any lack of imagination about rape in the many male narratives of it that abound—fictional or theoretical—but with the failure to acknowledge the meanings of rape for women. In that sense, this particular type of imagination is, in fact, based on a clear but denied knowledge of the *importance* of rape.

Imagining Rape

Rape is sexualized violence[18] and it is a gendered practice. Even if we temporarily accept Monique Plaza's argument that men are raped *as women*, i.e. as powerless and therefore as feminine and rape-able, raped men are rarely shown dealing with rape in a 'feminine' way. They are shown to deal with it and its consequences more actively and effectively, indicating an imaginative proficiency which suggests that 'failures' of imagination are a function of the refusal to acknowledge the meanings of rape for a woman.[19] However, there is *no erasure of violation* in either case (rape of men or women) since that would take away the power and meanings of rape.[20] Violation and violence are erased only by establishing ownership. After that violence is deemed either a prerogative, or it is not fully cognized as violence (in marital or caste rapes). Contrary to Plaza's understanding, men get raped *as men to be womanized*, and they may be shown to deal with it *as men* even if altered forever by the experience, raising the interesting issue about whether men experience rape as an elision of or insistence on gender. In *Hey! Ram* (2000, dir. Kamal Hassan) the protagonist Saket Ram's response to his near rape situation during the riots is interesting because it points to how gender is based on the meanings of sexual difference.[21] He performs a feminine masquerade: he turns submissive, disarms his assailant, and then, abandoning masquerade, kills his assailant and, unlike his wife Aparna, averts becoming the grounds of a discourse. Saket Ram's (Muslim) assailant highlights the gendered and communalized view of the 'effeminate and cowardly' Hindu, a view that is overturned by Saket through his successful escape of rape and the murder he commits, but 'confirmed' and magnified by the rape of 'his woman', Aparna, that is underway in the adjoining room. It is not idly that one speculates on what possible masquerade Aparna could have resorted to. It is necessary to note that while men may be 'raped as women', insofar as they are at that moment relatively powerless, they are *also raped as men*, because the acknowledgement of their sex and gender is a necessary part of the rapist's assertion of power. Men are raped as men who must be feminized, and rape is often punitive, consolidating the suggestion that femininity is punishment. We may argue that the type of alteration that men undergo after rape is a consequence of having to review the taken-for-granted relation between *women and rape*, and the stability of the power of masculinity itself. This is an *exact inversion* of the reiteration of gender in the rape of a woman.

The loss of 'manhood' is not the same as the loss of purity; the elements that are deemed 'corrupted' and the devolving shame in both cases are of a completely different order. The first may be recovered through re-manning oneself—rediscovering the power of masculinity (gender) usually through a killing spree—but 'feminine purity', especially in the light of curtailed agency, cannot be recuperated, only asserted or bestowed (by the rightful 'owner' of her sexual self). This bestowal could entail a forfeiture of male proprietal rights and hence, the narrative cul-de-sac of death that follows rape in cinema. The systemic, institutional, and embodied means of installing and ensuring gender subjectivity disallows women the agency of recovery whereby the importance of a rape may be denied, curtailed, or forgotten. It remains and is retained as a fetish of a masculine imagination of it.

But the most significant manifestation of gender difference in both the real and the represented rapes of women lies in the presence of a third participant—the 'legitimate' male partner—who *permits* the recognition of the rape as violence,[22] even while changing its figuration. Female testimony being insufficient and female sexual agency being suspect, assertion of rape by her is not necessarily true nor is the averred rape necessarily violent. In the process, there is a deflection of victimhood away from the woman to the third party, which may be husband, lover, family, community, or 'society'. This results in a further violence: the fetishization of rape that has cost the female subject the experience of it in the first place is thus accompanied by the conversion of her from victim to violator—cause of shame and pain. The discursive and ideological investment in rape as emblematic, whether of moral worth or the 'improper' expropriation of sexuality, partially explains why rape (in cinema) need not occur, but simply *present itself as a possibility*.

The conversion of the visceral experience of rape, as shown above, into the ideational and the ideological achieves a magnification of its significance and effects. The result is a conversion of value in which the raped body is devalued so that it may acquire an ideological worth that correspondingly appreciates the entitlements of patriarchy. In this sense, the mandatory gender violence on the screen may be classified into 'private' violence (domestic discipline arbitrarily differentiated from violence but including sexual harassment by the hero, especially during courtship, intimidation, slapping by the intimate male partner) and 'public' violence. The latter is distinguishable from the former and deemed violent only because a stranger commits it, constitutionally linking violation again to the issue of ownership. The Censor Board eventually found these distinctions untenable, and both—physical punishment of wives by husbands/male partner and lascivious rapes by strangers—were considered degrading to women.[23] The Censor Board's position on the proper treatment of women cognized that differentiated violence on screen is the effect of multiple violations of female subjectivity—actual, discursive, and representational—coming together in a continuum.

When detached from subjectivity and selfhood, rape is no more about the personal anguish of a violated self, but is reified into a narrative prop in which the moving force is usually male desire.[24] The several protests against Shekhar Kapur's representation of the rape in *Bandit Queen* had to do with what Arundhati Roy called his 'Woman-as-Victim-Arithmetic'.[25] Female agency and victimhood in the difficult contexts of patriarchy and the structural violence and power disparities that it facilitates gain interesting, if controversial, visibility in the representations of mainstream Bombay cinema.[26] Often these get defused, even warped, and surface simultaneously to recuperate dissent ('I said "no"') and to measure 'provocation' ('she asked for it'). Many films depict rape as violation and yet contest women's structural vulnerability, impugning consent and recording the tension between representing vulnerability as a structural condition and as an ontic condition (women are physically and morally weak or women are sexually unreliable/insatiable).

Mainstream Bombay cinema routinely tends to opt for the shorthand of the latter even while the sense of the former is retained peripherally to the plot. Hence, women are easily threatened and helpless but for the timely intervention of the divine or the hero. If a woman gets raped, however, she is converted to a sacrificial victim at the altar of social purification, which is undertaken by the active agent, the male protagonist. Once voided of historical context, independent subjectivity, and a valid voice, the female body is nominated as immanently vulnerable (it wants to be raped, it must be raped, or it gets raped anyway), thereby diminishing or naturalizing the violence (it is in the nature of things, it can't be helped, pain is a part of a woman's life). Once this discursive tactic is implemented, subjectivity and, therefore, pain are effectively eliminated from the equation; rape gets transformed into pleasurable spectacle and a male fantasy of control. The moral condemnation that accompanies rape indicts both the rapist and the woman as complicit in dishonouring *her man*. It is through this displacement of violence from the woman onto the man, and through the shift in attention on male pleasure, that the discourse of female pain metamorphosizes into one 'on her sexiness', that rape becomes titillation.[27]

Depictions of rape capture resistance and violation, purity and despoliation, pain and pleasure, shame and triumph at once, through a discourse of (mis)represented, violent sexuality in which a transcription of reality is transformed into a discourse. The field of representation itself, as will be demonstrated shortly, comes under pressure to accommodate this seductive but transgressive pleasure. The cinematic employment of the screen as both mirror and veil in Hindi cinema is an escape that allows that which cannot/will not be said to be shown, and that which cannot/will not be shown to be veiled but visible, *on screen*. In practice, this involves a representational violence that attempts to conceal (injunctions) while suggesting everything (titillations). Discourses, technique, and technology are all pressed into service by Hindi cinema to dodge supervision, structure 'pleasure', and keep the patriarchal discursive investment in rape intact.

Excess and Containment

For instance, in the film *Bhrashtachar*, a blind woman, Sunaina (Shilpa Shirodkar), is drugged, abducted, and raped by the villain Purushottam (Anupam Kher). In the process of coming out of her drugged stupor, and just before she is raped, from a symbol of purity and innocence, over an unbroken period of two minutes, she emerges as a dishevelled sex object. It is not merely in that the condition of her clothes now signifies both vulnerability as well as a moral disordering, but the seductiveness is reinforced by the fact of her blindness to it—both literally and in her state of semi-stupor. The oppositional relation, always hovering over the film text, of blindness–inferior–not-human–insentience: gaze/sight–superior–human–sentience, is then reinforced and reinscribed in gender terms of blind–disempowered–immoral–female: sighted–empowered–moral–male. The rapist–villain Purushottam rotates the circular bed on which Sunaina lies. The camera translates as his gaze as it traces the contours of her body in voluptuous detail. The victim herself participates 'involuntarily' in this by making small orgasmic sounds and shifting her legs and gradually raising her sari, ostensibly because she is emerging insensibly from her stupor, but actually to accommodate Purushottam's/the viewer's gaze. In one particular shot, images of the moaning, semi-naked woman are superimposed on Purushottam's eyes, which are seen along with her image through his spectacles, which become the mirror–screen within the screen, identifying both Purushottam and the viewer as spectators of the body. Here, several complicities are registered: the woman with her victimization, with the conversion of herself from victim into seductress and the corresponding shift of responsibility away from rapist to victim, the camera with the gaze and intention of the villain, and the director's with the ideologies of machismo that dictate this scene even if the film otherwise attempts to offer a critique of this discourse. But it is in the subsequent rape scene that the ambiguity of the mirror-veil proves insightful.

Unable to show penetration, the camera organizes the gaze quite literally onto a series of mirrors in the room that image the fragments of the central but off-screen violence. The object of desire is imaged not as absence, but as an alluring, partial yet vastly multiplied presence in the mirror-veil of the screen, the multiplicity functioning as an apologetic compensation for the denial of the consummation of viewing penetration. The masculinism is furthered through erratic camera movements that seem to draw toward, rather than escape from, the violence, without ever reaching it except in mime. The viewer participates involuntarily in the violence, in this mimicry of it. The parody of female resistance, already decreased here by the confusion of blindness (e.g. she runs into his arms to the sound of stimulating music), finally effects erasure of the violated object. Her distortion and her blindness get identified as a *natural* condition, a gender attribute whereby the *woman herself* cooperates in a parodic negation of her sexuality, subjectivity, and pain. Hence the audacious representation of Purushottam's pleasure at the moment of penetration through the woman's contorted face as it hangs upside down, over the edge of the bed. The elision of feminine subjectivity and the woman as subject of pain and resistance is legitimized, and the mistranslation of pain as pleasure occurs. Though startling, it is not surprising then that this rape scene has been extrapolated and posted as a pornographic clip.[28]

The representational paradoxes of visible invisibility, narration, and the denial of narrative are characteristic of mainstream films that attempt to deal with women's sexuality, violation, or subjectivity. Even a film like *Bandit Queen* (1994), which was commissioned by Britain's Channel Four to do an account of Phoolan Devi's life, and which saw itself as self-reflexively politically correct, deals mainly with the (imagined) meanings of rape in ways that are idiomatically in line with the mainstream discourse. *Bandit Queen*'s overt preoccupation with issues of caste, sexual violence, and poverty as well as its point of origin announced it as a liberal film. Though it remains an important film because of its attention to the neglected issue of caste inequalities in India, its gendered ideological and discursive orthodoxy were gradually unveiled. In the analysis that follows, I will show the extent to which representation of rape and feminine subjectivity hinge on the denial of women's narratives. I will also show how during the controversy over the film, this strategy of erasure manifested itself off screen, again as denial of narrative space and subjectivity, providing a crucial frame for signification.

Bandit Queen in Context

The exchange of meanings between the female body and the social body in India has been interrupted historically by the axis of caste that complicates questions of purity and hierarchy. Issues of caste, especially those of lower-caste women, are topics rarely touched by mainstream Bombay cinema. One of the strengths of *Bandit Queen*,[29] the story of Phoolan Devi's life, was its willingness to consider the intersections of caste and gender in constituting structural inequalities. Its greatest weaknesses were that it sexualized vulnerability, and then converted that vulnerability into a feminine trait, and effected a masculinist appropriation of the meanings and truths of a woman's life. Phoolan Devi (played by Seema Biswas) is a low-caste, low class woman in a rural, feudal set-up. The combination of these disadvantages that render Phoolan at least four times removed from privilege, security, and effective agential action are corroborated by child marriage (in exchange for a cow and a bike as a child of 11 to a man of 35), conjugal rape, caste-based rape, vengeful rape, and yet more rape, leading to Kishwar's exasperated '...film makers have an unhealthy obsession with sex and sex related violence'. Yet according to the title of the film, its concern is not with structural or historical vulnerabilities, but with the transcendence of these, with the transformation of a woman into India's most wanted and feared dacoit—'Bandit Queen'. However, through this project Shekhar Kapur retains a focus on vulnerability which then attaches to a notional femininity that jeopardizes causality and makes nonsense of the title of the film: how she became the Bandit Queen remains a mystery. The film forgets its raison d'être—to explain how Phoolan Devi became a legendary bandit—and doesn't bear much resemblance to the book that inspired it, irrespective of whether the original film script was altered or not.[31]

The first, immediately evident difference between Mala Sen's literary version and Shekhar Kapur's cinematic one of Phoolan Devi's life is in the erasure of the 'narratee'/listener (with the exception of the opening and closing sequences to which I return later), the person to whom the story is recounted, in the film version of her life. Where Mala Sen's account is as much about accessing and acquiring the Phoolan story as it is about Phoolan,[32] Kapur's film has no such commentary to draw attention away from the central spectacle of the Bandit Queen herself. Her life unfolds not as a past that is being mapped hesitantly, tentatively, because of the uncertainty of the terrain and the reluctance of the subject of the narrative; but as an immediately happening present that of necessity is oblivious of its future. While the consciously retrospective literary narrative bears within itself the implications of that life (Phoolan's) for the subject of the narrative (Phoolan), the film proved to be obdurately inattentive to these considerations. Most telling of this was the way in which the film implicated Phoolan in the Behmai massacre (see below). The future of the protagonist is 'discovered' by the viewer along with the eponymous protagonist heroine, but as if the camera was recording her life through her own eyes, staking a truth claim. Yet, the camera here is clearly not the protagonist's eye, not only because she is often the unknowing object of its gaze, but also because it is privy to other spaces and lives that she is not. Rather, though the camera functions as if it were a 'mute' witness space—almost as if it were the earth or the sky or both (literally the site of the scene itself) —neutrally registering a series of events unfolding in one life, it is also revealed to be voyeuristic. Its anonymous eye can be located anywhere in this undefined site—in fact, it defines this site in the coverage it gives it—in *any* body (recording the scene as it is registered on that body) or outside *all* bodies, as an 'immaterial' spectator. Yet, one specific and very important effect that this self-neutralization into anonymity allows, is the transformation of the camera—in its (unexplained) concern with Phoolan's life and its apparently transparent access into her most private events—into an invisible eye that, though not the protagonist's, can occupy its space, see through it. It is a strategy that permits the camera an apparently deep intimacy with the experiences of Phoolan's life, *without accounting for the source or the logic of that intimacy*.

Phoolan's protests at the appropriation and distortion of her life, the ban she sought on the film, and the support she received on the matter were linked to the very issue of the truth claims that the film made. This included the baseline of the film—'This is a True Story'—and Kapur's introductory remark at its premier screening: 'I had a choice between Truth and Aesthetics. I chose Truth, because Truth is Pure'.[33] Yet Kapur never met his legend even once, a decision that his producer Bobby Bedi defended, 'Shekhar would have met her if he had felt a need to do so'.[34] This fairly common appropriation of material would not have acquired great significance had it not been for the dispute between Phoolan and the filmmakers. After the film was made, Phoolan's request to see the rushes was first ignored and then denied by the producers who claimed that they had bought the 'rights' to her life story. As if this bizarre statement constituted a reason in itself. Subsequently, when she heard scenes of the film, she challenged and then protested inaccuracies in the representation of her life and events. She stated that the film was fictitious, misleading, and damaging to her. She was at this time facing trial for the Behmai massacre in which she denied having any hand, but which the film showed her orchestrating. She obtained a stay order on the grounds that the film was prejudicial to her legal interests as it indicted her in the massacre despite her legal position on it. She also denied the rapes (as Mala Sen records in her book)[35] and distanced herself from the shame that devolved from being raped, a fact that the film was aware of, given the single-minded focus on rape. Shekhar Kapur and Channel Four's reaction to Phoolan's position was most instructive. First, abandoning truth claims, they claimed artistic licence. Then, in an exceptionally appropriative and exploitative mode, they claimed ownership over Phoolan's story. Eventually, they called *her* a liar (an accusation that was not restricted to the dispute over the contract), money mad and ironically enough, hard and exploitative.[36] Their outrage at her opposition and grit show the extent to which their cinematic representation of her life, her rape, and her subjectivity rested on the *denial of her narrative*, the extent to which Kapur had successfully manipulated and contaminated the 'truth' of Phoolan in his own mind, turning her into the pure victim and diversion that the film had made of her. But most exploitative of all was Kapur's insistence on his own victimhood in relation to Phoolan. And as the controversy grew, Phoolan was dubbed as a part of an ever-growing gang of perpetrators as Shekhar positioned himself to the white world as a persecuted artist and classic third world political victim in the line of Rushdie.[37] After the stay order, Channel Four had to negotiate with her and add to the meagre amount that they had paid initially; a small price since the film launched Shekhar Kapur into the international circuit, which, Madhu Kishwar[38] believes, was the real reason for choosing and treating the subject as he did.

Representing Rape: The Truth of the Gaze

This circumventing of the 'truth' problems of recounting the past, this ability to affect intimacy—in a way impossible for Mala Sen, as self-conscious *literary* biographer—is specifically an effect of Kapur's *use* of the medium. His camera neither announces itself as omniscient, nor does it problematize its narrative by grounding itself in the corporeal limits of any one body, not even that of the protagonist. In this seeming insubstantiality–neutrality–anonymity achieved by minimizing traces of its own presence in the narration, the camera seeks to 'fictionalize' itself—as if by doing so it could close the gap between its own (and by implication the viewer's) historical moment and that of Phoolan's—a gap that inevitably fictionalizes any history that chooses to ignore it. In thus attempting to fictionalize itself, to simulate authenticity in its representations, however, it engages in a significant and deliberate duplicity which, paradoxically, serves to enhance the effect it seeks, rather than subvert it. This duplicity lies primarily in two vital exceptions to the strategy of self-minimization or neutralization: the movie begins with a shot of the adult Phoolan staring straight into the camera and announcing her identity, proudly and abusively, '*I* am Phoolan Devi, sister-fucker, *I*!' The construction of this identity as the theme of this film is conclusively emphasized at the very end of the film with another, analogous shot—except that this time it is the young adolescent Phoolan who snarls at the camera, '*I* am Phoolan Devi, sister-fucker, *I*!' These two shots serve as the brackets that enclose and encapsulate

Phoolan's life. They signal an odd and disturbing run on between the child and the woman, especially given the susceptibility to rape.

An analysis of the need to write the true story of Phoolan Devi can be no more than conjectural. It is nevertheless necessary to speculate on the imperatives that dictate the textualizing and contextualizing of the figure of Phoolan, its transmission into the combated ideological spaces of discourses on rape and gender *as an authentic figure*. The two shots are the quotation marks by which we (are supposed to) recognize that the narration they contain is essentially 'true': in having Phoolan address the camera directly at these points, Kapur is indicating that the narrative in between is hers alone, even if there is no evident 'listener'. Or rather, the listener is marked off as the anonymous spectator addressed directly by Phoolan, the spectator who in *his* anonymity *becomes* the eye of the camera *invited* by Phoolan (because addressed directly by her) to explore in intimate detail the story of her life. The logic of the camera's intimacy therefore lies not in the narrative, nor in the research, but in the cinematic strategies by which the hypothetical anonymous spectator may be positioned as *both spectator of and participant in her life*. This, however, is not an entirely easy fit.

That the intended spectator is masculine is clear from the epithet 'sister-fucker' flung at the viewer by Phoolan. This is reinforced through one powerful sequence of shots in the film: after she is brutally abused and repeatedly gang raped by the *thakurs* of Behmai, Phoolan is shown lying clothed in rags, whimpering in pain and shock, left almost unrecognizably battered and bleeding outside her cousin's house. When he approaches her, not recognizing him she stiffens, then scrambles up and, with hips jutting out, screams in hysterical defiance, 'Come on, take me, take me again!' *at the camera*, which is approaching her with him. The 'harmless' viewer and the 'harmless' cousin are equally implicated in this scream of 'misrecognition'; they are equally addressed as potential rapists, though 'illusorily' so: the cousin because he *is not* recognized and the viewer because he *can never be* recognized. At this moment then, in the film, an irreconcilable contradiction erupts into the complicitous relation that the camera seems to share with the viewer. The viewer is jolted out of the apparent anonymity of his gaze which allows him his intimate access into Phoolan's life and into the raw reality of the (capability for) violence in his gendered sexuality. Even if, similarly, Phoolan's directly abusive 'sister-fucker' does implicate the viewer, it is in this sequence of shots that the complicity is established beyond doubt.

Why this should be the case is a matter of some significance. When Phoolan abuses the viewer through the camera, the address is lost as rhetoric (sister-fucker, besides being common slang, is an appellation that probably would not apply to all viewers) and therefore lost in the dark spaces within which Phoolan is viewed and in which the address is made. The two framing abusive shots are effective not because of the content of the appellation used, but because Kapur, in deploying sexually abusive language freely, is breaking a long-standing proscription within the world of Hindi cinema. More importantly, that such language should be used by a woman *at the viewer* is both, a claim to the (forbidden) power of 'masculine' language and through that, a direct attack on the masculinist sensibilities of the viewer. In this definition of gender positions through antagonistic provocation, however, the viewer is only addressed, not implicated. In the sequence described above, in contrast, the address is made not to the 'man' in the audience but *to his gaze*. It is the gaze itself that is implicated by Phoolan as rapacious, appropriative, intrusive. Following her rape by the Behmai *thakurs*, Phoolan is paraded naked before the village as a spectacle, the object of hundreds of male eyes and the camera too gazes at her similarly;[39] she is seen through the eyes of the *thakurs* throughout the rape and parade sequence. Immediately after this, when she is seen by the viewer through her cousin's eyes, and *offers herself* to the viewer through him in the same terms, the complacent anonymity of the view and viewer is shattered. He is revealed as implicated in her rape in having shared in the *spectacle* of it. If the camera derives its intimacy from its ability to position the viewer as both spectator and participant, here that intimacy is revealed, for one powerful moment, as being deeply exploitative, because deeply perhaps deliberately gendered.

In many senses, *Bandit Queen* is a film about gaze and perception. Kapur uses the camera complexly, ambiguously: rich, sometimes clashing colours suffuse stark, minimalized scenes—bare stretches of the Chambal ravines, unembellished village huts, shots of skeletal bridges towering over minuscule figures. In terms of montage, the *mise en scène*, framing and composition of these is rarely particularized or focused entirely on one object; there is invariably another presence, usually contrastive, that diffuses the central image, literally or metaphorically. For instance soon after their first meeting, when Vikram Mallah comes to watch Phoolan bathing at the river, the shot-reverse-shot sequence reveals Vikram's gaze as containing not just Phoolan but the mammoth pillars of the railway bridge, while Phoolan's view of him is partially obscured by the rocks he is standing behind. The camera steadily refuses to work its way around these objects that partially obscure the scene being shown, almost as if unwilling to engage with or immerse itself in anything in its totality. One reason for this holding back could be to affect objectivity, to maintain the sense that the camera's gaze is impartial, engaging in the scene multidimensionally, unwilling to distort the 'truth' even slightly by a full display of its object, or reveal itself as 'interested' in actively seeking to reveal the total object.

It ends up, curiously enough, as a secret, spying eye, peering through bars in windows and chinks in walls, gaps in curtains, whether it is when Phoolan is raped for the first time by her husband, or in the police station, or in Behmai by the *thakurs*. The camera seems to be caught in a double bind of its own making: its objectivity lies in its refusal to actively engage in the scene through total focus, but this technique seems more voyeuristic than anything else when recording rape. In fact, these scenes—and specifically the self-imposed discomfort of the camera in recording them—reveal the complicity of the camera's attempted objectivity of gaze in the violently masculinist situations it records. At the specific moment of acknowledging and recording rape, it becomes unclear whether the camera is recording it 'objectively', or whether it is a voyeur, enthralled by the spectacle of rape, celebrating its tragedy with Nusrat Fateh Ali Khan's haunting music woven into Phoolan's screams.

Mythifying Truth

Shekhar Kapur exploits Phoolan's story while offering a critique of that very exploitation. The issues of gaze and perception now get embodied within its directing principles, so to speak. *Bandit Queen* is an exercise in mythography, disguised in the intent of unravelling the myth. Any biography involves the narration of a life, its conversion into a text, and the allocation of a context. This may or may not entail the use of causality, sequentiality, cogency, multiple significations, beginnings, and endings (besides, of course, birth and death), but frequently does. These tropes of narration function as the organizational means to produce the significance(s) of 'character' that render a life intelligible. The problem is—what kind of intelligibility does Kapur produce out of the vast information available to him and why? Beset by rapists and only momentarily sexually happy, Kapur's film ignore its own title, offering no account of her many skills, leadership, and the processes by which she acquired them, giving no evidence of how Phoolan became and remained the queen of the ravines. The narrative is so constrained by the limits of *Kapur's* fetishized imagination of rape that it fails the moment victimhood is relinquished by the female subject who evidently learnt how to deal with men severely and control and lead them as well, master weaponry, negotiate ravines, harsh territory and governments. Within the context of the film, Phoolan's vocation is a confused one. Is it to avenge the outrage and violation of her fragile feminine honour or to defend the rights of her caste and women, as the book claims? Both apparently, as the deprivations of caste and gender are woven together as indeed they are in everyday life. Yet if we consider what motivates her violence in the film—beating her husband senseless, the Behmai slaughter—it is the experience of rape; caste becomes incidental. A hypothetical but revealing question is: What if the story were about a man? Would it have invested the sexual explanation with a greater value than a caste-based one? This question indicates the narrative and ideological investment in sexual difference in a film whose protagonist defied most rules of sexual difference.

An additional reason for the disappearance of the bandit queen lies in the relation tracked between masculinity and violence—an equation that isn't established in the book—which breaks down when Phoolan has to turn violent, which she did to become and remain first a bandit and then the Bandit Queen. Though Phoolan is often spoken of as the reincarnation of bloodthirsty Kali, especially after Mallah institutes her as the goddess, the relation she has with violence is shown as forced and occasional. The mythologizing is happening here at least at two levels: on the one hand, Phoolan is woman, vulnerable and prone to violation and on the other, she is the indomitable Woman who cannot be destroyed because the violence *makes* Woman—fierce, indestructible. In other words, it is the occurrence of violence that engenders Woman. To locate the transformation of Phoolan into vengeful goddess via rape is to draw that very mode of the goddess into the realm of the violable. If this is the case, in what precise way does female violence come to be distinguished and distinguishable from male violence, especially since Phoolan had 55 charges against her, of which 22 were for murder? Masculine violence seems easier to explain: it is unproblematically self-evident. Men rape, brutalize, plunder, kill, and plot as if born with the will and talent to do so. The problem being addressed is a conflation between the statistical fact of greater male violence and a definition of masculinity, which is accounted for in the film as simply masculinity.

Female violence needs not just explanation, but a sexualized one in order to make it both feminine and comprehensible. Through this, both male and female violence are first differentiated and then mythologized. For it is only through her Kali avatar that Phoolan is understood, as if to say that in order to transcend historicity and achieve the immortal status of Woman, women must first be violated, understand and learn the logic of that violence, and teach it to men. It seems that in Kapur's imagination, Phoolan could be heroized only if she was victimized as woman and retained as woman in essential ways—victim and non/apolitical, private creature. The lesson to be learnt is that feminine wrath may be kept in check through some passable and regular sex, adequate food, and male protection. There is simply no space left to record the Bandit Queen—ruthless strategist, leader, and negotiator who brought three state governments and the central government to the negotiating table and whose formidable familiarity with the ravines allowed her to remain undisputed leader of a gang, some of whom were higher caste men. We have seen how these omissions emerge from and implicate the entire narrative. *Bandit Queen* is not a biographical record of the life of a female bandit; it is a watered down account of a middle-class female vigilante determined by her sexuality and a personal history of rape.

The narrative, discursive and cinematic devices that are routinely deployed in the representation of rape manifest the importance of visibilizing women but silencing them and absenting their subjectivities. Rape, as a stock narrative device to facilitate the expression of male subjectivity and patriarchal values, demonstrates the inseparability of representations of violence from the notations of gender. Both of these, as Teresa de Lauretis has argued, are contingent on the reciprocal relation between power and sexual difference.[40] The violence of this representation lies also in the way in which the subject of pain, the context of rape, the body of the raped woman, and her response are deployed to perpetuate and validate masculinities that engendered the violence in the first instance and are used as narrative opportunities to present masculine subjectivities and advance the consolidation of homosociality. The transformation of (feminine) body into dematerialized site, subjectivity into compliant void, history into myth, and action into metaphor, which is achieved through the transformation of the visceral experiential into the ideational and then the ideological, signals the patriarchal uses of rape. The consequent paradoxes that ensue include a conflation between female pleasure and female pain, a conceptual predicament that only guarantees the continuance and eroticization of violence.

Notes

1. While now the amended rape laws grant a privileged status to the raped person's claim, they do so only to the extent that they have shifted the onus of proof. Rape trials, on the other hand, continue to rely on the old practice of denying rape by impugning consent through various means, including character assassination.
2. Rajeswari Sunder Rajan, 'Life After Rape: narrative, theory and feminism:', in M. R. Higonnet, ed., *Borderwork*, Ithaca (NY): Cornell University Press, 1994, p. 73. In this context, C. S. Lakshmi states, 'And attempts are made to write this notion of tradition on the body of the woman to dictate its movement, needs, attire, aspirations and spheres of existence, even while this body is moving over time, space and history', C.S. Lakshmi, 'Bodies Called Women: Some Thoughts on Gender, Ethnicity and Nation', *Economic and Political Weekly*, vol. XXXII, no. 46, 15 November 1997, p. 2953.
3. The stakes are clarified by two instances: first, in the differential treatment by both media (type and extent of coverage) and institutional response such as the unprecedented speed with which the cases were dealt with legally in cases where the victim was a white, well-placed foreigner. Implicit in such a response are the imagined meanings of the rape for the national community to which that woman

belongs. The heightened sensitivity towards (international) perceptions of the 'Indian man' and sexual trauma during cross-racial rape clearly concede the investment in discourses of sexual ownership. Similarly, this is the case with inter-communal/ethnic/class/caste rapes. In contrast to this, we have the typical, slow callousness with which umpteen rape cases of Indian women are treated.

4. This is implicit in Monique Plaza's 1981 critique of Foucault's position on rape.
5. I have deliberately not cited consensual sex as the opposite of rape. The prevalence of marital rape, and the general and persistent legal trend toward erasing the possibility of rape having occurred ('Did she actually want/provoke it?' and 'Did she actually mean 'no'?'), are not ways of denying rape, but of continuing the practice of it through the elision of the meanings it has for women.
6. Lévi-Strauss observes how rape constitutes a violation of the customary rules of exchange of women between men (marriage). See Joplin in L.A. Higgens and B.R. Silver (eds.), *Rape and Representation*, New York, NY: Columbia University Press, 1991.
7. The association of penetration with power gets expounded linguistically in the aggressive use of sexual terminology such as 'fuck', 'screw', or 'bugger' or 'nail' to refer to experiences of defeat, violation, and hierarchy.
8. Rape laws are an extension of property laws that protect men's interests (Brownmiller, 1975, pp. 16–17). S. Brownmiller's rather ahistorical and blunted understanding of private property (the phenomenon and notions of it have changed) and social relations (people are not treated as chattel even if consigned thus) ignores several causal relationships. It is more useful when elaborated by the social denial of autonomy on which rape is based and by the varying practices of rape. The issue of rape may arise only within the context of a prior acknowledgement of freedom. Therefore, even if rape becomes an issue in the case of slaves or the lower castes, it may arise as issues of proper treatment or as administrative matters, e.g. compensation, the neglect of or rights of bastard children, etc. In India, rape is still not an issue of violation of integrity in caste rape, as the political processes and judicial rulings in the Mathura and Bhanwari Devi cases show. Practices like *doli* or the *devadasi* system underscore the ownership issue as one where the violation is not absented, but in fact becomes a marker of status within social relations.
9. Veena Das, 'Sexual Violence, Discursive Formations and the State', *Economic and Political Weekly*, vol. 31, 1996.
10. That women are taken by surprise and to 'safe' spots, normally by a friend or acquaintance, overpowered physically and by shock, that they prefer to be raped rather than be battered, to remain anonymous and silent rather than be exposed and ostracised and stigmatised (as loose and fallen) are factors that, strangely enough, are hardly considered.
11. For instance, rapes committed by Japanese soldiers are somehow worse than those committed by American or European soldiers; rapes committed by Muslims are worse than those committed by Hindus; and rapes committed by 'native' men are less objectionable and violative than those committed by 'foreign' men. Likewise, the rape of 'decent' women—middle or upper class, educated—is worse than the rape of less privileged women. The rape of men is deemed to be more appalling than that of women.
12. J.R. Schwendinger and Herman, *Rape and Inequality*, Beverly Hills, CA: Sage Publications, 1983.

13. Rapists or sexual aggressors who are powerfully situated within society are hardly ever convicted. Madhu Kishwar (1999) discusses the importance of slander as a means of controlling women. Whether to prevent them from forms of sexual agency, or from seeking reparation for acts of sexual aggression through police, legal, or community action, slander is permanently attached to women. This brings me back to the point of woman as causal agent in rape and the ways in which women get implicated in rape willy-nilly. Studies of crime in American society show how accusations of rape, fuelled by sexual myths and anxieties, are used as a weapon against black and ethnically marginalised men (Schwendinger, 1983). War tribunals have rarely convicted rapists. Rape in war is on the borderline between individualistic and institutionalised rape (ibid.). Sexual harassment—whether it results in rape or not—is treated as a prerogative by the men who commit it, and as an occupational hazard by those who hear about it and by the women who suffer it.
14. P. Agarwal, 'Savarkar, Surat and Draupadi', in T. Sarkar and Urvashi Butalia, eds., *Women and Right-Wing Movements*, New Delhi: Kali for Women, 1996, p. 43.
15. T. Sarkar and Urvashi Butalia, eds., *Women and Right-Wing Movements*, New Delhi: Kali for Women, 1996, p. 77.
16. Syeda Hameed et al., *The Survivors Speak: Fact-finding by a Women's Panel*, 2002, p.14.
17. This radical and essentialist position is denied by the ample evidence of the familiarity of a 'male imagination' with rape, as we see from the popularity of the rape fantasy within literature, cinema, pornographic literature, and films, the Freudian slip that women eagerly anticipate rape. Several works document the agility of the male imagination when it comes to the question of rape and the implications of that for women.
18. Monique Plaza, 'Our Damages and Their Compensation. Rape: The Will Not to Know of Michel Foucault', *Feminist Issues*, vol. 1, no. 3, 1981.
19. These include the belief that women experience and recover from rape differently from men, that they enjoy it/never recover from it, and so on. Yet women do experience rape differently from men. It is established that anticipated social ostracism, a hostile juridical apparatus, and inadequate support mechanisms expand the significance of rape—even psychologically—beyond the act. Very importantly, an unwanted pregnancy may make it even more difficult for a woman to conceal or forget a rape, as we see in incidents of ethnic cleansing. Equally, the social premium of premarital female virginity makes rape socially hazardous for her.
20. Lata Mani (in Niranjana et al., 1993) points out that sati is an exception to a routine erasure of violence, since the death and sometimes the pain of the women have to be recorded to confirm the significance of the act for patriarchy. However, I argue that there is never an erasure of violence committed against women, only a denial or reinterpretation of it, which indexes and magnifies the scope of violence.
21. For a detailed analysis of the film, see Karen Gabriel, 'Draupadi's Moment in Sita Syntax: Violations of the Past and Construction of Community in Kamal Hassan's *Hey Ram!*' in T. Abraham, ed., *Women and the Politics of Violence*, New Delhi: Shakti Books, 2002.
22. Das in Veena Das and Ashis Nandy, *The Word and the World: Fantasy, Symbols and Records*, New Delhi: Sage Publications, 1986.
23. The Central Board of Film Certification as Explanation to Clauses (E) and (F) of General Principles maintained that the 'importunation of women' was to be

included in objectionable material (see Sarkar, 1982, p. 114). See also The Indecent Representation of Women (Prohibition) Act, 1986 and The Indecent Representation of Women (Prohibition) Rules, 1987 for views on depictions of disciplinary tactics such as slapping the wife or beloved and courtship through eve-teasing.

24. Teresa De Lauretis has argued that masculine desire invests all narrative. See de Lauretis (1982) and especially 'The Violence of Rhetoric' in de Lauretis (1986). While that narrative power needs to be challenged, a challenge at that level is insufficient to counter the power of masculine desire. A nuanced understanding of the activation and practices of masculine desire and power may be found in Sangari (1993, pp. 867–82).
25. A. Roy, 'The Great Indian Rape Trick (Parts I and II)', *Sunday Observer*, 26 August–3 September and 11–17 September 1994, p. 62.
26. In India, these debates have rarely been polarized in the way in which they have been in the West and have been alert to the ways in which social stratifications like caste, religion, and class intersect to complicate relations between men and women, and between women and structural power.
27. Das, in Veena Das and Ashis Nandy, *The Word and the World: Fantasy, Symbols and Records*.
28. The clip is available on http://indianmasalaclips.blogspot.com/2007/09/shilpa-shirodkar-rape-vdo-from.html.
29. See also Karen Gabriel, 2005a and 2005b for a discussion of this film.
30. Madhu Kishwar, 'The Bandit Queen', *Manushi*, vol. 84, September–October 1994, p. 35.
31. Mala Sen, who wrote the book *India's Bandit Queen: The True Story of Phoolan Devi* (1991) on which the film was based, also wrote the script of the film. However, the film makes several important and hazardous departures from the book and apparently from the script as well. One of these is a single-minded focus on rape and the implication of that for Phoolan. In her scathing critique of the film, Arundhati Roy noted that Phoolan Devi spent three-and-a-half years in the ravines. She was wanted on 48 counts of major crime, 22 murder, the rest kidnaps-for-ransom and looting. Even simple mathematics tells me that we've been told just half the story.... How about changing the title of the film to: Phoolan Devi's Rape and Abject Humiliation: The True half-Truth? (In A. Roy, op. cit., p. 8.)
32. 'Sometimes various versions of the same event—versions that totally conflict with each other i.e. Phoolan's version, a journalist's version, or an eyewitnesses account—are all presented to the reader in the book. What emerges is a complex, intelligent and human book full of ambiguity, full of concern, full of curiosity about who this woman called Phoolan Devi really is' (A. Roy, op. cit., p. 1).
33. Cited in A. Roy, ibid.
34. A. Roy, ibid.
35. Mala Sen's book records how Phoolan Devi never acknowledged her alleged rapes, never used the word *balatkar* (rape) in relation to her ordeals but rather referred to them as *mazaak* (fun) that was had at her expense.
36. However, when Channel Four commissioned the film, Phoolan Devi, then in prison, was paid the paltry amount of 'less than one percent of the six hundred and fifty thousand pound budget of the film' (A. Roy, op. cit.).
37. Shekhar Kapur also lambasted the Censor Board which had ordered minor cuts of what they felt was gratuitous violence in the film or an Adult certificate for the film. He cashed in on a misplaced western sympathy for even his treatment of

Phoolan, and claimed that the Censor Board and indeed the nation were not very sympathetic to serious artists. In short he claimed that he (like Rushdie) was being victimized, a cry that found an echo only in the West. Phoolan was marginalized except as a part of an ever-growing gang of perpetrators. Unfazed by the counter arguments that came from several quarters including women's groups, the press, and the CBFC, Kapur continued to claim victim status, even through the diatribe against Phoolan.

38. Madhu Kishwar, op. cit.
39. The camera pulls back into a long shot that documents the smallness of Phoolan at that moment of exposure. Ghosh [in Kapur and Cossman, eds., 1996] feels that the rape scenes are pornographic though P. Gopal believes that the film was more ambiguous than that. Cf. P. Gopal, 'Of Victims and Vigilantes: The Bandit Queen Controversy', *Thamyris*, vol. 4, no. 1, 1997, pp. 73–102. I am inclined to agree with Gopal.
40. de Lauretis, 1986, op. cit., p. 43.

REFERENCES

Agarwal, P., 'Savarkar, Surat and Draupadi', in T. Sarkar and Urvashi Butalia, eds., *Women and Right-Wing Movements*, New Delhi: Kali for Women, 1996.

Bourke, Joanne, *Rape: A History from 1860 to the Present*, London: Virago, 2007.

Brownmiller, S., *Against Our Will: Men, Women and Rape*, London: Penguin, 1975.

Das, Veena, 'Sexual Violence, Discursive Formations and the State', *Economic and Political Weekly*, vol. 31, 1996, pp. 35–7.

Das, Veena, ed., *Mirrors of Violence: Communities, Riots and Survivors in South Asia*, New Delhi: Oxford University Press, 1990.

Das, Veena, and Ashis Nandy, *The Word and the World: Fantasy, Symbols and Records*, New Delhi: Sage Publications, 1986.

de Lauretis, Teresa, *Alice Doesn't: Feminism, Semiotics, Cinema*, Bloomington, IN: Indiana University Press, 1982.

———, *Technologies of Gender: Essays on Theory, Film and Fiction*, Bloomington, IN: Indiana University Press, 1986.

Gabriel, Karen, 'Draupadi's Moment in Sita Syntax: Violations of the Past and Construction of Community in Kamal Hassan's *Hey Ram!*', in T. Abraham, ed., *Women and the Politics of Violence*, New Delhi: Shakti Books, 2002, pp. 76-124.

———, *Imaging a Nation: The Sexual Economies of the Contemporary Mainstream Bombay Cinema (1970–2000)*, Maastricht: Shaker Publishers, 2005a.

———, 'Dethroning the Queen: Gender, Sex, Caste and the Bandit Queen', in Abhilasha Kumari, ed., *Communicator, Journal of the Indian Institute of Mass Communication*, vol. XXXX, no. 1, January–June 2005b.

Gopal, P., 'Of Victims and Vigilantes: The Bandit Queen Controversy', *Thamyris*, vol. 4, no. 1, 1997, pp. 73–102.

Gopalan, L., 'Avenging Women in Indian Cinema', *Screen*, vol. 38, no. 1, 1997, pp. 42–59.

Hameed, Syeda et al., *The Survivors Speak: Fact-finding by a Women's Panel*, 2002.

Higgens, L.A., and B.R. Silver, eds., *Rape and Representation*, New York, NY: Columbia University Press, 1991.

Kapur, R., and B. Cossman, eds., *Feminist Terrains in Legal Domains: Interdisciplinary Essays on Women and Law in India*, New Delhi: Kali for Women, 1996.

Kishwar, Madhu, 'The Bandit Queen', *Manushi*, vol. 84, September–October 1994, pp. 34–7.

———, *Off the Beaten Track: Rethinking Gender Justice for Indian Women*, New Delhi: Oxford University Press, 1999.

Lakshmi, C.S., 'Bodies Called Women: Some Thoughts on Gender, Ethnicity and Nation', *Economic and Political Weekly*, vol. XXXII, no. 46, 15 November 1997, pp. 2953–62.

Mani, Lata, 'Reading Eyewitness Accounts of Sati', in Tejaswini Niranjana, P. Sudhir, and V. Dhareshwar, eds., *Interrogating Modernity: Culture and Colonialism in India*, Calcutta: Seagull, 1993, pp. 273–90.

Plaza, Monique, 'Our Damages and Their Compensation. Rape: The Will Not to Know of Michel Foucault', *Feminist Issues*, vol. 1, no. 3, 1981, pp. 25–35.

Roy, A., 'The Great Indian Rape Trick (Parts I and II)', *Sunday Observer*, 26 August–3 September and 11–17 September 1994.

Sangari, K., 'Consent, Agency and Rhetorics of Incitement', *Economic and Political Weekly*, vol. 28, no. 18, 1993, pp. 867–82.

Sarkar, K., *You Can't Please Everybody! Film Censorship: The Inside Story*, Bombay: IBH Publishing Company, 1982.

Schwendinger, J.R., and Herman, *Rape and Inequality*, Beverly Hills, CA: Sage Publications, 1983.

Sen, Mala, *India's Bandit Queen: The True Story of Phoolan Devi*, London: Harvill, 1991.

Sunder Rajan, Rajeswari, 'Life After Rape: narrative, theory and feminism:', in M. R. Higonnet, ed., *Borderwork*, Ithaca, NY: Cornell University Press, 1994, pp. 61–78.

———, ed., *Signposts: Gender Issues in Post-independence India*, New Delhi: Kali for Women, 1999.

Virdi, J., 'Reverence, Rape—and then Revenge: Popular Hindi Cinema's "Woman's Film"', *Screen*, vol. 40, no. 1, 1999, pp. 17–37.

9

Frames of Cinematic History: *The* Tawa'if *in* Umrao Jan *and* Pakeezah

Shweta Sachdeva Jha

HISTORY AND popular Hindi films have a long and complex relationship. Films such as *Mughal-e-Azam* (1960) and *Gandhi* (1982) are still remembered for their brilliant recreation of famous historical figures and milieu.[1] On one hand genre-based categorization in film scholarship defines 'historical films' as those films that recreate 'historical' pasts. Such categorizations are anchored in frameworks of 'event histories' or 'life histories' of famous people. On the other hand historians of subaltern groups and practitioners of women's histories have emphasized the significance of rethinking 'event' or 'persona' based history writing. In this article, therefore, rather than focusing on such 'event histories' or 'life histories', I shall try to determine the coordinates of the cinematic imagination of history through a study of the cinematic *tawa'if*, locating her within a larger social and cultural context.

Popular Hindi films have an intricate relationship with the postcolonial imaginary in India. Studies on spectatorship, film stars, and the emergence of multiplex theatres in India have shown us the significance of understanding films in a broader cultural context. Consequently, in order to understand how popular Hindi films negotiate history through the *tawa'if*, I shall study the cinematic imagination of the *tawa'if* within the historical context of these films as well as the wider relationship between the actresses who play the *tawa'if* and their star images amongst spectators.[2]

This article has emerged out of my ongoing attempt to write a social history of the *tawa'if* in colonial north India.[3] And it is an attempt to raise a few questions about the complexity of reading history through popular Hindi films. As case studies, I discuss two films—Kamal Amrohi's *Pakeezah* (1971) and Muzaffar Ali's *Umrao Jan* (1981)—and their cinematic framing of the *tawa'if* as a historical subject. Although scholars have studied them as part of the 'courtesan genre', these films also imagine the *tawa'if* as a historical artefact and as an embodiment of the nation. While discussing *Umrao Jan*, for instance Sumita Chakravarty rightly points out that 'although the story has primarily Muslim characters, the film draws upon Hindu elements as well in its music and lyrics'.[4] This re-imagination of the *tawa'if* culture as representative of a desirable cultural and religious unity has been part of the popular cinematic discourse on the nation. Yet this desirability needs to be contextualized in terms of the emergent conflicting discourses on communal and religious identities in postcolonial India. In this context, the reimagination of Lucknow as the seat of *ganga–jumna tahzib*, or composite Hindu-Muslim culture, symbolized an ideal moment in history where the *tawa'if* became one of its main representatives. The films to be discussed in this article come together in their re-visioning of this *nawabi* past, usually symbolized by Lucknow. According to Chakravarty,

> Although courtesans were located in all parts of India, it is Lucknow that popular culture has identified as their representative site. For the minority Muslim population and for Indians generally, Lucknow connotes the 'civilized' outpost or remnants of bygone Muslim imperial splendour, the elegance of the Urdu language, and lived social graces. Such a complex of sentiments, in light of occasional but ongoing tensions between communal groups, makes the task of the Bombay film a delicate one and notions of authenticity (to a prior text, to history, to contemporary life) highly complicated at best.[5]

For Mukul Kesavan, the representation of the *tawa'if*, and the use of Urdu and the backdrops of Awadh and Lucknow, are means by which popular Hindi films construct an 'Islamicate' culture where 'Islamicate would refer not directly to the religion, Islam, itself but to the social and cultural complex historically associated with Islam and the Muslims, both among Muslims themselves and even when found among non-Muslims'.[6]

In her reading of these 'Islamicate films', Rachel Dwyer has problematically argued that both *Pakeezah* and *Umrao Jan* are enjoyed by Muslims and Hindus for different reasons. Muslims, she suggests,

> feel a sense of nostalgia for a glorious past, which could be interpreted as being destroyed by the advent of modernity and westernisation. This could be augmented by sorrow at the present low status of Muslims in India... There may also be sadness at the loss of the pleasures shown in many elements of performance, which, since they are unacceptable to orthodox Islam that rejects alcohol, illicit sex and performance of dance and music, are no longer available to those who wish to remain within the Muslim community of India.[7]

She further sees the *tawa'if* as a representation of decadent femininity, which in turn locates Muslims in the past and therefore as anachronistic in the present, thus visualized as the 'other'. She contextualizes this reading in the rise of a *Hindutva*-ized state and sees the filmmakers Amrohi and Ali as figures who 'mourned the passing of an era'.

To the contrary, I wish to argue that the relationship between films, history, filmmakers, and the audience is not so simple. Through close textual reading of these films, I wish to show that both films imagine the past in different ways. Although they are similar in certain aspects of their cinematic re-imagination of the *tawa'if*, yet they need to be understood for their own specific methods of negotiating history. These films cannot just be seen as visions of nostalgia nor can the pleasures of any community be so easily categorized. I feel it is important to look at these films as individual texts and to map their variations and similarities in the wider discourse on films and history. In determining this relationship, I choose to focus on the cinematic narratives, *mise-en-scène*/sets, and the choice of famous actresses whose 'star texts' further add to the imagination of the *tawa'if* as a performer. [8]

Films and History

As early as the 1960s, philosophers of history had started analyzing the relationship between the content and form of history writing. Seminal to these theories of historiography were arguments that shifted the focus from questions on objectivity, causation, and explanation to questions on historical narratives. Scholars such as Louis O. Mink and Hayden White focused on the centrality of the narrative in 'historical enterprise'. For Mink, the narrative structure was itself a 'cognitive instrument' or a 'mode of comprehension', and for White, historical narratives needed to be analyzed as 'verbal fictions, the contents of which are as much invented as found and the forms of which have more in common with their counterparts in literature than they have with those in sciences'. [9] Some of the key issues that this raises for us are the ways in which films fit into our readings of history and the specificities of cinematic narratives of history. We need to locate the modes through which cinematic adaptations of novels such as *Umrao Jan 'Ada'* recreate a socio-cultural milieu and to compare them with literary narratives of the past.

In the last few years, films and their relationship with history have attracted rich debate and research amongst scholars. [10] Genre-based criticism of films discusses history in relation to what are called 'history films or historical films'. These films are theorized as being based on 'historical events' or 'historical personae'. Pierre Sorlin defines and categorizes films as 'historical films' or 'history films' on the basis of their characters, dialogue, and representation of the past. [11] Rosenstone further argues:

> There are two ways of looking at the inventions of characters, dialogue, and incidents that are an inevitable part of the dramatic history film…not in terms of the specific details they present, but rather in the overall sense of the past they convey, the rich images and visual metaphors they provide to us for thinking historically. You may also see the history film as part of a separate realm of representation and discourse, one not meant to provide literal truths about the past (as if our written history can provide literal truths) but metaphoric truths which work, to a large degree, as a kind of commentary on, and challenge to, traditional historical discourse.[12]

Thus, a 'history film' deals consciously with a certain past, although our opinions, as an audience, of its depiction of the past may differ from the intention and the practice of the filmmaker. In the context of commercial Hindi films, Chakravarty asserts that the cinematic language of a 'historical film' is distinct.

> The choice of representing history on the screen is also made by the filmmaker to articulate a 'new' language of desire vis-à-vis the cinematic apparatus itself. The historical film, in short, makes a distinct break with normative expectations of realism and transparency of the text and strains toward the grand, the opulent, the classical.[13]

These studies of history/historical films warn us against searching for a 'truthful' or 'accurate' rendition of the past. Rather, they reiterate that popular films have a unique relationship with history. Sometimes, however, as in the case of films like *Veer Savarkar* (2001), questions over 'historical accuracy' become contentious fields for ideologically variant representations and reconstructions of the past.

If the use of spectacle and the representation of characters in popular memory are characteristic of historical films, then both *Pakeezah* and *Umrao Jan* fit into this genre as they try to negotiate the *nawabi* past through their reconstruction of the *tawa'if* as a historical subject. In their attempt to recreate or re-present this historical past, both *Umrao Jan* and *Pakeezah* invest in elaborate sets, props, and costumes, wherein a whole team of editors, music directors, art directors, costume designers, and script writers try to recreate the *tawa'if* of a historical milieu. They attempt to create audio-visual narratives of a quintessential *lakhnawi* culture in nineteenth and twentieth century north India through melodious Hindustani music, including ghazals in Urdu, and stylized *kathak* performances by famous actresses who play the role of the *tawa'if*.[14] However, I will theorize, that both these films share and differ in their historical re-imaginations. Also, these films should not be confined to a study of genres; rather, they should be analyzed for their specific cinematic vocabularies and their location as cultural referents and co-ordinates in popular memory. Through the *tawa'if*, these films revisit a historical and cultural past and become part of the postcolonial imaginary. Before studying the *tawa'if* within the frames of cinematic history, let us see how the *tawa'if* is perceived in academic scholarship.

The Historical *Tawa'if*

Most literature on the *tawa'if* has denied her a history of her own by equating her with the *ganika*, the *vaishya*, the *nautch* girl, and even the Japanese *geisha*.[15] By using the term *tawa'if* interchangeably for a courtesan and a prostitute without a specific regional or cultural location, scholars have denied her a specific identity as a historical subject. Although she is often remembered as a cultured woman, she entertained elite nawabs in nineteenth century Lucknow. Known to excel in the arts of courtly etiquette, poetry, music, dance, and the art of seduction, she became a symbol for a nostalgic courtly past considered lost in the aftermath of the rebellion of 1857.[16] According to Kumkum Sangari, 'The courtesan also became a recuperative "heritage" figure laden with the baggage of ancient India and *nawabi* Awadh.'[17]

The *tawa'if* first became a subject of historical enquiry in the work of Veena Talwar Oldenburg, who had conducted interviews with the surviving generations of the *tawa'if* during her fieldwork trips to Lucknow between 1976–84. Her study revealed the hierarchical and varied institution of the *kotha* or salon as a site of performance and contestation. The owner of the *kotha* was called a *chaudhrayan* and was the senior-most *tawa'if*. The *kotha* women included different types of performers, who differed in terms of their clientele and nature of work. She argues that the *kotha* was both an institution of performance and a household unit. In the aftermath of the rebellion of 1857, changes in *nawabi* patronage and changing policies by the colonial state in the late nineteenth and early twentieth century eventually led to the marginalisaton of the *tawa'if* and the *kotha*. Oldenburg argues that the *tawa'if* mocked the patriarchal institution of marriage or heterosexual relationships as normative by leading a lifestyle of resistance as lesbians. [18]

After the rebellion of 1857, new municipal polices of the colonial state, especially the Contagious Diseases Act (1868) and the wide-scale attempts to restructure and 'sanitize' the city drastically affected the *tawa'if*. They were forced to register as common prostitutes and were sometimes even forced to sell their *kotha* and move outside the confines of the city. Charu Gupta has shown that both the colonial state and Indian reformist associations such as the Arya Samaj shared similar ideologies and pushed for 'sanitized' city spaces and the removal of the *tawa'if* to the outskirts to ensure 'clean' and clearly demarcated spaces of habitation and indulgence. The famous among them continued to perform at grand occasions but many others resisted the reformist propaganda through formal protests.[19]

Scholarship on the links between the state and prostitution in colonial India is still emerging. Sumanta Banerjee has shown us the rich possibilities of a historical and cultural enquiry by studying the prostitutes and performers of nineteenth century Bengal.[20] However, most studies on the *tawa'if* share a nostalgia for the *tawa'if* culture but do not perceive them as active subjects. There has scarcely been any study on the *tawa'if* as performers and poets in courtly cultures or urban contexts that attempt to understand their location across a broader historical and cartographic framework. Elsewhere, I argue that the *tawa'if* need to be seen as historical subjects whose subjectivity and agency can be configured by rethinking ideas of 'archive', 'sources', and discursive categories of performance and history.[21] In this article, I confine my study to the 'imagined *tawa'if*' in literary and cinematic representations.[22]

Literary and Cinematic Representations of the *Tawa'if*

The *tawa'if* was a prominent subject in early Urdu novels such as Sajjad Husain 'Anjum' Kasmandavi's *Nashtar* (The Surgeon's Knife, 1893), an Urdu translation of a Persian autobiographical novel written by Hasan Shah of Kanpur in 1790, and Mirza Muhammad Hadi 'Ruswa's *Umrao Jan 'Ada'* (1899–1901).[23] Later, in *Bazaar-e-Husn* (1917) and *Yeh Kothewalian* (These Women of the Kotha) (1958?), both Premchand and Amritlal Nagar wrote of the *tawa'if* within a socio-realist framework.[24] Nagar based his text on interviews conducted with the *tawa'if* in the 1950s in Lucknow. Both the authors brought to the fore the terrible condition of prostitutes in the cities and critiqued the social apathy and moral condemnation of prostitutes as degraded women. Both these authors continued a long tradition of literary representations of courtesans in Hindi/Urdu literature, where the 'courtesan–dancer in "classical" times becomes the receptacle of the ideological concerns of the day'.[25] It needs to be seen if the cinematic *tawa'if* was imagined in a similar way as the literary *tawa'if*.

Pakeezah (The Pure One) was planned in the 1950s by Kamal Amrohi, who had started his career as an independent film director of a ghostly psychodrama and a classic of the black and white era, *Mahal* (1949), starring Ashok Kumar and Madhubala. His creation of an eerie backdrop through a combination of scenic and sound effects, use of light and dark spaces, bare sets, mesmerizing music, and haunting lyrics, especially the song '*Ayega ayega...anewala*' (He will come...) marked him as a filmmaker with a style unique to himself. Later, Amrohi went on to write the dialogues for the big budget *Mughal-e-Azam* while planning for *Pakeezah*. In 1956, *Filmfare* magazine carried a report on the start of the shooting.[26]

The film was eventually completed in 1971, about 15 years after this announcement. The story revolved around the life of a *tawa'if*, Sahib Jan. Meena Kumari played the roles of Sahib Jan as well as the *tawa'if's* mother Nargis. Meena Kumari had married Amrohi in the 1950s but by the time the film was complete, they had been divorced for about seven years. The film was completed a few months before her premature death in 1972. Her co-star in the film was Raj Kumar, who played her love interest, Salim. Earlier, Amrohi had wanted Ashok Kumar to play the role of Salim, but by the time the film actually materialized, Ashok Kumar was to play the role of Salim's uncle, Shahabuddin.

Pakeezah begins with a scene in which a *Kathak* dancer dances around a candle flame and a voiceover tells us the story of the *tawa'if* Nargis and her lover Shahabuddin. The scene and the tone of the voice set the moral tone of the film where the *tawa'if* belongs to a sullied world of moral decadence and her profession as a dancer and singer mark her as a public woman. The inherent purity of the *tawa'if* is the prominent theme of the film. '*Pakeezah*' literally means the pure one, or one of the pure heart. The repeated use of *pak* (pure) and *napak* (impure) within the film, the use of metaphors in dialogues, and the use of visuals and colours make the semiotics of the film heavily symbolic. For instance white is foregrounded as the colour of purity, and whenever the *tawa'if* are not performing in their colourful and glossy attire, they wear flowing white cottons.

Sahib Jan uses disturbing metaphors to argue that the presence of the *tawa'if* symbolise the lack of humanity in a society. She compares the *tawa'if* to corpses on display whose souls are dead. The bazaar for her is like a cemetery where the *tawa'if* are like corpses left in open graves, displaying their 'glittering finery'. Through visual images such as a bird in a cage, a bird with its wings clipped, and a kite caught on a tree, the film establishes visual and linguistic codes that run parallel to the main narrative. At the same time, these codes reiterate the inhuman nature of the institution of prostitution in contrast to the pure soul of the *tawa'if* herself. The film shows that even women of elite backgrounds such as Sahib Jan, who is the daughter of Shahabuddin, a nawab whose father prides himself on his lineage, can end up being a *tawa'if* in a society that accepts prostitution as an institution.

Pakeezah begins in a bazaar in Delhi but moves on to Suhagpur, Ramnagar, and Patiala, and refers to Panipat and Hyderabad. It does not have one continuous, specific spatial or historical location; rather, it uses mythic spaces such as the idyllic forest and the consumerist bazaar as opposing locations. It is this conjunction of the specific and the mythic which is unique to popular Hindi films and their cinematic imagination of the past. The imaginary setting wherein the romance blossoms between the two main characters, the *tawa'if* Sahib Jan and her lover Salim, is also located in a moment between historical time and contemporary time in the nationspace.

In the plot, Nargis has to take refuge in a cemetery after being ostracized by her husband, Shahabuddin's father and the patriarch of the household. Shahabuddin's father is a *hakim* (doctor) who takes pride in his privileged lineage and refuses to accept Nargis as his son's bride as she is a *tawa'if*. She runs away from the house and dies a lonely death while Shahabuddin continues to search for her. Before dying she leaves a letter for him informing him of the birth of a daughter, Sahib Jan. However, the letter reaches him after a gap of 17 years; by then, his daughter has become *tawa'if* Sahib Jan who is brought up in a *kotha* by her aunt. Later, Shahabuddin's nephew Salim falls in love with Sahib Jan. Initially, Salim doesn't realize that she is a *tawa'if* but when he does, he still offers to marry her and renames her *Pakeezah*—the one with a pure heart. This renaming is significant as it is meant to recognize her as a woman of honour, unlike a performer in north India who would be identified with a name with a suffix such as *Jan* or *Bai*. However, Sahib Jan considers herself to be a woman of ill repute. She runs away moments before she is about to get married and does not offer any explanation to Salim. As part of a series of misunderstandings, Salim's marriage is fixed elsewhere and Sahib Jan is invited to perform a *mujra* (dance performance) in his household.[27] In a dramatic unfolding of events, Shahabuddin realizes that she is his daughter and she is eventually married to Salim. In the final scene, Sahib Jan is recognized as the daughter of a man of honour and her wedding procession leaves from the *kotha* for Salim's household along with the corpse of her father, who is accidentally killed by Sahib Jan's authoritarian grandfather.

One of the key issues is the way in which the film visualizes the *tawa'if* and her milieu. In terms of the construction of a historical setting, the film uses elaborately designed sets, *ghazals*, choreographed performances accompanied by musicians and *kathak* dancers, and sets and décor within the studio space which are inspired by Mughal miniatures. For example the song '*Inhi logon ne le lina dupatta mera*' (These people who took away my veil…) foregrounds Sahib Jan as a performer, with the bazaar as a backdrop where we can see other *tawa'if* dancing in courtyards. To create a world of late nineteenth and early twentieth century princely culture, rich nawabs are shown to lead lavish lifestyles and patronize the *tawa'if*.[28] These actors wear expensive costumes and visit palatial *kothas* such as Ghulabi Mahal with its lavish interiors and beautiful fountains and pools.

The film uses rich carpets, huge chandeliers, silver spittoons, and betel nut cases as historical artefacts.

The visualization of the song '*Thare rahiyo o banke yar*' (Stay my handsome lover) is another example. In it, Sahib Jan appears similar to a *tawa'if* in a courtly setting as painted in miniatures with a backdrop of a palatial house, a garden, and a fountain. The dancers perform behind her in postures and costumes that also show the influence of nineteenth century company paintings and photographs of famous *tawa'if*. There is a similarity with the later film *Umrao Jan* here in the use of lavish costumes and rich jewellery.

However, the film also gestures towards the changing contours of this aristocratic world wherein a contractor can compete with an aristocrat like the Nawab of Panipat for the attentions of a *tawa'if*. Although the contractor says that he is aware of his 'lower' status and sits separately from other aristocrats, yet when it comes to showering money on the *tawa'if*, he dares to compete with the Nawab, who in turn takes it as an act of great social misdemeanour. Yet this upward mobility, which makes the contractor gain access to wealth and an aristocratic lifestyle, is a reminder of the rise of certain moneyed groups as new patrons of the *tawa'if* in the late nineteenth and early twentieth centuries.

In an interesting intertextual reference, Amrohi uses the name Gauhar Jan for the character of the famous *tawa'if* played by Nadira, whom Sahib Jan joins in Suhagpur. This *tawa'if* is shown to own the famous Ghulabi Mahal, where Sahib Jan starts performing after leaving Delhi. Both Gauhar Jan and Sahib Jan take rides in their *tonga* (horse cart) in the city. They dress up in all their finery and jewellery and enjoy a celebrity status. The famous *tawa'if* and gramophone singer Gauhar Jan (1870?–1931) was also known to take such rides in early twentieth century Calcutta.[29]

In contrast to this popular public image of the *tawa'if*, the film continues to voice the nationalist discourse on the significance of women as wives and mothers. Women thus embody the nation space, including the cultural and historical ideals of domesticity and morality. *Pakeezah* participates in this discourse and shows women to inhabit two spaces: the bazaar and the home. The *tawa'if* inhabit the public space where they are on display in the bazaar and are like commodities to be bought. This is dramatized through the use of symbols such as bags of money. In the song '*Thare rahiyo o banke yar*', Sahib Jan plays the seductress and her patrons express praise for her by throwing bags full of money at her feet. The patron with most money can hope to have an exclusive audience with her. When she visits the bazaar to meet her friend Bibban, we are shown a view of the other *tawa'if* as if on display in their courtyards and windows—on view for the people/consumers walking along the streets.

Meena Kumari (Courtesy: *Pakeezah*, 1971, Kamal Amrohi)

Rekha (Courtesy: *Umrao Jan*, 1981, Muzaffar Ali)

Yet even though the film critiques society for objectifying the *tawa'if* as a body on sale for pleasure, the gaze of the camera does the same with the actress Meena Kumari. It objectifies her through shots of her eyes, her graceful gestures, her painted feet, her hair being washed in fragrant water, and her elaborate dressing ritual. Sahib Jan's feet become a visual fetish representing her sexuality. Her painted feet arouse desire in Salim, who leaves a note tucked between her toes, asking her not to sully them by stepping on the ground. The feet also work as a semiotic code for a woman's virginity. To be accepted as a woman of honour, the *tawa'if* will have to pass through a test of pain and blood; dramatized through the final performance when Sahib Jan dances on broken shards of glass till her feet are drenched with blood. This display of her bleeding feet is meant to remind her father of his failure to 'give her his name'. In order for her to be accepted by society, her father has to come and take her palanquin from the *kotha* to the groom's household as part of the wedding procession—a symbolic journey from the public space where she is called Sahib Jan to the private one, where her name gets linked with her father's lineage.

The nature of this opposition between public and private is not a simplistic distinction based on gender, as male or female space. Spatial distinctions were complex in colonial India and spaces were demarcated according to codes of sociability.[30] Decent women did not interact with men who were not related to them although within private spaces of the home, such as the courtyard, or on occasions such as weddings or festive celebrations, women of the household could meet men from their extended families. Only prostitutes socialized with men in public. Thus the *tawa'if* was a 'public' woman, as she entertained men who were unrelated to her in a public space.

Freedom from the institution of the *kotha* is marked by an interchange of spaces between the closed world of the *kotha* and the domestic space of the household. When Sahib Jan meets Salim in the forest, she is shy and talks to him from behind the partition. The partition is like the veil, a symbol that is a reminder of her 'innate' decency, morality, and shyness. According to the film's ideology, respectable women observe 'purdah' and are shy in front of strange men. As a *tawa'if*, Sahib Jan may have transgressed into public space, yet she is inherently a decent woman who initially observes purdah with Salim. Fareed Kazmi asserts that in popular Hindi films, the *tawa'if* becomes a subject for the exploration and assertion of the domestic ideal for Muslim women and of their identity as women in purdah. In a feminist reading of *Pakeezah* in relation to other Muslim socials, she writes:

> Since most female protagonists in Muslim socials are courtesans or prostitutes they are on public display. Their profession is such as they have to 'perform' before

men, and are therefore presented as isolated, glamorous, sexualized objects on display. But as the narrative progresses, they fall in love with the main protagonist and become his property, losing their outward glamorous characteristics, their generalized sexuality and show girl connotations, so that their eroticism is subjected to the male star alone.[31]

In the case of *Pakeezah,* once Salim enters the narrative, Sahib Jan is shown as a subject in relation to him, and she can no longer continue to be a *tawa'if* whose profession is to charm other men or to entertain them. Through the character of Salim, we get a few glimpses of the film's ideological vision.

Negotiating Modernization in Postcolonial India

The film shows a corrupt world of nawabs and contractors who treat the *tawa'if* as objects. Change is brought in by a man marked by his 'modern' outlook when he chooses to marry a *tawa'if* for love. He is shown to be a 'modern' man, whose modern outlook is symbolized by his western dress, his cigar, and his profession as a forest officer who belongs to the era of industrialization but protects forests and nature. He will play this role again as the protector and caretaker of the honour of Sahib Jan. He stands up for his love of a *tawa'if* and is unafraid to disagree with his grandfather, who symbolizes conservative social tradition and thinks *tawa'if* are women of the bazaar and cannot be a part of decent homes.

In contrast to an oppressive world of artifice, created through the use of staged sets, choreographed music, and dance performances, Salim's character is sketched in relation to nature. The film builds a dichotomy between the natural space of forests and the consumerist city. When the boat carrying Sahib Jan and the Nawab of Panipat is caught in a storm, the unconscious Sahib Jan finds herself in a forest where Salim has his outpost, away from the city. A close-up shot of her eyes flashes onto the screen and her gaze leads us to wide-angle shots of the beauty of nature. Her love for Salim is shown as naturally beautiful like the stars and the sky and nature's bounty, distant from the oppressive and consumerist world of the *kotha* and the bazaar. The film builds up contrasts between harmony in nature and discordance and hierarchies in the world of the city.

In a scene where the contractor tries to rape Sahib Jan, his attempt is shown as an act against nature. Like the mysterious and evil world of sound, space, and ghostly figures of *Mahal*, in *Pakeezah* too Amrohi reiterates that fear and evil desires are the workings of the human mind, but sometimes, real life can embody these fears. In this case, the contractor's desires take the shape of a hissing cobra. The cobra is in Sahib Jan's room earlier, but it has been harmless. For the contractor, though, the cobra becomes a symbol of his own fear to which he succumbs.

Salim does not just play the role of a protector; he is also a man who is representative of the forces of modernization and cultural change. Another powerful 'character' that symbolizes this change is the train. Salim's first encounter with Sahib Jan is on a train journey. Throughout the film, the sound of the train reminds Sahib Jan of her encounter with her lover. A train journey can bring people from different backgrounds into close proximity; it is a marker of social equality and progress. It is on the train that Sahib Jan is first seen by Salim as a woman and not as a *tawa'if*.

The train in the film becomes a harbinger of change, a technological innovation that not only helps cover distance, but points towards a future world of social equality and universal progress. Even when Sahib Jan's dress gets entangled on the railway tracks, the train stops just in time to save her. The crowd that gathers around her mention the alacrity of the engine driver and his ability to save her. Thus the train is a symbol for technological change that will benefit humanity. It is because of this belief in progress, industrialization, and modernization that *Pakeezah* appears to be moulded in Nehruvian ideology. The period between the 1950s and the 1970s was one of belief in nationalism and there was an impetus towards industrialization. This was part of Nehru's vision wherein India needed to 'modernize' and to progress like the nations in the West.

Historically, the railways had played an important role in increasing the mobility of performing communities, such as the *tawa'if* for travelling from one region to another. The *tawa'if* often travelled from one city to another to perform at weddings, festivals, and musical gatherings. In an interesting anecdote, Amritlal Nagar recalls an incident about the rivalry between two *tawa'if* and their quarrel at the railway station leading to performances to outdo each other.[32]

Expressing a complex relationship with the historical past and its conceptualization of modernization in postcolonial India, the film participates in the Nehruvian vision of visualizing a shared cultural and historical past that subsumes regional and religious identities as part of an emergent nationalism. In tandem, there is the idea of modernization and change, which would bring greater equality between the elite and the poor and a better future for the marginalized such as the *tawa'if*. *Pakeezah* tries to negotiate the historical past and the debates on Muslim women's identity, prostitution, and the meaning of modernization through the subject of the *tawa'if*. In the following section, we will see how Muzaffar Ali's *Umrao Jan* shares or differs from this vision of the past.

Remembering a Cultural Past

Muzaffar Ali based *Umrao Jan* on Mirza Muhammad Hadi Ruswa's novel *Umrao Jan 'Ada'* (1899–1901), celebrated as one of the best amongst early Urdu novels. Literary historians of Urdu literature have called Ruswa (1857–1931) one of the first sophisticated novelists in Urdu. The film and novel tell the story of the transformation of an ordinary girl into a famous *tawa'if*. Amiran is a young daughter of a Shi'a caretaker of the mausoleum of Bahu Begum (the wife of Nawab Shuja ud Daulah) in Faizabad. Dilawar Khan, her neighbour, plans to kill her to avenge the years he had spent in prison due to the testimony given by Amiran's father. He abducts Amiran but instead of killing her, sells her to Khanum, a *chaudhrayan* of a *kotha* in Lucknow.

Ruswa's novel uses a narrator who claims to retell the true story of the life of a *tawa'if*, Umrao Jan. Parts of the novel are narrated by Umrao Jan herself and are interspersed with discussions with the narrator Ruswa on poetry, wine, love, and issues such as religion and prostitution. The novel has a multi-layered narrative with a plot full of clever coincidences, digressions on poetic gatherings, satires on *maulvis* (scholars who are not necessarily priests), critiques of elite begums and fake poets; in sum, it is one of the best reconstructions of a socio-cultural milieu.

Critics have long debated the 'infidelity' or 'violation' done by filmic adaptations of novels to the literary text. As argued by Robert Stam and others, rather than focusing on issues of 'fidelity' in filmic adaptations, we need to look for the means by which an adaptation 'becomes' another text. Using a different 'archive of tropes and concepts' such as adaptation as reading, rewriting, critique, or incarnation', Stam, Alessandra Raengo, and Kamilla Elliott argue for a shift towards intertextuality.[33] Thus, films should be analyzed as individual art forms with semiotics and modes of imagination specific to them.

In the case of *Umrao Jan*, the film does not always closely adhere to the complex narrative of the novel although its rendition of the main plot is close to it. It begins with casting credits that have the backdrop of a Shi'a home where there is an engagement ceremony going on. Close-up shots of jewellery, garlands of roses and jasmine, the dress of the young bride-to-be, and the wedding songs sung by women set the scene in Amiran's household in Faizabad. The credits for costume designs and art direction appear along with photographs of a *hookah* and the costumes, interspersed through the engagement scene. Later on, the film recreates the *tawa'if* in her cultural milieu of Lucknow through the backdrop of historic monuments, the use of the royal fish emblem, old *hookahs*, silver betel nut cases, and the keeping of pigeons, all remnants of *lakhnawi* culture.

The film uses material artefacts and paintings as intertexts to a historical and cinematic text. Paintings are used as reference points in the visual narrative of the film. The similarity between the appearance of the cinematic *tawa'if* and the painted subjects are attempts to add 'authenticity' to the recreation of a past milieu.[34] This intertextual use of visual images is unique to *Umrao Jan* and needs to be understood in relation to the director's own life. Ali's interest in the scenic, visual, and cultural past of Lucknow is related to his own princely lineage as the Raja of Kotwara. His use of specific socio-historical symbols, the emphasis on local cultural traditions such as *missi* (blackening of gums) that marked a girl's coming of age and her ability to take patrons as a *tawa'if*, the Shi'a engagement ceremony, the reference to the practice of the *kotha* being closed during Muharram, are all signifiers of his personal interest in stressing a historically specific culture.

The depiction of the spaces of the *kotha* and the *mujra* are visually framed as paintings showing the reclining Khanum Jan adorned with jewellery, smoking the *hookah* and the *tawa'if* performing for the nawabs in a hall lit by chandeliers and decorated with carpets. The use of paintings as visual texts embedded within the narrative suggests that this film attempts to be a part of the tradition of painting as well as a cultural artefact in itself. It is significant that *Pakeezah* does not make this intertextual use of paintings a part of its cinematic narrative. However, it also uses elaborate views and framed visions, which make scenes appear like paintings. Yet there is no deliberate attempt to emphasize this inter-referentiality.

Like *Pakeezah*, this film boasted of a popular star cast. Rekha, one of the popular actresses of the time, plays Umrao Jan, with Fahrukh Sheikh playing Nawab Sultan, her lover. Ali's choice of a child actor and not a familiar face in Hindi films to play Amiran makes her transformation into a *tawa'if* played by the famous actress Rekha a transformation representative of a much broader cultural and social change when a simple girl from Faizabad became a famous *tawa'if* in Lucknow. In *Pakeezah*, Meena Kumari played Nargis as well as Sahib Jan, suggesting a continuity in the *tawa'if* tradition but also symbolic of changing times which bring a better future for the daughter. Nargis and her socially unacceptable love for Shahabuddin are finally given social respectability through the marriage of Sahib Jan and Salim. Unlike *Pakeezah*, *Umrao Jan* concentrates on the life of one girl and her life as a *tawa'if*.

Umrao Jan the film is a Bildüngsroman, like the novel, in its plotting of the transformation of a girl into a performer. In the novel, Umrao Jan recounts an incident during her musical training when the *chaudhrayan* got annoyed with her *ustad* for not paying adequate attention to her training. She also refers to the reluctance amongst *ustads* to share all their musical knowledge. By the late nineteenth century, established musicians who were also known as *kalawant* were known to distance themselves from the *tawa'if*.[35] Ali ignores this attempt amongst the famous musicians to dissociate themselves from the *tawa'if* and chooses to represent the relationship between musicians and the *tawa'if* as one of respect and great esteem. In the film, musical apprenticeship marks the beginning of a *tawa'if*s training. When Khanum Jan introduces Khan Sahib, she emphasizes his greatness as an *ustad* under whose tutelage Umrao would receive her musical training. The film shows the tying of the thread, a ceremony that marked musical apprenticeship amongst the community of musicians and their disciples. By foregrounding the musical apprenticeship and later showing her interest in poetry, and her request to Maulavi Sahib for *isslah* or advice in her poetic composition, the film shows Umrao Jan receiving training to be a singer, dancer, and a poet.

Unlike *Pakeezah*, these insights into the ceremonies and lifestyle of the *tawa'if* show them as a community of performers. In a deeper engagement with the *tawa'if* culture in Lucknow, the film locates performers in a socio-political milieu and a specific cultural locale in the late nineteenth century. In *Pakeezah*, we get a few glimpses of music and dance rehearsals in the backdrop but not such a close engagement either with the life of a *tawa'if* as a performer or with her training as an artist. Both films, however, emphasize the oppressive institution of the *kotha*, which makes the *tawa'if* a subject on the margins of power and social acceptability. In one of the most touching scenes of the film, when Umrao/Amiran performs in her home town of Faizabad, she recognizes her house and meets her mother but is disowned by her younger brother (someone she took care of and played with as a child), who shuns her and asks her to leave.

A contrast between the novel and the film is in the character of Umrao Jan as a woman with agency. In the novel, Umrao Jan recalls her love for Nawab Sultan, her ideal lover but at the same time she recounts that a *tawa'if* cannot really fall in love as she is trained to be manipulative and charming. The novel critiques the immorality and exploitative nature of the institution of the *tawa'if*, but the narrator also insists that he is not interested in writing a reformist narrative. Umrao Jan is shown to be saucy and rational: she engages with Ruswa in erotic banter, and is quick to retort to every accusation and to critique marital love.

On the other hand, in the film, Umrao Jan is constantly pining for true love and eventually leads a lonely life. The film has moments when the *nawabi* practice of visiting the *kotha* is criticized. For instance Nawab Sultan hears Umrao Jan's voice for the first time when he is passing through the bazaar. When he meets her in person, he insists that he does not go to *kotha*s, a practice that he disapproves of. It is her poetry that has attracted him. As in the novel, Nawab Sultan and Umrao Jan share a loving relationship that includes sharing their poetic compositions. There are peripheral voices as well, such as that of Faiz Ali, a highway robber and a patron of Umrao Jan, who accuses the nawabs of being weak pawns in the hands of the British.

Faiz Ali's statement is an allusion to the rebellion and an impending change. He reminds us of the colonial critique of the effeminacy and effete culture of the nawabs of Awadh. Although the film tries to follow the novel and to recreate a historical milieu, these critiques of the *nawabi* culture and practices remain peripheral to it. On the other hand, in *Pakeezah,* the immorality of the *tawa'if* culture is strongly reasserted throughout, even though the film simultaneously attempts to create a grand past through the use of costumes and décor.

Umrao Jan was completed in 1981, and conceived during the post-Emergency years of political and social turbulence. These years were marked by the rise in movements to formulate separate regional, linguistic, and religious identities and by disillusionment with the emergence of authoritarianism in governance at the centre. At this time, *Umrao Jan* seemed to express nostalgia for a past that represented a time of socio-cultural unity and artistic creativity.

The nature of this nostalgia was, however, different from that of the novel which, sharing some of the nostalgia, was still very much a product of the changing perceptions, practices, and market of an emerging print culture. Recent scholarship on the vernacular print sphere has shown the need to trace print cultures and literary practices of nineteenth century India in their broader contexts. In the late nineteenth century, some printed texts such as song-books were continuations of practices that were part of oral traditions, while others such as detective novels were new genres that did not have any precursors in earlier literary practices.[36]

Thus the characterization of the *tawa'if* Umrao Jan as pert, her digressions on the ability and the need for the *tawa'if* to feign real love, the comic descriptions of the activities in the *kotha*—its internal hierarchies and tales of love and jealousy—all make the novel an interesting read. As an author, Ruswa was also prolific in the production of what some have called the 'penny dreadfuls', books that brought him financial success. This is how the translators Khushwant Singh and M. A. Husaini describe him:

> ...a dual personality—an earnest minded Dr Jekyll burning the midnight oil writing sublime prose, working out a system of Urdu shorthand...and the vulgarian [*sic*] Mr Hyde, doing the rounds of the city's brothels and churning up cheap trash to bring in filthy lucre...[37]

Rather than reading Ruswa's authorship as schizophrenic, *Umrao Jan 'Ada'* can be seen as a novel that bordered on the literary and the popular. This distinction between 'cheap trash' and 'sublime prose' needs to be understood as a product of new critical standards of literary writing and scholarship that had emerged.

In contrast to the novel, in the film, Umrao Jan is shown to have hardly any agency; rather, her character elicits sympathy from the audience. In terms of relationships, the film tends to idealize the bonding between the *tawa'if* in the *kotha* through the imagined friendship between Bismillah and Umrao, ignoring the rivalries and hierarchies within the institution. Towards the end of the novel, the *tawa'if* Umrao Jan is known as a poet who chooses to participate in small literary gatherings and is no longer part of a *kotha*. She takes solace in religion and reading Sufi texts, yet the narrator mocks religious figures such as the *maulavi*. The film stays away from satirizing any religious figures.

Alain Desoulières sees another link between Ruswa's narrative and cinema. He argues that the novel's narrative seems like a proto-cinematic narrative. He gives the example of the mirror scene, which works like a flashback and refers to the 'retrospective and cinematographic rhetoric of the novel', which also displays the author's interest in stage drama. In a footnote, he reflects that in the absence of a definitive version of Ruswa's text, if we were to know when the 'mirror scene' was written or modified, then we would have some hints about the relationship between the narrative and cinema. His hypothesis is that if this scene was included in the 1905 edition, it would reveal Ruswa's interest in cinema. The first public film show was held in Bombay in 1896, and Lucknow was the subject for a short British film *Delhi, the Rome of Asia and Lucknow* (*c.*1897).[38] However, the film does not use the mirror scene as a flashback, rather it shows Umrao Jan looking sad and lonely and unsure of herself. Whereas in the novel we have an old and mature Umrao Jan thinking of the various moments of her past, the film does not show an aged *tawa'if*; rather, she remains a young woman desirous of love and affection, possibly an embodiment of the film's nostalgic vision.

Therefore the relationship between the literary text, the film, and history could possibly be understood through what I call the 'concept of echoes'. As an echo is simultaneously an exaggeration and a silencing of the originating sound, films and literary texts too, echo history. The echo is a new sound as it is different from the originating sound yet related to it. Similarly, literary and cinematic texts are historical texts but are still new texts in their own right. Both the literary and the cinematic *tawa'if*, therefore, become echoes of the historical *tawa'if*. In the next section, I will show how reading the 'star text' can further make us aware of the nuances of this relationship.

FILMS, STAR TEXTS, AND HISTORIES

While studying star images in Hollywood, Richard Dyer states:

> A film star's image is not just his or her films, but the promotion of those films and of the star through pin-ups, public appearances, studio hand-outs and so on, as well as interviews, biographies and coverage in the press of the star's doings

and 'private' life…Star images are always extensive, multimedia, intertextual…. Star images have histories and histories that outlive the star's own lifetime… [39]

Both *Umrao Jan* and *Pakeezah* had famous actresses play the role of the *tawa'if*. In these films, the *tawa'if's* sexuality is framed and reconstructed through the image of these actresses or their 'star texts'. In the context of popular Hindi films, film stars are popular icons in people's imagination. Their lives are discussed and read in film magazines, on internet sites and blogs, and they inspire fan clubs. Jyotika Virdi calls these parallel discourses on the lives of the stars, 'star texts':

…the extra-text about the stars' lives—are sometimes parallel to or at an angle from the film narratives. Film texts can reflect or refract star biographies. The play between the film and extra-text heightens tension and dramatic potential, expanding the possibilities of reading multiple meanings in the interchange between the two that the audience reads simultaneously. In this context Hindi film culture is a continuous film text, which includes not just the film's narrative but also adjoining discourses…. Read against and parallel to films, star texts offer a wealth of information about cultural politics… [40]

Recent scholars of women in early cinema have also shown how archival research on the lives of women actors can become a useful tool for feminist historiography in early cinema.[41] I will use one film magazine and its articles to see what it can tell us about the women performers. In the case of Meena Kumari, it will give us a glimpse of her life as a star and her struggle to survive in an industry that uses the currency of the 'star image'.

Pakeezah was a film that was planned in the 1950s, when Meena Kumari (1932?–72) was married to Amrohi. By the time the film was completed, they had already been divorced and Meena Kumari had become known as the famous 'tragedy queen'. Her role in *Sahib Bibi aur Ghulam* (1962) has been read by Virdi as a text that runs counter to *Pakeezah* in the portrayal of a wife who tries to be a *tawa'if* to gain her husband back from the *kotha*. Initially, *Pakeezah* did not do too well at the cinema halls but Meena Kumari's premature death added to the film's eventual success and, as argued by Virdi, led on to make Meena Kumari a real life 'tragedy queen', a romantic poet, an alcoholic, and a woman with a melancholic temperament.[42] Her mother, Iqbal Begum, was a stage actress who had a short-lived career in early films. There have been allusions to her links with the *tawa'if* culture, yet these hints have often been seen as too scandalous to be included in obituaries celebrating her as an actress. In 1979 Sohrab Mody made a documentary, *Meena Kumari ki Amar Kahani* (The Unforgettable Story of Meena Kumari) to commemorate her life as an actress, but had to struggle with her real life background.

Historically, the relationship between the *tawa'if* and actresses is complex and deserves extensive research in the context of early cinema, which is at present beyond the scope of this article. In an article that Meena Kumari wrote for a film magazine, she recounted her struggle to be an actress as being due to financial need rather than because of a desire for fame or popularity:

Self-Portrait
...how and why I have become so good an artist is something I don't know... in my case, the question of my taking up my profession out of personal interest or preference, that is with consciousness of what I was going to do, does not arise. As a matter of fact, I later realized that I had entered my profession from sheer necessity. The thrill of earning fame, or the thought of it, had no part in the business.[43]

Nimmi (b. 1930), another famous actress of the 1950s, also wrote a similar article in the same issue of the magazine and recounted the troubles that she had to undergo to be financially independent. These rare glimpses of early actresses as working women, trying to achieve financial independence through the film industry, can provide us with rich archival material for an understanding of the lives of these actresses. As another example of the relationship between film actresses and the audience in the 1950s, here is another article that Meena Kumari wrote in *Filmfare.* It reminds us of the scene in *Pakeezah*, when Sahib Jan is accosted by Salim in public and is ashamed when men whistle at her and treat her like a commodity.

My Ideal Fan
It is not a matter of pride for me to say that I am actually afraid to go out shopping because of what my 'fans' who invariably collect wherever I go, will say. It can be humiliating...at Indian theatres [the public] never lets us pass *without making our ears burn* (my emphasis)... I do not want to be praised and pampered, but I appreciate sympathy from fans.[44]

These articles in the early film magazines show us the attitude of auidiences towards film actresses in real settings and point towards the changing configuration of the star image. In the context of Hindi film magazines, Dwyer has shown how readers use Indian film magazines such as *Stardust* as 'ways of dealing with...everyday life' and of interpreting their status as individuals in a consumerist society.[45]

In some ways, Rekha appears to be a contrast to Meena Kumari in terms of her star image. She has continued to hold an iconic status as the *femme fatale* of Hindi cinema. Rekha (b. 1954) began her career in the film industry as a child artist. After initial years of struggle, she established herself as a popular actress by the 1980s. She played the role of the *tawa'if* Zohra

Bai with Amitabh Bachchan in *Muqaddar ka Sikandar* (King of Destiny) in 1978. By this time, Bachchan had established himself as one of the most popular stars of all time. Soon he came to be known as the one-man industry. The release of *Umrao Jan* was accompanied by another film, which further added to Rekha's growing popularity as a star. This was Yash Chopra's *Silsila* starring Rekha, Amitabh Bachchan, and his wife, Jaya. *Silsila* was a story about an extramarital relationship and love beyond the bounds of marriage. The rumours about the film as based on the real life affair between Rekha and Bachchan made the film immensely popular, revealing how powerful star texts can be in cultivating star images. By the 1980s, Rekha fashioned herself as an actress with a signature look very different from her early years as a struggling actress. This transformation was often referred to as that of an ugly duckling! In interviews and film magazines, Rekha claimed that she had achieved this by changing her lifestyle, healthy eating practices, and doing yoga. Soon she had inspired a whole fashion trend and had film magazines raving about her affair with Amitabh Bachchan. Such publicity added to her image as a symbol of seduction and glamour. She was seen as a woman who could challenge patriarchal norms by remaining single and being famous.

This change in being able to cultivate a star image and a star text was possible with the rising significance of film magazines and their consumption by the audience. Referred to as the 'ancillary industry' by Virdi, these magazines made the stars and their lives a part of the social lives of their readers. Reading these as star texts and social texts needs further research in relation to the changing nature of film publicity, film journalism, and patterns of readership over the years.

Returning to the links between star texts and film texts, both Meena Kumari and Rekha held iconic status as women who were glamorous and unattainable. Films such as *Pakeezah* and *Umrao Jan* engaged with their contemporary images as romantic, unattainable, and lonely women in order to recreate the image of the *tawa'if* as a woman who is seductive, charming, and yet leads a tragic life at the margins of power and seclusion. The *tawa'if's* persona is framed and reconstructed in these films through these popular star personae.

Conclusion

The *tawa'if* has been a popular subject amongst Hindi films; yet another version of *Umrao Jan* has been released in 2006. The historical *tawa'if* was an accomplished singer, poet, and dancer, in essence, a talented performer who later came to be despised as a prostitute. This combination of a talented performer and a marginalized subject made the *tawa'if* an attractive subject for Hindi films. The cultural context of *ghazals* and *kathak* made these narratives ideal blends of poetry, music, and dance.

Yet it is also through the *tawa'if* that films participate in and engage with popular perceptions of *nawabi* culture and a desirable past of unity across socio-religious identities. One could reject popular films as being historically 'naïve' or one could try to comprehend them as audio-visual narratives of popular history. The *tawa'if* in films is a subject whose history is closely intertwined with the star image. The cinematic *tawa'if* is the result of the slow percolation and interpellation of perceptions of the historical *tawa'if* into the domain of public reception and cultural memory. Even today, the *tawa'if* is a cinematic palimpsest whereby popular films negotiate links between women, performance, and history.

NOTES

1. Terms such as 'popular Hindi film' or 'commercial Hindi films', 'Bollywood', 'art cinema', 'new wave cinema' have been questioned in contemporary scholarship. For the purpose of this article, I retain the term 'popular' to read the relationship between films and history whereby people negotiate history through everyday practices such as storytelling, watching films, reading *Amar Chitra Katha* comics. I use the term 'popular' to draw connections with those films that became cult classics for their depiction of a glorious and nostalgic past and had famous actors playing historical characters.
2. I argue that films such as *Pakeezah* or *Umrao Jan* attempt to recreate the past through the *tawa'if* but differ in their imagination in relation to their ideological present.
3. I choose *not* to translate the Urdu term *tawa'if* into courtesan or dancing girl in order to avoid the a-historical and universalized assumptions of the 'courtesan'. I prefer to locate the *tawa'if* as a specific historical subject in a particular historical milieu from the late eighteenth century to the early twentieth century. In this article, I study the imagined *tawa'if* as a subject in two popular Hindi films released in the late twentieth century.
4. Chakravarty, 1993, pp. 287–8.
5. Ibid., p. 288.
6. Kesavan, 1994, pp. 244–57.
7. Dwyer, 2004, pp. 78–92.
8. I will elaborate upon this aspect in a separate section.
9. Hayden White, quoted in Roberts, 2001, pp. 1–10.
10. See issues of the journal *Film and History: An Interdisciplinary Journal of Film and Television Studies;* Rosenstone, 1995 and 2006, Rosenstone, and Landy, 2001.
11. Sorlin, 1980.
12. Rosenstone, *History on Film,* pp. 1-4.
13. Chakravarty, *National Identity in Indian Popular Cinema,* p. 159.
14. An Urdu *ghazal* is a brief lyric poem which can be romantic or mystical in tone and evokes the feelings of a lover separated from his beloved. For more on the Urdu *ghazal* as a song, see Manuel, 1988–9, pp. 93–113.
15. Chandra, 1973; Nevile, 1996; Trivedi, 2002, pp. 153–64; Chatterji, 1998.

16. Sharar, 1975. The first attempt to locate the *tawa'if* in a historical context was made by Veena Talwar Oldenburg in the 1990s. Oldenburg, 1990, pp. 259–87. Ethnomusicologists have tried to historicize the *tawa'if* as an artist. Qureshi, 2006, pp. 312–21; Maciszewski, 2006, pp. 332–68; Manuel, 1999; Neuman, 1990. The events of 1857 are variously referred to as 'mutiny', 'rebellion', 'first war of independence' in historiography. Recently events were organised around the commemoration of the event in India and the United Kingdom. New research and debates are constantly emerging, for example Dalrymple, 2006; Narayan, 2006.
17. Sangari, 2006, p. 264.
18. *Thakahi, randi* were affiliated to the *kotha* but held a lower rank and mainly provided sexual services; *Khangi* were women who were married or observed purdah but made use of the *kotha* for secret liaisons. Oldenburg, 1990, pp. 259–87. For a different perspective on resistance see Rajan, 1996, pp. 122–49.
19. Gupta, 2001, pp. 85–22.
20. For studies on prostitution from the imperial perspective see Ballhatchet, 1980; Walkowitz, 1980; Levine, 2003. Hubel, 2005, pp. 121–40; Das Gupta, 2005, pp. 454–84; Banerjee, 2000; O'Shea, 1998, pp. 45–63.
21. I present this argument in my thesis while situating and configuring questions of agency and representation of the *tawa'if* as a historical subject in colonial north India. Sachdeva, 2008.
22. For a theoretical discussion of the representation of women as historical beings subject to real social relations that include gender see de Lauretis, 1987, p. 15.
23. Shah, Mirza Muhammad Hadi 'Ruswa', 2005. The English translators of Ruswa's novel mention that there were various versions of the novel from 1889 to 1938.
24. Premchand, 1958.
25. Dalmia, 2006, p. 206.
26. *Filmfare,* 3 August 1956, vol. 5, no. 61, p. 43.
27. *Mujra* could refer to salutation and not just a dance performance. Qureshi, 19–22 May 2005.
28. Princely states or successor states is a term used for the states of Jaipur, Hyderabad, Murshidabad, and Awadh which emerged as independent states in the later phase of the eighteenth century. Although they were independent of the Mughal empire, yet they saw the Mughals as sovereigns for a long time. Many of these states remained independent till they were finally incorporated into the Indian nation state.
29. Chandvankar, 2002.
30. Orsini, Introduction, *Love in South Asia*, pp. 1–39.
31. Kazmi, p. 240.
32. Nagar, 1958, p. 68.
33. Stam and Raengo, 2004; Elliot, 2003.
34. A more in-depth study of cinema and painting is beyond the scope of this article but there is interesting work such as Vacche, 1996.
35. Neuman, 1990, p. 140.
36. Blackburn and Dalmia 2004, pp. 1–24.
37. Ruswa, 2005, p. 10.
38. Desoulières, 1998, pp. 67–87.
39. Dyer, 1986, pp. 2–3.
40. Virdi, 2003, pp. 136–7.
41. Bean, 2002, pp. 2–26.
42. Her recordings of her own Urdu compositions are available.

43. Kumari, 1956, pp. 4–5.
44. Kumari, 1956, p. 19.
45. Dwyer, 2000, p. 35.

References

Ali, Muzaffar, *Umrao Jan* (DVD), 1981, Sacramento, CA: Bollywood Entertainment, 2001.

Amrohi, Kamal, *Pakeezah* (DVD), 1971 Mumbai : Shemaroo Video, s.d.

Ballhatchet, Kenneth A., *Race, Sex and Class Under the Raj: Imperial Attitudes and Policies and Their Critics, 1793–1905* London: Weidenfeld and Nicolson, 1980.

Banerjee, Sumanta, *Dangerous Outcast: The Prostitute in Nineteenth Century Bengal*, Calcutta: Seagull Books, 2000.

Bean, Jennifer M., 'Toward a Feminist Historiography of Early Cinema', in Bean and Diane Negra, eds., *A Feminist Reader in Early Cinema*, Durham and London: Duke University Press, 2002, pp. 2–26.

Blackburn, Stuart, and Vasudha Dalmia, eds., *India's Literary History: Essays on the Nineteenth Century*, Delhi: Permanent Black, 2004.

Chakravarty, Sumita S., *National Identity in Indian Popular Cinema 1947–1987*, Austin: University of Texas Press, 1993.

Chandra, Moti, *The World of Courtesans*, Delhi: Vikas Publishing House, 1973.

Chandvankar, Suresh, 'My Name is Gauhar Jan: First Dancing Girl, Calcutta', http://www.mustrad.org.uk/articles/gauhar.htm, accessed 16 November 2002.

Chatterji, Shoma A., *Subject: Cinema, Object: Woman, A Study of Women in Indian Cinema*, Calcutta: Parumita Publications, 1998.

Dalmia, Vasudha, 'The Spaces of Love and the Passing of the Seasons: Delhi in the Early Twentieth Century', in Francesca Orsini, ed., *Love in South Asia*, Cambridge: Cambridge University Press, 2006, p. 206.

Desoulières, Alain, in Vasudha Dalmia and Theo Damsteegt, eds., 'The Three Lives of Umrao Jan Ada', in *Narrative Strategies: Essays on South Asian Literature and Film*, New Delhi: Oxford University Press, 1998, pp. 67–87.

Dwyer, Rachel, 'Representing the Muslim: The "Courtesan Film" in Indian Popular Cinema', in Tudor Parfitt and Yulia Egorova, eds., *Jews, Muslims and Mass Media: Mediating the 'Other'*, London, New York: Routledge Curzon, 2004, pp. 78–92.

———, *All You Want is Money, All You Need is Love: Sex and Romance in Modern India*, London: Cassell, 2000.

Dyer, Richard, *Heavenly Bodies: Film Stars and Society*, London: BFI, Macmillan, 1986.

Das Gupta, Amlan, 'Women and Music: The Case of North India', in Bharati Ray, ed., *Women of India: Colonial and Post-Colonial Periods*, Delhi and London: Sage Publications, 2005, pp. 454–84.

Elliot, Kamilla, *Rethinking the Novel/Film Debate* Cambridge: Cambridge University Press, 2003.

Gupta, Charu, *Sexuality, Obscenity, Community: Women, Muslims, and the Hindu Public in Colonial India*, Delhi: Permanent Black, 2001.

Hubel, Teresa, 'The High Cost of Dancing: When the Indian Women's Movement Went After the Devadasis', in Laura B. Lengel, ed., *Intercultural Communications and Creative Practice: Dance, Music and Women's Cultural Identity*, Westport, Conn. and London: Praeger, 2005, pp. 121–40.

Kazmi, Fareed, 'Muslim Socials and the Female Protagonists: Seeing a Dominant Discourse at Work', in Zoya Hasan, ed., *Forging Identities: Gender, Communities and State*, Delhi: Kali for Women, 1994, pp. 226-43.

Kesavan, Mukul, 'Urdu, Awadh and the Tawaif: The Islamicate Roots of Hindi Cinema', in Zoya Hasan, ed., *Forging Identities: Gender, Communities and State*, Delhi: Kali for Women, 1994, pp. 244-57.

Kumari, Meena, *I Write, I Recite*, Universal Records, 2001.

———, 'Self Portrait', *Filmfare*, 20 July 1956, pp. 4–5.

———, 'My Ideal Fan', *Filmfare*, 31 August 1956, pp. 19.

Landy, Marcia, ed., *The Historical Film: History and Memory in Media*, New Brunswick, NJ: Rutgers University Press, 2001.

Lauretis, Teresa de, *Technologies of Gender: Essays on Theory, Film, and Fiction*, Hampshire and London: Macmillan Press, 1987.

Levine, Philipa, *Prostitution, Race and Politics: Policing Venereal Disease in the British Empire*, New York: Routledge, 2003.

Maciszewski, Amelia, 'Tawa'if, Tourism, and Tales: The Problematics of Twenty-First-Century Musical Patronage for North India's Courtesans', in Martha Feldman and Bonnie Gordon, eds., *The Courtesan's Arts: Cross-Cultural Perspectives*, New York: Oxford University Press, 2006, pp. 332–68.

Manuel, Peter L. , 'A Historical Survey of the Urdu Ghazal-Song in India', *Asian Music*, vol. 20, no. 1, Autumn 1988–Winter 1989, pp. 93–113.

———, *Thumri in Historical and Stylistic Perspectives*, Delhi: Motilal Banarsidass, 1999.

Muhammad Hadi 'Ruswa', Mirza, *The Courtesan of Lucknow: Umrao Jan 'Ada'*, trans. and ed. Khushwant Singh and M.A. Husaini, New Delhi: Orient Paperbacks, 2005.

Nagar, Amritlal, *Yeh Kothewalian*, Delhi: Ruchika Printers, 1958.

Neuman, Daniel M., *The Life of Music in Northern India: The Organisation of an Artistic Tradition*, Chicago and London: University of Chicago Press, 1990.

Nevile, Pran, *Nautch Girls of India: Dancers, Singers, Playmates*, New York and Delhi: Ravi Kumar Publishers, 1996.

Oldenburg, Veena Talwar, 'Lifestyle as Resistance: The Case of the Courtesans of Lucknow, India', *Feminist Studies*, vol. 16, no. 2, Summer 1990, pp. 259–87.

O'Shea, Janet, 'Traditional Indian Dance and the Making of Interpretive Communities', *Asian Theatre Journal*, vol. 15, no. 1, Spring 1998, pp. 45–63.

Premchand, *Courtesans' Quarter: A Translation of Bazaar-e-Husn*, trans. Amina Azfar, Oxford, New York: Oxford University Press, 2003.

Qureshi, Regula Burckhart, 'Female Agency and Patrilineal Constraints: Situating Courtesans in Twentieth Century India', in Martha Feldman and Bonnie Gordon, eds., *The Courtesan's Arts: Cross-Cultural Perspectives*, New York: Oxford University Press, 2006, pp. 312–21.

———, '"*Mujra* Poetry" and the Female Performance of Male Desire', paper presented at *Music and the Art of Seduction*, Tropentheater: Amsterdam, 19–22 May 2005.

Roberts, Geoffrey, ed., *The History and Narrative Reader*, London and New York: Routledge, 2001.

Sachdeva, Shweta, 'In Search of the *Tawa'if* in History: Courtesans, *Nautch Girls* and Celebrity Entertainers in India, 1720s–1920s', Ph.D. diss., SOAS, University of London, 2008.

Sangari, Kumkum, 'Love's Repertoire: Qurratulain Hyder's *River of Fire*', in Francesca Orsini, ed., *Love in South Asia*, Cambridge: Cambridge University Press, 2006, pp. 259–85.

Shah, Hasan, *The Nautch Girl: A Novel*, trans. Qurratulain Hyder, New Delhi: Sterling Paperbacks, 1992.

Sharar, Abdul Halim, *Lucknow: The Last Phase of an Oriental Culture,* trans. and ed. E.S. Harcourt and Fakhir Hussain, Boulder, Colorado: Westview Press, 1975.

Sorlin, Pierre, *The Film in History. Restaging the Past*, Oxford: Blackwell, 1980.

Stam, Robert, and Alessandra Raengo, *Literature and Film: A Guide to the Theory and Practice of Film Adaptation*, Oxford: Blackwell, 2004.

Sunder Rajan, Rajeshwari, 'The Prostitution Question (s): (Female) Agency, Sexuality and Work', in Ratna Kapur, ed., *Feminist Terrains in Legal Domains: Interdisciplinary Essays on Women and Law in India*, Delhi: Kali for Women, 1996, pp. 122–49.

Trivedi, Madhu, 'Female Performing Artistes in North India: A Survey', in Ahsan Jan Qaisar and Som Prakash Verma, eds., *Art and Culture, vol. II*, Jaipur, 2002, pp. 153–64.

Vacche, Angela Dalle, *Cinema and Painting: How Art is Used in Film*, London: Athlone Press, 1996.

Virdi, Jyotika, *The Cinematic Imagination: Indian Popular Films as Social History*, New Jersey, London: Rutgers University Press, 2003.

Walkowitz, Judith, *Prostitution and Victorian Society: Women, Class and the State*, Cambridge: Cambridge University Press, 1980.

PART IV
LITERARY AND CINEMATIC IMAGINARIES

10

The Art of Film Adaptation: The Remains of the Day*

Seymour Chatman

PRACTICALLY FROM its birth, cinema has been inspired to make film versions of nineteenth and twentieth century novels. By 1921, for example, over a hundred adaptations of Charles Dickens' novels had already appeared on the screen, 10 of *Oliver Twist* alone. There is a superfluity of articles on individual adaptations, many of them devoted to the tedious question of 'fidelity'. But theory about the subject is rather unimpressive. Conventional wisdom, much of it from the industry itself, argues that only bad novels make good films because film is innately committed to the visible, and pulp fiction is the readiest source of photogenic action. The other side of this truism is that good novels make bad films, and until recently, Hollywood has either stayed away from the challenges of the great novels, or in attempting them, produced laughable results. For example two versions of *Madame Bovary* were made, one in 1934 deliciously entitled *Unholy Love*; and a glossier but no less naive 1949 version, directed by Vincent Minnelli, starring Jennifer Jones as Emma and James Mason as (of all people) Gustave Flaubert, on the witness stand, defending his book against a morals charge. So much for Hollywood's understanding of the novelist who so fiercely struggled to refine the author's voice out of existence! Fortunately, a fine version of the novel appeared in 1991 directed by Claude Chabrol and starring Isabel Huppert. In general, the French have done the best in filming masterpieces among their novels. A recent exquisite example is Raul Ruiz's adaptation of the last part of Proust's *Remembrance of Things Past*.

But in the last 20 or 30 years, some of the best American directors have adapted serious novels to the screen. Stanley Kubrick did fine versions of *Lolita, A Clockwork Orange*, and *Barry Lyndon*. Coppola used *Heart of Darkness* as the basis of *Apocalypse Now*. Martin Scorsese adapted Edith Wharton's *Age of Innocence*. The most dedicated of film adaptors is James

Ivory, who works regularly with producer Ismail Merchant and screenwriter Ruth Prawer Jhabvala. The team has adapted novels and novellas like Henry James' *The Bostonians, The Europeans,* and most recently *The Golden Bowl*, E.M. Forster's *Howards End*, *A Room with a View*, and *Maurice*, Katherine Anne Porter's *Noon Wine*, Jean Rhys' *Quartet,* and Carson MacCullers' *Ballad of the Sad Café*. One of their finest is the adaptation of Kazuo Ishiguro's 1989 novel *The Remains of the Day,* which appeared in 1993.

The discussion of film adaptation, both in popular and scholarly publications, has focused too extensively on the question of 'fidelity', as if the sole task of the film were to render some precise replication of the novel. That sort of faithfulness, of course, is impossible because the two media are so different. A letter-perfect adaptation would be a simple reading of the novel by a voice over a blank screen. The real issue is not literal fidelity, but whether a film gives a good cinematic *equivalent* of the novel. There is a broad range of equivalencies: a successful adaptation may stick quite closely to the details of the original or, at the other extreme, use the original only as a jumping-off point. *The Remains of the Day* exemplifies the former, Coppola's *Apocalypse Now* the latter. The historical difference between the turn-of-the-century Belgian rape of the Congo and the Vietnam war is, of course, great. But the central theme—a western intellectual driven mad and bloodthirsty by unlimited power over a primitive people—is common to both works.

But the loose adaptation is not my subject. Rather, I will try to illustrate how a film can use certain techniques to present interesting equivalencies of a novel's effects. How are the words printed on a book's pages transformed into a satisfying equivalency on the screen? I will concentrate on changes in form to accommodate the new medium, but of course I cannot avoid implications for content as well. I am not going to pass judgment on whether the filmmakers were 'right' to make such changes, but rather to speculate on how the technology of cinema might have prompted them to do so.

If you haven't read Ishiguro's novel, let me summarize it quickly. It recounts the memories of a butler named Stevens who managed the house of a British nobleman, Lord Darlington, in the 1920s and 1930s. After the sale of the house in the 1950s he stayed on in the employ of a rich American who purchased it. Lord Darlington was sympathetic to the German cause, and through Stevens' impeccable household expertise, arranged under his own roof a series of secret meetings among British and European dignitaries, culminating in the one between von Ribbentrop and Chamberlain that led to the sell-out of Czechoslovakia.[1] As first-person narrator, Stevens recounts these events from the self-restricted viewpoint of a servant whose sole purpose in life has been to help his employer achieve 'those great things' that milord meddled in. Stevens' unquestioning support of his master is challenged throughout by various characters. Stevens defends himself, using words like 'professionalism', 'duty', and 'dignity'. He denies complicity in the evil consequences of appeasement by arguing that his sole responsibility was to ensure that the meetings were well-catered, and that it was not up to such an insignificant person as himself to have an opinion about the political motives and methods of the participants.

As Stevens reminisces about these events he recalls his own personal affairs, in particular his relations with Miss Kenton, the chief housekeeper, and the illness and death of his father, William Stevens, once a great butler himself, but reduced by age to the position of underbutler. Stevens' very manner of speaking reveals how his exclusive commitment to domestic service has squeezed his own life, especially his capacity to love. We surmise from his memory of remarks of Miss Kenton, which he was too obtuse to understand at the time, that she was attracted to him but could only express herself in a teasing away. Ultimately, despairing of his incapacity to reciprocate her love, she married another butler and resigned from service. After the War, Lord Darlington, publicly impugned as a Nazi sympathizer, dies in sorrow and disgrace. Stevens stays on at Darlington Hall because it is bought by an Anglophilic American anxious to preserve its way of life. But the house can no longer enjoy the luxury of a large staff, and Stevens has to manage with only three other servants. Unexpectedly, he receives a letter from Miss Kenton, reminiscing nostalgically about the old days and hinting at dissatisfaction in her marriage. Still unable to articulate his affection for her, but wondering at 'what might have been', Stevens rationalizes his desire to see her under the guise of professional responsibility. He hopes to invite her back to reassume her duties as chief housekeeper.

His American employer offers him the car for a vacation to the west country. The novel's structure consists of Stevens' narration of his adventures on the road, the chapter titles naming the places where he spends the night, mixed with memories of the old days at Darlington Hall that come to mind as he drives along. These memories are either stated in general terms or presented scenically, as flashbacks to actual dialogue and action.

So, presumably, what a film version of this novel must capture is the butler's half awareness of the price he has paid for fending off life's opportunities in the name of service. The missed opportunities are both moral and emotional. He is blinded by personal loyalty to the evil enterprise being hatched in the house that he so devotedly manages, and he loses the companionship of a fine woman who, we infer, respects and perhaps loves him. By making Stevens a first person narrator, the novel gives a slanted view of his intense loss. The very way Stevens tells the story, for example raises questions about his ability to understand its full ramifications. A name often applied to this technique is 'unreliable narration', and Jim Phelan and Mary Martin have published a fine article examining the issue.[2]

As narrator, Stevens is our only source for the story, and since he refuses to understand either the implications of his master's political dabbling or Miss Kenton's feelings for him, the text he generates constitutes a flawed interpretation. Except, that is, for occasional speculations about how things might have been different had he pursued closer communications with Miss Kenton. And most particularly, one sentence, just six pages from the end. Up till that point, the reader can only infer what Stevens cannot confess even in the privacy of his own mind. The sentence occurs at the novel's climactic moment, when he hears Miss Kenton wondering about the sort of a life she may have had with him instead of her husband. Stevens is stabbed by the belated recognition of his loss. Here is how he narrates his reaction:

> I do not think I responded immediately, for it took me a moment or two to fully digest these words of Miss Kenton. Moreover, as you might appreciate, their implications were such as to provoke a certain degree of sorrow with me. Indeed—why should I not admit it?—at that moment, my heart was breaking.

The passage sums up not only the man's inhibitions but how they are filtered through the faux Oxbridge upper class lingo spoken by this elite servant. Almost instinctively, his first reaction is the incredible understatement that Miss Kenton's remark 'provoked a certain degree of sorrow' in him. But his façade cracks immediately, and he ends admitting his heartbreak.

To the extent that a novel comes to the screenwriter, Mrs Jhabvala, already scenic in character, that is full of quotable dialogue and filmable actions in identifiable surroundings, adaptation is relatively easy. For instance Stevens' first encounters with Miss Kenton pretty directly match the words on the page. But transferring other novelistic passages to the screen was harder. Consider a character's abstract generalization, for example Stevens' frequent meditations on what constitutes the highest standard of domestic service. Such a monologue would make for very boring cinema. Other problems were difficult, but subject to ingenious solutions. There is, for instance, the question of time. Every narrative, whether novel, film, play, opera, comic strip, or ballet necessarily utilizes *two* kinds of time. One can be called 'story-time', the time taken by the events in the plot. Novels like Tolstoy's *War and Peace* or Proust's *Remembrance of Things Past* go through many years of events. Joyce's *Ulysses,* on the other hand, covers only a day. The other kind of narrative time is that required to 'read' or otherwise experience the story events: a film typically lasts two hours, a novel much longer, depending on the number of pages and the reader's pace. This kind of time is often called 'narrating', or 'discourse-time'.

Film adaptations almost always have a problem reducing discourse-time. Typically, they must squeeze the novel's reading time of many hours into little more than two hours of viewing-time. Fortunately, cinema's multiple tracks of information make such consolidation possible. Consider, for example that part of a novel traditionally called the 'exposition', that is the introductory summary of past events to establish a 'present moment', the moment of the first scenic action. Such exposition, especially in nineteenth century novels, could go on for many pages.

Ishiguro's novel recounts two stories: the earlier story of Stevens' relations with Miss Kenton at Darlington Hall against the background of Lord Darlington's involvement with the Nazis, and the later story, that of Stevens' motor trip to the west to see Miss Kenton. I'll refer to these as the 1936 story and the 1956 story. The novel begins with a 'Prologue' of 20 pages, say, 20 to 40 minutes of discourse time, which recounts the 1956 story, mostly as Stevens' summarized exposition of events since the acquisition of Darlington Hall by its new American owner and the problems that loss of staff has caused.

The film version, on the other hand, reduces exposition time to only a minute or two by cleverly mixing visuals with a voiceover soundtrack. As we watch Stevens' current labours at Darlington Hall, heavier because of staff losses, we hear Mis Kenton's voiceover reading the letter she has

[clip 1: 00.10–0:1:36]

written him, reminiscing about her career there, and guessing that the staff *has* been reduced. This guess is verified by a visual dissolve or *erasure* of footmen who used to serve under Stevens in the more affluent past. Then, Stevens' own memory of Miss Kenton is represented through another erasure as he peeps through a round window into the servants' hall: she too vanishes. Note that the motif of long elapsed time is visually captured by the two grandfather clocks framing the door through which he passes, and that the odd round window is studded at intervals like those of numerals on a clock face. The rhythm of the music also emulates a ticking clock's sound.

The novel provides its exposition of the 1936 story piecemeal during Stevens' adventures on the road. This kind of exposition was called 'distributed' by the novelist and narrative theorist Ford Madox Ford, who much favoured it over 'bunched' or 'lumped' exposition, especially at a novel's beginning. Stevens' account of his visit to the west follows the orderly progression of the six-day trip itself, whereas the 1936 story occurs in bits and pieces as these randomly occur to Stevens in freely associated memories.

Because cinema is by definition an external art, an art of surfaces, the filmmaker's hardest task is to communicate in a visual way a character's inner life, his or her thoughts and feelings. Here is an example of the problem in the novel. Early on, Stevens-as-narrator expresses obliquely, through his ostensible preoccupation with staffing problems (which he admits to himself are minor), his hopes of seeing Miss Kenton again and perhaps persuading her to return to service at Darlington Hall. Her letter has come unexpectedly and from a considerable distance, a distance that matches the emotional gulf between them. It is also distanced in time, as she recalls a painful incident in the 1936 story that had touched her deeply: Stevens' father, grown old and unemployed, was hired below his customary rank, namely, as underbutler. She remembers how the elder Stevens stumbled on the lawn, dropping a laden tray he was about to serve to Lord Darlington and his guests in the summerhouse. Acutely embarrassed, he had to be carried to his bed. A few days later, she watched the old man from an upstairs window retracing his steps, 'looking down at the ground as though he hoped to find some precious jewel that he had dropped there'. The dropped jewel obviously symbolizes his precious professionalism, lost in an instant in this grotesque fall. As he reads the letter, Stevens remembers sharing that long ago moment at the window with Miss Kenton in terms so much warmer than his usual bureaucratic prose as to seem almost poetic.

It is something of a revelation that this memory from over thirty years ago should have remained with Miss Kenton as it has done with me. Indeed, it must have occurred on just one of those summer evenings she mentions, for I can recall distinctly climbing to the second landing and seeing before me a series of orange shafts from the sunset breaking the gloom of the corridor... [I saw] Miss Kenton's figure, silhouetted against a window, turn and call softly: 'Mr. Stevens, if you have a moment' ... Down below, the shadows of the poplars were falling across the lawn. To the right of our view, the lawn sloped up a gentle embankment to where the summerhouse stood, and it was there my father's figure could be seen, pacing slowly with an air of preoccupation.

Note the phrase 'something of a revelation'. That he had shared an intimacy with Miss Kenton is just occurring to Stevens—20 years too late. Even now, he avoids the full implications of that revelation. His distance from Miss Kenton, both temporal and spatial, is preserved by the discourse. In the novel, it is hard to know how much in the way of romantic attraction Miss Kenton feels since Stevens so inveterately underreads her reactions.[3] Not that he is totally insensitive to emotion; it's just that he is so devoted to service that he only attends to the needs—practical and emotional—of Lord Darlington and his guests.

In both the 1936 and 1956 stories, the film version eschews first person narration, restricting itself to a here-and-now representation of every scene. Events and characters are no longer filtered solely through Stevens' memory but appear, visually, in their own right, and so we can measure for ourselves the mutual attraction of the two. We infer it from clues like the flowers with which Miss Kenton tries to brighten Stevens' room. It also is implied by her teasing raillery, or to use Stevens' word, 'bantering'. In the film, Miss Kenton's emotions can be read on her face, as in the scene at the window:

[clip 2: 31:54 S and K looking out of the window down at father]

Note how only Miss Kenton's emotions are evoked; Stevens remains stony-faced, as he should, since it is only much later that he can allow himself to recognize the intimacy of the moment. The verbal simile of the elder Stevens' 'lost jewel', of course, is missing, but something of the impact of the event is preserved by his pantomimic movements in the garden.

Certain nuances of novels cannot be captured satisfactorily by the visual medium and wise directors don't even try. What, for instance is the visual counterpart of a specifically named emotion—say 'heartbreak?' Can any filmmaker really hope to convey an exactly named thought to the audience? Hardly. Except for experimental films, usually only two means are available to convey a specific word for an inner state. The more obvious is to have the word actually spoken, either in a straightforward manner in dialogue; or, less often these days, by the device called voiceover, that is an utterance on the soundtrack but independent of any lip movement. But direct verbalization of the word 'heartbreak' would be inappropriate to a film like *Remains of the Day,* whose very theme is the protagonist's inability to articulate his feelings even in his own mind.

The other means is to rely solely on the actor's performance to suggest the feeling—through facial expression, body language, and movement, supplemented perhaps by lighting and mood music. Even if these are very well done, as they are in *Remains of the Day*, they cannot achieve the *precise* specificity of the novel's wording but only a general sense of the feeling invoked. Ask viewers and they're likely to propose a variety of words—'sad', 'disconsolate'; 'depressed', all are just as probable as 'heartbroken'.

This film relies on the great talents of the actor Anthony Hopkins to convey the sense of heartbreak in three separate moments. The first occurs as the couple walk along the boardwalk reminiscing about the old days. Like the novel, the film has Miss Kenton admit to having made a mistake with her life. Upon hearing that, Stevens murmurs 'Yes', more to himself than to her, as if to acknowledge how clearly it applies to his own situation. He looks straight ahead, his eyes enormously round with dismay. Recovering his façade, he partially masks his heartbreak with a paternalistic platitude: 'We all make such mistakes,' he says.

[clip 3, 2:18–3:10]

In the novel, we read that Stevens puts Miss Kenton on the bus and then goes to the pier. There, as chance would have it, he strikes up a conversation with a retired butler. As he describes his service to Lord Darlington and his fears that he can no longer match that standard for his

American employer, he sheds a tear. The retired butler tries to comfort him with a slightly used hankerchief and good advice. 'Don't look back,' he says. 'Enjoy yourself... The evening's the best part of the day.' The man leaves, and Stevens sits alone watching the pier lights go on. He is struck by the way the vacationers, pleased by this modest event, start to chat, or as he puts it, banter with each other. Stevens' narration ends as he vows to study bantering skills more ardently, the better to please his new employer. This belated attention to bantering, to what we would call 'kidding around', is ironic, given Stevens' inability to understand the affection hidden behind Miss Kenton's bantering in the old days. It is characteristic that Stevens can only validate this practice by making it a professional responsibility. The plan and its belaboured characterization as a task mitigates any sense of tragedy that Stevens' situation might otherwise evoke, rendering him more pathetic than tragic. As one critic put it, Stevens is 'an emotionally challenged Englishman who mistakes etiquette for morality, a man with a good heart that is buried beneath a pathological fetish for order'.[4] Or in the words of another, he is 'a portrait of heroic futility, heartbreaking fatuity, and purblind doggedness'.[5]

The film drops the retired butler, and puts Miss Kenton instead on the bench with Stevens. *She* is assigned the observation that people always cheer when the lights go on. Stevens contemplates the cheering crowd as if they were space aliens, and mutters 'I wonder why'. She replies that for many people the evening is the best part of the day. Then she asks Stevens what he is looking forward to. 'Work, work, and more work', he says. In the film, the remains of *his* day are clearly bleaker than those suggested by the novel:

[clip 4, 3:10–4:18]

The final sign of heartbreak is purely visual: it takes place as Miss Kenton and Stevens shake hands goodbye. In a close-up, Stevens' hand is left empty, as the bus pulls Miss Kenton away for the last time.

[clip 5: 3:10–4:18]

The film ends by adding a scene showing Stevens and his employer releasing a pigeon trapped inside the Hall—a somewhat heavy-handed symbol for Stevens' own entrapment to his profession.

Anthony Hopkins is a consummate screen actor with an astonishing range of facial expressions: remember his portrayal of the cannibalistic psychiatrist Hannibal Lector in *The Silence of the Lambs.* On the contrary, the character of Stevens requires great constraint and a narrow range of facial expressions. For this purpose, Hopkins uses only a few to reveal feelings that not even this repressed butler could conceal. One such expression is a sidelong glance of...what is it? Deference? For instance in the amusing conversation in which Lord Darlington, played by James Fox, feeling discomfited by his guardian's duties, assigns to Stevens the task of explaining

[clip 6]

the birds and bees to his charge, Mr Cardinal. Cardinal, played by Hugh Grant, is a quite worldly young reporter who is about to be married.

The dialogue is very close to the original, but the film additionally communicates, through the sidelong glance and other facial business, Stevens' confused embarrassment and automatized deference.

Stevens' facial expressions in dealing with Miss Kenton are more complex. In the early stage of their association, when he is still firmly on professional terms, he has no problem. Conscious of his superior rank in the servants' hierarchy, he rejects her attempt to brighten up his den with flowers, and then, with flourishes of his cigarillo, orders her to be more respectful of his father. When she answers him tit for tat and walks out, he adopts a tight smirk that ends in a strained mirthless laugh, as if she had acted beyond the pale.

[clip 7]

The finest moment in Hopkins' performance is the embarrassed vulnerability he exhibits when challenged at the truly emotional level. Here, the film adds an intensity that cannot be inferred from his narration in the novel. The setting is again his room, but this time Miss Kenton is the aggressor, teasingly inquiring about the nature of the book that he reads in his spare time. Here is how the novel's Stevens-as-narrator describes his reaction:

> I looked up to see Miss Kenton advancing towards me. I shut the book, and clutching it to my person, rose to my feet...Miss Kenton was continuing to advance and I must say it was a little difficult to assess what my best course of action

would be. I was tempted to thrust the book into the drawer of my desk and lock it, but this seemed absurdly dramatic. I took a few paces back, the book still held to my chest...Then she was standing before me, and suddenly the atmosphere underwent a peculiar change—almost as though the two of us had been suddenly thrust on to some other plane of being altogether. I am afraid it is not easy to describe clearly what I mean here. All I can say is that everything around us suddenly became very still; it was my impression that Miss Kenton's manner also underwent a sudden change; there was a strange seriousness in her expression, and it struck me she seemed almost frightened...She reached forward and began gently to release the volume from my grasp. I judged it best to look away while she did so, but her person positioned so closely, this could only be achieved by my twisting my head away at a somewhat unnatural angle. Miss Kenton continued very gently to prise the book away, practically one finger at a time. The process seemed to take a very long time, throughout which I managed to maintain my posture... I believe it was around this point that I decided there was no need to tolerate any more. I cannot recall precisely what I said, but I remember showing Miss Kenton out of my pantry quite firmly and the episode was thus brought to a close.

The film sequence captures much of this subtlety, but with a few interesting differences.

[clip 8]

The film does not alter the action, but adds some brilliant visual details. As Miss Kenton steps forward to grasp the book, her face only a few inches from his, Stevens raises his right hand to his face in a defensive way, like a child about to be scolded by its mother. The low-key lighting from above, which in a horror movie would be a cliché for sinisterness, here merely accentuates his bashfulness. As he stares at her unblinkingly, his eyes seem at once full of helpless reticence and a yearning which he cannot express or even acknowledge. She pries his fingers away from the book as he continues to stare shyly into her face, never altering his posture. (The prying away of fingers, by the way, richly echoes another scene in which Stevens has to pry his father's fingers away from the utility cart to which he has been subjugated after his first stroke. In other words, both father and son have to be torn physically from their sense of duty in order to experience emotion). After Miss Kenton discovers that the book is not 'scandalous at all but only a sentimental old love story', he delicately retrieves it with his left hand, explaining that he reads to improve his English, and begs her, in the softest tones, not to disturb the few moments that he has to himself. Unlike the novel, in which he regains some composure and authority, he does not escort her to the door, but remains forlornly back in the corner. In a televised interview, by the way, Hopkins said that he played the scene as if Emma Thompson were trying to seduce him.

In the novel, Stevens finally gains some insight into his affection for Miss Kenton, but not into his attitude toward his profession. Despite his voyage of discovery and the admission about Darlington's mistakes that history has forced upon him, Stevens' philosophy of life has not really changed. He comments that

> The hard reality is, surely, that for the likes of you [that is, the reader] and I, there is little choice other than to leave our fate, ultimately, in the hands of those great gentlemen at the hub of this world who employ our services. What is the point in worrying oneself too much about what one could or could not have done to control the course one's life took? Surely it is enough that the likes of you and I at least *try* to make our small contribution count for something true and worthy. And if some of us are prepared to sacrifice much in life in order to pursue such aspirations, surely that is in itself, whatever the outcome, cause for pride and contentment'. (p. 244)

No such self-consolation, however misguided, ends the film. Instead, our final sight of Stevens is the brief glance he gives to the outside world as the pigeon, unlike him, escapes to its freedom.

In their openness, both the novel and the film are modernist or postmodernist endeavours, but they achieve openness in different ways, unique to their respective media. The novel achieves it through the use of unreliable narration. To use Phelan and Martin's terms, the character-narrator both under reads and under reports the events he recounts. Under reads in the sense that he did not and in some ways still cannot fully understand their full ramifications; under reports in the sense that he does not fully admit to his reader what he knows and what the reader suspects. The film, on the other hand, eschewing direct verbal access to Stevens' mind, requires us to read out of Anthony Hopkins' face and gestures what his inhibitions do not permit him to say.

* This is the version of the paper that Professor Chatman presented at the video conference for the seminar on 'Reflexions: Literature, Film, and Culture', organized by the Department of English, University of Delhi, in March 2004.

NOTES

1. Darlington and his associates were apparently modelled after the so-called Cliveden Set. For a discussion of these men, see Quigley 1966, chapter 12, and 1981. Carroll Quigley writes: 'They were gracious and cultured gentlemen of somewhat limited social experience who were much concerned with the freedom of expression of minorities and the rule of law for all, who constantly thought in terms of Anglo-American solidarity, of political partition and federation, and who were convinced that they could gracefully civilize the Boers of South Africa, the Irish, the Arabs, and the Hindus, and who are largely responsible for the partitions of Ireland, Palestine, and India, as well as the federations of South Africa, Central Africa, and the West Indies. Their desire to win over the opposition by cooperation worked with Smuts but failed with Hertzog, worked with Gandhi but failed with Menon, worked with Stresemann but failed with Hitler, and has shown little chance of working with any Soviet leader.'

   Quigley's characterization sounds very much like the denunciation of Lord Darlington and his guests as 'amateurish' by the American congressman, Mr Lewis, in both the novel and the film. In the novel he says: 'You gentlemen here, forgive me, but you are just a bunch of naive dreamers. And if you didn't insist on meddling in large affairs that affect the globe, you would actually be charming. Let's take our good host here. What is he? He is a gentleman...decent, honest, well-meaning. But his lordship here is *an amateur*... He is an amateur and international affairs today are no longer for gentlemen amateurs... You here in Europe need professionals to run your affairs ... A toast, gentlemen. Let me make a toast. To professionalism' (Ishiguro, 1990 p. 102). Lord Darlington's amateurism ironically contrasts with the professionalism of his butler.
2. See Phelan and Martin, 1999, pp. 88–109.
3. A good example occurs when Miss Kenton remarks (doubtless ironically) that she cannot imagine what more Stevens could want from life than being at the top of his profession. He answers with the most explicit statement in the novel of his goal in life:

   As far as I am concerned, Miss Kenton, my vocation cannot be fulfilled until I have done all I can to see his lordship through the great tasks he has set himself. The day his lordship's work is complete, the day *he* is able to rest on his laurels, content in the knowledge that he has done all anyone could ever reasonably ask of him, only on that day, Miss Kenton, will I be able to call myself, as you put it, a well-contented man.

His obtuseness about her feelings is caught in the observation that immediately follows:

She may have been a little puzzled by my words; or perhaps it was that they had for some reason displeased her. In any case, her mood seemed to change at that point, and our conversation rapidly lost the rather personal tone it had begun to adopt.

The reader wants to shake Stevens—can't he at least *ask* her what's bothering her about what he's said?

4. Johnson, 1993.
5. Simon, 1993.

REFRENCES

Ishiguro, Kazuo, *The Remains of the Day*, New York: Vintage International, 1990, p. 102.

Johnson, Brian, *Macleans*', vol. 106, no. 46, 1993, p. 93.

Phelan, James, and Martin, Mary Patricia, 'The Lessons of Weymouth: Homodiegesis, Unreliability, Ethics and *The Remains of the Day*, in *Narratologies: New Perspectives on Narrative Analysis*, Columbus: Ohio State University Press, 1999, pp. 88–109.

Quigley, Carroll, *Tragedy and Hope: a History of the World in our Time*, New York: Macmillan, 1966.

———, *The Anglo-American Establishment from Rhodes to Cliveden*, New York: Books in Focus, 1981.

Simon, John, *National Review*, vol. 45, no. 24, 1993, p. 61.

11

Screening Reality: The Remains of the Day *as Fact, Fiction and Film from a Postcolonial Perspective*

Ved Prakash Baruah

Often we just don't know enough about what's going on out there, and I felt that's what we're like. We're like butlers.

—Kazuo Ishiguro from Allan Vorda, (ed.), *Face to Face: Interviews with Contemporary Novelists*

I knew in England that since my great-great-grandparents hadn't been born there I didn't have a chance, so it never occurred to me to try to fit—and I took it for granted I was an outsider, and that was fine. And the same for India.

—Ruth Prawer Jhabvala from Antony Korner, *Art forum*

THE INTELLECTUAL and cultural legacy of *The Remains of the Day* is a veritable mélange of people, places and purposes; the author is an émigré of Japanese birth and ancestry settled in Britain; the screen adaptation is by a novelist of Jewish descent who spent her childhood in Nazi Germany and then lived as a refugee in England and as a wife in India married to an Indian, settling later in New York; the filmmakers are an unusual Indo-American team who specialize in British 'heritage cinema' and adaptations;[1] and the tale itself is of a 'real' English butler who wanders in the rooms of his memory trying to understand his 'then and now', and in doing so, inadvertently gets entangled with the larger picture—Britain's history. Needless to say, then, the compass of the tale, as novel or film, is larger than the tale itself; and what lies outside the 'frame' might just be what Seymour Chatman overlooks in his keenly argued and thoroughly enlightening article, 'The Art of Film Adaptation: *The Remains of the Day*'.[2]

Writing a response to an article, I feel, is in many ways very similar to the process of adaptation of a novel for the screen when viewed from the aspect of 'fidelity', and the 'ambivalencies' (the elisions and the alterations), I contend, are as important as the 'equivalencies', if not more. My argument, since it establishes ambivalencies as its cornerstone, will engage, therefore, directly with (and even contest) what I interpret as Chatman's tacit undermining of the correlation of form and content (their similitude of status and value) in the case of adaptations, as evidenced in his asseveration that he will 'concentrate on changes in form to accommodate the new medium, but of course [he] cannot avoid implications for content as well'.[3] Consequently, I will discuss the subject of adaptation of *The Remains of the Day* from the vantage point of content, particularly from a postcolonial perspective, foregrounding what inclusion effectuates as well as what is effectuated by exclusion. I shall also attend to how such negotiations connect with the formal aspect of cinematic representation.

My response to Chatman's article, therefore, will be centred on what I think constitutes the 'without the frame',[4] namely, the tensions that inhabit and determine Kazuo Ishiguro's novel (focusing primarily on the first person narratorial perspective and its connection with history, private and public), the manoeuvres that Ruth Prawer Jhabvala (and the Merchant–Ivory team) invest(s) in the adaptation and the implications of these strategies, as well as the factors that determine adaptation, effected as it is by the formal and contextual demands of the medium; using Chatman's article as a point of reference—both in terms of convergence and divergence.

Ishiguro's *The Remains of the Day* does not fall into the bracket of what is generally classified as 'the historical novel',[5] but no commentary on the novel is possible without entering the arena of negotiations 'affected' by what should be interpreted as the imaginative reconstruction of the 'past', using the 'present' as a device subjected to critical inquiry. The novel reads more as a narrative of personal reminiscence—a sort of autobiographical account—than as any kind of historical fiction, but the presence, albeit in the background, of historical figures like Ribbentrop, Oswald Mosley, H.G. Wells, and G.B. Shaw, and of fictionalized versions of Unity Mitford and the Duke of Windsor reinforces its intimacy with the genre. The book, then, needs to be viewed under the lens of what can be called the distinction between 'historical' and 'historicized' fiction, between fiction about history and fiction about its own historically relative construction of history.[6] Such a reading of the text immediately foregrounds the significance of the author's 'subject position' and of its reciprocity with cultural epistemes. The subject position, in Ishiguro's case, manifest in his fiction and elsewhere, is troubled terrain, to say the least, and a whole range of identities, from a genuine Japan-in-his-soul writer to a masquerading 'whiteface', as well as the more commonplace tag of an Anglo-Japanese writer, have been attached to him.

While the universality of Ishiguro's stories (I refer to his oeuvre and not just to the novel in question) conceals his ancestry, it is impossible to divorce the writer from his writing. Sheng-mei Ma contends that 'Ishiguro's dream of post-ethnicity turns out to be a veiling and an intensification of his minority complex', which Ma understands as the motivating force behind his use of English characters and their peculiar 'Englishness'. Ma even goes on to say that the 'characters' denial of emotions parallels a minority writer's innermost neurosis, a deep-seated anxiety over identity'.[7] What is so evidently flawed in Ma's proposition is that this persuasion translates in terms of Ishiguro's characters becoming Ishiguro himself, or some facet of his self, coming to terms with his own history, his ethnicity. I argue for a need to recognize Ishiguro's identity politics differently, understanding his fictional characters as projections of the minority onto the majority, calling upon the majority to perceive and to recognize the mutual kinship of the 'other' and themselves, suggestive not of any 'neurosis' but of eudaemonia. In my estimation, then, Ishiguro emerges as an 'assimilated' figure (and a genuine post-ethnic), exhibiting none of the anxieties that Ma's thesis forwards. The narrative of *The Remains of the Day* symbolizes this aspect of performance of identity, played out through the apposition of Stevens' professional and private roles, one masking the other.

The 'novel of history'[8] attempts to investigate the possibility of conferring sequence, direction, and narratability upon the past as well as the present, in relation to the present, and my discussion of the novel will be from this vantage point. History as conventionally and institutionally constructed is not, in most cases, concerned with the intimate, the obscure, and the idiomatic, but with the outward, the visible, and the typical. In *The Remains of the Day,* however, the emplacement of the two 'forms of history' (the private and the public) in simultaneous ordering within the narrative, enables each to exist in its own right and allows scope for direct authorial intervention, when the substance of the tale is understood in terms of causality. Consequently, then, the novel is as much 'about' the period between the Wars, as it is about its protagonist–narrator, the very 'unreliable' Mr Stevens, the paradigmatic English butler representative of the 'traditions' of England.

Ishiguro constructs Stevens by tapping into (and manipulating) a kind of myth (or stereotype) about the English butler and English country life—one that has been transmitted around the world not through highbrow history books, but through popular culture, comic books, movies, and fiction—and he uses the figure metaphorically to reconstruct a life lived in historical anonymity, representing an 'underclass' (or a subaltern, to use the more favoured jargon), writing, as it were, a 'history from below'.[9] By focusing on the intersection of personal (or private) and historical (or public) events played out within a very narrow framework, he employs what has been called an 'alternative history' conceit, where Stevens' narrative represents a (mis)recognizing of history which is at times deliberate. Stevens' main concerns pertain to the quality of his professional performance, and the ensuing topic of what constitutes greatness in a butler that runs throughout the narrative as an apparent digression proves to be the key to his character as well as to the novel's perspective on history.

The central concern of the novel is the first person narrator's attempt to come to terms with his values and identity, set against a backdrop of historical change where, although the historical context may be accurate to a greater or lesser degree, the author's main interest is in historical processes and their imprint upon individuals rather than in their view of history itself. Ishiguro's use of history in the narrative, therefore, mirrors Margaret Scanlan's understanding of its role in post-War novels. She suggests that history in these novels is repeatedly decentred and experienced through the lives of individuals detached from history, and it is

> … neither glamorous nor consoling. It is too diffuse to offer lessons, too unfinished to constitute a space into which we can escape; and we ourselves, implicated in the failures of the past, cannot even enjoy its ironies comfortably. Whatever the authors' professed politics, their novels resonate with a profound pessimism about the consequences of public action. What actuates in these fictions is not, then, a confidence that the past will teach us how to behave, but a quieter conviction that it is better to know than to remain ignorant, even though what we learn is the enormous difficulty of understanding our lives historically.[10]

In the process of writing his journal—the novel, so to say—Stevens is suddenly thrust into history and is forced to recognize that actions and even the omissions of actions have consequences. Through him, perhaps, Ishiguro reminds us that public as well as private history is no more than the summing up of such actions and omissions.

For instance, in the novel Stevens recalls his life through his commitment to professionalism and duty, and he seems not to comprehend the ways in which his own narrative—where his relationship with Miss Kenton plays such an important role—reveals the processes by which his identity, vocation, and values were formed and determined. The unreliability of Stevens' narrative questions, further, this aspect of unverified and self-spoken 'truths'. While aspiring to serve (and achieve through it) greatness, he facilitates his employer's efforts to promote Nazi appeasement, however naively, and comes across as a man unable to see the larger picture in his pursuit of order within the rather insular universe he knows and inhabits.

His investment and commitment to the discourse of 'butlery' determines Stevens' identity, historically pertinent and valid at the time in which it is adopted but not necessarily valid forever. The narrator's investment in this particular set of values allowed him to function in perfect harmony in relation to his social environment. However, the passing of time has made his value system redundant, putting him out of step with the immanent present. The effect of such an anachronistic situation is that the narrator's identity (that of a butler's) no longer suffices, demanding a 'revision'.[11]

This aspect is best represented in the novel (as in the movie) in Stevens' encounter with Harry Smith and his take on 'dignity', which foregrounds this 'revision' very succinctly. Since the future generation (Harry Smith's) has already 'consented' to a different and emergent hegemony (democracy/communism in this instance) Stevens, comfortable in his cocoon until now, needs to accept the reality of the changed circumstances brought about by the breakdown of the Empire (and the public denunciation of his employer) and he needs to (re)present his self and his narrative differently. The unreliability of the narrative, then, stems from Stevens' realization of the ramifications of real history, and he uses his professional capacity as a mask to defend himself and his complicity (or not) with pro-Nazi activities.[12] This opening up of a gap between the individual's value system and the surroundings makes it imperative for Stevens to remember (or reconstruct) his life from a different perspective.

The novel is set in July 1956, unmistakably the period of the Suez Canal crisis, which is an episode that marks, de facto, the end of the British Empire, but there are no outward references to these events.[13] Instead (and more pointedly so), Ishiguro's narrative is driven by the 1936 story which is made up of personal memoirs wherein the cognizant unreliability of the narrator is often subverted by the thoughtful workings of memory itself, pinpointing the significance of its ellipses and elisions, its divisions, conflating the distortions of the past and its conflicts with present experience.[14] Stevens' attempt to rekindle his ruined personal life fails, and he is left in a state of having no other alternative but to assimilate the values of his new American master in order to carry on with his 'duties'. The much talked about 'bantering' that he recognizes as vital to his assimilation into the new order indicates this, and his resolve to master it effectively sums up all that he has learnt during the week-long trip.

The first question that crops up, then, is what does one do when one adapts a novel which its writer declares (in spite of its apparent presence) has no element of realism in it?[15] Underlying all adaptations (and perhaps all acts of reading and/or writing), I would say there is a three-step process, namely, representation, imagination, and interpretation (not necessarily in that order). So the screenwriter either underplays and delimits the realistic potential of the novel, or heightens it. It is difficult to deny that the movie has realistic foci, and this not merely because the Merchant–Ivory team[16] specializes in realistic cinema but also (and largely) due to Jhabvala, the screenwriter. As both Ishiguro and Jhabvala attest the independence of a novel and its adapted movie version as final products,[17] it is crucial to grant a certain amount of credit to the screenwriter, as it is through exercise of the three-step process by this agent that a novel starts its afterlife as a screenplay.[18] Chatman's non-appreciation of the complexities of Jhabvala's screenplay and her manoeuvres stems largely from his disavowal of the primacy of content in the visual medium, as iterated above, which in effect silences the question posited in the beginning of the paragraph.

When considering the adaptation I shall attempt to investigate the nature of the effected changes in content alongside an appreciation of the formal ones, attempting to understand and isolate the motivation behind the modifications executed. Indicative of the change of content effected in the adaptation is the fact that the movie both starts and ends differently from the novel, and I stress that such changes exhibit what embodies the crux of Jhabvala's attitude regarding adaptation: the unshackled expression of a scriptwriter's subjective position and intellect.

Ishiguro's narrative, coming as it does in the form of the novel, undergoes transformation through Jhabvala's vision;[19] the 'insider' perspective of the former meets the 'outsider' position of the latter, both literally and symbolically (because of their respective subject positions), and Ishiguro's first person narrative is modified into a drama that, while preserving the ironies of Stevens' interior landscape, expands the socio-political world that he inhabits. The drive behind such a shift can be attributed to Jhabvala's preoccupation with the question of (non)identification in her writings, which can be efficaciously summed up as the paradox of belonging and exile through which she construes herself: 'Not really having a world of my own, I made up for my disinheritance by absorbing the worlds of others.'[20] In a rare fragment of autobiography, the 1979 Neil Gunn fellowship lecture 'Disinheritance', Jhabvala described herself as a 'writer without any ground of being out of which to write: really blown about from country to country, culture to culture, till I feel—till I am—nothing'.[21] Caryl Phillips, recognizing the facet of 'disinheritance' in Jhabvala, proffers her the tag of postcoloniality:

> Ruth was postcolonial before the term had been invented. She understood loss of language, land and history in a brutal and visceral way, and reinvented herself, first in the heart of the old empire, then in the cradle of a newly independent country, and now in the centre of the new American empire.[22]

Caryl Phillips fails, in my view, to understand the real nature of her 'homelessness', and he ignores the existence of a certain sense of ambiguity about 'loss' in her writings that I feel is so definitive of Jhabvala's imagination, and for which the word 'mimicry' is a close synonym.[23] My contention is that for Jhabvala the sense of 'loss' is a deliberate construct which can be (and is) remedied by 'masking' as a 'chameleon hiding [her] self in false or borrowed colours'.[24] In an interview, Jhabvala says:

> When I was in England I was pretty young, still a student, but even then I would always write from an English standpoint. Wherever I am, I just turn around and pretend I'm from there.[25]

What distinguishes her from Ishiguro is her perception of the lack of a sense of belonging or rootedness and an acute sentience of being in exile, starkly contrasted with Ishiguro's 'assimilation'. Hence the insider–outsider paradigm defines their respective positions and the upshot of this is keenly corroborated in the explication offered in their fiction.

The opening sequence in the movie establishes its realistic foci, starting as it does in the middle of things with Miss Kenton's voiceover, reading out a letter addressed to Stevens which not only reduces the exposition time (as Chatman indicates) but also sets the tone of the obviously digressive nature of the adapted version. The first and the most striking instance of departure (in the movie) from the novel is the dissolution of one of the most prominent aspects of the novel, the demise of the unreliable narrator and his 'controlling' narrative (which effectively effaces the trope of the unreliability of the narrative in the movie).[26] He exists in the movie only as a character, even if the central one. As discussed above, the unreliable narrator is the mainstay of all Ishiguro's textual apparatus(es) and commentary (individual as well as collective). It is noteworthy that Anthony Hopkins, in his subtle and penetrating portrayal of Stevens, effectively depicts this fettering of his character's control over the narrative through the use of a tight shoulder stance and breathy hesitations that punctuate his dialogue delivery.

The emergence of the visual free play of unfiltered imagination and the spatio-temporal construction of events (the here-and-now portrayal) is a phenomenon related to the digression referred to above, since the narrative unfolds now without Stevens' agency. This does provide greater autonomy to the filmmakers' vision but since this intervention occurs at the stage of scripting the movie, the credit (or discredit) goes to Jhabvala. It is important to undertake an analysis of what such an intercession achieves. The most striking parallel that I am reminded of is the adaptation of Vladimir Nabokov's *Lolita* by Stanley Kubrick. The screenplay written by the author himself retains the unreliable narrative of Humbert, sticking to the 'literal' narrative model. Jhabvala, in an interview expressing her views on adaptation, provides a counterpoint to this model by asserting that:

> Any adaptation you do it diagonally. You can take up the theme but you can never, never, never do it literally. You'd come up with a kind of travesty, if you tried to interpret anything literally.... Fidelity is not the first [thing]. No I don't think so. Like I said, the theme and the feel of the characters...the ambience and their relationships...that is what you try...but never, never literally.[27]

It is noteworthy that there is a marked difference in the respective visions of Kubrick and the Merchant–Ivory team regarding adaptations. While Kubrick revels in exploiting the comic potential of a narrative by creating a chasm between the verbal (the written) and the visual (the filmic), achieving a very highly marked irony,[28] the Merchant–Ivory team (I include Jhabvala here) hungers for realism, in dialogue and in visual similitude, across the ostensibly different surfaces of the two mediums. As I understand it, then, adaptation in Jhabvala's terms being effectively realized 'diagonally' (understanding it symbolically in view of the connotations of its synonymous meanings) brings in the aspect of the adapter's socio-cultural discourses and subject position into play.

With the redundancy of the 'intradiegetic' or internal narrator, the very first thing that ensues in the adaptation is that it enables a finer depiction of the space and time co-ordinates of the narrative, liberated as it is now from the unidimensionality of the first person narrative.[29] This accords a more central role to the visual elements (or the depictive representational elements) of the narrative, enabling the movie to achieve a heightened sense of realism. This effecting of spatio-temporality can be manifested in two ways; it can either be achieved through the use of visual temporal elements like period architecture or clothing, or through non-visual temporal elements like period music.[30] The movie uses both to heighten the realistic depiction, the former being so evocatively presented in the title credits as well as in the opening sequence when the camera zooms in with Darlington Hall, forming the backdrop [00:00:29–00:01:54],[31] while the latter can be instanced in the scene in Stevens' parlour where

he is in conversation with Mr Benn, and he plays a gramophone record [01:02:06–01:03:54].

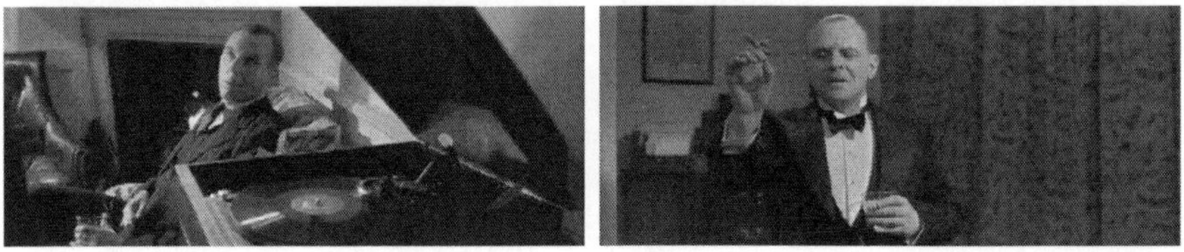

Moreover, while the presence of the frame narrator hinders the function of the temporal properties of the storyline, very pointedly so in this instance because of the prominence of the analepses, the 'here-and-now' representation makes possible the enactment of an independent 'time-structure in the plot.[32] The temporal properties of cinematic representation (words in conjunction with images) serve to represent the temporality of the events represented,[33] highlighting the difference between 'then and now' (something that the novel achieves through the unreliability of the first person narrative), and it is from these images that we are able to determine the temporality of the fictional characters and events depicted. The visual fades and dissolves illustrate this facet and function as qualitative representations of temporality, indicating a distance in time that may not be contextually represented. This facet is very finely captured in the movie,[34] where the richness of the past is visually depicted through paintings lining both sides of the corridor walls as Miss Kenton walks down and her 'erasure' mirrors the barrenness of the wall, effectively combining the private loss of Stevens with the (symbolic) public loss of Empire [00:04:40–00:04:56].

In the novel there are only two outward references to the East, the first being the classic instance of the English butler and his encounter with a tiger in India, and the other being the Chinaman incident. Although both instances appear in the movie almost unfiltered from their rendition in the novel, however, small but significant changes lend them a distinct political import. While the scope of the Chinaman incident, in the novel, is restricted to heightening the notion of place (and position) that every object in Darlington Hall (as a microcosm of the Empire and its 'order') is allocated, and the need to preserve these (as the inadvertent exchange by Stevens Sr leads to the disruption of a competent running of the household, remedied only by the intervention of the staff), the movie incorporates a visual metaphor, a continuous nodding Chinaman, suggesting servile assent [00:23:45–00:24:04].

The tiger under the table incident does even more. It is one of the many tales that put the spotlight on a butler's achievement of greatness and dignity in service, but this particular account has an inherent connection with the colonial burden ('the butler's burden', as it is here) and its associations with the civilizing mission is apparent. The successful obliteration of the savage, symbolically represented by the tiger under the dining table which in turn symbolizes 'culture', leaving no 'discernible traces' or causing 'upset' to the tea ceremony and the dinner of the 'lords' and their 'ladies', is suggestive not only of the efficiency of the butler's service, but also foregrounds the master–servant complicity in the 'mission', thus going beyond the commonplace reinforcing of typical colonial perceptions. The movie version of the account [00:17:17–00:18:33], however, deviates from the novelistic account with the addition of a seemingly harmless, 'They don't think nothing of it. In India, they're used to anything', in an undertone by Stevens Sr. This very potently introduces Jhabvala's notion of India which, although ambiguous for the most part, also comes out as detestation, evidenced in these lines:

> India ... will attack you in every possible way: it'll attack your morality, it'll destroy your personality, it'll bring out your worst qualities. It'll make you irritable, bad-tempered, arrogant.[35]

The subsequent fundamental departure from textual fidelity is seen in the (re)creation of the Mr Lewis character. Mr Farraday, the new American owner of Darlington Hall, does not find a place in the movie's scheme of things and Mr Lewis, the American Senator present at the conference in March 1923, takes his place. In the novel, Mr Farraday symbolically represents American dominance in the new world configuration and acts as the representative of a new hegemony, revealing Stevens' inadequacies, an aspect I have already dealt with in my discussion of the novel's political import.

This intervention is also vital because it intensifies the implications of the novel's political stance about the role that America plays in post-Empire Britain beyond the obvious, foregrounding Jhabvala's personal impressions of the Second World War as through it, she not only avows her Jewish roots but also the sufferings of her family due to Nazi prosecution.[36] In the movie, however, Mr Lewis (and not Mr Farraday), the same Senator Lewis who had famously denounced Darlington and his associates calling them 'amateurs' as opposed to the 'professionalism' that he subscribes to—at the last dinner of the 1923 conference—ends up, post-retirement, as the owner of Darlington Hall, and this is pregnant with purpose. Through this, I feel that Jhabvala, by endowing the original Mr Lewis' incisive political outlook to the new 'master' persona, effectively transfers the paradox of 'professionalism' and 'amateurism' that defined the Senator Lewis and Lord Darlington relationship. However, as he enters the 'master' persona only after he has retired from political life, he ceases to exist in his 'professional' avatar, his earlier identity. This, in effect, makes the question of any qualitative difference between the two masters redundant, uniting them in purpose and in kind.

A new facet to the master–servant relationship emerges when attention is focused on another change that is effected (and which is definitely in the same vein as above) in the movie. I refer to the transformation of the innocuous Ford[37] that Mr Farraday owns and offers to Stevens for his holiday (in the novel), to a Daimler[38] in the movie:

> LEWIS: I tell you what, you take the car. [Pause] Take the Daimler.
> STEVENS: Good Lord, sir, I couldn't.
> LEWIS: *You and that Daimler belong together. You were made for each other.*
> STEVENS: That's most kind of you, I must say, sir. Most kind.
>
> (Emphasis added)
> [0:06:06–00:06:18][39]

The substance of this change, I contend, modifies the basic premise of Stevens' complicity/innocence paradigm in the movie as opposed to the novel. In the movie, Stevens' association with fascism is determined in a more forthright manner and his intimate 'belonging' ('You and that Daimler ... were made for each other') with this political ideology is no longer (and not only) enacted through (and because of) the 'master', but more directly. The sense of gratitude that Stevens expresses to Lewis ('That's most kind of you....Most kind') marks a lineament of his persona that is denied him in the novel (in part because he acts in the capacity of an unreliable narrator): his need to be identified (and appreciated) for his contributions to 'international affairs' in his 'personal' capacity. The movie's use of the *cinema verité* technique of a shaky camera heightens the realism in the portrayal of Stevens' departure from the precincts of Darlington Hall into the world outside, the 'real world' as it were [00:08:08–00:08:18].

This aspect finds evocative expression if the motoring trip is viewed as a metaphor for liberation from his 'profession' and from his livery, divesting himself of the role of the gentleman's gentleman, becoming a 'real' gentleman. In such a case, during the week-long trip Stevens is free and acts in his personal capacity, hence his 'boast' of being involved in affairs of 'foreign policy' (the scene at a pub in Moscombe [01:11:04–01:13:23]) should be interpreted in the above light:

> STEVENS: Not directly as such, no, particularly in these days. Perhaps more so in the early 1930s and just before the war. My concern was more international affairs. Or foreign policy, so to speak. Not that I ever held high office, mind you. No, any influence I exerted was in an unofficial capacity.
>
> [01:11:40–01:12:06]

To come full circle (and back to the exposition), a notable dimension of my approach is to foreground instances like Chatman's neglect of the significance of the model for Lord Darlington and his associates, the 'Cliveden Set'—which he introduces only as a mere footnote.[40] While narrating the novel's sequence of events Chatman refers to Darlington's political role and its connection with the 'sellout of Czechoslovakia', and in the cited footnote he refers to Carroll Quigley's assessment of the men and their activities quite liberally, but summarily ends the discussion by stating that 'Quigley's characterization sounds very much like the denunciation of Lord Darlington by ... Mr. Lewis.' While this observation has its own merits, it does not quite satisfy the demands that Quigley's statement, seen from my perspective, exacts. Quigley mentions that the 'Set' was 'convinced that they could gracefully civilize the Boers of South Africa, the Irish, the Arabs, and the Hindus, and [they were] largely responsible for the partitions of Ireland, Palestine, and India....' The implications of this assertion significantly open the novel to a postcolonial reading (effectively an 'outside the frame' approach), a prospect denied in Seymour Chatman's article.

This article is a response, to reiterate my stance, directed against Chatman's non-acknowledgement of an essential feature of criticism: the political implications of the nature of the author's (and the adapters') as well as the interpreter's individual position and its germane connection with content as well as with form. Since this response countervails Seymour Chatman's paper, it is woven around instances which Chatman does (or does not), discuss, not only to offer an interpretation of the novel and the movie from my 'contrapuntal' position, but also to supplement his argument and to emphasize that what is said (or not said) is as important, if not more so, as how it is said.

NOTES

1. Ismail Merchant (lately deceased) was a Bombay-born Muslim who worked most of his life in the West, and James Ivory is an American Protestant with a keen interest in and understanding of India.
2. See Chapter 10, pp. 195–209 in this volume.
3. Seymour Chatman, 2009, p. 196.
4. With obvious roots in what I understand as Edward Said's 'contrapuntal' method. Although he does not use the term, Said's methodology involves referring back to the text from a perspective that seeks to reveal the hidden subtexts that would inform an 'against the grain' reading. See Edward Said, 1984, 'Introduction' and pp. 238–42.
5. I refer to Georg Lukács's ostensive definition. See Lukács (1969), 1981.
6. Commentators on fiction beginning in the late 1960s have established this distinction as a prerequisite to any inquiry into the post-War British novel.
7. Shang-mei Ma, pp. 72, 83.
8. I use the phrase 'novel of history' (with its incongruent syntax) in preference to the more widely used term, 'the historical novel', to highlight the distinction established above.
9. Ishiguro is not really interested in describing a world that he knew well and at firsthand, and in an interview with Don Swain, he refers to this metaphorical sense in which he understands the butler figure as representative of all those who do not really understand the political world but nevertheless do vote (video interview, http://www.wiredforbooks.org/, accessed on 19 March 2008).
10. Margaret Scanlan, 1990, p. 16.
11 This reading is heavily influenced by my understanding of Edward Said's use of Antonio Gramsci's and Michel Foucault's notion(s) of discourse and hegemony. See Shelley Walia, 2001.
12. Ishiguro's own relationship with England is fraught with a certain anxiety and he envisions both Japan and England from an imaginary position. Japan assumes the status of a dreamscape (interview with Don Swaim, refer to note 9) and England becomes a 'mythical place' with which he has no 'deep links' (interview with Alden Mudge, http://www.bookpage.com/0009bp/kazuo_ishiguro.html, accessed on 19 March 2008).
13. 'On 26 July 1956 the Egyptian President, Colonel Gamal Abdel Nasser, announces the Egyptian nationalization of the Suez Canal [and] on 27 July the British Prime Minister, Sir Anthony Eden, forms the Egypt Committee to co-ordinate Britain's intent to recover her access to the Suez Canal. Not only did the 1956 Suez Crisis result in deep political and public division in Britain, it also caused international uproar. It has come to be regarded as the end of Britain's role as one of the world powers and as the beginning of the end for the British Empire. In future British foreign policy would be conducted in concurrence with American diplomatic support' (http://www.bodley.ox.ac.uk/dept/scwmss/projects/suez/suez.html, accessed on 19 March 2008).

14. Seymour Chatman, 2009, pp. 199–200.
15. Refer to note 9. This aspect is discussed in the section (29:13–40:40) of the 55-minute interview.
16. I refer to Ismail Merchant and James Ivory and not to the third member of the team, Ruth Prawer Jhabvala. For my purposes I will see her as distinct from the other two who, in my schema, represent the filmic aspect and the scripted respectively.
17. Commenting on the movie, Ishiguro says, 'It's a different work from mine. It's James Ivory's *Remains of the Day* which is related to my *Remains of the Day*.' Ishiguro also refers to his literary agent's perceptive comment on what she considered the crucial difference, 'She said: The movie is about emotional repression. But the book is about self-denial... And I thought, yes, that's probably right. They are crucially different themes.' (Ishiguro in conversation with Linda L. Richards, http://januarymagazine.com/profiles/ishiguro.html, accessed on 19 March 2008.)
18. Seymour Chatman, in his article, views the adaptation of Ishiguro's novel as a relatively easy task, since it comes to Jhabvala, as it does, 'scenic in character...full of quotable dialogue and filmable actions in identifiable surroundings'.
19. It should be noted here that she is a major novelist in her own right, the winner of a Booker among other awards. Jhabvala (as evidenced by her interviews and non-fiction writings) understands the art of adaptation as a process of simplifying the complexities of a novel, enabling the characters to emerge in their own right.
20. Cited in Antony Korner, 1987, p. 99.
21. Maya Jaggi, 2005, http://www.guardian.co.uk/film/2005/mar/19/books featuresreviews, accessed on 19 March 2008.
22. Ibid.
23. I refer to her ambiguous stance regarding the contribution of her Jewish roots, of her English education, and of her life in India, and the very apparent strategy of appropriation that she employs in viewing (and constructing) herself as a writer.
24. In her 1979 lecture 'Disinheritance' cited in Maya Jaggi, 2005.
25. Antony Korner, 1987, p. 99.
26. As Seymour Chatman most rightly points out. But he does not delve into the issue.
27. Interview with Philip Horne in *The Guardian*, 27 October 2000. Excerpts from their conversation are also reproduced at http://merchantivory.com/goldenbowl/ruth.html, accessed 19 March 2008. Here, the question was with reference to adapting Henry James, but she answers in a general sense.
28. I have in mind Stanley Kubrick's *A Clockwork Orange* (1971) with its intradiegetic narrator and his *Barry Lyndon* (1975) with its extra-diegetic narrator. In both movies the first person narrative of the novel undergoes a striking qualitative metamorphosis due to the interplay of the visual/pictorial and the linguistic elements of the movie. Note that Thackeray's novel did not have a first person narrator.
29. I agree with Seymour Chatman's understanding that certain narrative statements use the mode of '*telling*' (mediating, presenting, diegetic) and others, the mode of '*showing*' (unmediated, exposing, mimesis) as also the distinction that he draws between diegesis and mimesis from the narratorial perspective; in the former the narrator is revealed, while in the latter this does not have to be the case. See Seymour Chatman (1978) 1993.
30. More often than not, this is the contribution of the director, the art director and other members of the film team, and not the scriptwriter. The instances I refer to are likewise.

31. All references to movie footage are from the Columbia Tri-Star (UK) DVD, 2001.
32. In positing the notion of an independent time-structure, I advance Seymour Chatman's idea of the 'two' kinds of time—'story-time' and 'discourse-time'—that function in all narratives, by bringing in another aspect of time that I feel operates in and differentiates diegetic and extra-diegetic elements in film—the distinction between representational time and represented time, especially due to the 'play' of non-visual elements like sound.
33. George Currie, 1995, pp. 96–103.
34. As Seymour Chatman has noted, and what he calls 'visual dissolve or *erasure*', in the instance of the footmen. I disagree, though, on his insistence on the identification of the grandfather clock as a motif for long-elapsed time and his equating the round window to a clock face. In my view, the former is symbolic of the vestiges of the past (and Empire) and the latter is an instance of 'tunneling of time', the horizontal depiction of time.
35. Yolanta May, 1975, p. 53.
36. This in spite of her established disavowal of her Jewish roots: 'I can trace no influence of my Jewish background in myself or my writing'. From 'A letter dated 13 May 1991', cited in Roland Shepherd, 2004, p. 10.
37. The company started by Henry Ford who pioneered mass production. Ford once (in)famously said that 'all History is bunk', to which Joseph Heller in the Epigraph to his novel *Picture This* (1988) ironically added, 'who knew almost none'.
38. Ironically, the marque refers to two different companies, one British and the other German. Both companies trace their roots to Gottlieb Daimler (1834–1900), the German engineer who produced the first high speed internal combustion engine. However, symbolically a Daimler represents German ascendancy and power.
39. The transcription of the above exchange (and elsewhere) is excerpted from the English subtitles to the DVD version of the film (refer to note 31). The time corresponds to this version's actual running time.
40. Seymour Chatman, 2009, p. 208, note 1.

References

Chatman, Seymour, *Story and Discourse: Narrative Structure in Fiction and Film*, London and Ithaca: Cornell University Press (1978), 1993.

———, 'The Art of Adaptation: *The Remains of the Day*', in Manju Jain, ed., *Narratives of Indian Cinema: Postcolonial to the Global*, New Delhi: Primus Books, 2009.

Currie, George, *Image and Mind: Film, Philosophy and Cognitive Mind*, Cambridge: Cambridge University Press, 1995.

Heller, Joseph, *Picture This*, New York: Putnam, 1988.

Horne, Philip, 'In Conversation with Ruth Prawer Jhabvala', 27 October 2000, http://www.guardian.co.uk/film/2000/oct/27/2, accessed 19 March 2008.

Ishiguro, Kazuo, *The Remains of the Day*, London: Faber and Faber, 1989.

Ivory, James, (dir.), *The Remains of the Day*, 1993.

Jaggi, Maya, 'Brave New Worlds', *The Guardian*, 19 March 2005, http://www.guardian.co.uk/film/2005/mar/19/booksfeaturesreviews, accessed 19 March 2008.

Korner, Antony, 'Three's a Company', *Art forum*, November 1987.

Kubrick, Stanley, (dir.), *A Clockwork Orange*, 1971.

———, (dir.), *Barry Lyndon*, 1975.

Lukács, Georg, *The Historical Novel*, trans. Hannah and Stanley Mitchell, Harmondsworth: Penguin (1969), 1981.

Ma, Sheng-mei, 'Kazuo Ishiguro's Persistent Dream for Postethnicity: Performance in Whiteface', *Post Identity*, vol. 2, no. 1, Winter 1999, pp. 71–88, http://liberalarts.udmercy.edu/pi/PI2.1/PI21-Ma.pdf, accessed on 19 March 2008.

May, Yolanta, 'Ruth Prawer Jhabvala in conversation with Yolanta May', *The New Review*, vol. 2, no. 21, December 1975, pp. 53-7.

Mudge, Alden, 'Ishiguro Takes a History Approach to the Detective Novel: Interview by Alden Mudge', *Book Page*, September 2000, http://www.bookpage.com/0009bp/kazuo_ishiguro.html , accessed on 19 March 2008.

Said, Edward, *The World, the Text and the Critic*, London: Faber and Faber 1984.

Scanlan, Margaret, *Traces of Another Time: History and Politics*, Princeton, NJ: Princeton University Press, 1990.

Shepherd, Roland, *Ruth Prawer Jhabvala in India: The Jewish Connection*, New Delhi: Chanakya Publications, 2004.

Swain, Don, [Interview with Kazuo Ishiguro], video interview, 1990, http://www.wiredforbooks.org/kazuoishiguro, accessed 19 March 2008.

Vorda, Allan, ed., 'Stuck on the Margins: An Interview with Kazuo Ishiguro', in *Face to Face: Interviews with Contemporary Novelists*, Houston, TX: Rice University Press, 1999.

Walia, Shelley, *Edward Said and the Writing of History*, London: Icon Books, 2001.

12

'Filmi' Shakespeare

Poonam Trivedi

IN THE FILM *Agneepath*, Amitabh Bachchan, playing a mafia don and inevitable killer, comes to have a meal with his mother who strongly disapproves of his dealings. As he washes his hands in preparation for the meal, which is meant to be a gesture of appeasement of the parent, the mother quips, 'all the water of Bombay will not cleanse your hands...', in an obvious and succinct use of one of the most well-known lines of Shakespeare—from the sleep-walking scene of *Macbeth*. The message about the indelible taint of the immoral is unexceptional; it could have been said in a countless different ways. That the commercial Hindi potboiler chooses to borrow lines from as canonical a figure as Shakespeare is significant. It is this unnoticed and unacknowledged presence—a unique appropriation, intertextuality, and absorption of Shakespeare in the Indian film— which is the basis of the seemingly unholy conjugation in the title of this article, 'Filmi' or film '*me*' Shakespeare, i.e. the conjugation of the Indian film and Shakespeare.

The popular Indian film has in the recent past been subject to considerable critical attention and exegesis, particularly in its embodiment of a public domain which is expressive of a people's desires, quests, and achievements. From being dismissed as crass and commercial, the popular film, particularly the Bombay Hindi film, has now acquired a legitimacy, even an authority, as a marker in the evolution of mass culture. Indian cinema, its production and reception, is being read as a text that quintessentially articulates the space of a pan-Indian identity and nationalism. However, little attention has been paid to the hybrid genealogy, the diverse seeding sources, or the inspirational resources that have provided the ground for the growth of something which has become so recognizably indigenous as the Hindi film. To look for Shakespeare in the Indian cinema may evoke suspicions of bardolatory or even seem like a colonial throwback. Yet, a long look into the history of the Indian, and particularly the Hindi, film reveals this correlation as neither whimsical nor contrived. Shakespeare was a leaven to the initial growth of Hindi cinema and has since nourished it in diverse forms, legitimate and illegitimate, as appropriations, recreations, relocations, and as 'afterlife' or presences. To trace this varying use of Shakespeare in the Hindi film is not just to navigate the changing attitudes to the colonial bard, but more crucially, to chart the shifts in the politics of an inter-culturalism which provides another inroad into the cultural imaginary of mainstream Indian cinema.

It is well-known that Indian cinema sprang up on the floorboards of the Parsi theatre. What is less known is the contribution and influence of Shakespeare in providing an inexhaustible source of plots, scenes, characters, and dialogue to be exploited. Like many of the plays of the Parsi theatre, the early films too were broad adaptations, which borrowed freely, changed liberally, and interpolated without qualms and usually without acknowledgements. The earliest Indian cinematic engagement with Shakespeare goes back to the silent era and is generally recognized to be *Dil Farosh* (1927), based on a popular stage adaptation of *The Merchant of Venice* by the same title by Mehdi Hasan 'Ahsan'. Two other films of the silent era, *Khoon-e-Nahak* (1928) and *Mitha Zahar* (1930), were based on adaptations of *Hamlet* and *Cymbeline* by Ahsan and Narain Prasad Betab, both stalwarts of the Parsi theatre. With the coming of the talkies, in the 1930s and into the 1940s, the translation and transmission of Shakespearean rhetoric, already circulating on stage, was exploited and several of the successful stage adaptations of Shakespeare, in Urdu, were readapted for the screen. Beginning with *Hathili Dulhan* (*The Taming of the Shrew*, 1932), *Khudadad* (*Pericles*, 1935), *Khoon-ka-Khoon* (*Hamlet*, 1935) to *Said-e-Havas* (*Richard III* and *King John*, 1936), *Zan Mureed* (*Anthony and Cleopatra*, 1936), and *Pak Daman* (*Measure for Measure*, 1940).[1] Like the stage versions, these films were as much 'using' Shakespeare as 'abusing' him. Betab, who translated and adapted only two Shakespeare plays, nevertheless ran a magazine titled 'Shakespeare' to popularize his plays and ideas; Aga Hashr Kashmiri, the most gifted of the later Parsi theatre dramatists, who translated and adapted five plays, was accorded the *nom de plume* of 'Indian Shakespeare', so that when he started his own theatrical company, it is no surprise that he decided to call it the 'Indian Shakespeare Company'. Mehdi Hassan Ahsan was more open and is reported to have admitted that in his opinion Shakespeare's way of thinking did not harmonize with the Indian ways of thinking, and that is why the plays were being altered.[2]

Of these *Khoon-ka Khoon* (*Hamlet*, 1935) by Sohrab Modi, credited as 'the man who brought Shakespeare to the Indian screen',[3] is the best known and the most typical. Based on one of the most popular stage adaptations of the 1920s, it was filmed with the same principal cast: Modi as Hamlet, Naseem Bano as Ophelia, and Shamsadbai as Gertrude. A hybrid mixture of styles, characteristic of Parsi theatre as a whole, was reproduced in the production: apart from the main roles, the other characters were all Indianized, their costumes and sets were a mixture of the Elizabethan and Muslim–Indian, 17 songs, some characters, and much protracted clowning were added. Yet, the film advertised itself as '*Hamlet alias Khoon-ka-Khoon*' and Modi himself, as Hamlet, was dressed in the customary black and posed in characteristic pensive stances, and several scenes, e.g. the closet scene and the play-within-play were visualized in the English theatrical manner. An influence of the imagery of the silent Shakespeare films, particularly in the case of the female roles, is to be noted in the stylized feminine look of highly arched eyebrows, large smouldering dark eyes, and dark painted bow-lips. The formal properties, too, of these early Indian Shakespeare films remained marked by their theatrical origins: Modi's account of the filming of *Khoon-ka-Khoon* is revealing, 'As the play had proved popular, it was decided to film it in the way it was presented on the stage—in the same chronological order of scenes, with the movie camera replacing the audience'.[4] A frontality of presentation, a declamatory and histrionic vocalization with a rhetorical and visual flamboyance were their characteristic modes, traces of which may still be seen today in the continuing heightened expressionism of Indian cinema. The main contribution of these early Shakespeare films was to popularize the iconic poet and assimilate him into the mass consciousness, often without the audiences' knowledge. Further, their bold and subversive appropriation of Shakespeare in the vernaculars and in a hybrid performative mode which took place during the high noon of the empire and within the context of an aggressive propagation of the study of English (in 1844 Lord Hardinge, the Governor General, passed a resolution assuring preference in government jobs for those acquainted with European literature) may be seen as acts of cultural resistance, 'upstaging', at the popular level, the official dictates of the empire. Imitation and simultaneous displacement was an assertion of the local modes of pleasure in the face of the growing hegemony of English.[5]

In the 1940s and 1950s, with another class of more literary Indians being attracted to the film industry (Indians had begun being literally 'schooled' into Shakespeare and English literature in India with the establishment of Hindu College in Calcutta in 1817, and the universities in the metropolitan cities in 1857), there were attempts to bring a more 'authentic' Shakespeare on the screen. Kishore Sahu's *Hamlet* (1954) is an acute illustration. Sahu was an unusual actor, writer, director, and producer who came into films after a university degree in literature. He scripted, directed, and starred in several films based on classic European sources.[6] His film on *Hamlet* not only retained the title, the Shakespearean names, settings, and most of the plot, but more crucially, modelled itself on, or rather 'mimicked' closely the visualizations of Lawrence Olivier's film

Hamlet (1948). While Modi's Hamlet was only fitfully imitative, in some scenes and costumes, of the Western cinematic styles, Sahu's film strove to be completely so. Sahu's Hamlet, visualized as a replica of the traditional prince, like Olivier's, was also costumed in black doublet and hose with gold chains on his chest and a poniard by his side. But the dark interiors, misty battlements, enframing arches, stair imagery, even the unfolding of scenes, especially in the beginning, were straight out of Olivier's film. No other Indian Shakespeare film has come so close to suggesting an Elizabethan/Western ambience. Nevertheless, the film had to concede to Indian taste and generic compulsions: Ophelia was given a flashback in which she sang and danced with her companions, confessing her love for Hamlet, the gravediggers were used for comic effect, many mandatory songs were interpolated, and the psychological complexity of the whole was simplified into an emotional pathos. In this second stage of negotiation with the English bard, the anxieties of authenticity versus populist appropriation were more sharply manifest. Sahu's faithful recreation, in the context of post-independence, was an attempt to measure up to the might of the master, doing it like them. It was also an attempt to harness the cultural capital of the original in the international arena—India had just hosted its first International Film Festival in 1952. But its replications, manifestations of a narcissistic desire to be the same as a canonical subject, had to be decentred and fragmented to become the consumerist, commercial spectator.

Yet Sahu was not content to mimic and displace; he had to comment and inscribe too. In an unusual gesture of intertextuality and interculturality, the result, probably, of Sahu's literary leanings, key moments of the dialogue (largely from Ahsan's *Khoon-e-Nahak*) were punctuated by apt quotations in the form of couplets from classical Urdu poets. Hamlet and Ophelia, therefore, quoted couplets from Ghalib in a romantic scene; Polonius used well-known Urdu proverbs in his advice to Laertes; Ophelia in her madness sang not a bawdy ballad, but lines of a fatalistic pathos from Bahadur Shah Zafar's much loved poem '*Na kisi ki ankh ka noor hun...*'; and Hamlet, in his dying speech to Horatio, exhorting him to live to tell his story, adds another well-known couplet by Zauq on the preparedness or readiness of man, '*Layee hayaat aaye, kazaa le chali, chale/Apni khushi na aaye na apni khushi chale*'.[7] Kishore Sahu's *Hamlet* was not just measuring up to Shakespeare, but re-coding and improving him too!

The reception of Sahu's *Hamlet* highlighted the tensions of this kind of interculturalism. The film did reasonably well at the box office but its critical assessment was mixed. While the *Filmfare* critic lauded the film, the *Filmindia* critic tore it to pieces. The debate was, as with all Shakespeare films, polarized around the burden of the book, i.e. around authenticity and appropriation: the former critic saw the rendering as 'creditable',[8] the latter as a 'slander' to Shakespeare's memory, 'stupid' and 'selfish', while yet another indicted it for its 'lack of Indianness'.[9] Dame Sybil Thorndike, who was, surprisingly, present for the premiere in Bombay, praised both Gertrude as 'magnificent', and Ophelia as 'perky, impassioned, human'.[10] The Indian intelligentsia, however, still under a colonial hangover, could only accept Shakespeare either pure and pristine or bowdlerized and indigenized!

This attempt to prove oneself as a filmmaker through a faithful reproduction of the codes of filming Shakespeare had been initiated earlier: a Tamil *Shylock* in 1940 had taken great pains to recreate an authentic Venetian 'look', through costume and setting, for its narrative. In Hindi, a *Romeo and Juliet* (1947) scripted by Kamal Amrohi not only eschewed Indianization, but also tried to copy the Hollywood version of Norma Shearer and Leslie Howard (1936). Similarly, *Cleopatra*, in Hindi (1950), was largely derived from Cecil B. De Mille's Hollywood extravaganza. All these films failed at the box office, despite the presence of well-known actresses such as Nargis as Juliet and Bina Rai as Cleopatra.

The only way of being 'faithful' to Shakespeare, in the intercultural context, it seems, is to relocate him fully. Or so it was shown in the next stage in the negotiation of this colonial legacy, which chose to inflect the main concerns of the plays into a pervasive local mise-en-scène. It led to a Shakespeare transformed and expropriated, but paradoxically 'true'. Of these, Gulzar's *Angoor* (1981), a complete Indianization of *The Comedy of Errors*, has been the most successful, in fact, the most commercially successful Indian Shakespeare film to date, as is proved by its continuing sales on DVD. Yet, perhaps because earlier films based on Shakespeare did not do well at the box office, *Angoor* nowhere, in its credits or posters, acknowledges its debt to Shakespeare, except at the very end in an ironic self-reflexive gesture, when it flashes a portrait of Shakespeare winking at the audience! The story of comic confusions caused by the misrecognitions between two sets of identical twins is tailor-made for cinematic treatment; the tricks of the camera can concretize what is left to the imagination on stage. Before *Angoor*, two other film versions of *The Comedy of Errors*—*Bhrantibilas*, in Bengali (1963) and *Do Dooni Char* (Hindi, 1968)—were ventured. The success of *Angoor*, ably scripted by Gulzar, an Urdu poet in his own right, however, went beyond its localization, which nevertheless rang true. It lay more in its obvious delight in its own virtuosity; Shakespeare's comic structures were preserved and merged into the indigenous *hasya* traditions. A consummate performance by Sanjeev Kumar as Antipholus, of perfect timing and comic insouciance, added to it. Other localizations in regional cinema, for instance of the *Taming of the Shrew* in Kannada, *Bahadur Ganda* (1976), and *Nanjundi Kalyana* (1989) have similarly proved very successful.

An extension of the dialogics of this relocation into a critical intervention is achieved by *Kaliyattam*, an award winning film by Jayaraaj (1998), in which the relocation of *Othello* becomes a means to examine the circulation of power within class and caste structures in rural Kerala. It uses the indigenous folk ritual theatre of *theyyam*, its conventions and community, to foreground the key issue of racism in the play by transposing it on to the iniquities of the caste system. Fair and winsome Thamara, a Brahman landlord's daughter, falls in love with Perumalayan, a revered *theyyam* master, but dark, bulky, and a pockmarked low-caste. Their happiness is poisoned by Paniyan, the Iago figure, a junior *theyyam* artist confined to the minor comic roles, who covets Perumalayan's skills and position. A third *theyyam* artist, Kanthan/Cassio favoured by Perumalayan, unfortunately cannot hold his drink during the wedding celebrations and is made the scapegoat by Paniyan. Cheerma/Emilia, his wife, is persuaded to steal the handkerchief/consummation sheet which is used to stoke the fires of jealousy. Thus, despite the relocation into a completely different ambience, the film manages to incorporate most of Shakespeare's plot and dialogue quite closely, adding only one character, an elder female confidant for Desdemona, and some scenes setting the *theyyam* festival. The film is promoted as an 'adaptation of William Shakespeare's *Othello*' in its publicity handouts, but its skill and sophistication produce an unfamiliar take on a familiar myth, going beyond adaptation, or even relocation, to create a critical reinterpretation of the original in postcolonial terms. Not only does it use Shakespeare to examine and expose the tensions of contemporary Kerala society, its reworking provokes insights into aspects of the play buried under centuries of learned response. There has been a somewhat lukewarm response to *Kaliyattam* by some of the Malayalam intelligentsia, holding its depiction of a romantic union between a *theyyam* personator, always a low-caste, and a brahman's daughter as entirely implausible. However, the value of the film lies in driving home this very point, that Shakespeare's romantic pairing of Othello and Desdemona was as unbelievably transgressive in his own time, something readers and viewers are apt to forget given the familiarity of the story. Fire, as a symbol of this transgressive passion—both within and without—is central and is given a live presence through the cinematography. It is seen both as a propitiatory fire, integral to the ritual of the *theyyam*: Perumalayan achieves his transformation into a godhead by walking on fire and therefore it is the source of his mystery and attraction—as he says to Thamara, 'I have no other fire'; and at the end, as the funeral pyre into which Perumalayan throws himself. The handkerchief, an object which in the play is talismanic of the sexual union of Othello and Desdemona, frequently seems too common and trivial to sustain its symbolic meaning. In *Kaliyattam* it is substituted by a red and gold patterned *patta* that functions as a consummation cloth, the multiple associations of which are instantly available. On their wedding night Perumalayan hands this *patta* to Thamara with the words, 'It's my life', reinforcing its association with his passion/sexuality/fire. When Thamara spreads this *patta* on their bed in preparation for their second tryst, it becomes a symbol which mediates her 'appetite' and legitimizes female desire. Jayaraaj even betters Shakespeare here (dare we say so!) for the red cloth also represents fertility and this is suggested as a reason why Cheerma steals it from her mistress she is so devoted to—something left ambiguous in the play—for she is shown caressing it and the implication is that perhaps she too may conceive via the *patta*, such is the longing that is stoked in her. When Paniyan/Iago finally gets hold of it, he rolls and cavorts on it, laughing in a kind of illicit joy as if he had got hold of Peru and Thamara's sexuality. Othello's murder of his blameless wife is almost always seen in criticism as a sign of his innate savagery. In *Kaliyattam*, Perumalayan comes to the bedchamber with part of his make-up/*kollam* on—dark eyes in a vermilioned face—a half-human, half-god, unhinged by the dualities and divisions of his being. As he bends down to give his wife a last kiss and she wakes up, he threatens to kill her, but she suddenly clings to him, grabbing his bare chest for protection. Her touch on his bare chest sends a quiver through Perumalayan: in a flash love seems to assert itself and for a second he melts, looking as if he will change his mind. Othello's turmoil, 'of one that loved not wisely, but too well' (5.2.353) was never more poignantly realized: the visual imagery—his chest painted with coiled snakes, part of the *theyyam vesham*—and the camera's forensic close-up of his erotic shiver, lift it beyond the dimensions of stage performance. The film creates an intercultural 'intertext', bringing to scopic satisfaction significant subtexts of the play, which more than often remain unarticulated, forcing us, literally, to see anew.

This kind of re-visioning that adds to and expands the canonical text leads to the fourth and current stage in the engagement with, by now, a globalized bard, which is of a postcolonial confidence to 'play around' with and deconstruct Shakespeare for our own needs. Here the critical issue is no longer how much of the play is retained, but how succinctly it can be dovetailed into local concerns. Two recent films *Maqbool* (2004), and *Omkara* (2006)—in Hindi, by the same director, Vishal Bharadwaj, are outstanding examples of this trend.[11] Hailed as 'cross-over' films, they take this negotiation with Shakespeare several steps further. They demonstrate not only a postcolonial 'play' with Shakespeare's text, but also a confident postmodernist reimagining of literary heritage, convincingly turning the war-torn Scotland of *Macbeth* into Mumbai's gangland presided over by the ageing don Jehangir Khan alias Abbuji and his right hand man, Maqbool, and the Mediterranean worlds of Venice and Cyprus into the small town badlands of western Uttar Pradesh held in thrall by the wily politician, Bhaisaab and his prime henchman, Omkara. While both the films together constitute a paradigm shift in the Indian reconfiguration of Shakespeare on screen, they also reveal a significant evolutionary progress. *Maqbool*, the first film, was described gingerly by its director/script writer and music composer, Vishal Bharadwaj, as 'a loose adaptation'[12] of Shakespeare's *Macbeth*. Anxious to sell his film as a commercial entity, Bharadwaj played down the Shakespearean source in interviews and press releases: 'My film is not meant for Shakespeare scholars'.[13] 'My interpretation is not textbookish' … 'I have tried to be true to the play's spirit than to the original text'.[14] The critical success of *Maqbool* at various film festivals, however, emboldened Bharadwaj, two years later, to market his *Omkara* openly as an 'adaptation of Shakespeare's *Othello*'. Not only did he flaunt his canonical source, promos and websites also traced earlier cinematic adaptations, positioning his film within an international/global tradition, rubbing shoulders with the likes of Orson Welles. Reviewers of *Maqbool*, by and large, were taken in by Bharadwaj, and did not see more than a soup spoon of Shakespeare in the film. But it seems that India's English schooled generations had not carried home much of their Shakespeare. For, what it is strikingly significant about the film is how much of the original text is retained, and engaged with, within the adaptation, in terms of the plot, character, imagery, and not just theme and atmosphere. That this had largely gone unmarked and unnoticed, at least in print, is not altogether surprising, for much of the textual detail of the source is presented in an oblique fashion, though seamlessly dovetailed into the translation, localization, and cinematic visualization. As one has seen, there has existed a practice in India of exploiting Shakespeare's plays as stageable or screenable fodder; the Indian film industry is notorious for plagiarizing almost everything. But *Maqbool* blazed a new path; within the terms of its appropriation it found innovative ways of presenting and even enhancing the concerns of the text, becoming, in the process, a 're-textualization' of Shakespeare. *Omkara*, on the other hand, released as a mainstream commercial film, rode on the acclaim of *Maqbool*, garnering considerable box-office success in India, and even more abroad. It received more assured critical approbation: 'He captures the essence of the original in a blanket of innovation, intelligence and integrity…' (*Indian Express Group*); 'I've never seen the play so perfectly tuned to a time (present) or a place (Uttar Pradesh)' (*Times of India*), and 'What you take away from *Omkara* is the knowledge that a classic script always has the power to move us, provided it is handled by a director who knows his craft, and actors who understand their job. Shakespeare would have smiled', said Lindsay Pereira on www.rediff.com.[15] More than even its adaptative success, it was seen as a film that broke the conventional Bollywood mould ('into smithereens', *Times of India*) with panache. 'The most arrogant piece of kitsch ever made…

Startling...', was the verdict of *The Times*, London.[16] Clearly, both films merit a longer discussion.

Maqbool retains and even expands all the major relationships and events of Shakespeare's *Macbeth*. Duncan/Abbuji's trust in Macbeth/Maqbool, the prophesying witches/cops who plant the seed of ambition, the seduction of Maqbool into treachery by his beloved wife, here Abbuji's mistress Nimmi, the drunken guard, the killing of Abbuji in his sleep, the ensuing suspicion and fear, the poisoning of the bond with fellow captain/henchman, Banquo/Kaka, and his subsequent slaughter by Maqbool, the escape of his son Fleance/Guddu who survives to be the inheritor, the setting in of guilt and nemesis, the hallucinating Lady Macbeth, the beguiled Macbeth, the avenger Macduff/Boti and the tragic end (unusual for Bollywood)—all these form the central structure of the film. After a basic transposition of the cultural milieu into a largely Muslim gang in Mumbai, there are continuous and consistent parallels with Shakespeare's text despite Bharadwaj's disclaimers.

This reimagining is, however, not without its mandatory *masala* formula features like comic bumbling cops, family scenes of festivity and weddings, catchy music, dances and songs, religious and romantic, even an 'item number' with a vamp cum would-be moll in a backless *kurti*, hospital scenes, and the populist picture of communal harmony—of Muslims and Hindus working and marrying together. But the film unrolls not as what is defensively termed 'a loose adaptation', but rather as a close and acute appropriation. And, as a Shakespeare film, it bears the burden of the book with some finesse.

Significant changes/interpolations in plot and character clarify areas of obscurity or ambiguity in the original. For instance giving Duncan/Abbuji a young daughter, Sameera (instead of two sons), who is in love with and is going to marry Fleance/Guddu establishes a more immediate moral equity and structural neatness and coherence than Shakespeare's own use of Fleance as an elaborate compliment to King James I, who was said to be an eighth generation descendant of Fleance. The Lady Macbeth/Nimmi figure is here made the don/Duncan's mistress, who is attracted to Maqbool/Macbeth instead and seduces him into the murder of the don. Not only does this amplify the dominant theme of treacherous transgressivity, but it also literally fleshes out the suggestion in Shakespeare's play that Lady Macbeth uses her sexual command over Macbeth to subdue his scruples and make him agree to kill to fulfill her ambitions too.

It is in the range and depth of its re-textualisation, however, that *Maqbool* becomes a contemporary 'literary film', 'symptomatic of the contemporary imagination' which needs to be read not from the centre, but from its spaces of discursive difference.[17] It locates itself in the popular genres of the Bollywood gangster and the Muslim social film; it is a direct inheritor of recent critiques of urban violence like *Satya* and *Company*, which are generally accepted as fictionalizations of real life gangsters like Dawood Ibrahim and Chota Rajan and their mafia-like hold on the people and institutions of Mumbai. The radicalism of *Maqbool* lies in its use of a canonical text to ally itself to such exposures of festering urban culture. Both these films, *Satya* and *Company*, like *Maqbool* and *Macbeth*, are narratives of people who depend on bloodshed and violence for their living; who, to consolidate their positions, are sucked into treachery and revenge; and who end by eliminating each other. All these films position women in a seductive, but ultimately destructive role, and though they valorize violence as a livelihood, they end by asserting the moral that violence does not pay.

Retelling in a literary film initiates its own alternative referentiality. In a postmodernist 'play' and self-reflexivity, *Maqbool* dares to talk of itself, its own lifeline, i.e. Bollywood, with tongue-in-cheek jibes at the recent exposures of the deep nexus between the underworld and the film industry in Bombay. There are several references to Bollywood, all of which reveal it to be another field of action for the mafia, where the financing and fixing of films, like gold smuggling, illegal occupation, and contract killing are admitted to be part of their *dhanda* or business. In the one family scene of relaxation after dinner, the conversation turns to the fortunes of Bollywood and Kaka/Banquo quips that Abbuji's life was worthy of being filmed, and then goes on to brag that it will not auger well if this year they cannot get out a film with 'Bhabhi', i.e. Nimmi, Abbuji's mistress. 'Tell me, Bhabhi, which director do you want, Karan Johar, Ram Gopal Verma, Mani Ratnam', he grandiosely reels off, offering her the pick of the best, only to be reduced to a stammer by an icy stare from Abbuji who is definitely not pleased. The business or *dhanda* of Bollywood will not include family because, as Maqbool has let fall earlier in the conversation, in a kind of double irony, the gangsters believe Bollywood is peopled by the cheap and low kind—*ghatiya*. Another glance at the equation between the film world and the underworld is made through Om Puri/Inspector Pandit's observation regarding Abbuji that 'had he not been in the underworld, he would have been in films, what an actor he is', after watching him enjoy a *nautch* with some composure immediately after an emotional shake-up—which is strategically simulated—at being reminded of the police raid at his own wedding which had left him bereft of his godfather figure, again something we suspect was stage-managed by Abbuji himself. Such seemingly casual self-referrals in the film are not simple narcissism, but function as searing critiques, tearing off the veil of make-believe which covers the underhand dealings of both the film and the extortion industries. They also establish a parallel between the king-making delusions of the underworld/Bollywood and the royalist ambitions in the theatre of war in *Macbeth*. 'There's no art/To find the mind's construction in the face' (4.1.11–12)—Duncan's observation on the traitor Macdonwald self-reflexively exposes Abbuji, and by analogy, casts back a doubt on the Scottish king's manipulations.

The film ventures bravura quotation and parody too. A delightful bit of pastiche, verging on parody, occurs in the seduction scene between Maqbool and Nimmi, where she forces him to accept her at the point of a gun, and which ends with him ferreting around with a lighted faggot to recover, among the stones, her fallen earring. This, of course, is recognizable as a reworking of a well-known romantic song sequence from a hit of the 1960s, *Gunga Jamuna*, '*dhoondo dhoondo re saajanaa, mere kaan ka bala*'. While the original was a celebration of married love, dramatizing the morning after, here, in a literally dark (*noir*) film it becomes the summation of a transgressive love, showing how Maqbool has finally been caught in Nimmi's net. These self-reflexive stances, on Bollywood and its genres, intersect with the reflexivities of *Macbeth*: if Macbeth comes to the conclusion that 'life's but a walking shadow, a poor player that struts and frets its hour upon the stage', (5.5.24–5) Inspector Pandit too is made to remark on role playing in life.

Most of all, it is in the cinematic visualizations of the poetic images of the play that the seamless blend of the popular with the postmodern is to be seen. One of the strengths of the film is its power to surprise. Unusual placements of Shakespeare's images accost one at unexpected turns in the narrative, forcing at times a revelatory extension of meaning. These cinematic enactments do not call attention to themselves and are integral to the new narrative, yet they resonate fully with the old. A loud raucous chatter of crows and other birds, for instance imaging Lady Macbeth's statement, 'the raven himself is hoarse that croaks the fatal entrance of Duncan under my battlements', (1.5.38) forms the background 'music' to Maqbool and Nimmi's first long scene, by the roadside, where she plants the seed of treachery in his mind. The cawing of crows, in fact, becomes a choric comment on any talk of murder: it accompanies the new ACP Devasare's questioning of the inspectors on his first day; it forms the background of Abbuji's questioning of the dead Moghul's son Boti; it chimes in with Nimmi's aggressive stoking of the fires of ambition and eroticism in Maqbool.

The festivity of the engagement party celebrations takes the place of the banquet in honour of Duncan, in the backdrop of which Macbeth and Lady Macbeth plot the murder. A huge steaming cauldron, that in the play is full of 'Double, double, toil and trouble: Fire burn and cauldron bubble', (4.1.10–11) is glimpsed in the kebab makers' shop, where a rival gang gathers to plot further machinations of crime and revenge. The atmosphere of fear and terror unleashed by Macbeth reflected in the line:

'Each new morn, /New widows howl' (4.3.4) is graphically and aurally picturized in Sameera's wild scream of anguish and hate when Maqbool pretends to commiserate with the break-up of her engagement after Kaka's death and Guddu's flight. The dagger soliloquy is encapsulated in a brief sequence in which Maqbool hallucinates that the blood of the goat butchered for the wedding feast has not been washed clean. The haunting of Banquo's ghost is given a fresh spin when Kaka's body is brought in, disrupting Abbuji's prayer meeting, and as Maqbool touches the body in a pretended show of grief, the eyes of the dead body suddenly flip open completely, throwing Maqbool off his guard. The most creative transposition and illustration, however, is of the central image of the play, 'Pity like a naked new born babe...shall blow the horrid deed in every eye/that tears shall drown the wind' (1.7.21, 24–25). This is visualized in Nimmi's newborn son, seen lovingly cradled by Guddu/Fleance and Sameera at the end, the very sight of which weakens Maqbool's blood-lust, blowing his horrid deeds in his own eyes, making him drop his gun and walk out in a gesture of surrender, leaving the camera to mark a tear staining the glass visor through which Maqbool was looking at the babe. Pity, as the naked babe, remains the unborn child in the play *Macbeth*, emphasizing the sterility of the Macbeths. In *Maqbool* its embedded meaning is released to force a final moment of anagnorisis, a self-realization of the futility of a life of bloodshed in *Maqbool*. Since in the film the child is born of premature labour, it is also a visualization of the child that was 'untimely ripped' ... 'from his mother's womb' (5.8.15–16), the figure who was forecast as the one which will vanquish Macbeth. It thus becomes the twice-fold instrument of the reassertion of the good. Finally, at the very end, in the play, Macbeth's head is cut off and brought on stage, a sign of the just desert for the 'butcher king'. In the film, Maqbool walks out of the hospital, having dropped his guns, and is shot down by Macduff/Boti who happens to see him outside. But no shriek or blood is shown; instead the camera pans, then tilts its line of vision to ground level, cuts to a view of the sky above and then cuts back to a close-up, framing only Maqbool's head as fallen and rolling on the ground. As the viewer looks from Maqbool/Macbeth's field of vision, spiritual music begins, there is another cut, the camera swivels up to show a clear blue sky, rare in the film, heralding the closing mood of 'the time is free' (5.9.21). Such cinematic visualizations create a 're-textualization' of the source, adding to and releasing embedded meanings, almost as if the deferred possibilities of Derrida's *différance* were being caught!

Yet, the stroke of genius in the reimagining, and which is the summation of the popular and postmodern blend, is the recasting of the witches as a pair of conniving cops. The three Weird sisters of the play are turned into a duo of comic cops, both corrupt and bumbling. This has to be a first, an entirely original turn, for though there have been dozens of adaptations of *Macbeth*, in gangland situations too, the witches have almost always remained female (in *Joe Macbeth,* 1955, dir. Ken Hughes, they are a pair of street eccentrics—a hot chestnut seller and a sandwich board man—and in *Men of Respect*, 1991, dir. William Reilly, they are turned into occultist groupies). But never have they been visualized as policemen who monitor and control the underworld through their prophecies. This breaks free of and reverses several traditions of casting and performing the witches who, in fact, always pose something of a challenge in staging *Macbeth*, for how do we embody the unnatural/supernatural? Polanski, for instance imaged them as a cultist feminist group, which almost threw the text overboard. There is a risk in modernizing the witches too much; they lose their mystery and menace. On the other hand, the prophesying astrologer/witch is a familiar figure in India, but in relocating them as two policemen, Inspectors Pundit and Purohit who compulsively draw horoscopes and foretell the future—using ketchup to sketch the chart and tidbits of food, cigarette stubs, or pebbles to mark the planets on it—in their daily line of duty, Bharadwaj and Tyrewala, the scriptwriters, do not just naturalize and make believable the unnatural and the supernatural but peg it down into a gamut of known material relations and inferences. As an interfering pair, the comic cops intersect with the vice/evil, clown/fool tradition. In their bumbling attempts at duty they are the scapegoat cops of every Bollywood film. As conniving abettors and simultaneous upholders of the law they form an exposé of the role and function of the police in India, a sly, ironic glance at the recent scams and prison escapes in which the police are being proved to have given a helping hand. But, most of all, they acquire shades of the Shakespearean wise fools and take on some of the critiquing and ribald function of the Porter when they are caught by the camera pissing in unison, into the night rain off the first floor balcony ('drink, Sir, is a great provoker of three things. ...nose-painting, sleep, and urine. ...he took up my legs sometime...'(2.3.26, 28, 41)!

These cop witches thus constitute the radicalism of the reimagining which inexorably hangs a new question on a canonical text: for who are the witches/weird sisters, what is their power of magic? 'Weird', in Middle English, meant not evil but fate. Are the witches marginal people trying to assert power by 'prophesying' or 'equivocating' on both sides? In Shakespeare's play the witches kill, avenge, trade in body parts, and lead Macbeth on. In the film, the cop duo promises much but delivers little. They attempt to chase, encounter and interrogate, but instead let off prisoners and fail to make them speak. They act as go-betweens, being privy to the deals hatched and the payoffs made. They seem to be hand-in-glove with Abbuji's gang, turning up in the nick of time to bail them out. They seem like sponges, out to milk their situations. It is only through their prophesying that they retain some credibility and exert power. Maqbool is impelled to go to them after the murder of Abbuji, to find out what lies further for him. Yet they justify all their actions as an expression of their own grassroots philosophy, of maintaining a balance of power, a '*shakti ka santulan*', by letting fire and water confront and confound each other: '*aag ko pani ka dar bahut bada hai*'. They believe in letting the gangs fight it out among themselves, let dog eat dog. The witches in *Macbeth*, too, are called 'juggling fiends' (5.9.19) and Macbeth a 'wayward son' (3. 5.11). Were the witches in *Macbeth* also trying to wrest a little control/power? The ambiguities of the text are extended in the film and by the end a suspicion begins to creep up at the back of our minds whether this prophesying, instigating ambition, and power struggle was not a ploy, planted by the witches/police, to seduce the chieftains/gangsters into liquidating each other? So cleverly is reality and unreality juggled around that one begins to doubt one's straight perceptions.

Omkara, a more polished and assured cinematic rendering of Shakespeare in the Indian milieu, takes the adaptive layering a stretch further. Like *Maqbool*, it too retains most of the basic plot, interpolating situations to flesh out the new location of the story. Thus, several gang fights and summary dismissal of opponents are etched in to underline the ethos of ruthless violence in which the hero, Omkara/Othello is drenched; Dolly/Desdemona is betrothed to Rajju/Roderigo, making her elopement, on the eve of the wedding, more transgressive; a family and a home are visualized for Omkara/Othello, lending greater credence to his obsession with the *kardhani*/cummerbund/handkerchief as a precious family heirloom. Bianca the prostitute becomes Billo, a chanteuse, providing the license for the Bollywood trademark song and dance routines. Yet, paradoxically, these features which give ballast and root the story in its new milieu simultaneously work against it. While Vishal Bharadwaj's adaptation 'explains' much, ironing out the perplexing ambiguities of the play, it sacrifices, too, crucial shades of the tragic inevitability and pathos. Narrowly identifying Omkara with a violent macho culture robs him of that valorous heroism, or of an artistic edge like Perumalayan's in *Kaliyattam*, which forms the basis of Desdemona's undying love for him. Giving him scenes of a familial domesticity opens out and dilutes the tension of a tight claustrophobic play, Othello's isolation being part of the reason for his downfall. And Billo/Bianca's 'item' numbers, though they have become the hit songs of the season, do not add, but rather, detract from the localization. Bharadwaj's most successful re-visioning, of Iago/Ishwar '*Langda*' Tyagi, seen as a believable loyal comrade at arms alienated at being passed over for a promotion, is nevertheless shorn of his bedevilling misogyny and racism in the realistic singularity of his presentation. Similarly, the racism of the play, transposed into the endemic casteism of north Indian society, is pegged at a credibility: unlike in *Kaliyattam*, Omkara is not a low-caste, but a half-caste Brahman, more befitting his position as a trusted general/*bahubali*, but which, nevertheless, dilutes the rationale for his murderous insecurities. So does the playful tease by Indu/Emilia, of the contrast between Omi's dark colour and Dolly's white complexion, render superficial and skin deep the huge class and race divide of the original.

Yet there is more to Bharadwaj's adaptive prowess than merely providing recognizable Indian equivalents to Shakespeare's classic. It lies, as seen in his *Maqbool*, in creating innovative cinematic imagery out of the suggestions and insinuations of the text. In *Omkara*, he goes a step beyond imagification to evolving a *trope*, a visual/descriptive shorthand, which patterns and problematizes many occurrences. The most arresting of these is a witty deployment of the technologies of the mobile phone which do not just narrate, but also intervene, record, and assert surveillance. The plot of *Othello* turns crucially on 'hearsay'; 'calling', 'telling,' 'listening,' are salient actions in a play which dramatizes a poisoning of the mind through whisperings in the ear. In this tragedy, it is not so much the 'eye' as the 'ear' which leads the hand, as for instance in *Macbeth*. Right at the start we are told by Othello how Desdemona would 'with a greedy ear/devour up my discourse' (1.3.149–50) of how 'telling my story' [which]...wish'd she had not heard' (1.3.161) became a story through which 'the bruised heart was pierced through the ear' (1.3.219). Desdemona pleads with the Senators: 'to my unfolding lend a gracious ear' (1.3.244) when she wishes to accompany Othello to Cyprus. Later Iago plots to 'abuse Othello's ear' (1.3.393), whilst Othello fears that Iago 'makest his ear /A stranger to thy thoughts' (3.3.146–7). Such critical communication via the 'ear' is captured in the film through the many uses of the mobile phone. From the opening scene, with the *baraat* party's mobiles being confiscated, the instrument progressively becomes embroiled in the elopement; it intervenes during the confrontation with an irate Brabantio who is threatening to blow out Omi's brains, when the Godfather, Bhaisaab's, voice and salutary authority is relayed through the mobile's speaker phone. A video clip on a mobile phone provides irrefutable ammunition in the blackmail and liquidation of a political opponent. Later, the mobile phone becomes essential to Iago's machinations, establishing alibis and, finally, it is used to provide proof of Desdemona's so-called infidelity. From an instrument, a mere means, the mobile phone becomes an agent, its instrumentality layering echoes and resonances into a network of connections. The circuit of deceptions, lies, and misunderstandings, which add up to the tragedy of 'hearsay' in *Othello*, is neatly enfolded in *Omkara* into the mobile circle of the telephonic. Needless to add, these scenes also document and comment on the local exponential boom in the use of the mobile phone and its varying functionalities as the new tool of empowerment, as fair in love as in crime.

It is in attempting this blend, a balancing of the 'global' (bard) with the recognizably 'local' (regional Indian) that takes *Omkara* a step further in the appropriative trajectory: not only does it reconfigure its 'local' genre of the commercial Bollywood gangster film, it also projects itself strategically into an internationalism of the by now globalized Shakespeare. This straddling of two worlds—*Omkara* does not so much break the mould as it stretches the gangster film to turn the spotlight on the battle within (the depiction of the warring hinterlands of Uttar Pradesh never did ring so unsentimental and true), its box-office success abroad,[18] its sweep of awards at home (seven Filmfare awards) —has pitched the Indian Shakespeare film into a mainstream format and won for it an acceptance beyond that of the art house film. In contrast, *Kaliyattam*, which eschewed commercial dimensions, but was more completely immersed in its local cultural context, and thus could present an acutely felt, and argued, intertextual evocation of Othello, remained nevertheless tethered to the niche art cinema circuit. The runaway success of the songs and music score of *Omkara* is another testimony of its achieving a position in the mainstream 'popular' film market. *Maqbool*, on the other hand, though more playfully inventive, and closer to Shakespeare's imagistic text, perhaps because of it, could not command that level of box-office success as *Omkara*.

Maqbool and *Omkara*, then, as a mix of art and commerce, are positioned as third generation postcolonial adaptations, not in awe of Shakespeare, neither plagiarizing him, like the Parsi theatre film, nor genuflecting to his canonical authority, like the faithful imitations discussed earlier. Shakespeare forms a kind of a benchmark; our responses to him determine our own distance from our past. On stage, there have been several successful adaptations of *Macbeth* and *Othello* performed in our own indigenous theatre styles. But with *Maqbool* and *Omkara* we have hit another level of appropriation. Here it is neither ethnicity nor authenticity that is aimed at but, rather, a postcolonial maturity in contemporizing the universality of Shakespeare into our own current concerns. While *Omkara* domesticates Shakespeare, *Maqbool* rewrites him in Indian terms.

This third generational postcoloniality is reinforced through the persona of Vishal Bharadwaj, the director, scriptwriter, and music director of the films. A backwoods boy from Bijnor, Uttar Pradesh, Bharadwaj, by the creativity shown in *Maqbool* and *Omkara*, has unfixed Shakespeare from the grip of the English medium school and made him a free floating signifier available for anyone with the nous to take him on. Like cricket, then, we seem at last to have appropriated another imperial icon and have been shown to do it well.

These full-fledged Shakespeare films notwithstanding, the equally, or perhaps, more, significant and surprising dimension of Shakespeare in the Indian cinema, as noted at the start of the article, is his continuing circulation in 'bits and pieces', or as an 'afterlife'. This is to be found in diverse modes—in the form of fleeting images (a silent film titled *Indian Shylock*), lines of dialogue (as seen in *Agneepath* [*Macbeth*] or *36 Chowringee Lane* [*Lear*]), as fragments of scenes and sequences (the performance of the balcony scene of 'Romeo and Juliet' in *1942: A Love Story*, and of an opera, 'Troilus and Cressida', in *Dil Chahta Hai*), as citations or quotations (a boat named 'Much Ado' is sighted in the harbour when the love triangle in *Dil Chahta Hai* gets very involved—to name an obvious few) as characterization or themes—the heroine in male disguise, the female lawyer, the doomed young lovers, feuding families, the hardheaded money lender, the taming of the shrew, identical twins, the return of the uncanny, the revenge tragedy, etc.—instances of which are too ubiquitous to need enumeration. The repeated resurfacing of such Shakespearean traces shows that Shakespeare is no longer the other, but exists as absorbed into the cultural imaginary of the nation, the result of a process elucidated by the cannibal theory of translation[19] in which the original has to be 'devoured' for the colonized to break free, and where the act of devouring is both a violation and an act of homage. This cannibalistic metaphor helps us to reconfigure the dynamism of the film industry with its borrowing or 'consuming' of texts and their reproduction only in tangentially identifiable forms. Journeying through Indian cinema, via Shakespeare, takes us through a history of negotiation with what was once the colonial book, to its transformation and unnoticed acceptance into a public domain of the nation.

NOTES

Earlier versions of this article have been published in the *Communicator: Journal of Indian Institute of Mass Communication*, vol. XXXX, January–June 2005 and in *Literature Film Quarterly*, May 2007.

1. For an account of Shakespeare in early Hindi cinema see Verma 2005.
2. For a history of the Parsi theatre see Gupta 1981.
3. Rajadhyaksha and Willemen, 2002, p. 150.
4. Verma, 2002, p. 84.
5. For an account of the place of Shakespeare in the growth of the modern Indian theatre, see my 'Introduction' to *India's Shakespeare*, op. cit. For a performance history of *Hamlet* in India, see Trivedi, 2002.
6. Rajadhyaksha and Willemen, 2002, p. 203.
7. For other such intertextualities, see Verma, op. cit.
8. Quoted by Verma, p. 85.
9. Rothwell, 1999, p. 169.

10. Ibid., p. 169.
11. Another film which would also fall into this category but which is more in the nature of an 'art' film, not being commercially released, is *Othello* by Roysten Abel, a cinematic take off of his own, far more successful, play-*Othello: A Play in Black and White*, which had won the best first award at the Edinburgh Festival in 1999. Abel's play was the first such innovative postcolonial intervention into the staging practice of Shakespeare in India: it used the outsider theme in the play to highlight the discrimination in metropolitan India against those of the provinces; it thus debated the issue of identity and nationalism. Its success was due to its timing, in the contemporization of a canonical text, and in its performative finesse. But the film, which tries to elaborate these ideas, failed to communicate the immediacy of the play and was lost in a welter of esoteric images. An earlier Bengali film, *Saptapadhi* (Seven Steps of Marriage) 1961, is a more complex postcolonial extension of the *Othello* theme, in which a Brahman boy, Krishnendu, falls in love with his Anglo-Indian college mate, Rina Brown, during a college performance of *Othello*. He converts to Christianity to marry her, is separated because of class and racial differences, but is finally reunited after some years. See Chakravarti, 2003.
12. Interview by Singh, 2004.
13. Interview by Pais, 2003.
14. Interview with Subhash K. Jha, *Deccan Herald*, 15 February 2004.
15. As quoted in the DVD promotional flyer.
16. Ibid.
17. Villasur, 2002.
18. *The Times of India*, 2006, quotes *Forbes* magazine to show how Bollywood reaped an American windfall in 2006 with its films making up half of the 14 foreign language films that grossed more than $2 million in the US — more than any other language, and that the seven Hindi hits of 2006 in the US offered 'another sign that India's film industry is capturing broad, even global, appeal'. 'Bollywood is hot,' the magazine observed. It also mentions an overall estimate of $14.7 gross takings for *Omkara* in 2006.
19. As proposed by Oswald de Andrade's *Manifesto Antropofago* (1928) and developed by Haraldo de Campos. See Vieira, 1999.

References

'Bollywood hits jackpot in the US', *Times of India,* 24 December 2006.

Chakravati, Paromita, 'Modernity, Postcoloniality and *Othello*: the case of *Saptapadhi*' in Pascale Aebisher, Edward J. Esche, and Nigel Wheale, eds., *Remaking Shakespeare: Performance Across Media, Genres and Cultures,* London: Palgrave, 2003.

Gupta, Somnath, *Parsi Thiyetar: Udhbhava aur Vikas*, Allahabad: Lok Bharti, 1981.

Pais, Arthur J., www.rediff.com, 6 November 2003.

Rajadhyaksha Ashish, and Willemen Paul, eds., *Encyclopaedia of Indian Cinema*, New Delhi: Oxford University Press, 2002.

Rothwell, Kenneth S., *A History of Shakespeare on Screen*, Cambridge: Cambridge University Press, 1999.

Singh, Vijay, www.rediff.com, 29 January 2004.

Trivedi, Poonam, '"Playing is the thing": *Hamlet* on the Indian Stage', *Hamlet Studies,* vol. 24, 2002.

Vieira, Else Ribeiro Pires, 'Liberating Calibans: Readings of *Antropofagia* and Harold de Campos' Poetics of Transcreation', in Susan Bassnett and Harish Trivedi, eds., *Post-Colonial Translation: Theory and Practice,* London: Routledge, 1999.

Verma, Rajiva, '*Hamlet* on the Hindi Screen', *Hamlet Studies*, vol. 24, 2002.

———, 'Shakespeare in Hindi Cinema', in Poonam Trivedi and Dennis Bartholomeusz, *India's Shakespeare: Translation, Interpretation, and Performance*, Newark: University of Delaware Press, 2005.

Villasur, Belan Vidal, 'Classic adaptations, modern reinventions: reading the image in the contemporary literary film', *Screen*, vol. 43, no. 1, Spring 2002, pp. 5, 17.

13

A Dramatic Film: Performative Politics in Peter Brook's Mahabharata

Sonali Pattnaik

> IT IS indeed a matter, as Artaud puts it, 'of bringing cinema together with the innermost reality of the brain', but this innermost reality is not the Whole, but on the contrary a fissure, a crack.
>
> —Deleuze, 1989, p. 167

THE USES OF THIS article may not be too many if the reader is interested in further commentary on Peter Brook's film as a successful or failed adaptation of that vast unwieldy epic, the *Mahabharata.* David Williams' book on the production, albeit only on the theatrical version, exhaustively discusses Brook's vision for theatre, the CIRT (the international theatre group that he initiated), and the polemics of Orientalist and Humanist readings of the text as well as its ramifications for both theatre and the epic itself. I propose to engage with something slightly different here. I wish to ask a question about cinema and its relationship to literature and writing via Brook's radicalization of cinematic space and simultaneously to open a discussion about what this means for the reading and reception of the *Mahabharata.* Primarily, the article will focus on the way in which cinema can contribute to ongoing controversies around textuality and reading practices. The performative politics espoused by the filmic text will be analyzed to examine how it expands, alters, and debunks received notions of textuality in order to restitute orality to the epic as well as to problematize the dichotomy between text and context. I am less interested here in Brook's approach as a 'western' reader to the 'Indian' epic and more curious about the method of representation deployed by the film which, I wish to argue, contests not just false divisions between texts and their contexts, but critiques the larger thematic debate between constructivism and essentialism.[1]

The epic has many beginnings but the film has only one. It begins with an opening shot where the camera tracks the movement of a young boy who, it has been suggested, represents an ignorant audience, following a path marked by objects/props to find his way to his teacher/narrator/author, Vyasa. The boy appears amazed and curious and touches and scrutinizes the objects as if he were in a museum that exhibits things from a distant culture. This is a telling moment as the boy/audience is being asked to journey into a plethora of material things that are dislocated from their local meaning to acquire an antiquarian value. Like Brook, who also uses these multicultural props in his production, 'we' (as ignorant audience) are invited to participate in this part archeological and part spiritual quest for origins which I will explain in a while. For the moment, I wish the reader to turn her attention towards the setting itself. Throughout the film the scene remains as it appears in this opening shot, minimalist and 'primal', a term that occurs often in David Williams' analysis of the philosophy embraced by Brook and the CIRT. The desire to reach a naive and simple truth, a basic and universal language, is not hidden to anyone who has read through the director's interviews. For instance he argues that 'the language of dramatic imagery is a language which is deceptive, because it is naive on the surface [...] It seems to be the hilt of primitive naivety [...] However, on the other side of that muddle are levels which cannot be put into words'.[2] Along the same lines, Williams explains that the choice of theatres such as the *Bouffes du Nord* was propelled by Brook's desire for a 'growing asceticism' of space where the actor is free to communicate intimately and directly. This shared space, a utopic elemental bowl that allows the actor intimacy with his environment and his audience, is recast in the film as a rocky, cavernous terrain divested of geographical and cultural specificity. This poses an immediate problem, for the cinematic audience cannot share with the actor a space in the same way as a theatre audience can. While theatre is momentary, in that it is a single performance where the spectator witnesses a final and direct relation with the actor, in cinema this relationship is deferred temporally and spatially; the filmic set is an artificial device, which the actor inhabits repeatedly in the presence of a camera. Thus the particular stage device employed would achieve quite different results when used in the cinematic setting. While the reasons for the emptying out of space can be appreciated in the cultural context of a theatre overburdened with artifices aimed at achieving realism, such a move does not result in a similar aesthetic revolt in cinema. Brook, who was part of a group of postmodernist directors who rejected familiar conventions of theatre to create a new school of thought that believed in engagement with the audience and greater political and social responsibility for theatre, which led to the birth of the atelier, tries to import that strategy to cinema.[3] His school of theatre argued for a need to place actors in a theatrical and mental tabula rasa so that they could perform and create drama afresh.

Stale conventions would be thrown out of the window in a process of unlearning in order to arrive at a new language of communication, and for this to occur, arrangement of space was significant. While the desire for rejecting the familiar is politically crucial, we must not forget to ask what foundational myths are deployed in maintaining the idea of cleansing and unlearning or for that matter, what effect such a transposition of ideas from one medium to another would have on cinema.

Problematically, the filmmaker is surprisingly unconcerned about the artifice involved in presenting the much sought after 'innocence' and equally unaware of the dangers involved in taking recourse to the idea of the stage as a tabula rasa. The imperialist will to knowledge that this act of forgetting involves is sanctioned by the notion that the mind/stage is a surface which may be erased and inscribed upon at will to arrive at an original innocence, no matter where and who you are. The stance assumes the existence of this surface because it conceals the tools of production that are employed in maintaining the illusion of a surface, creating another false dichotomy between surface/depth. Brook is quite naturally silent about who it is that stands anterior to the process of unlearning/learning and who it is that does the act of wiping out and reinscribing, thereby subscribing to the idea of an essentialist a priori subject. We, however, must ask after this person since she/he is (not unlike Brook himself) an instance of the privileged first world actor/spectator/student who assimilates the other without a moment of confrontation or dissonance. Yet, what such a deployment of a myth of surfaces does to theatre is quite different from the way in which it operates within cinematic realism. Although as theatre it enters into an appropriation of 'nature' as an unwritten and acultural space, as cinema it contains the potential of subverting the very notion of the 'real' as it appears in conventional screen space.

For the cinematic spectator is rarely called upon to suspend her disbelief, and yet Brook's aesthetics of natural primacy demands of her a recognition of the boundaries of space, jolting her into an awareness of a dissonance of sorts. Although Brook's intention is to present the space as if it did not have a history, the introduction of a stage-like set into the frame of cinema creates quite another effect. The spectator in a theatre may not be able to identify with the actor on the stage and is aware of the shortcomings of her position vis-à-vis the stage which may not allow for complete and absolute viewing, but the cinematic spectator is usually meant to experience the privilege of complete and absolute sight which, among other factors, helps her transgress her self and become the other whom she is watching. André Bazin argues, in his discussion of the fallacy of filmed theatre, that not only does cinema free the audience from their seats and produce angles that stage viewing cannot, it also removes the problem of realism encountered in theatre by capturing real time and space through the camera. Cinema, on the one hand, allows for greater 'realism' to enter the theatrical experience and on the other, he claims, robs the spectator of her active participation in the act of viewing. The 'act of will' that is essential to theatre is absent in cinema, which requires a submission of will through passive identification. Theatre is always based on a sense of opposition between audience and actor, which is primarily caused, he demonstrates, through décor.[4] While the dichotomy that Bazin draws between cinema and theatre is one that must be dismantled in order to show the interdependence of one on the other, I wish to alter his theory in order to discuss the other dichotomy of which he speaks—that between stage/screen. Bazin is, in a way, right about cinema 'solving' the 'problem of realism', but is unmindful of the fact that this creates a myth of presence where theatre is meant to lack absolute reality, while cinema gains it.[5] Besides, he also forgets that cinema introduces its own kind of opposition, or rather, duality, between spectator and screen. The spectator is complacent not because of a total identification with the actor but rather because of a fissure between her immersion in the other and her ability to know (at an unconscious level) that she is not altogether the other, the reason why it is possible to 'enjoy' being horrified at films. It is precisely this split (an act which constitutes our recognition of ourselves), this play of identity and difference that disallows total assimilation and creates a newer kind of opposition, one can argue, even a more self-reflexive opposition than the one required in the conscious 'act of will' of theatre. It is this sense of difference that is heightened by Brook's use of stage space and stage conventions on the cinematic screen to create dissonance that debunks a Bazinian faith in the realism of the cinematic shot.

Further, Bazin convincingly demonstrates that the success of adaptation rests on the intelligent management of the décor of cinema. Since his primary objection to filmed theatre is the fact that it does not take into account the need for a reconstruction of space that the cinematic field necessarily demands, it follows that for a play to be successfully adapted onto the screen, the director must keep in mind certain theatrical conventions of the stage while resetting them for the celluloid. This, he holds, will save theatre, as cinema can now be its carrier, while retaining its own uniqueness as cinema.[6] I wish to interrogate, first, the kind of realism that cinema engenders which can salvage theatre's loss of 'truth', and second, how the anti-realism (if realism is seen as an aesthetic device predicated on lending consistency to the image) of the theatre shatters the cohesiveness of the cinematic image. Deconstructing the performative politics of the film in this way urges us to rethink the realism of space and the ability of the mechanical tools of cinema to acquire political and cultural value.

In Brook's work the elemental bowl is no longer an actual quarry or ancient theatre (as it is in the theatrical versions) fetishized into a primal space where the bodies of the actors can stretch into newer possibilities and return to a state of 'innocence—a state of wholeness and natural creativity, present in childhood but lost in the passage to adulthood', but rather a constructed materiality rendered 'unreal' through the mechanical production of the scene by the camera and ingested into another space—the cinema theatre (or, for that matter, a radical reorientation of cinematic space is made apparent through home videos, DVDs, and laptop screening).[7] If the boundaries of the cinema screen are invisible and the conventional director uses this to create a semblance of universality, the intrusion of the stage/theatrical space into the cinematic screen robs the spectator of this frontier-less realm. Following the argument that through an erasure of the suspension of disbelief cinema has resurrected the 'real', in Brook's cinema that erasure of suspension is problematized and the audience is reminded of their willful forgetting. The nowhere land presents itself unintentionally as a constructed or at least a dehistoricized artifice, thus undercutting the intended universalism of Brook's film, gesturing toward the contingency of reality itself. Read against the grain of *auteurial* intention, the question of space stands radically resignified in this film as it sheds its certitude to signify a layered and contingent reality made from the bric-a-brac of theatrical and cinematic tools. The rocks do not mean 'sheer nature' any longer, but foreground the artifice involved in spatial construction; the scenes of the film denaturalize the presence of nature to remind us that it is always available to us as cultural artifact.[8]

The beginning of the film makes fresh sense read as a deliberate reminder of the lack of linear time with which the reader of the epic is confronted and accurately problematizes a simplistic notion of origins by tracking the boy's movement through historical events marked by theatrical props strewn around his path like the signposts of an event available for reconstruction. Immediately, this journey through a museum of the past alerts the spectator to the film's /text's performative aspect. Is the filmmaker suggesting, she finds herself asking, that there is no past but only a construction of it, only a repetition of events through performance? At one stroke, cinematic realism contructs the world of the *Mahabharata* as that of the spectators, breaking down the barriers between stage and seat through the centrifugal screen (as Bazin's argument has demonstrated), and at the same time it suspends such a realism by reminding the spectator of the make-believe that comprises theatrical realism, presenting it as an aesthetic choice. This technique would not have entailed subversion of realism on stage, for one is asked to suspend one's disbelief about an actor masquerading as a character, or since an unreal set passing off for the 'real' is a familiar enough dislocation for the audience.

Now we may turn to the relationship between cinematic defamiliarization and the meaning of the epic itself. Alf Hiltebeitel's deconstructive method of reading the *Mahabharata* rightly claims that an analogy between the Western epic and the Indian epic is futile, as the Indian epic may have developed as a reaction to the didacticism of ancient Sanskrit literature and thus resembles the fictional hybridity and polysemic possibilities of the Western novel (a form that consciously critiqued the conventions of the epic) rather than the conventional epic form.[9] The form of the text signals a departure from universalism and stability of meaning which may be in sharp contrast to Brook's allegorical reading of it as a tale with a central theme of threat, written for all mankind in a time of chaos. Structurally, it is impossible to find a single notion of truth or dharma in the *Mahabharata*. It is a text that is acutely self-reflexive and performative, where (one of) the author(s) is/becomes a character and inserts himself into the text putting, in the process, the sanctity of the clan's genealogy in grave doubt. Further, as Vijya Mishra has demonstrated, the knowledge of this genealogical truth is with the women alone.[10] One may add, the secrets of authorship are known only to women who 'imagine' their co-authors into existence. Both Vyasa and Krishna (as Hiltebeitel has deciphered) appear and disappear magically and at the call of women.[11] Male and female seem to be constantly changing roles in this sense, birthing and vanishing at whim. Cinema, naturally, has the means of producing such effects of appearance and disappearance through technological manipulation. But that would be a point about cinema's power over the spectator and less about the significance of the play of appearances and divinity as far as the epic is concerned. The cinematic text would, in other words, be saying quite the opposite of what the written (let us assume a single written text for the moment) text suggests through such interplay of orders. The use of spectacle could serve to present a magical text but also a monumental one as well, where technological production could awe the spectator into silence rather than foreground reflexivity.[12]

As Hiltebeitel has argued exhaustively, the written epic often produces itself infinitely through such ruses, blurring the gaps between character, author, and reader, which makes the *Mahabharata* an extremely complex text. The very form 'Vaisampayana said … Duryodhana said … Sakuni said' tells us that the text unfolds through speech acts, constructing itself through various utterances rather than omniscient and singular narration with reference to an absolute event or moment of truth. We must not forget that the reader is often invited to draw the links herself as in the case of the disappearance of Krishna which, as Hiltebeitel explains, is in keeping with the cosmic order and the dichotomy present between Shiva and Vishnu at that level.[13] Finally, the labyrinthine weave, the contingency of dharma, and the overweening presence of description in the narrative can be self-reflexive to the point of being frustrating. Frustrating, that is, if you are looking for a single kernel of meaning.

Brook's reading of the epic as an allegory can be read as a desire to straighten the narrative, to find that (perhaps non-existent) singular grain of truth. Although the *Mahabharata* makes a similar claim, that 'what is not here is nowhere', the structures of storytelling promise contingency and performativity.[14] The open-ended nature of the text has often been commented upon, but I wish to make a slightly precocious point that goes beyond semantic plurality. The fact that the epic is a living text, and that it continues to exist in various forms, highlights not only its orality but also its resistance to totality. Similarly, the narrative strategies within the epic indicate an admission of the impossibility of arriving at Meaning in itself, as it is always dependant on an utterance that substitutes terms for meaning. It can only be as Vaisampayana or Duryodhana says, that there can only be other stories with similar themes that reflect on the main story, no singular utterances but a strategy that disseminates meaning to local rather than a universal site(s). The epic alerts us to a structure of signs that is metaphorical, where one version or one story always stands in for the (real) meaning which is always deferred to another time or story. Brook ignores this performative narrative in his search for a single and linear one as his reading of the epic as a tale that represents a universal truth reveals. His reading of the epic as an allegory that stands for human suffering is not far from the philological endeavour of Max Müller, who sought in India a single religion above all other religions, a spiritual essence that may be culled out of a labyrinthine spread and applied to the whole universe at large.[15]

This should also remind us of what Deleuze says of cinema. Through the films of Eisenstein and Artaud, he argues that most cinema, even that of the dialectical montage of Eisenstein, reads the language of cinema as containing the possibility of arriving at thought in its totality. Each shot is meant to represent a meaning that is borne into existence through a nervous impulse, a shock wave that forces us to think thought itself. But as Deleuze deconstructs this notion, via Artaud's claim that cinema represents, rather, the impossibility of thought, the shots are moving images that stand in for thought itself, blocking our ability to think outside the ever present images. Thus the language of cinema, based on identity in difference, shows us that thought is metaphorical. The language of cinema is made up of a sign-chain of moving images that defer the meaning with each shot, only standing in for themselves, defined through their difference from the next shot. We can only think what the images stand for, not the entirety of the sign-chain. Cinema, then, represents the inability of thought, the lack that inhabits our very being, the lack that propels our very movement. For Artaud (as Deleuze puts it) cinema 'is essentially suited to reveal this powerlessness to think at the heart of thought'.[16]

There are three scenes that I would like to focus on, which will bring the Deleuzinan/Artaudian critique of presence in cinema together with the subtexts within the film. Perhaps, despite itself, the politics of performativity employed lead us, in Brook's text, to that dissociative force which Deleuze outlines, and it is left to us to work out whether or not that force rescues the text from its dominant representation as allegory. The scene depicting the birth of Gandhari's 100 sons is visually powerful and challenging to a cinema-going audience, for it brings to the frame techniques and conventions of the theatre to such an extent that cinematic realism is undercut to make way for exaggeration. The actress' gestures, intensely dramatic, increase the oppositional element between spectator and actor and keep easy identification at bay. The stick that the maid uses to beat the ball of lead out of Gandhari's womb is again marked with the tools of theatre where, at the back of the camera's expository eye, the spectator must believe that there is a gown hiding a ball, and a gesture of birth where the ball is let out by the actor and set rolling on the stage as childbirth. In Brook's film, the camera's eye is reordered to film a theatrical gesture, bringing into the frontier-less frame of cinema the constructedness of theatre. If cinema disallows thought by showing that no whole can be arrived at through the montage of images, then Brook introduces a set of images that also rob the spectator of a complacency of cinematic realism, which often guises this dislocation of meaning through an appearance of stability and essence. The repeated order of Gandhari, 'strike! strike!' limits language to what Brook would believe to be a 'primal' utterance. Yet it has the effect of alienating the character from realist dialogue to produce sounds that parody the fluency of realist cinema. Alienation must, however, rely on accepted conventions and beliefs in order to play with them. Where Brook's film runs into a serious problem is in the execution of such techniques of alienation against the framework of a universalist, allegorical reading which appears more subtly and more forcefully throughout the film. It is precisely for this reason that despite the imaginative use of props and characters, the film often appears as cultural kitsch, losing its radical edge to a tokenist end.

The international cast clearly challenges atavistic and nationalist–hegemonic interpretations of the *Mahabharata*.[17] Often, productions such as the B. R. Chopra televised series promulgate a tinsel, melodramatic version of the epic that aim to sequester the text from its historical context and present it through a contemporary dominant cultural sensibility. There is, in the movements and gestures of the actors in Brook's film, a desire to unlearn such dominant conventions of art in order to take recourse to marginal and oral forms of production. Yet, in the end, such a project must be subjected to critical attention for its anthropological biases and Brook's cast, despite its plural make-up, is ridden with a desire for seamless multiculturalism, which is only the polished face of neoimperialism. When Brook claims that his cast went through a process of unlearning, one is left to wonder who and what are unlearnt. There seems to be an anteriority of (Eurocentric) presence that the stance presumes. The being who has the economic and political privilege of documenting other cultures in order to wipe and reinscribe them is not brought into a crisis by the film. While conventions of American theatre are challenged by an assimilation of techniques from Africa and India, the same process of anthropological quarrying is not granted to the un-American spectator, who cannot turn the gaze backwards. The norm here is the privileged spectator who still wishes to find in the many cultures of the world 'a sense of wonder'. Trans-culturalism can only have its uses when the stability of a host culture is threatened, but in the case of Brook's humanist reading of the play and the project of trans-cultural activity, there is no instability but rather assimilation. This is, I submit, the reason why Brook cannot resist the temptation of casting black actors for the two characters that are embodiments of a certain brute ferocity. Ultimately, it is not dissonance that the film seeks, but rather absorption that leads to wonder. The lack of a complex reading of trans-culturalism (for instance he seems to believe that cultures can be picked up and abandoned, just as a conglomeration of ethnic origins can show interculturalism) sanctions the deployment of a stereotype for the creation of horror, such as the black body as a surface that triggers fear and contains natural ferocity. Ghatotkacha, the ferocious *rakshasa* son of Bhima, known for his terrible features and great physical prowess, is depicted as an African tribal, as both he and his father Bhima are played by actors of African origin.

The point is not about cultural piracy, but rather a question of the use of forms and the end it achieves. It is a question of methodology. To return to the earlier idea about the rejection of presence through the yoking together of disparate forms, one would also have to say that the multi-racial cast, in its attempt to remain harmonious, does not go far in the critique of presence. In fact, Brook uses the actor's body in such a way that, rather than dislocating the truth of the body, as evident in the case of the black actors, the cast cannot escape the materiality of the body. Why, one wonders, does Brook not use the techniques of cinema to pose questions to the theatrical overuse of the materiality of the body to find the fluidity that he seems to desire?[18] There are moments, however, that escape this reliance on the material body: one such instance of questioning the materiality of the actor's body is the scene where Ganesha abandons his mask to reveal himself as Krishna (we know this, as it is the face of the actor who will play Krishna, and because of the answer he gives to the boy's question about where Krishna is) and Vishnu (we know this because of the reclining posture he assumes). Identity, the scene suggests in a fantastic moment of self-reflexivity, is not fluid and continuous but rather contingent upon the props of the world, the cultural and epistemological norms that allows us to construct and reconstruct ourselves through them. The actor's identity is available through his character, which in itself is defined through conventions like the mask or the posture and so on.

It is possible, then, to read this text against its main current of thought via other props that it employs. It is then that certain moments, such as the few discussed, erupt from the uncritical celebration of universal harmony and Truth to pose questions about the means employed to reach this state of seamless cohesiveness, bringing the allegorical/universalist reading into crisis. Such moments exhibit not 'disorder', a term that Brook uses to describe his theatrical practice which I have attempted to show as politically problematic, but rather the contingent nature and performative aspects of the very tools that are used to achieve that illusion of disorder. The film, despite itself, raises these questions about the relation between the cinematic and written texts to shift the focus from the essence of a text to a textual practice predicated on a search for the means and conditions of signification. Its use of theatre through the imagistic language of cinema tells us about the very manner in which it tells the story, thus foregrounding the conditions of textuality rather than *the* text in itself. It opens up a discussion about textuality that asks for a more critical appreciation of the language of cinema and all that it brings, not to a reading of the *Mahabharata* alone, but to our study of textual utterances. To borrow and resignify the Artaudian theory of cinema, the film recounts a fundamental problem with textual utterance; that the innermost reality of a text is not the Whole, but on the contrary a fissure, a crack.

Notes

1. While it is a fallacy to assert that pure essentialism can exist, as most of what we understand as reality is a product of social, political and man-made processes and cannot be extricated from their fields of instantiation, it is equally dangerous to think that since reality is constructed, it cannot have an essence. While the latter errs in thinking that there is pure human agency in the making of reality, the former errs in attributing no agency whatsoever to the construction of reality. Suffice it to say that reality is constituted by social processes but is also independent

of them, so that we can and must speak of constructed/strategic essences, debunking that false binary.

2. David Williams, ed., *Peter Brook and the Mahabharata: Critical Perspectives*, London: Routledge, 1991, p. 52.
3. Christopher Baugh archives the history of the growing and changing relationship between technology and performance and brackets Brook with directors such as Criag and Grotowski, who embodied a growing disengagement and outright rejection of the past to construct the atelier phenomena.
4. André Bazin, *What is Cinema?*, ed. and trans. Hugh Gray, Berkeley: University of California Press, 1967, pp. 76-124.
5. Ibid., pp. 76-94.
6. Ibid., pp. 16-124.
7. Williams, op. cit., p. 6.
8. Ibid., p. 54.
9. Alf Hiltebeitel, *Draupadi among Rajputs, Muslims and Dalits: Rethinking India's Oral and Classical Epics*, Delhi: Oxford University Press, 2001, pp. 11-20.
10. Williams, op. cit., pp. 195-205.
11. Alf Hiltebeitel, *The Ritual of Battle: Krishna in the 'Mahabharata'*, New York: State University of New York Press, 1990, p. 73.
12. I am aware here that Robert Stam has drawn attention to the fact that it is cinema that is criticized for its embodied presence. I think that the notion of presence in flesh and blood that is hidden in a steady dichotomizing of theatre and cinema can be dismantled by showing that even though cinema engages with flesh-and-blood actors, it problematizes presence by removing them into another temporal and spatial framework where you are both with and not with the actors.
13. Hiltebeitel, *The Ritual of Battle* pp. 85, 86-111.
14. For this brilliant insight I am indebted to Christopher Baugh's book about the relationship between theatre, technology, and power. The larger argument about the nexus between knowledge production, here image production, and power is, of course, what Michel Foucault has adumbrated through the entire corpus of his works in order to search for the rules of formulation for any discourse.
15. I use the term performativity in the sense that Judith Butler uses it to describe gender. For Butler, performativity means a repetitive construction of identity that is not natural or essential but involves a routinization of gestures and discourses. I suggest that the epic's tale-within-a tale form is reflexive of the text's refusal to submit to an essential or natural meaning, thus unfolding itself through repeated speech acts within and without the text.
16. Gilles Deleuze, *Cinema 2:The Time Image*, trans. Hugh Towlinson and Robert Galeta, London: Athlone Press, 1989, p. 166.
17. See Vijay Mishra, 'The Great Indian Epic and Peter Brook', in David Williams, ed., *Peter Brook and the Mahabharata: Critical Perspectives*, London: Routledge, 1991 and Peter Van Der Veer, *Imperial Encounters:Religion and Modernity in India and Britain*, Princeton: Princeton University Press, 2001 for the uses of the epic in a nationalist agenda.
18. See Peter Van der Veer for the philological and Orientalist agenda in the search for ancient Sanskrit texts such as the *Mahabharata* that led to the collation of a critical edition.

References

Bazin, André, 'The Myth of Total Cinema' and 'Theatre and Cinema, Part One', *What is Cinema?*, vol. 1, ed. and trans. Hugh Gray, rev edn. Berkeley: University of California Press, 2004, pp. 1-24, 76-124.

Baugh, Christopher, 'The scene as machine, 1: Scenography as a machine for performance', 'The scene as machine, 2: constructing and building the scene as machine', *Theatre Performance and Technology: The Development of Scenography in the Twentieth Century*, New York: Palgrave Macmillan, 2005, pp. 46-81.

Butler, Judith, 'Preface', 'Bodily inscriptions, performative subversions', *Gender Trouble: Feminism and the Subversion of Identity*, New York: Routledge, 1990, pp. xv-xvi, xxiii-xxvii, 185-93.

Deleuze, Gilles, 'Thought and Cinema', *Cinema 2: The Time Image*, trans. Hugh Towlinson and Robert Galeta, London: Athlone Press, 1989, pp. 151-9.

Foucault, Michel, 'Part I: Introduction' and 'Part II: The Discursive Regularities', *The Archaeology of Knowledge and the Discourse on Language*, trans. A.M. Sheridan Smith, New York: Pantheon, 1972, pp. 3-76.

Hiltebeitel, Alf, *The Ritual of Battle: Krishna in the 'Mahabharata'*, New York: State University of New York Press, 1990.

———, 'Introduction', 'The Oral Epics', 'The Elder Brothers and the Heroes of Palnadu', *Draupadi among Rajputs, Muslims and Dalits: Rethinking India's Oral and Classical Epics*, Delhi: Oxford University Press, 2001, pp. 1- 87.

Mishra, Vijay, 'The Great Indian Epic and Peter Brook', in David Williams, ed., *Peter Brook and the Mahabharata: Critical Perspectives*, London: Routledge, 1991

Stam, Robert, and Raengo, Alessandra, eds., 'Introduction: The theory and Practice of Adaptation', *Literature and Film: A Guide to the Theory and Practice of Film Adaptation*, Malden, USA: Blackwell, 2005, pp. 1-46.

The Mahabharata, dir. Peter Brook, Perf Maurice Benichou, Marmadou Dioume, Mireille Maalouf, screen writer Peter Brook, Jean-Claude Carrier. Productions du 3ème Etage and Reiner Moritz Productions, 1989.

Williams, David, ed., 'Theatre of Innocence and of Experience: Peter Brook's International Center- An Introduction', 'The Presence of India- An Introduction', 'Theatre, Popular and Special, and the Perils of Cultural Piracy', 'The Great Indian Epic and Peter Brook' and 'Peter Brook's Orientalism', *Peter Brook and the Mahabharata: Critical Perspectives*, London: Routledge, 1991, pp. 3-28, 41-4, 52-8, 195-205, 262-7.

Van Der Veer, Peter, 'Monumental Texts: Orientalism and the Critical Edition of India's National Heritage', *Imperial Encounters: Religion and Modernity in India and Britain*, Princeton: Princeton University Press, 2001, pp. 101-33.

Editor and Contributors

VED PRAKASH BARUAH is currently pursuing an M.Phil. from the Department of English, University of Delhi. After completing his Bachelor's degree with a first class, he went on to obtain an MA in English from St. Stephen's College, University of Delhi. His research interests include colonial Assam, twentieth century literature, and Indian diaspora fiction.

NANDINI CHANDRA is a Senior Lecturer in the Department of English at Hansraj College, University of Delhi. Her book *The Classic Popular: Amar Chitra Katha (1967–2007)* was published by Yoda Press in July 2008. Her interests include the social history of South Asian popular culture, childhood studies, Hindi cinema, and Hindi minor genres.

SEYMOUR CHATMAN is Emeritus Professor of Rhetoric at the University of California, Berkeley. His research focuses on the filmmaker Michelangelo Antonioni and on narrative structure, particularly in literature and cinema. Besides several seminal articles on rhetoric, narratology, and cinema, his publications include *Michelangelo Antonioni: The Investigation* (Cologne, London, Los Angeles, Madrid, Paris, Tokyo: Taschen, 2004), *Reading Narrative Fiction* (New York: Macmillan, 1992), and *Coming to Terms: The Rhetoric of Narrative in Fiction and Film* (Ithaca: Cornell University Press, 1990).

RASHMI DORAISWAMY is Professor (Central Asia) at the Academy of Third World Studies, Jamia Millia Islamia, New Delhi and its Honorary Deputy Director from October 2005 to May 2007. She was associated with *Cinemaya* from 1988 to 2001. She was the recipient of the National Award for the Best Film Critic in 1995. Her entry on 'Film and Literature (India)' has appeared in the *Encyclopedia of Postcolonial Literatures in English* (Routledge, 2005). Her entries on Indian and foreign cinemas have appeared in *The Little Black Book: Movies* (London: Cassell Illustrated, 2007). She is co-editor of *Being and Becoming: The Cinemas of Asia* (Macmillan, 2002), editor of *Cultural Histories of Central Asia* (Aakar, 2009) and author of *The Post-Soviet Condition: Chingiz Aitmatov in the 90s* (Aakar, 2005) and Guru Dutt: *Through Light and Shade* (Wisdom Tree, 2008). She has served on several film festival juries in India and abroad and was international observer for the presidential elections in Uzbekistan in 2007.

KAREN GABRIEL is a deputed Senior Fellow with the Centre for Women's Development Studies, and also teaches English Literature at St. Stephen's College, University of Delhi. She is particularly interested in the relations between media and its technologies, culture, society, and developmental agendas and policies and has published widely in these areas. Her book *The Sexual Economies of the Contemporary Mainstream Bombay Cinema (1970-2000)*, was published by Shaker in 2005. Two of her forthcoming books are: *The Melodramatic Nation: Gender, Sexuality, Bombay Cinema*, to be published by Women Unlimited, and *Translating Gender: A Text and its Contexts*, to be published by Katha. She is currently working on two project: 'Media Censorship and the Postcolonial Regulation of Sexuality and Culture' and 'National Iconography'.

PRIYA JAIKUMAR is Associate Professor in the Department of Critical Studies at the University of Southern California's School of Cinematic Arts. Jaikumar's research has focused on interpreting historical change in cinema. Examining the collapse of British imperial power, her book *Cinema at the End of Empire* (Duke University Press, 2006) details the intertwinned film histories of Britain and India from 1927 to 1947. Her writings on state power, cultural regulation, film form and feminism appear in *Cinema journal, The Moving image, Post Script, Screen, World Literature Today*, in the anthologies *Hollywood Abroad,* and *Transnational Feminism in Film and Media*, and in forthcoming collections such as *Outsider Films* and *Border Crossing: Silent Cinema and the Politics of Space.* She is currently working on a book on location shooting in photography and film, and co-editing an anthology on the cultural turn in readings of state institutions titled *Undoing Leviathan.*

ANUJA JAIN is a Ph.D. Candidate at the Department of Cinema Studies, Tisch School of Arts, New York University. She graduated with an M.Phil. in English Literature from the University of Delhi. In 2005, she was awarded the Tisch School of Arts Corrigan Fellowship by New York University for her doctoral studies. She is currently working on her dissertation project which analyses the various visual representations of sectarian violence in India.

MANJU JAIN retired as Professor, Department of English, University of Delhi. She is the author of *T.S. Eliot and American Philosophy: The Harvard Years* (Cambridge: Cambridge University Press, 1992) and *A Critical Reading of the Selected Poems of T.S. Eliot* (Delhi: Oxford University Press, 1991). She has translated Premchand's novel *Rangbhoomi* into English, published by Penguin India, Delhi (2011).

LALIT JOSHI is Professor in the Department of History at the University of Allahabad. His areas of teaching and research include Cultural

Globalisation and the History of Cinema. He has published extensively both in Hindi and English in national and international journals and anthologies. His manual on Hindi cinema titled *HOUSE FULL* is going through a second edition.

SONALI PATTNAIK is a lecturer in the Department of English at Kirori Mal College, University of Delhi. She completed her M.Phil. in English with a distinction from the University of Delhi in 2006. She has read research papers at several international seminars on areas such as the War of 1857, physiognomy and colonial ethnography, gender, and representations of the body within a postcolonial context. Her publications include 'The Trial and Errors of Warren Hastings' for a special edition of the *Yearly Review* (Department of English, University of Delhi), a book review of 'Lesbian Voices: Canada and the World' in *Intersections* and 'The Second Sex of *Chak de India*' and 'Reel Real Women' for the electronic news journal *Tehelka*. Her poetry can be found on Sonali-s-musings@ over-blog.com.

M. MADHAVA PRASAD is Professor of Cultural Studies, The English and Foreign Languages University, Hyderabad. His publications include *Ideology of the Hindi Film: A Historical Construction* (Oxford University Press, 1998), and several essays on cinema, politics, caste, and other social issues. He is currently working on Indian political ideology, with particular emphasis on the language question.

POONAM TRIVEDI is a Reader in English at Indraprastha College, University of Delhi. She received her doctorate from the Shakespeare Institute, University of Birmingham, U.K. She has co-edited a collection of essays, *India's Shakespeare: Translation, Interpretation and Performance* (2005), authored a CD *King Lear in India* (2006), and published articles on women in Shakespeare, on Shakespeare performance and film in India, and on Indian theatre. She was Secretary of the Shakespeare Society of India (1993–9).

SHWETA SACHDEVA JHA teaches English at Miranda House, University of Delhi. She was awarded the Felix Scholarship for her doctoral studies at the Department of History at the School of Oriental and African Studies (SOAS), University of London. Apart from presentations at conferences, her forthcoming publications include papers in journals such as the *Asian and African Studies.*

VALENTINA VITALI is a Reader in Film Studies at the University of East London. She is co-editor, with Paul Willemen, of *Theorising National Cinema* (BFI, 2006) and the author of *Hindi Action Cinema: Industries, Narratives, Bodies* (Oxford University Press, 2008). Her work has appeared in a number of journals and anthologies, including *Boundary2*, *Inter-Asia Cultural Studies*, *Kinema*, *Framework*, *Women: a Cultural Review*, and *Hong Kong Connections: Transnational Imagination in Action Cinema* (Duke University Press and Hong Kong University Press, 2005).

Index

36 Chowringee Lane 245
Aadhi Haqeeqat, Aadha Fasaana 136
Abbas, Khwaja Ahmed 24, 25, 125, 126, 127, 128
Ab Dilli Door Nahin 128, 129
Achhut Kanya 23, 27, 32
Advani, L.K. 89, 92
Agneepath 229, 245
Agra 26
AIADMK 102
Ajanta Cinetone of Bombay 20
Ali, Faiz 182
Ali, Muzaffar 167, 176, 179, 180
Allahabad 21, 26
Amar Jyoti 32, 40
Ambedkar, B. R. 126
Amrit Manthan 32, 36, 40
Amrohi, Kamal 167, 172, 176, 233
Angoor 233
Apocalypse Now 195, 196
Art forum 211
Arya Samaj 171
Asceticism 114
Ashk, Upendranath 20, 21
  Maskebazon Ka Svarga 21
Asian American International Film Festival 99
Australia 4
Ayodhya Ka Raja 39

Babri Masjid 85, 86, 89, 92
Bachchan, Amitabh 56, 59, 60, 61, 62, 187, 229
Badmaash ka Beta 38
Bahadur Ganda 233
Balidan 23
Banaras Hindu University 26
Bandish 139
Bandit Queen 146, 151, 153, 154, 158, 159, 160, 161
Bandopadyaya, Jogiban 30
  Kheyali 30
Barnouw, *Indian Film* 54
Barrister's Wife, The 39
Barua, P.C. 23
Barua, Pramathesh 39
Bazaar-e-Husn 172
Bedi, Bobby 155
Bedi, Rajendra Singh 29
Behind the Curtain 36
Benares 26, 33
Bengal Presidency Council of Women 15
Benjamin, Walter 70, 71, 72, 77
Bhabha, Homi 70
Bhaduri, Murari 23
Bhagyachakra 36
Bharatiar 101, 102, 103, 104
Bharati, Subramania 100, 101
Bhaskar, Ira 88, 91
Bhatnagar, Ram Kishan Lal 40
Bhrantibilas 233
Bhrashtachar 146, 147, 152
Bicharak 23
Bihar 29
Bioscope 30
Bioscope Ke Chhipe Rahasya 37
Biswas, Seema 154
Bollywood 86, 236, 237, 238, 239, 241, 242, 244
Bollywoodisation 97
Bombay 4, 9, 20, 21, 22, 23, 24, 26, 28, 29, 32, 36, 40, 41, 54, 55, 56, 57, 58, 59, 61, 79, 80, 85, 86, 90, 115, 125, 127, 128, 145, 146, 151, 154, 168, 184, 229, 233, 238
  American-Indian Picture Palace 22
  Bombay Talkies 32, 40, 54
  Filmistan 20
  Roxy Theatre 23
Bombay 85, 91, 92, 93, 98
Bombay Entertainments Duty Act 9
Bombay's Blood Yatra 85, 91, 93
Boot Polish 125, 130, 131, 132, 135
Bose, Devakikumar 39, 40

Bose, J. C. 38
Bose, Nitin 39
Bose, Satyen 126
Bose, Subhash Chandra 114
Bresson 72
Bridegroom Wanted 32
Brook, Peter 249, 250, 251, 252, 253, 254, 255, 256, 257, 258
Bulgakov, Mikhail, *Master and Margarita, The* 72
Burma, National Council of Women 5
Butalia, Urvashi 148

Calcutta 3, 12, 20, 26, 38, 40, 54, 175, 231
  New Theatres 20, 23, 32, 36, 39, 40, 54
Canada 99
Casteism 25, 54, 73, 88, 89, 101, 102, 106, 123, 126, 127, 129, 130, 131, 141, 147, 149, 153, 154, 159, 160, 234, 243
censorship 3, 4, 5, 9, 10, 14, 16, 25, 34, 86
  guidelines 16
  principles and methods of the 3
  strict 25
Central Circuit Cine Association (CCCA) 58
Certeau, Michel de 70, 73, 74, 75
Chabrol, Claude 195
Chakravarty, Sumita 113, 168
Chalta Purza 38
Chamberlain 196
Chand 20, 32, 33, 34, 37, 41
Chander, Krishna 29
Chandidas 36, 39
Chatterjee, Partha 11
Chatterjee, Vamadasa 38
Chatterji, Saratchandra 39
Chattopadhyaya, Bankimchandra 28
Chaudhry, Ramashankar 39
Childhood 124, 126, 128, 131, 132, 133, 136, 138, 139, 140, 141, 142, 211, 253
Children 33, 34, 37, 87, 89, 92, 107, 124, 125, 126, 127, 128, 129, 130, 131, 132, 133, 135, 136, 137, 138, 139, 141, 148
China 60, 61
Chitrapat 30, 31, 41
Chopra, B. R. 256
Cinema
  action 38, 60, 62
  adaptations 169, 180, 195, 196, 198, 211, 212, 215, 216, 217, 218, 230, 234, 236, 237, 241, 242, 244, 249, 252
  advent of 11, 14
  American 4, 6, 7, 8, 15, 21, 33, 34, 36, 54, 55, 63
  art 33, 36, 86
  aspects of 32
  audiences for 4
  ballad 32
  ban on 15
  Bengali 12, 27, 28, 29, 30, 33, 54, 233
  British 5, 6, 7, 15, 21
  cartoon 32
  children 128
  church 33
  cinematograph 3
  commercial 39, 236
  connoisseurs of 31, 44
  conventions in 82
  criticism 30, 169
  dimensions of 53, 54
  documentary 85, 86
  English 10, 12, 13, 15, 26, 30, 101, 102, 103, 124, 134, 207, 211, 213, 217, 219, 231, 232, 236, 241, 244
  epic 33
  essays on 21
  ethics of 33
  European 36
  exhibitions 3, 5, 7, 57
  fantasy 33
  foreign 13, 35, 55, 58
  functioning of 53, 56
  good 30, 33, 36, 44
  Gujarati 27, 28, 29, 30
  Hindi 19, 20, 21, 26, 27, 28, 29, 30, 31, 33, 38, 40, 41, 43, 44, 45, 54, 56, 58, 59, 60, 62, 64, 85, 86, 87, 90, 91, 92, 97, 98, 99, 101, 102, 112, 123, 124, 131, 133, 137, 139, 152, 158, 167, 168, 170, 172, 174, 177, 181, 185, 186, 187, 188, 229, 230, 233, 235

historical 167, 169, 170
history of 53, 169
impact of 11, 33
Indian 3, 5, 7, 8, 12, 13, 21, 23, 24, 25, 28, 32, 34, 35, 36, 37, 40, 42, 44, 45, 55, 56, 81, 82, 86, 112, 113, 115, 186, 229, 230, 231, 236, 245
influence of 4, 5, 7, 128
institution of 6
Italian 55
jungle 33
language 19, 21, 23, 26, 27, 28, 29, 30, 32, 35, 73, 92, 97, 98, 99, 101, 102, 108, 113, 126, 127, 147, 158, 168, 170, 202, 216, 250, 251, 255, 256, 258
limitations of 54
literature and 69, 78
low-cost 38, 59
make-up 37, 235, 257
make-up in 37
Marathi 22, 27, 28, 54
nationalist ambivalence 22
misrepresentation 6
modalities of 54
musical 32
pedagogical aims of 35
play 32
production 5, 7, 53, 54, 55, 56, 57, 59, 61, 63, 128
quality of 7
reviews and critiques of 38
screening of 5
silent 23
special effects in 37
standards of 36
star and corporate profiles 38
story 33
stunt 38, 55
swadeshi 23
Tamil 57, 97, 98, 99, 104
techniques and inventions 37
terrorism in 97
trends in 21
Urdu 26, 27, 28, 29, 168, 170, 172, 180, 183, 230, 232, 233
Western 5, 8, 9, 34, 44
Cinema hall 34, 43, 59
Cinematograph Act 4
City Under Siege, The 74
Colonialism 15, 69
Comedy of Errors 233
Communal conflagration 86, 89
Company 23, 238
Constructivism 249
Contagious Diseases Act 171
Coomarswamy, Ananda 26
Coppola 195, 196
Coulson, Mrs V.G. 15
CPCI 58
Crime 5, 62, 112, 127, 129, 147, 239, 244
Criminals, The 60
Culture 7, 8, 10, 19, 22, 25, 26, 29, 32, 44, 64, 86, 97, 98, 168, 170, 172, 174, 180, 181, 182, 183, 185, 188, 213, 216, 220, 229, 238, 242, 250, 257
Indian 8
Islamic 29
lakhnawi 170, 180
nawabi 183, 188
swadeshi 25
Western 7, 10
Czechoslovakia 196, 223

Dakshyaksh 33
Daku Mansur 39
Dalia 23
Darlington, Lord , *Remains of the Day, The* 196, 197, 199, 200, 201, 202, 204, 221, 223
Das, Veena 147
Decency 9, 177
notions of 9
Deleuze 81, 249, 255, 256
Delhi 26, 29, 30, 44, 58, 128, 129, 173, 175, 184
Delhi, the Rome of Asia and Lucknow 184
Democracy 13
Derrida, *différance* 240
Devdas 27, 33, 36, 39
Devi, Phoolan 153, 154, 155, 156, 157, 158, 159, 160
Dey, K. C. 39
Dhoop Chhaon 32
Dialectical progression 113
Dickens, Charles, *Oliver Twist* 195

Dignity 13, 130, 140, 141, 197, 215, 220
Dil Chahta Hai 245
Dil Farosh 230
Dil Se 99, 111, 112, 113, 114
Directors 125
Dirks, Nicholas B. 99
Divorce 5
DMK 102, 106
Do Bigha Zameen 125
Do Dooni Char 233
Doordarshan 139
Dostoevsky 71, 72
Meek One 72
Dwyer, Rachel 168, 186
Dyer, Richard 90, 184

Education 135
Eisenstein, Sergei 33, 70, 77, 255
Battleship Potemkin 77
Emma, *Madame Bovary* 195,
England 4, 6, 7, 15, 23, 33, 153, 211, 213, 217, 221
British Social Hygiene Delegation 5
Essentialism 249
Evans, W. 4, 5
Evils 25, 37, 127
Excuse Me Sir 36

Face to Face: Interviews with Contemporary Novelists 211
Ferry 125, 129, 130, 131, 133, 134
Filmfare 30, 128, 137, 173, 186, 232, 244
Film Finance Corporation 24
Filmindia 25, 30, 137, 232
Filmmaker 23, 24, 26, 27, 28, 34, 35, 36, 37, 41, 54, 80, 85, 86, 91, 92, 93, 98, 126, 127, 128, 129, 131, 135, 155, 169, 170, 172, 196, 200, 202, 211, 217, 233, 251, 253
documentary 85, 86
Indian 23, 36, 37
Film Producers' Guild of India 58
Film production 7, 53, 54, 55, 56, 57, 59, 61, 63, 128
modalities of 56
First International Film Festival of India 24
Flaubert, Gustave 195
Fleming, Ian, *From Russia with Love* 78
Forster, E.M. 196
A Room with a View 196
Howards End 196
Maurice 196
Four, Channel 155
Fox, James 204
France 4, 70, 77
Frankenstein 37
Freidberg, Anne 69, 75
French New Wave 81, 82
Fundamentalism 88

Gambling 25, 63, 127
Gandhi 167
Gandhi, Indira 61
Gandhi, Mahatma 7, 24, 25, 26, 27, 114, 123, 127, 133, 134, 135
views on cinema 7
Gandhi, Rajiv 109
Gargya, Lakshman Prasad 30, 31, 32
Germany 4, 34, 211
Ghatak, Ritwik 80, 81, 82
Ghosh, Aurobindo 26
Ghosh, Jyotishchandra 30
Giribala 23
Goel, Hanuman Prasad 19
Goncharov, *Oblomov* 71
Gopalan, Lalitha 99
Gorky, Maxim 39
Green, Mr 9
Grihadaah 39
Gujarat 89, 148
Gulzar 233
Gungadin 34
Gunga Jamuna 239
Gupta, Charu 171
Gupta, Hemen 126
Gupta, Mohan Lal 34
Guzdar, Mushtaq 28

Habermas, *Structural Transformation of the Public Sphere* 26
Haig, H.G. 5
Hathili Dulhan 230
Hatimtai 33
Heart of Darkness 195
Hey! Ram 149

Hiltebeitel, Alf 254
Hindi Sahitya Sammelan 26, 29, 31
Hinduism 86
Hindu–Muslim conflict 87, 88
Hindu subjectivity 88
Hindutva 86, 91, 93, 99, 169
  karsevaks 89
  rath yatra 89
  Sangh Parivar 89
Hogg, H.W. 13
Hollywood 4, 7, 11, 34, 36, 54, 55, 62, 63, 64, 184, 195, 233
Hughes, Ken 241
Hugo, Victor 39
Humbert 217
Hum Sub Chor Hain 60
Hunch Back of Notre Dame, The 37
Huppert, Isabel 195
Husaini, M.A. 183

Identity 19, 74, 86, 87, 88, 89, 90, 91, 92, 94, 98, 100, 102, 103, 105, 106, 107, 115, 130, 131, 134, 136, 140, 142, 146, 148, 156, 171, 177, 179, 213, 214, 215, 221, 229, 252, 255, 258
  caste 102, 106, 130, 131
  collective 146
  ethnic 100
  fractured 88
  national 86, 87, 88, 90, 91, 92, 94, 100, 146
  regional 98, 100, 106, 107, 115
  religious 91
  secular 90
  Tamil 100, 103, 105, 106
Imagination 22, 37, 148, 149, 150, 159, 160, 167, 168, 169, 174, 180, 185, 215, 217, 233, 237
  irrational 37
IMF 61
Imperial Conference 3, 6
Imperial Film Company 42
India
  American distributors in 62
  British 8
  censorship of films 3, 4, 5, 9, 10, 14, 16, 25, 34, 86
  communities of 13
  films to defame 34
  growth of cinema in 42
  Hindi Periodicals in 19
Indian Cinematographic Committee 3, 24, 33, 55
Indian documentaries 85
Indian Film Festival of Los Angeles 99
Indian Motion Picture Congress 24, 42
Indian Motion Picture Producers Association (IMPPA) 58
Indian National Congress 22
Indian People's Theatre Association (IPTA) 80, 124, 125, 126, 127, 129, 135, 140
Industrialization 53, 60, 79, 178, 179
Inqalab 39
Irani, Daisy 124, 136, 137, 139, 140
Ishiguro, Kazuo 196, 199, 211, 212, 213, 214, 215, 216, 217
  Remains of the Day, The 195, 196, 202, 211, 212, 213
Ivory, James 196

Jacobs, Lewis, *The Rise of the American Film: a Critical History* 53
Jaffer, Sir Haroon 3, 7
Jagdeep 136, 137, 138
Jagriti 125, 130, 131, 133, 135
Jain, Hrishamcharan 30
Jambu Kaka 32
James, Henry 196
  The Bostonians 196
  The Europeans 196
  The Golden Bowl 196
Jan, Gauhar 175
Japan 4, 212
Jawaharlal Nehru University 123
Jeevan Prabha 32
Jeevan Prabhat 32
Jhabvala, Ruth Prawer 196, 198, 211, 212, 216, 217, 218, 220, 221
Jones, Jennifer 195
Jones, Major W. Ellis 11, 13, 14
  Written Statement 12
Joshi, P.C. 129
Joshi, Umesh 28
Josson 85, 91, 92, 93
  Bombay's Journey of Blood 85, 91, 93

Journalism 19, 30, 33, 44, 111, 187
  Hindi 19, 33
Jurassic Park 63
Jyotindranath 42, 44

Kalbus, Oskar 53
  Vom Werden Deutscher Filmkunst 53
Kaliyattam 234, 235, 242, 243, 244
Kamalahasan 97, 104
Kannathil Muthamittal 97, 98, 99, 100, 102, 103, 104, 105, 107, 108, 109, 110, 111, 112, 113, 114, 115
Kanpur 26, 172
Kanwar, Amar, *Season Outside* 80
Kapoọr, Prithviraj 38
Kapoor, Raj 126, 135
Kapoor, Shyamnarayan 27, 37
Kapur, Shekhar 146, 151, 154, 155, 156, 157, 158, 159, 160
Karloff, Boris 37
Karorepati 32
Kaun 19, 39
Keats, John 39
Kenton, Miss, *Remains of the Day, The* 197, 198, 199, 200, 201, 202, 203, 205, 206, 207, 214, 217, 219
Kesari 22
Khan, Karim 75
Khayal 42
Khemka, Bajranglalji 40
Khoon-e-Nahak 230, 232
Khoon-ka-Khoon 230, 231
Khosla Commission on Censorship 24
Khudadad 230
Kierkegaard 113, 114
King Kong 60
Kissing 7, 9, 13, 14, 20, 35
  public 14
  screen 14
Kitaab 139
Kodai 101
Komal Gandhar 81
Kracauer, Siegfried, *From Caligari to Hitler* 53
Krishna, Sri 40
Krishnaswamy 54
  Indian Film 40, 54, 99
Kubrick, Stanley 195, 217
  A Clockwork Orange 195
  Barry Lyndon 195
  Lolita 195, 217
Kudhyadi, Nandan 79
Kumar, Amar 129
Kumar, Ashok 139, 172, 173
Kumari, Meena 139, 173, 176, 177, 181, 185, 186, 187

Lage Raho Munnabhai 123
Laila Majnu 39
Lector, Hannibal, *Silence of the Lambs, The* 204
Lekhak 21
Liberation Tigers of Tamil Eelam (LTTE) 98, 104, 105, 108, 109, 112, 114, 115
Life of Christ 22

MacCullers, Carson, *Ballad of the Sad Café* 196
Madame Bovary 195
Madan Theatres 55
Madhubala 172
Madhuri 20, 27, 39, 43
  Chhaya 20
Madras 3, 6, 34, 56, 59, 98, 101, 111
Madurai Conference, 1931 23
Magic Flute 33
Mahabharata 249, 253, 254, 255, 256, 258
Mahal 172, 174, 175, 178
Mahatama 32, 40
Mahua 33
Manbhanjan 23
Manmayi Girls School 32, 33, 36, 124
Mansur, Mallikarjun 79
Manto 76, 77
  Thanda Gosht 76
Manzil 27, 39
Maqbool 235, 236, 237, 238, 239, 240, 242, 243, 244
March, Fredrick 37
Mauj Majah 30
Maya 19, 32
MDMK 102
Meena Kumari ki Amar Kahani 185
Meerabai 36
Mehboob, *Mother India* 112

Mehmood, Junior 136, 137, 138
Mehra, Prakash 61
Mehta, Deepa 73, 75, 80
  1947—Earth 73, 75, 80
Men of Respect 241
Merchant, Ismail 196
Mhatre. R.K. 9
Mickey Mouse 32
Milton 39
Minnelli, Vincent 195
Mira 32, 76
Mir, Ezra 37
Mishra, Lakshmishankar 35
Mishra, Vijya 254
Misrepresentation 5, 6, 9, 10, 11
Mistri, Babubhai 60
Mitha Zahar 230
Mitra, Rajendra Lal 28
Miyan, Ghani 71
Modernism 70, 71, 82
Modernity 11, 19, 69, 70, 71, 74, 75, 76, 78, 80, 82, 88, 102, 113, 114, 168
Modernization 178
Modi, Sohrab 230
Moral values 6, 41, 43
Mosley, Oswald 212
Mother India 30, 112
Motion Pictures Export Association of America (MPEAA) 62, 63
Movement
  cultural 80
  Dravidian Anti-Hindi Imposition Movement 99
  Dravidian movement 102
  national 22, 24, 25, 43, 44
  Self Respect Movement 101
  Swadeshi 22, 38
Movietone, Wadia, *The Indian Screen Gazette* 30
Mr Jekyll and Mr Hyde 37
Mughal-e-Azam 167, 173
Mukherji, Bhudeva 28
Mukhopadhyay, Kailash, *Rupamancha* 30
Mukti 23, 32
Mullick, Pankaj 23
Mulvey, Laura 100
Mumbai Express 97
Munna 125, 129, 130, 131, 134, 137, 138, 140
Munshi, K.M. 42
Muqaddar ka Sikandar 187
Murder 5, 71, 129, 145, 148, 149, 160, 235, 237, 239, 242
Muslim 4, 5, 9, 29, 74, 87, 88, 89, 90, 108, 126, 136, 148, 149, 168, 177, 179, 231, 237

Nabokov, Vladimir 217
  Lolita 195, 217
Nagar, Amrit Lal 20
Nagari Pracharini Patrika 20
Naidu, Sarojini 23
Nanjundi Kalyana 233
Nargis 173, 174, 181, 233
Nashtar 172
Nationalism 22, 27, 38, 62, 88, 99, 126, 129, 134, 141, 179, 229
  hegemonic 99
Natir Pooja 23, 32
Naukadubi 23
Navinchandra 38
Navyug 22
Nayakan 98
Nehru, Jawaharlal 23, 24, 25, 56, 123, 124, 128, 129, 130, 135, 179
  preliminary statement on Indian cinema 23
Nepali, Gopal Singh 20
New Theatres 20, 23, 32, 36, 39, 40, 54
Nigam, Sachidananda 38, 39, 40
Nihalani, Govind 77
Nimmi 186, 237, 238, 239, 240
Nirala, Surya Kant Tripathi 20
Niranjana, Tejaswini 88

Omkara 235, 236, 242, 243, 244
Optimism 36, 131
Orsini 26, 27

Pak Daman 230
Pakeezah 167, 168, 170, 172, 173, 174, 175, 176, 177, 178, 179, 181, 182, 183, 185, 186, 187
Palm Springs Film Festival 99
Pandey, Gyanendra 72, 89

Pant, Govind Ballabh 31
Pantulu, V. Ramadas 5
Pasternak, Boris, *Dr. Zhivago* 78
Patel, Baburao 25, 30, 128
Patil Committee of Enquiry 24
Patna 26
Pawagarh ka Patan 38
Phalke, Dhundiraj Govind 22, 23, 54
Philadelphia Film Festival 99
Phillips, Caryl 216
Pooranbhakt 36
Porter, Katherine Anne, *Noon Wine* 196
Prabhat Film Company 32, 36, 40, 54
Pradeep 20
Pragmatism 40, 131
Prakash, J. Om 57, 58
Premchand, Munshi 20, 21, 27, 29, 172
  Cinema aur Sahitya 21
Prem, Saryuprasad 38, 41
Progressive Writers' Association (PWA) 125
Proust, *Remembrance of Things Past* 195, 198
Punjab 13, 28, 29, 58
Punjab Boy Scouts Association 13
Puranbhakta 39

Qawwali 130
Queen Christina 33

Radio Ceylon 58
Rai, Lala Lajpat 14
Rajadhyaksha, Ashish 97
Raja Harishchandra 22
Raju, Master 136, 138, 139, 140
Rakesh, Mohan, *His Heap of Rubble* 71
Ramachandran, T.N. 103
Ram Rajya 25
Rangabhoomi 31
Rangachariar, Diwan Bahadur T. 3, 5, 6, 8, 10, 14, 24
Rang De Basanti (RDB) 123, 141
Rani, Devika 23
Rao, Rao Saheb Dr U. Rama 5
Rao, Vidya 42
Rape 145, 146, 147, 148, 149, 150, 151, 152, 153, 154, 155, 156, 157, 158, 159, 160, 161, 178, 196
  discourses on 145, 157
  gang 147
  imagining 149
  languages of 146
  marital 147
  nature of 145
  taxonomies of 147
Rasayatra 79
Rasul, Sheikh Iftikar 35
Ratnam, Mani 85, 86, 87, 88, 89, 90, 91, 92, 97, 98, 99, 100, 101, 102, 106, 107, 108, 110, 111, 112, 113, 114, 115, 238
Ray, P.C. 38
Realism 13, 54, 71, 80, 81, 82, 92, 93, 126, 130, 131, 132, 136, 170, 215, 218, 222, 250, 251, 252, 253, 256
  cinematic 251, 253, 256
  emotional 92, 93
Regionalism 27
Reilly, William 241
Rekha 176, 181, 186, 187
Representationalism 11
Rhys, Jean 196
  Quartet 196
Ribbentrop, von 196, 212
RICC 15
Riots 72, 74, 80, 85, 87, 89, 90, 91, 92, 115, 148, 149
Rise of the American Film, The 53, 54
Roja 98, 99, 100, 115
Romi, Master 136
Rooplekha 36
Rosenstone 169
Roy, Arundhati 151
Roy, P.C. 33
Ruiz, Raul 195
Ruplekha 33
Rushdie, Salman 156
Russia 34, 71, 78, 79, 128
Ruswa, Mirza Muhammad Hadi 180
  Umrao Jan 'Ada' 169, 172, 180, 183

sadhana 41
Sahib Bibi aur Ghulam 185
Sahni, Bhisham 71, 72, 77, 78, 79, 81
  Tamas 71, 72, 73, 75, 76, 77, 81
  We Have Arrived in Amritsar 79

Sahu, Kishore 231, 232
Said-e-Havas 230
Sammelan Patrika 20
San Francisco International Film Festival 99
Saraswati 20
Sathe, V. P., *Sound* 30
Satya 238
Savitri Satyavan 39
Scorsese, Martin 195
Sectarianism 85, 87
Secularism 88, 90, 91, 99, 100, 126, 129
Sehgal 39, 44
Sen, Keshub Chandra 28
Sen, Mala 154, 156
Sex 5, 7, 127, 146, 147, 149, 152, 154, 160, 168
  conduct 5, 7
  legal 146
Shahana 30
Shahani, Kumar 79
  Kasba 79
  Tarang 79
Shah, Chandulal 39
Shah, Hasan 172
Shakespeare 229, 230, 231, 232, 233, 234, 235, 236, 237, 239, 241, 242, 243, 244, 245
  Anthony and Cleopatra 230
  Cymbeline 230
  Hamlet 230, 231, 232
  King John 230
  Macbeth 229, 235, 236, 237, 238, 239, 240, 241, 242, 243, 244, 245
  Measure for Measure 230
  Merchant of Venice 230
  Pericles 230
  Richard III 230
  Romeo and Juliet 233, 245
  Shylock 233, 245
  The Taming of the Shrew 230
Shantaram (director) 39
Shantiniketan 134
Sharatchandra, Chatterji 27
Sharma, Gajanand 30
Sharma, Kamalkumar 32
Sharma, Krishna 148
Sharma, Narendra 20
Sharma, Rajkishore 32
Sharma, Ramasrey 32
Shastri, J.R. 31
Shaw, G.B. 212
Shelley, P.B. 39, 101
Shirin Farhad 39
Shoesmith, Brian 4
Sholay 62
Shri Gaurang 33
Shukla, Ramchandra 21
Silly Symphony 32
Silsila 187
Singh, Dara 60, 62
Singh, Kapildev 32
Singh, Madan Gopal 79, 80, 82
Singh, Rajbahadur 41
Sippy, Ramesh 62, 146
Sita 33
Sivathamby, Karthigesu 101, 102
Social order 8, 11, 14, 16
Society 4, 14, 15, 27, 38, 39, 44, 86, 88, 93, 99, 102, 114, 124, 148, 150, 173, 177, 186, 234, 243
  English 15
  white 14
Solidarity 4, 15, 105, 110
  ethnic 15, 110
Somnath temple 89
Son of India 36
Sorlin, Pierre 169
South Korea 60, 63
Sri Lanka 97, 98, 103, 104, 105, 107, 108, 109, 110, 111, 112, 114, 115
  Genocidal attacks 108
  Indian Peace Keeping Force (IPKF) 109
  Tamil militancy 97
  See also LTTE
Srivastava, J.P. 31
  Cinema Tatha Rangmanch 31
Stardust 186
Star Wars 63
Stenson, J. 9
Stevens 196, 197, 198, 199, 200, 201, 202, 203, 204, 205, 206, 207, 208, 213, 214, 215, 216, 217, 218, 219, 220, 221, 222
Storm Over Bengal 34

Subah Ka Sitara 39
Sudarshan 20, 27
Sudha 19, 20, 31, 32, 33
Sampadakiya Sahmati 20
Sundaram, P.S. 101, 103

Tagore, Rabindranath 23, 25
Tamasha 33
Tamil Nadu 23, 99, 100, 101, 102, 106, 107, 109
Tamil Nadu Actors Association 23
Tarana 80
Taruni 36, 171
Tawa'if 42, 131, 133, 135, 167, 168, 169, 170, 171, 172, 173, 174, 175, 177, 178, 179, 180, 181, 182, 183, 184, 185, 186, 187, 188
Temple Wells 39
Terrorism 97, 98, 99, 100, 109, 113
Theatre Owners Association 58
Theatres 8, 9, 35, 55, 167, 186, 250
Thompson, Emma 207
Thumri 42
Tilak, Bal Gangadhar 22, 23, 25
Times of India 236
Times, The 77, 237
Tolstoy, *War and Peace* 198
Toronto International Film Festival 99
Trader Horn 33
Trivedi, Harish 29
Turgenev, Ivan 39

Umrao Jan 167, 168, 169, 170, 172, 175, 176, 179, 180, 181, 182, 183, 184, 185, 187
Unholy Love 195
United States of America (USA) 15, 53, 60, 61
Unity
film industry 54
imaginary 15
national 88
symbolic 15
Universalism 97, 98, 115, 253, 254

Vasantsen (art film) 33
Vasudevan, Ravi S. 88, 99, 100
Venkataram, R. 10
Verma, Bhagwati Charan 20
Verma, Mahadevi 44
Vidyapati 32
Vietnam war 196
Vijaya Pictures 42
Violence 33, 75, 77, 85, 86, 87, 90, 91, 93, 94, 97, 99, 108, 111, 112, 133, 146, 147, 148, 149, 150, 151, 152, 153, 154, 157, 159, 160, 161, 238, 242
sectarian 85, 86, 87, 90, 91, 93
Vivekananda, Swami 114

Walking in the City 70, 73, 75
Wells, H.G. 212
Wharton, Edith, *Age of Innocence* 195
Williams, David 249
Womanhood 13, 14, 42, 43
Indian 13, 42
mockery of 42
Western 14
Women 5, 7, 8, 11, 12, 13, 15, 20, 34, 36, 37, 38, 40, 41, 42, 43, 45, 81, 89, 91, 92, 112, 124, 128, 135, 141, 145, 146, 147, 148, 149, 150, 151, 152, 153, 154, 157, 158, 159, 160, 161, 167, 171, 172, 173, 174, 175, 177, 178, 179, 180, 182, 184, 185, 186, 187, 188, 197, 238, 254
British 8
European 11
Hindu 148
lives of 7, 185
middle class 43, 91
Muslim 148, 177, 179
professional 43
raped 145, 146, 161
Western 15
white 5, 7, 8, 11, 13, 15
World War I 53, 55
World War II 53, 57, 61, 64

Young India 38

Zanjeer 61, 62
Zan Mureed 230
Zarina 37